AF600392

HOLY SCRIPTURE SPEAKS: THE PRODUCTION AND RECEPTION OF ERASMUS' *PARAPHRASES ON THE NEW TESTAMENT*

Edited by Hilmar M. Pabel and
Mark Vessey

Erasmus' *Paraphrases on the New Testament* provides an extraordinary example of the adaptation of the Bible to the religious and rhetorical ideals of Renaissance humanism. Yet very little is known about the production and reception of the *Paraphrases*, which comprises nine volumes of the Collected Works of Erasmus. This collection of twelve essays, edited by Hilmar Pabel and Mark Vessey, aims to address this gap in Erasmus studies. The contributions reflect recent critical scholarship in three main areas: Erasmus' promotion of the ideals of Renaissance humanism; his work as an editor, translator, and interpreter of the New Testament; and the impact of his published writings on the culture of early modern Europe.

Holy Scripture Speaks represents the most concerted collective study of Erasmus' *Paraphrases on the New Testament* since the completion of the first English translation by scholars during the reign of Edward VI (1548/9). It reveals the rich complexity of the literary, theological, and cultural dimensions of the *Paraphrases*, and indicates future directions that research in this area should take.

HILMAR M. PABEL is an Associate Professor in the Department of History at Simon Fraser University.

MARK VESSEY is an Associate Professor in the Department of English at the University of British Columbia. He holds a Canada Research Chair in Literature/Christianity and Culture.

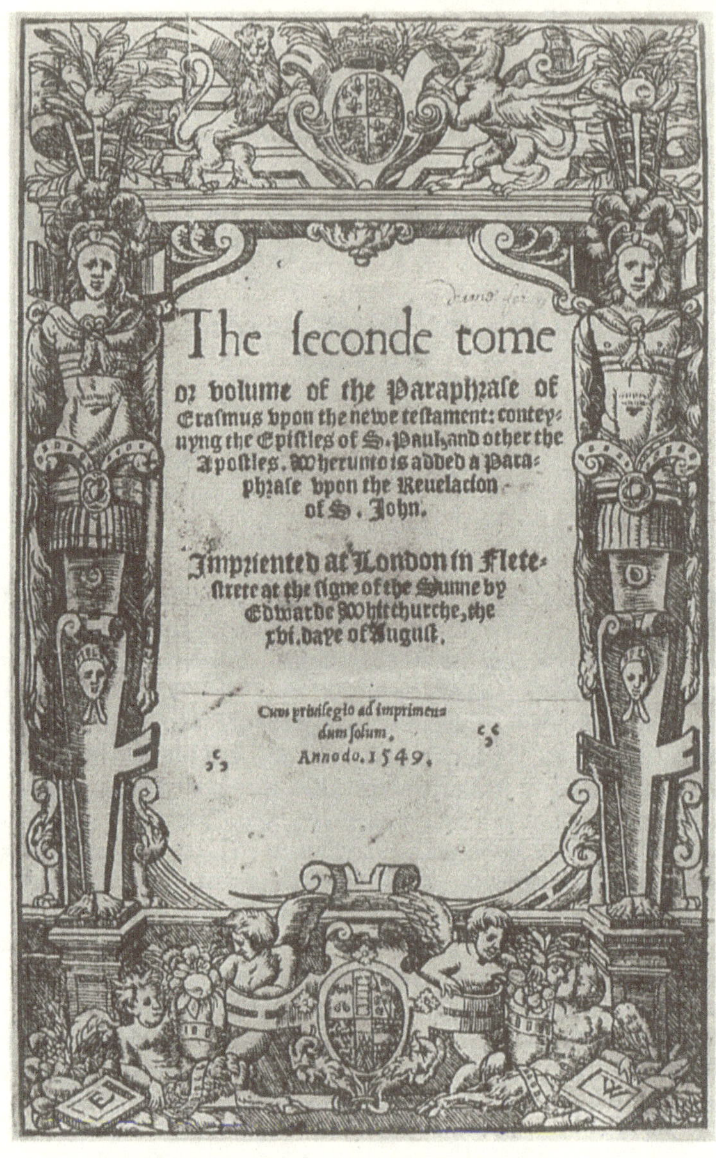

The ſeconde tome
or volume of the Paraphraſe of
Eraſmus vpon the newe teſtament: conteynyng the Epiſtles of S. Paul, and other the
Apoſtles. Wherunto is added a Paraphraſe vpon the Reuelacion
of S. John.

Imprinted at London in Flete-
ſtrete at the ſigne of the Sunne by
Edwarde Whitchurche, the
xvi. daye of Auguſt.

Cum priuilegio ad imprimen-
dum ſolum.
Anno do. 1549.

Title page of the second volume of the English translation of Erasmus' *Paraphrases on the New Testament* (1549). Courtesy of Special Collections and University Archives Division, University of British Columbia Library.

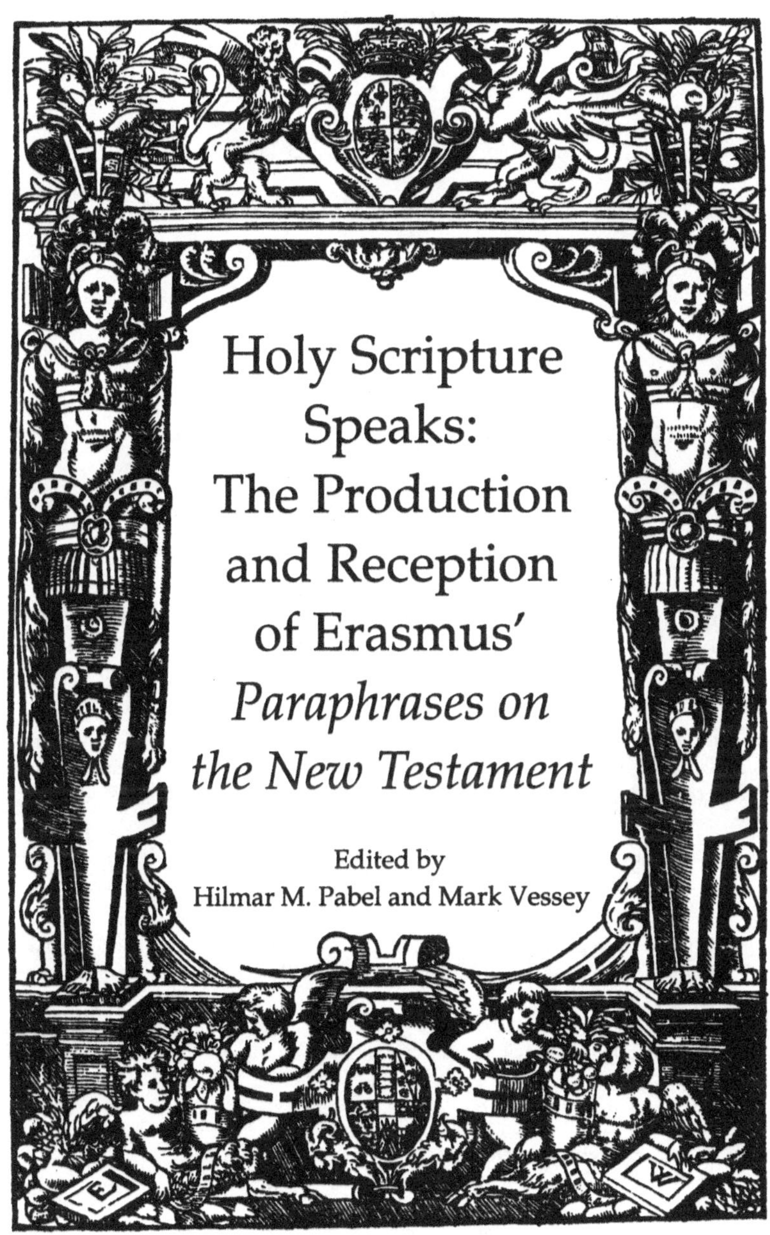

Holy Scripture Speaks: The Production and Reception of Erasmus' *Paraphrases on the New Testament*

Edited by
Hilmar M. Pabel and Mark Vessey

University of Toronto Press
Toronto Buffalo London

© University of Toronto Press 2002
Toronto Buffalo London
utorontopress.com

Reprinted in paperback 2019

ISBN 978-0-8020-3642-1 (cloth) ISBN 978-1-4875-2492-0 (paper)

Library and Archives Canada Cataloguing in Publication

Title: Holy Scripture speaks : the production and reception of Erasmus' Paraphrases on the New Testament / edited by Hilmar M. Pabel and Mark Vessey.

Names: Pabel, Hilmar M., 1964– editor. | Vessey, Mark, editor.

Series: Erasmus studies ; 14.

Description: Series statement: Erasmus studies ; 14 | Paperback reprint. Originally published in hardcover in 2002. | Papers originally presented at a symposium held at Victoria University, October 1999. | Includes bibliographical references and indexes.

Identifiers: Canadiana 2019012119X | ISBN 9781487524920 (softcover)

Subjects: LCSH: Erasmus, Desiderius, –1536. Paraphrases in Novum Testamentum – Congresses. | LCSH: Bible. New Testament – Commentaries – History and criticism – Congresses. | LCSH: Bible. New Testament – Paraphrases, Latin – History and criticism – Congresses.

Classification: LCC BS2335 .H64 2019 | DDC 225.4/7 – dc23

This book has been published with the help of grants from the Social Sciences and Humanities Research Council of Canada and Simon Fraser University.

University of Toronto Press acknowledges the financial assistance to its publishing program of the Canada Council for the Arts and the Ontario Arts Council, an agency of the Government of Ontario.

Canada Council for the Arts Conseil des Arts du Canada

Funded by the Government of Canada Financé par le gouvernement du Canada

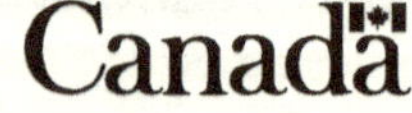

Contents

Acknowledgments

With one exception, the essays gathered in this volume originated in papers delivered at a symposium on Erasmus' *Paraphrases on the New Testament* held at Victoria College, University of Toronto, 1–2 October 1999, under the auspices of the Centre for Reformation and Renaissance Studies. Warm thanks are due to David Galbraith, Konrad Eisenbichler, and Michael Milway for their hospitality on that occasion, and to Robert Sider, Jane Phillips, James McConica, and Ron Schoeffel for constant and generous support rendered to the organizers, who are now the editors. Symposium and publication were made possible by a grant from the Social Sciences and Humanities Research Council of Canada, with further assistance from Simon Fraser University and the Canada Research Chair in Literature / Christianity and Culture at the University of British Columbia. Mark Vessey's contributions include material previously published in a review essay for the *Erasmus of Rotterdam Society Yearbook* 17 (1997), reproduced by kind permission of the journal's editorial board. We are grateful to Gretchen Minton and Stephanie Shirllan-Howlett for help in the preparation of the manuscript.

H.M.P.
M.V.
Burnaby–Vancouver, September 2001

Sequence and Dates of the Original Publication of the *Paraphrases*

THE EPISTLES

Romans	November 1517
Corinthians 1 and 2	February 1519
Galatians	May 1519
Timothy 1 and 2, Titus and Philemon	November/December 1519
Ephesians, Philippians, Colossians, and Thessalonians 1 and 2	January/February 1520
Peter 1 and 2, Jude	June/July 1520
James	December 1520
John 1–3, Hebrews	January 1521

GOSPELS AND ACTS

Matthew	March 1522
John	February 1523
Luke	August 1523
Mark	December 1523 / February 1524
Acts	February 1524

The Epistles were originally published by Dirk Martens in Louvain, except for Timothy, Titus, and Philemon, which were published by Michaël Hillen in Antwerp. The Gospels and Acts were all originally published by Johann Froben in Basel.

Order of the *Paraphrases* in the Collected Works of Erasmus (CWE)

CWE 42	Romans, Galatians	1984
CWE 43	Corinthians 1 and 2, Ephesians, Philippians, Colossians, and Thessalonians 1 and 2	
CWE 44	Timothy 1 and 2, Titus, Philemon, Peter 1 and 2, Jude, James, John 1–3, Hebrews	1994
CWE 45	Matthew	
CWE 46	John	1991
CWE 47–48	Luke	
CWE 49	Mark	1988
CWE 50	Acts	1995

Abbreviations

Allen	*Opus epistolarum Des. Erasmi Roterodami*. Ed. P.S. Allen, H.M. Allen, and H.W. Garrod. 12 vols. Oxford: Clarendon Press, 1906–58.
ASD	*Opera omnia Des. Erasmi Roterodami*. Amsterdam: North-Holland Publishing Company, 1969–.
CCSL	*Corpus christianorum, series latina*. Turnhout: Brepols, 1954–.
COE	*Contemporaries of Erasmus: A Biographical Register of the Renaissance and Reformation*. Ed. P.G. Bietenholz and T.B. Deutscher. 3 vols. Toronto: University of Toronto Press, 1985–7.
CSEL	*Corpus scriptorum ecclesiasticorum latinorum*. Vienna: 1866–.
CWE	*Collected Works of Erasmus*. Toronto: University of Toronto Press, 1974–.
DNB	*Dictionary of National Biography*. Oxford: Oxford University Press, 1885–.
ERSY	*Erasmus of Rotterdam Society Yearbook*.
Ferguson	*Erasmi opuscula*. Ed. W.K. Ferguson. The Hague: M. Nijhoff, 1933.
Holborn	*Desiderius Erasmus Roterodamus: Ausgewählte Werke*. Ed. A. and H. Holborn. Munich: C.H. Beck, 1933.
KJV	Bible, King James Version.

LB *Des. Erasmi Roterodami opera omnia*. Ed. J. Leclerc. 10 vols. Leiden: 1703–6.

NRSV Bible, New Revised Standard Version.

PG *Patrologia graeca*. Ed. J.-P. Migne. 162 vols. Paris: 1857–66.

PL *Patrologia latina*. Ed. J.-P. Migne. 221 vols. Paris: 1844–64.

RSV Bible, Revised Standard Version.

STC *A Short-Title Catalogue of Books Printed in England, Scotland, & Ireland and of English Books Printed Abroad 1475–1640*. Ed. A.W. Pollard, G.R. Redgrave, and K. Panzer. 2d ed. 3 vols. London: Bibliographical Society, 1976–91.

HOLY SCRIPTURE SPEAKS: THE PRODUCTION AND RECEPTION OF ERASMUS' *PARAPHRASES ON THE NEW TESTAMENT*

Introduction

Mark Vessey

> If we simplify history, we can say that before the 'modern' period, that is, until the sixteenth or seventeenth century, Holy Scripture speaks ... [T]he modern age is formed by discovering little by little that this Spoken Word is no longer heard, that it has been altered by textual corruptions and the avatars of history.
>
> Michel de Certeau

As a series of evangelical orations, Erasmus' *Paraphrases on the New Testament* (first published 1517–24) are a natural embodiment of their author's intent to make the Word of God effective in his own age: only if the gospel were *heard* again in its most persuasive form, the humanist rhetorician believed, could it move human beings to the life of Christ-like piety in which their salvation lay. At the same time, the *Paraphrases* are unmistakably the product of a highly evolved and rapidly developing textual and typographic culture. Virtual scripts for preaching rather than transcripts of sermons actually preached, they are the work of a man who was making the printing press his pulpit and who would always rely on others to give physical voice to the gospel message as he phrased it. Beyond the fact of their printed textuality from the moment of first issue, they are literate productions in another, more distinctive and generically specific sense too. As *paraphrases*, they depend upon and refer to a prior text, the Christian 'text' par excellence of Holy Scripture. Only if the gospel were *read* again in its primitive textual form, the humanist grammarian believed, could it be preached without error or loss.

Thus theorized, the relationship of scriptural text to paraphrastic discourse appears straightforward. In practice, as Erasmus' 1516 edition of the New Testament – Greek text, revised Latin version, annotations – sufficiently showed, there was no such thing as direct recourse to the visible letter of Scripture. For a scholar of the kind Erasmus had made himself, 'reading' and 'hearing' the Word of God faithfully in sixteenth-century Europe presupposed the review of an entire tradition of biblical transcription and commentary. While few were qualified to undertake the work, it was the responsibility of those who called themselves theologians to ensure that its fruits, once gathered, were distributed. By aiming at that distribution, the *Paraphrases on the New Testament* assume the whole burden of Erasmus' enterprise as scripturalist and orator, publishing scholar of the Bible and Christian exegete-in-print.

This volume of essays on the production and reception of the *Paraphrases* is meant to recomplicate the simplified history of the Western relationship to Scripture advanced by Michel de Certeau.[1] It aims to do so by consolidating and extending the gains of recent scholarship in three related domains: first, that of Erasmus' performance as an exponent of the literary, rhetorical, historical, and moral-philosophical ideals of Renaissance humanism; second, that of his work as an editor, translator, and expositor of the Bible, especially of the New Testament; third, that of the impact of his writings – more precisely, of the printed books which sixteenth-century publishers put onto the market under his name – on the culture of early modern Europe.

None of these subjects is new and none can be treated comprehensively in a work of this kind. For as long as Erasmus has been an object of scholarly interest outside confessional polemic, he has been studied as a humanist, as a biblicist, and as a figure of major cultural-historical importance – if only, in Lucien Febvre's crisp judgment, as one of history's losers. Moreover, the best students of his life and work have always known how to preserve the unity of a complex identity, to explain how a passion for Latin eloquence and zeal for the 'philosophy of Christ' were conjoined in a lifelong activity of teaching and preaching that found its main audience, and wrought its most lasting effects, through the new medium of print. Yet for all the clarity of this profile of Erasmus – which is essentially that of his own iconography – the challenge remains to establish detailed relations between his theory and practice as a reader and producer of texts in various genres, the corresponding and competing principles of his collaborators and critics, and the social and material conditions under which the traffic of books and ideas took place during and after his lifetime. It is in the area of these determinations that the contributors to *Holy Scripture Speaks* have concentrated their efforts.

Several factors appear to favour the undertaking. Chief among them is a growing awareness that Erasmus' notions of 'good literature' (*bonae litterae*) cannot properly be separated from his reflection on the sacred text of the Bible. After a long period during which the literary-humanistic and biblical-theological aspects of his oeuvre were divided between the monographs of literary or intellectual historians on the one hand and those of ecclesiastical historians on the other – that is, when they were not simply conflated under the rubric of 'Christian Humanism' – the last three decades have witnessed a concerted attempt to reconceive the Erasmian textual universe *as a whole*. In retrospect, the contrasting but complementary studies of Marjorie O'Rourke Boyle and Jacques Chomarat can be seen as decisive for this development; the latter is fundamental to the work presented here.[2] At the same time, and partly reflecting the progress of the Amsterdam (ASD) and Toronto (CWE) editions of the Complete Works, Erasmus' most patently 'biblical' productions – his edition of the New Testament with its *parerga* and defences, and such works as the *Expositions of the Psalms* and the *Ecclesiastes* – have been receiving closer scrutiny than at any time since the early eighteenth century. In the context of a movement towards a more encompassing view of Erasmus' literary theory and practice, this return to the biblical opus has yielded fresh insights into the relations between philology, theology, rhetoric, and hermeneutics, as they are worked out in and through Erasmian texts.[3]

Erasmus the biblicist has never, of course, been interpreted solely *ex Erasmo*. Comparative study of the theological and hermeneutical assumptions of leading sixteenth-century humanists and reformers has a long and noble record in modern scholarship. Still, it is another sign of the vitality of current research that Erasmus' initiatives are now being considered within a much broader framework than that formerly dictated by such well-canvassed issues as the nature of biblical inspiration, the authority of the Vulgate, the legitimacy of vernacular translation, or the claims of historical versus allegorical exegesis. Indeed, the history of the study, use, and influence of the Bible, in the Renaissance and Reformation as in other periods, is increasingly assuming the proportions of a history of culture, while retaining – albeit in a modified form – its traditional focus on the reproduction and reception of the sacred text itself. This new orientation is well exemplified by the 1989 volume co-edited for the series Bible de tous les temps by Guy Bedouelle and Bernard Roussel, the two parts of which are entitled 'Reading the Bible' and 'Bible, Culture and Society.'[4] Especially notable is the articulation of the first part, in which the expected inventory of confessional differences in approaches to and methods of interpretation of the Bible is preceded by two other substantial sections, the first on the social and technological conditions of access to the scriptural text in the later fifteenth and early sixteenth centuries, the second on the books, authors, and readers involved in the 'biblical' circuits of printed production and reception between 1530 and 1600. Already on the first page, allusions to Febvre and Martin's classic study of *L'Apparition du livre* and to Eisenstein's *The Printing Press as an Agent of Change* announce a fruitful convergence of 'the history of the Bible' with 'the history of the book.'[5] The work of Erasmus occupies a large place in the cultural narratives and bibliological taxonomies elaborated by Bedouelle, Roussel, and their colleagues. Except where it draws on a body of existing scholarship, however, a synoptic treatment of the type they offer can provide little more than hints for future research. To date, scholarship on Erasmus and the culture and commerce of the printed book in the early sixteenth century has been dominated by Lisa Jardine's finely iconoclastic *Erasmus, Man of Letters*, which takes his biblical oeuvre largely for granted.[6]

The following essays represent a range of positions within the disciplinary structure outlined above. By first profession either classicists, historians of the Reformation, or scholars of Renaissance literature, as students of Erasmus their authors have been obliged to become something of all these at once. By the same affinity and compulsion they are students of the Bible in and as culture. As will be seen from the Notes on Contributors, many of them are closely associated with CWE, especially with the part of that project devoted to Erasmus' New Testament Scholarship. By agreeing to participate in the symposium from which the present chapters derive, they signalled their interest in exploring the ways in which the impulses generated by Erasmus' *Paraphrases on the New Testament* affected the relationships of sixteenth- and seventeenth-century Christians to the mysterious and manifold reality that for them was Holy Scripture: uniquely authoritative book, inspired text, divine Word.

Simply stated, the task set for the symposium and this volume entails asking and trying to answer two series of questions, the first bearing on what may be thought of as issues of *production*, the second on issues of *reception*. (Customary and convenient as it is, the distinction is anything but watertight.) 'Production' in this context embraces both the literary-authorial and mechanical-commercial aspects of the process by which a discourse (*oratio*) is realized in forms in which it can act or be brought to act on the minds of readers or listeners. In the literary-authorial sense, such production is traditionally the province of grammar and rhetoric; in Erasmus' own terms it would fall comfortably under the heading used for one of his most marketable works, *De duplici copia verborum ac rerum* ('On the Double Supply of Words and Things'). Thus we ask: What kind of literary and rhetorical product is an Erasmian 'paraphrase' on a biblical book? What are the rules and models of the genre? How is a paraphrase created? What is its objective or claimed relation to the scriptural text? What is its implied or actual relation to the reader or hearer? How is the matter (*res*) of Scripture taken up and redeployed in the language (*verba*) of the paraphrase? What kind of character or voice does the paraphrast project and how closely does it fit that of the biblical author? These are among the issues addressed in Part I below, 'A Kind of Exposition,' which takes its cue as well as its title from Nicholas Udall, general editor of the first volume of Erasmus' *Paraphrases* to appear in English. 'For a paraphrase,' writes Udall, anticipating if not pre-empting the questions of genre to be considered here, 'is a plain settyng foorth of a texte or sentence more at large, with suche circumstaunce of mo [i.e., more] and other wordes as maie make the sentence open, clere, plain, and familiar whiche otherwise should perchaunce seme bare, unfruitefull, hard, straunge, rough, obscure, and derke to bee understanded of any that were either unlearned or but menely entreed [i.e., entered = instructed]. And what is this, but *a kinde of exposicion*, yea and that of the most piththie and effectuall sorte?'[7]

To account for the authorial forms of Erasmus' *Paraphrases* is, however, to tell at most half a story. Recognizing that the rhetorical *actio* or delivery of the Erasmian discourse will be mediated by the printing press, we therefore also ask: What printed forms did it successively assume? What role did the author (and others) play in its revision and correction? What typographic or bibliographic codes were used to preserve the difference, or assert an identity, between the paraphrastic text and the text of Scripture itself, as edited by Erasmus among others? At this point the boundary tentatively marked by the division into Parts I and II below is crossed, as issues of production become issues of reception. Other questions follow: How were the *Paraphrases* read and disseminated? How did they impinge upon existing theological discourses, and what was the reaction of other theologians to them? In what guises and under what circumstances did they pass from Erasmus' Latin to the European vernaculars? Finally, possibly the hardest and most important question of all: What difference did Erasmus' *Paraphrases* make to the consciousness that people had of being addressed, in Scripture, by Jesus Christ the Son of God, his apostles, and evangelists? Without pretending to offer exhaustive or even fully satisfactory answers in every case, the essays in Part II, 'A Full Library of Divinity Books,'[8] may serve to sharpen the terms in which such problems can be posed. And that, for the present, is perhaps ambition enough. As Hilmar M. Pabel remarks at the beginning of his essay, the *Paraphrases* have not been much studied in recent times. Now that a new English version of this work is coming to completion in CWE four and a half centuries after its first translation into that language, the moment is ripe for a fresh encounter with the most declamatory and clamorous of Erasmus' writings on the Bible.

Clamorous to the point of importunity, his earliest critics would allege. The *Paraphrases* were an anomalous and, to some, extremely disconcerting work. It is worth trying to recapture that initial experience of shock, to recreate the horizon of readerly expectations c.1517–24, lest Erasmus' texts in their pristine modern editions appear as dead letters of the kind he feared God's Scriptures had become for many of his contemporaries. The easy generalizations offered in the first paragraph of this introduction must now be suspended, so that the work of the volume can begin.

What in heaven's name did the author of the *Paraphrases on the New Testament* think that he was doing, and how can we know? 'Erasmus' concept of a paraphrase,' writes John J. Bateman, 'is not easy to describe' (CWE 44: xiv).[9] Nor is it easy to contextualize the biblical paraphrases that he produced, either diachronically with respect to prior and later traditions of Christian exegesis or synchronically within the discursive universe of Erasmus' own day. The first two essays below attempt to provide such contexts. In chapter 1 ('The Tongue and the Book: Erasmus' *Paraphrases on the New Testament* and the Arts of Scripture'), we begin by considering the relation between Erasmus' biblical work and that of his 'patron saint' and chief precursor among the Latin Fathers, Jerome. Like any genealogical analysis, this one opens onto a contemporary plane, enabling us to see how Erasmus' sense of his role as preserver of God's Word from 'textual corruptions and the avatars of history' (Certeau) conflicted with the institutional prerogatives of other Christian interpreters. The field of biblical studies – in which Jerome, ill-advisedly, once invited Augustine to 'play' with him[10] – was contested space, in the sixteenth century as in the fifth, and not even the choice of the less frequented genre of paraphrase could save Erasmus from the censure of professionals. Nor, as it turned out, could it guarantee his place in the history of the genre. Omitted from the canon of biblical paraphrasts in the *Bibliotheca sancta* (1566) of Sixtus of Siena, he is also overlooked in the *Cambridge History of the Bible,* where the survey of 'biblical paraphrase' as a genre in the period from the Reformation to the present day begins with the *Paraphrase and Annotations upon all the Books of the New Testament* (1653) by the Anglican divine Henry Hammond.

In chapter 2 ('Exegetical Fictions? Biblical Paraphrases of the Sixteenth and Seventeenth Centuries') Bernard Roussel begins to fill this literary-historiographical lacuna through a study of specimen texts of Erasmus and four of his successors in New Testament paraphrase, beginning with Francis Titelmans (whose *Elucidatio in omnes Epistolas apostolicas* was published in 1532) and concluding with Hammond. Conceding that the genre of biblical paraphrase, by its very nature, is likely to defeat any attempt to measure the indebtedness of later practitioners to Erasmus as putative 'inventor,' Roussel offers instead a comparative analysis designed to reveal the basic congruence of these writers' undertakings and the considerable diversity of effects that they produced. Both for its critical method and its breadth of reference (chronological, geographical, linguistic, and confessional) his essay can serve as a frame for those that follow. Roussel confirms that for later paraphrasts, as for Erasmus, the adoption of this form of exposition implied a willingness to enlarge upon or restrict the possible sense(s) of the source-text in obedience to other than purely philological criteria. While in theory the paraphrast reproduces the 'sense' of his biblical author, in practice 'every paraphrase constitutes an individual literary creation on an assigned theme.' The doctrinal commitments of the paraphrast are likely to play a particularly creative role. Roussel therefore proposes a sociolinguistic model of the biblical paraphrase that allows for differences in the 'addressees' envisaged and in the 'carriers' of communication used. Among the latter are such variables as bibliographic and typographic format, and mode of reception (e.g., public recitation or private meditation).

Towards the end of his essay, Roussel confronts the primary question for any literary-historical inquiry into 'Erasmian' biblical paraphrase: if Erasmus pioneered a genre, how are we to characterize it? His reply is forthright. The first-person biblical paraphrase is an 'exegetical fiction,' a kind of apocryphon whose apostolic attribution is sincerely disingenuous, deceiving no one. Precisely for this reason, such works provide excellent means of access to the 'communities of reading and interpretation' from which they issue. They are exceptional sources for the 'history of theologies and of culture' – and not only with respect to the Western, Christian tradition which they exemplify. The proliferation after Erasmus of these ostensibly 'canonical' apocrypha may, indeed, partly distinguish Christianity from other 'religions of the book.'

Answering Roussel's call for study of the processes of literary-doctrinal *communicatio idiomatum* between sacred and paraphrastic texts, Robert D. Sider's contribution in chapter 3 ('Historical Imagination and the Representation of Paul in Erasmus' Paraphrases on the Pauline Epistles') introduces a series of essays on Erasmus' intratextual relations with the actors and authors of the New Testament. Reminding us that the project of a commentary on the Pauline epistles was as old as Erasmus' sense of apostolic vocation, and noting how already in the *Paraphrase on Romans* (1517) Paul is assigned the first-person motto from the author's seal, Sider infers that Erasmus meant to 'make Paul his own,' if not by commentary then by paraphrase. A study of Paul's 'life and character' as they are revealed in the *Paraphrases* can thus help us understand Erasmus' historical vision of the apostolate and his writerly appropriation of the apostolic model. The choices made by the paraphrast in his adjustment of individual features of the biblical text to a general scheme of Paul's conversion, call, and missionary activity are minutely observed by Sider, down to such details as the selection of personal pronouns and possessive adjectives. 'For Erasmus,' he is able to show, 'the nerve centre of Paul's life as a Christian was the proclamation of the Word.' The Apostle of the *Paraphrases* is 'the prince of preachers rather than the first of theologians.' In order to create a dramatic context for Paul's preaching and display his character in action, Erasmus stresses the adversarial quality of his encounters, sometimes going beyond scriptural warrant to present the likeness of 'a man who defines himself in reference to the turbulent historical situation in which he is embroiled.' If this portrayal suggests a strong element of self-identification on the part of the paraphrast, other emphases detected here – on Christian preaching as revelation of a divine 'mystery,' for example, or on apostolic suffering as imitation of Christ – reinforce the impression. Little wonder that Noël Béda thought he could hear the voice of Erasmus through the persona of his Paul! Without going so far as to allow that Erasmus remade Paul in his own image, Sider supposes with good reason that '[t]he passion for preaching of the paraphrastic Paul must have been a theme personally congenial' to the author of the *Praise of Folly*.

Paraphrastic 'fiction' and biblical 'history' remain at the centre of both the next two essays. An Erasmian paraphrase, writes John J. Bateman, is 'designed ... to make Paul and ... the authors of the other epistles speak with the eloquence expected from a Roman without losing any of their authority and the plainness characteristic of the apostolic style' (ASD VII-6: 2, citing Allen Ep 710: 41–2). A particular quality of Roman eloquence is the object of Mechtilde O'Mara's study in chapter 4 of three 'Pauline' accounts of Christ's triumph over Satan and his coming in glory, from the *Paraphrases on Ephesians, Philippians, Colossians and 1–2 Thessalonians* ('Triumphs, Trophies, and Spoils: Roman History in Some Paraphrases on Paul by Erasmus'). The first biblical passage, Ephesians 4: 8 ('When he ascended on high he led a host of captives and gave gifts to men' [RSV]), is singled out by Bernard Roussel for the challenge posed to Erasmus and his successors by its citation of Psalm 68. O'Mara marks the paraphrast's insertion here and in the parallel cases of 1 Thessalonians 2: 19 and Colossians 2: 14–15 of imagery from the ceremonial of Roman military triumphs. Taking these features of the Erasmian text to be contributory to his overall 'purpose of making Paul's doctrine at home in the Latin language,' she explains its particular colouring as a reflex of his editorial work on the histories of Livy and Suetonius, carried out in the same period as his paraphrasing of the Pauline letters. She also draws attention to the 'oral' quality of Erasmus' discourse, itself an aspect of his fidelity to the Pauline prototype. Even as he interpolates the apostolic text with details gleaned from his scholarly reading, he 'enters into a kind of dialogue with the reader, keeping the latter's attention focused, with the skill of an extraordinary storyteller.'

A broader canvas for the study of biblical and parabiblical 'history' in the *Paraphrases* is provided by the paraphrase on the Gospel of Luke (published 1523), a text whose evangelist-author was reputedly both physician and historian. Erasmus' development of those roles is analysed in detail in chapter 5 ('*Sub evangelistae persona*: The Speaking Voice in Erasmus' *Paraphrase on Luke*') by Jane E. Phillips, who also provides a useful summary and discussion of Erasmus' statements of principle on his paraphrastic voicing or impersonation of biblical authors. The ethical-locutory situation of a Gospel-paraphrast, he recognized, would always be harder to specify than that of a paraphrast of the Epistles, but only in the preface to the *Paraphrase on Luke* does he give much consideration to 'the received character of the evangelist.' In the work itself, Phillips shows, Luke's historiographical and medical credentials are used to good advantage. The paraphrased author proclaims at the outset the salvific utility and reliability (*fides*) of his narrative, and thereafter consistently enriches its historical texture. As in the Pauline paraphrases analysed by O'Mara, the Vulgate Luke is overlaid by Erasmus with idioms and material details from classical sources. The resulting historical 'flavour' is markedly stronger than in the other Gospel paraphrases. Along with 'fuller historical contextualization,' the *Paraphrase on Luke* regularly makes 'typological connections ... between events on the historical plane and the spiritual transformations being set in motion.' Similarly, while medical images are elaborated by Erasmus on behalf of the other evangelists, his Luke is accredited as a specialist from the start, one in whose discourse '[i]llness, healing, and the art of medicine form the basis of a web of metaphors for individual sin and salvation, and can even be extended to the historical plane and applied to the health of nations.' In addition to these twin professional competences, Phillips identifies another aspect of the Lucan biblical persona that receives notable development, namely his 'self-presentation as an individual author addressing an individual reader.' It is not only the 'author' who grows paraphrastically. As successor to Theophilus, the implied reader or 'addressee' of the paraphrase inherits a larger place too.

With Irena Backus' essay in chapter 6 ('Jesus and His Family in Erasmus' Paraphrases on Luke and John') attention turns from the self-presentation of the paraphrased and paraphrasing author(s) to the characterization of the human actors in the gospel story. As an actor both human and divine, Jesus presents a special dramaturgical challenge. In the world-theatrical vision of the *Praise of Folly*, gods and humans inhabit separate realms, the former appearing only as spectators of the latter. The Gospel-paraphrast cannot maintain that division. From Juvencus' Virgilian account of the *gesta Christi* to Milton's 'brief epic' of *Paradise Regain'd*, versifiers of Christ's life favoured the heroic mode, where gods move freely in human society and human beings are routinely endowed with divine powers. For Christ's passion and (as O'Mara's study suggests) his triumphs, that register of expression was available to Erasmus too. How, meanwhile, does he represent Christ's early life? That is the question posed by Backus, partly in response to Jacques Chomarat's verdict that the Jesus of the *Paraphrases* is 'a failure as a literary creation.'

Before coming to the figure of Christ himself, Backus compares the paraphrast's treatment of Elizabeth, Zechariah, Mary, and Joseph in the opening chapters of Luke's Gospel with that of the patristic commentators upon whom he chiefly relied. On her findings, which may be compared with Phillips', the Erasmian Luke's historiographical expertise does not extend to placing such characters in a sharply differentiated historical setting; instead, Erasmus presents them as models of Christian behaviour of timeless validity, with a clear relevance to his own time. To that end, he often goes beyond both scriptural text and prior commentary in endowing these individuals with an intelligible humanity. His Elizabeth, for example, emerges as a woman 'with real suspicions, hopes and fears that any woman of [Erasmus'] era would have understood' and his Mary as one naturally fearful for her virginity. As Backus then goes on to show, the paraphrased Jesus in his human nature belongs fully to this company. 'The human Jesus at no point leaves the stage.' Because of the behaviour demanded of him by his divine nature, however, his character turns out to be largely unsympathetic.

Erasmus does little to mitigate the discomfort caused by this 'problem of two Jesuses.' Indeed, Backus argues, one of his objects may have been to counter the medieval tradition of piety represented by such works as Ludolph of Saxony's *Vita Christi*, which encouraged people to believe that they could come to know Christ on terms of individual familiarity. In the same way that the famous engraving of Erasmus by Dürer assures the viewer that a 'better image' of the author would be found in his writings, so, it seems, the paraphrast meant his readers and listeners to cleave to the *living* figure of the divine-and-human Christ represented in the Gospels, rather than to any devotional image fabricated in another text or medium.[11]

The chapters we have surveyed so far concur in attending first to the literary-rhetorical form or *verba* of the Erasmian paraphrase and only secondarily to its subject-matter or *res*. Yet '[i]t might be thought that these two aspects are so interconnected in reality that one cannot easily separate one from the other, and that they interact so closely that any distinction between them belongs to theory rather than practice' (Erasmus, *De copia* 1.7, CWE 24: 301). Always factitious, the separation of form and content is more than ever precarious when applied to a class of 'exegetical fiction' where the *verba* of the biblical text are, in a sense, the primary *res* and, conversely, any addition or alteration of subject-matter on the part of the paraphrast implicitly adds to or alters the *ipsissima verba* of Scripture. *In principio erat sermo* was Erasmus' scandalous rendering of John 1: 1, which we might now gloss, or paraphrase: 'In the beginning of paraphrase was the divine Word, and therein too lies paraphrase's end.' Jacques Derrida's paradoxical preface to Plato, *il n'y a pas de hors-texte*, would work equally well as a prologue to Erasmus' *Paraphrases*. However 'apocryphal' (Roussel's term) biblical paraphrase may sometimes be in practice, in theory it is always fully intratextual, that is, intra-Scriptural. That is the source of its power. Unlike normal commentary, which always declares its supplementarity with respect to the source-text, even when the commentator is merely explicating one biblical passage by another, paraphrase stands up – in its first-person, Erasmian mode, *speaks* up – in the name of Scripture itself.

A recent study of patristic exegesis has shown how resourceful the Church Fathers were in making the import of potentially dissonant biblical passages conform to their intuitions of the overall 'sense' of the Bible's teaching on such controversial topics as virginity, marriage, and divorce. One of their favourite ways of doing so was by the device of 'intertextual exegesis,' in which one scriptural text is used to exert interpretative pressure on another.[12] Such inter- or (as defined above) *intra*-textual versatility is an important aspect of the rhetorical-doctrinal method of the Erasmian paraphrase. In her discussion of his treatment of the union of Zechariah and Elizabeth, Irena Backus already finds the paraphrast, as 'Luke,' interpolating a passage from Matthew's Gospel in order to enliven his portrait of a pious Catholic marriage with a jibe at the moral laxity of the contemporary clergy. This mode of analysis is carried further by Hilmar M. Pabel in chapter 7 ('Exegesis and Marriage in Erasmus' *Paraphrases on the New Testament*'). By balancing the dignity of marriage with esteem for virginity and allowing for divorce in cases of adultery, Erasmus makes a decisive contribution to 'modern' theology and social thinking. His scriptural texts of reference are, however, necessarily the same as those used by ancient and medieval theologians. So how does he come to recommend these doctrines without (as some scholars have alleged) being in open breach with Christian tradition? The *Annotations* and *Paraphrases*, as primary sites of his engagement with Scripture and its prior exegesis, may be expected to provide the answer to that question.

Rejecting the facile distinction between Erasmus' hermeneutical theory and his practice as a scriptural theologian, Pabel subjects key passages of the *Paraphrases* to an 'Erasmian analysis,' one that takes due account not only of the relevant biblical 'intratexts' but also of the interpretative environment constituted by patristic and medieval exegesis in all its genres. The result is a philologically precise reprise of the Wife of Bath's exfoliation of the clerkly 'boke' on sex and marriage in *The Canterbury Tales*, which, though inevitably less rambunctuous than the original, conveys a similar sense of the adjustment of 'experience' to 'auctoritee' and vice versa. As in the Wife's discourse, Jerome's interpretation of texts such as 1 Corinthians 7 (in the treatise *Against Jovinian* and elsewhere) remains vividly present. If Pabel's paraphrast finally appears less radically reforming than Chaucer's, the independence of his readings and the directness of his rhetorical address are no less well assured. Here we see Erasmus the intrascriptural theologian moving deftly in and out of the tracks of his patristic precursors in that art, eliding the distinction of 'text' and 'gloss' that was so marked a feature of the apparatus of biblical interpretation transmitted from the Middle Ages.

Formal, bibliographical factors in the production of the *Paraphrases* receive closer scrutiny from John J. Bateman in chapter 8 ('The Textual Travail of the *Tomus secundus* of the *Paraphrases*'), which carries us beyond the limits of the author's control of 'scripture' and into the 'library' of printed divinity (Part II). Where previous essays in the volume focus on the Erasmian text as ideal product of the author's double store of (biblical) *res* and (parabiblical) *verba*, this one shows it assuming material shape in the collaborative domain of the printing shop. The ambiguity of the author's role as text-producer in a culture of print is nicely illustrated by contemporary portraits of Erasmus, including that by Metsys referred to in this chapter, which (in one of two surviving copies) shows him writing the beginning of the *Paraphrase on Romans* into a bound volume of blank pages, in a hand that imitates the form of printed characters. As Bateman reminds us, with an aptly anachronistic Virgilian turn of phrase, the 'licking into shape' of this and other 'offspring of his pen' was in fact the work, if not of many tongues, then of many hands, not all of them always tractable. Both the *castigator* (copy-editor and proof-reader) and the *typographus* (compositor) could, he observes, be 'minor authors in the making of a text ... [and] in the matter of orthography and punctuation [were] the principal authors.'

Erasmus was clearly most diligent in his efforts to ensure that the printed texts of his paraphrases represented as closely as possible his intentions at the moment of their issue, yet his success in this regard could no more be complete than could any other author's at this time. As one of the editors of the *Paraphrases* for the Amsterdam edition, Bateman is well placed to give an account of the vicissitudes of the Erasmian text (here, of the *Paraphrases on the Epistles* that made up the second volume in collected editions of the *Paraphrases* from 1523 onwards) down to the first *Opera omnia*, published at Basel in 1540, four years after the author's death. In the course of establishing a textual history and stemma for the twenty-eight editions 'directly or indirectly authorized' by Erasmus between the publication of the *Paraphrase on Romans* in 1517 and the *Opera omnia,* Bateman provides numerous insights into the author's and publishers' visions of the use of these works. From the title-page of the first Basel edition of the *Paraphrase on Romans* we learn that an Erasmian biblical paraphrase was designed to serve *vice commentarii* ('in place of a commentary'). Whereas commentary observes a distinction between biblical lemma and comment, paraphrase as such substitutes itself for the biblical text. Nevertheless, from 1521 onwards editions of Erasmus' paraphrases also included marginal extracts from the Bible, allowing text and paraphrase to be read side by side. Fuller suggestions for mode of use appear in the dedication to the *Paraphrases on 1 and 2 Corinthians* of 1519, whose addressee is imagined 'carrying Paul around' with him wherever he goes and being able to hear the Apostle 'talk clearly and intimately' to him without need of 'long-winded commentaries' (Allen Ep 916: 41–4: *quo Paulum ... tecum quocunque lubitum fuerit circumferas, posthac absque prolixis commentariis tecum dilucide familiariterque confabulaturum*). In keeping with the ideal of portability, Froben began in the same year to issue octavo editions of the *Paraphrases.* Bateman suggests that the public for these *enchiridia* or books-for-the-hand was probably the same as the one for which he published octavo Latin Bibles, that is, 'primarily ... the clergy but also ... the educated laity, female and male, who wanted books for private study and meditation or something to read at Mass.' From 1522 onwards, Froben also produced folio editions of the *Paraphrases* (first of the Epistles, then of the Gospels) in a format matching that of the *Novum Testamentum,* suitable for more scholarly use. By a combination of rhetorical and bibliographic manoeuvres, Erasmian paraphrase could thus claim to 'take the place' of conventional (text-and-)commentary in two distinct social-discursive locations. If the number of early editions is any kind of index, it found a ready market in both.

As Erika Rummel points out in chapter 9 ('Why Noël Béda Did Not Like Erasmus' *Paraphrases*'), it was their popularity that brought the *Paraphrases* to the attention of Noël (Natalis) Béda of the Paris faculty of theology, and so greatly alarmed him. Asked to approve the *Paraphrase on Luke* for reissue by a Paris printer in 1523, Béda quickly found matter for objection. In the ensuing epistolary and polemical exchanges he marked out the differences, as he saw them, between the officially sanctioned theology of the schools and the habits of a new breed of 'theologizing humanists' represented by Erasmus and Jacques Lefèvre d'Étaples. These men sought to distinguish themselves by attending closely 'to the reading of God's words themselves and to the biblical text,' but their neglect of the exegetical solutions long ago proposed by scholastic theologians laid them open to error and even heresy. Far from restoring the primitive sense of Scripture, as he claimed, Erasmus was a paraphrast in the pejorative sense, a 'wrong interpreter and corruptor.' His example was sufficient to prove that those without proper theological training should not embark on biblical exegesis. There are further grievances. The humanist exegetes exalted literary style over content, even daring to impugn God's own style in the Bible. Erasmus had the temerity to disagree with accredited theologians, including Thomas Aquinas. He published far too much, 'unceasingly writ[ing] one new book after another.' Most threatening of all, to one of Béda's profession and convictions, was Erasmus' belief that Scripture should be made available in the vernacular (*vulgari lingua*) to all persons, 'regardless of sex, age, or status.' At Béda's prompting, in December 1527 the Paris faculty of theology issued a formal condmnation of the *Paraphrases on the New Testament*.

Not surprisingly, given this kind of opposition, French translations of the *Paraphrases* were slow to appear in print. As Guy Bedouelle shows in chapter 10 ('The *Paraphrases* of Erasmus in French'), the person responsible for the French version of the *Paraphrases on the Gospels* printed by the Frobens at Basel in 1563 could plausibly claim that this was the first edition of the *Paraphrases* in that language, when in fact the version of the *Paraphrases on the Epistles* in the same volume reproduced a text published at Lyon twenty years before. Presumably the earlier work was not widely diffused. The 1543 Lyon translator, prudently anonymous, has little to say in his preface beyond the usual expressions of modesty; if he has rendered any service, thanks are due to God who has the power to make the dumb speak and reveals to the humble what he conceals from the worldly wise. The circumstances of the 1563 Basel translation, also anonymous, dedicated to Charles IX, are open to somewhat fuller reconstruction. Occurring at a time of rising tension between Catholics and Protestants, the work can be considered 'one of the last attempts to make Erasmian irenicism prevail.' The tone and slant of its preface enable us to associate it with the so-called *moyenneurs* or moderates, a party of reformers who followed Erasmus in emphasizing 'concord, union, the peace of hearts and, above all, of consciences' and who, like him, appealed to a few fundamental articles of faith as the basis for Christian belief and practice. The translator reports and rejects the opinion of some that the present religious troubles had been caused by the rendering of the Bible into French. What reason could there be for resisting 'the pure Word of God'? It was a pity that the *Paraphrases* not been translated earlier! Erasmus' work is represented as a continuous gloss or commentary derived directly from the Scriptures by a process of *collation*. As witnesses to the validity of this method of exposition, the translator summons the Church Fathers, who are said to have practised it themselves. Béda, as has been noted, saw matters differently. From the beginning, it would seem, the generic specificity, legitimacy, and ancestry of Erasmian paraphrase were as much in dispute as any of the author's opinions.

In promoting the French *Paraphrases* of 1563, the translator cites as precedents the German and English translations of Erasmus' work. In one notable respect both those versions exceed the Erasmian original: they include a paraphrase on the book of Revelation, made in German by Leo Jud and 'Englished' for inclusion with the *Paraphrases on the Epistles* in *The second tome or volume of the Paraphrase of Erasmus upon the newe testament* (London, 1549). Erasmus' exclusion of the last book of the New Testament and Jud's substitute paraphrase of it are the subject of current studies by Anne M. O'Donnell of the Catholic University of America.[13] In chapter 11 ('John Bale's *Image of Both Churches* and the English Paraphrase on Revelation'), Gretchen E. Minton considers the claims of a possible rival candidate for the place taken by Jud's work in the first English *Paraphrases*, and so enters on an investigation of the ways in which Erasmian techniques of biblical exegesis were exploited and adapted in the context of the English Reformation.

Bale's *Image of Both Churches*, completed around the time (1547) that Edward VI's injunctions were requiring an English version of the *Paraphrases on the Gospels* to be placed in every church in the land, announced itself as 'a frutefull exposicion or paraphrase ... wherein [the book of Revelation] is conferred with the other scripturs and most auctorised historyes.' In its method of 'conferring' scriptural texts (cf. the *collation* of the 1563 French translator's preface cited above) and its style of continuous first-person discourse Bale's work conforms broadly to the Erasmian model, on which it clearly depends. The principal difference, Minton shows, is in the author's manner of conflating the narrative of events prophesied by John of Patmos with those of other, more contemporary 'historyes.' It is Bale's personal and at times sharply polemical interest in interpreting the Apocalypse as a prophecy of the present age of the church and of the English as a godly nation – an interest stimulated by his experience as an exile in the later years of Henry VIII's reign and nourished by readings of Continental reformers – that shatters the mould of Erasmian paraphrase. Bale was certainly no 'moderate.' For a politic combination of Erasmian humanist principles and nationalist apocalypticism, Minton suggests, the English would have to wait for the appearance of John Foxe's *Acts and Monuments* or 'Book of Martyrs,' which injunctions of Elizabeth I in 1571 ordered widely diffused throughout the land, and which thereby came to form a supplement to the vernacular 'library of divinity' already constituted by approved English versions of the Bible and Erasmus' *Paraphrases*.

The story of the production, dissemination, and reception of the sixteenth-century English edition of Erasmus' *Paraphrases* is recapitulated and substantially enlarged by John Craig in chapter 12 ('Forming a Protestant Consciousness? Erasmus' *Paraphrases* in English Parishes, 1547–1666'), an essay that 'knits up' the present volume rather as Bale imagined Revelation did the Bible. Noting that scholarly interest in Erasmian influences on the religion of early modern England has flagged over the past three decades, as historians have devoted their main energies to the study of popular culture, Craig argues that the new historiography of the English Reformation has in fact made more pressing the questions raised in 1971 by Craig Thompson when he asserted, with respect to the 1547 royal injunctions ordering churches to acquire the *Paraphrases*, that 'what we want to know is first whether they did so, secondly whether the translations were used and what difference, if any, they made to readers.' Craig sets out to answer these questions through an extensive survey of parish and other records. First, however, he reviews the terms of the sixteenth-century injunctions and the publishing history of the English *Paraphrases*. He notes, inter alia, the different contexts of use, clerical and popular, that were envisaged for the Erasmian work in the injunctions; the restricted scope of the latter, which only ever specified the *Paraphrases on the Gospels;* the shifting designs of the editors of the English versions, progressively more reforming, between the first and second volumes and the first and second editions; and particular features of the layout of the printed text (biblical lemmata, paraphrase, marginal notes and cross-references, indexes) that could affect the ways in which it was read and understood.

Having prepared the ground for a fresh assault on Thompson's problem, Craig makes a search of the printed parish and ecclesiastical court records from fifteen English counties, from Cornwall to Cumbria, for signs of the purchase, ownership, and use of the *Paraphrases* between the reign of Edward VI and the Restoration. By 1553, he concludes, 'the *Paraphrases* [on the Gospels and Acts, if not also on the Epistles and Revelation] were probably to be found in most parishes.' There is some, but not much, evidence of loss and destruction of parish copies as a result of the Marian proscription of reformist books. Although the English *Paraphrases* were not reprinted after 1551/52, Elizabethan injunctions ordered their continued use (or at least availability) in churches, and records of visitation reveal their presence in parishes up and down the realm through the 1570s, 1580s, and beyond. An archdeacon of Derby was still asking for them on the eve of the Civil War!

Given these signs of ownership, what can be said about the use of the English *Paraphrases*? There are a few, fascinating hints that they were occasionally read aloud as part of the divine service, either as an adjunct to the Gospel reading itself or possibly in place of a homily. Clear evidence of extra-liturgical reading and study of the *Paraphrases,* either at the lectern to which this and other 'required' books were chained in church or at home, is harder to come by, though inventories of privately owned collections of books suggest some interesting possibilities. The data presented by Craig are sufficient, in any case, to cast serious doubt on previous arguments that the *Paraphrases* 'had only slight influence on Anglican thought.' Having established strong circumstantial grounds for believing otherwise, Craig ends with a call for closer study of the contents of the English translation, of its possible impact in the controversies of the Elizabethan church, and of its interaction in clerical and lay theological culture with other books that parishes are known to have acquired during the period. Fittingly, then, the present volume closes by opening a prospect on future research into the diverse ways that the printed Word of God was 'heard' and 'read' in the early modern period, not only in England but everywhere in Europe where the effects of Erasmus' style of scriptural rhetoric were felt.

Few passages in Erasmus' writings are more quoted than the place in the *Paraclesis* (1516) where he expresses a wish that the Scriptures be translated into the vernacular, that women be able to read the Gospels and St Paul, and that ordinary folk in every occupation and situation – the farmer at the plough, the weaver at the shuttle, the traveller on the highway – should have the words and stories of the sacred text constantly in their mouths (LB 6: sig. [*]3v). 'Let all Christian conversations rise from this source,' he continues, 'for almost all of us are as our daily conversation forms us.' Finding himself with blank pages to fill at the beginning of the *Paraphrase on Matthew* (1522), he warms again to his theme. A sixteenth-century English translator renders him thus:

> By my counsell and advyce, the ploughman and husbandeman of the countrey shall reade scrypture, the carpenter, the smyth, the mason, yea and harlottes also, and bawdes shall reade it / and to be shorte, the Turkes also shall reade it. *Yf Chryst dyd not kepe suche away from his owne voyce, I wyll not stoppe theym and kepe theym away from his bokes.*[14]

Even if the Latin Erasmus had to rely on other writers to vulgarize his version of the gospel, the example of his rhetorically free voicing of the sacred letter in the *Paraphrases* may have done much to change the daily conversation of Christian Europe. For historical evidence of a different order from that assembled by John Craig, we could cite the soliloquy – the conversation with a theatrical audience – of an English weaver of the 1590s, Nick Bottom by name.

> *Bottom wakes.*
> BOTTOM: When my cue comes, call me, and I will answer. My next is 'most fair Pyramus.' Heigh-ho. Peter Quince? Flute the bellows-mender? Snout the tinker? Starveling? God's my life! Stolen hence, and left me asleep? – I have had a most rare vision. I have had a dream past the wit of man to say what dream it was. Man is but an ass if he go about to

> expound this dream. Methought I was – there is no man can tell what. Methought I was, and methought I had – but man is but a patched fool if he will offer to say what methought I had. *The eye of man hath not heard, the ear of man hath not seen, man's hand is not able to taste, his tongue to conceive, nor his heart to report what my dream was.* I will get Peter Quince to write a ballad of this dream. It shall be called 'Bottom's Dream,' because it hath no bottom, and I will sing it in the latter end of a play, before the Duke.
>
> (Shakespeare, *A Midsummer Night's Dream* 4.1.198–213; emphasis added)

There is no reason to suppose that Shakespeare or his character had Erasmus' paraphrase on 1 Corinthians 2: 9 in mind. More interesting are the links that can be made between Bottom's comic ecstasy and the Christian transports promised by Dame Folly in her peroration.[15] Yet even those are perhaps of less moment for a cultural history than the freedom to (mis)take the part of Paul the Apostle that is tacitly assumed for the aspiring actor in Shakespeare's play, the one among those 'Hard-handed men ... Which never laboured in their minds till now' who would, if he could, play *all* parts. As the Oxford editor points out, the transformations of *A Midsummer Night's Dream* are more Ovidian than Christian; the comedy of the 'mechanicals' in rehearsal and performance arises from their awkwardness in speaking the lines and conveying the action of a classical plot, not a text of Scripture. Bottom's sensory confusion nevertheless has its Erasmian side. For he seems to have learned the lesson of the *Paraclesis* and related exhortations to the study of Scripture, including the one in the Edwardian and Elizabethan 'Book of Homelies,' a work of Erasmian inspiration that served alongside the *Paraphrases* as a resource for preaching in English parishes: 'These bokes [of Scripture], therfore, ought to be much in our handes, in our eyes, in our eares, in oure mouthes, but moste of all, in our hartes.'[16]

NOTES

1 The epigraph is from Michel de Certeau, *The Practice of Everyday Life*, 136; see also ch. 4 of his *The Writing of History*.

2 Marjorie O'Rourke Boyle, *Erasmus on Language and Method in Theology*; Jacques Chomarat, *Grammaire et rhétorique chez Érasme*.

3 See, e.g., Jerry H. Bentley, *Humanists and Holy Writ: New Testament Scholarship in the Renaissance*, ch. 4; Erika Rummel, *Erasmus' Annotations on the New Testament: From Philologist to Theologian*; Manfred Hoffmann, *Rhetoric and Theology: The Hermeneutic of Erasmus*; and Kathy Eden, *Hermeneutics and the Rhetorical Tradition: Chapters in the Ancient Legacy and Its Humanist Reception*, ch. 4.

4 Guy Bedouelle and Bernard Roussel, eds., *Le temps des Réformes et la Bible*.

5 Lucien Febvre and Henri-Jean Martin, *The Coming of the Book: The Impact of Printing 1450–1800*; Elizabeth L. Eisenstein, *The Printing Press as an Agent of Change: Communications and Cultural Transformations in Early-Modern Europe*. There is much of relevance to the history of the Bible in Henri-Jean Martin and Roger Chartier, eds., *Histoire de l'édition française*, vol. 1: *Le Livre conquérant: Du Moyen Âge au milieu du XVIIe siècle*. See also Jean-François Gilmont, ed., *The Reformation and the Book*; Jaroslav Pelikan et al., *The Reformation of the Bible / The Bible of the Reformation*; Paul Saenger and Kimberly Van Kampen, eds., *The Bible as Book: The First Printed Editions*; and Orlaith O'Sullivan, ed., *The Bible as Book: The Reformation*.

6 Lisa Jardine, *Erasmus Man of Letters: The Construction of Charisma in Print*, discussed in Mark Vessey, 'Erasmus' Jerome: The Publishing of a Christian Author.' See also J.B. Trapp, *Erasmus, Colet and More: The Early Tudor Humanists and Their Books*; and David R. Carlson, *English Humanist Books: Writers and Patrons, Manuscript and Print, 1475–1525*. The Erasmian edition of Jerome's *Epistolae* is now the subject of a detailed study by Benedetto Clausi, *Ridar voce all'antico Padre*.

7 *The first tome or volume of the Paraphrase of Erasmus upon the newe testamente*, fol. xiiii; emphasis added.

8 Again the phrase is Udall's. 'Thou hast here good Christian reader,' he begins his preface, 'the paraphrase of Erasmus upon the ghospel, that is to saye, a treasour, and in manier *a ful librarie of al good divinitie books*. For whatsoever thing any of the auncient doctours of the church leaft behynde hym, whatsoever in any catholike wryter is conteyned, whatsoever any notable good expositoure hath sette foorth for the syncere and playn declaracion of the newe testament, the pith and substaunce thereof hath this man with a clerkely judgement compendiously and briefly, as it were in a summe, couched together in this one worke' (fol. xiii v; emphasis added). He then recommends the work as one well designed 'to induce and traine the grosse and the rude multitude, aswell of Curates and teachers, as also of other private readers' (ibid), marking out the ground for a reception-study of the kind envisaged here.

9 For a summary of Erasmus' statements on the subject, see Bateman's

introduction to ASD VII-6, *Paraphrasis D. Erasmi Roterodami in omneis Epistolas Apostolicas*, pars tertia, 1–4.

10 Jerome, Epp 115.1 (CSEL 55: 396): 'in scripturarum, si placet, campo sine nostro invicem dolore ludamus'; 116.2 (Augustine's reply): 'equidem, quantum ad me adtinet, serio nos ista quam ludo agere mallem'! – passages perhaps already glanced at by Erasmus in his *De contemptu mundi* (ASD V-1: 80, line 111, where the Amsterdam editor, Sem Dresden, cites a clearer reminiscence in Allen Ep 936: 58–9, April 1519, by which time Erasmus was embroiled with his critics at Louvain and elsewhere). The Paris theologian Noël Béda proved equally resistant to the humanist's sense of exegetical 'play': see below, 271.

11 See the closing statement of the *Paraclesis*: 'An image, if it represents anything at all, represents only the form of the body, but these writings set before you the living picture of his sacred mind, Christ as he actually spoke, healed, died, and rose from the grave, rendering him so completely present that you would see less of him if you had him directly in front of your eyes' (trans. and ed. Robert M. Adams, *Desiderius Erasmus: The Praise of Folly and Other Writings*, 127).

12 Elizabeth A. Clark, *Reading Renunciation: Asceticism and Scripture in Early Christianity*.

13 Her paper at the 1999 Toronto conference was entitled 'Erasmus' Unwritten Paraphrase on the Book of Revelation.'

14 *An exhortation to the study of the Gospell*, printed as a sequel to William Roye's translation of the *Paraclesis* at London by R. Wyer (STC 10493.5, dated 1534?), sig. e.ii v. The Latin of the sentence here italicized reads 'Si hos non submovit a sua voce Christus, nec ego submovebo eos ab illius libris' (LB 7: sig. **2v).

15 On Folly's quotation of 1 Cor. 2: 9 and its context in Erasmus' thought, see M.A. Screech, *Ecstasy and the Praise of Folly*, 177–8, and, for the rapprochement of Bottom and Folly in Shakespearean scholarship, the indications given by Peter Holland in his introduction to the new Oxford edition of *A Midsummer Night's Dream* (Oxford: Oxford University Press, 1994), 83–4. The quotation from the play follows the Oxford text.

16 Ronald B. Bond, ed., *Certain Sermons or Homilies*, 62 (from 'A Fruitfull Exhortation to the Readyng and Knowledge of Holy Scripture'). See also Rivkah Zim, 'The Reformation: The Trial of God's Word,' 112–18 ('A People of the Book: Shakespeare's Audience').

PART ONE

'A KIND OF EXPOSITION':

THE PRODUCTION OF THE *PARAPHRASES*

ONE

The Tongue and the Book: Erasmus' *Paraphrases on the New Testament* and the Arts of Scripture

Mark Vessey

THE LEGACY OF JEROME

Readers of the Vulgate in Erasmus' day, and for centuries before that, had been used to finding a letter of Jerome to Paulinus of Nola as a general preface in their editions of the Bible. Written in the mid-390s, around the time that its author's idiosyncratic projects as translator and interpreter of the Bible assumed their full dimensions, the letter combines advice and invective in roughly equal parts. Paulinus is to be on his guard against those who simulate the exegetical expertise so laboriously acquired by his correspondent, for 'the art of Scripture is the only one in which all people everywhere claim mastery. As Horace says, "Trained and untrained alike, we all write poems" [Horace, Ep 2.1.117]. The gossipy old woman, the brainsick old man, the wordy solecist, one and all lay hold of this art and rend it in pieces, teaching what they have not yet learned.'[1]

Jerome's satire on amateur biblicists in this letter to Paulinus has tested the ingenuity of modern expositors, anxious to identify his unnamed targets. We want to know who played the parts of the *garrula anus*, the *delirus senex*, and the *soloecista verbosus* in his world. Erasmus, in his 1516 edition of Jerome's letters and other *opuscula*, is less curious. Understanding these references in a broadly topical sense, he does not even pause over them in his commentary (CWE 61: 211). Instead, he seizes the opportunity offered by a nearby mythological allusion to make his own addition to the rogues' gallery of inexpert interpreters. An English Franciscan, identified only as 'a certain theologian, highly esteemed by many but most of all by himself, from among those who preach in public,' had lately sought to discredit Erasmus' planned edition of Jerome, alleging that the texts were already plain to all readers. When challenged by their editor to explain the mythological reference in question, however, he had uttered only nonsense. In the story told by Erasmus, the venue for this exegetical trial was a tavern, its genre a drinking bout ('more of a compotation than a disputation'), its audience no better than the speaker deserved. A sequel thrusts the same theologaster into more illustrious company at a banquet attended by Erasmus' friend Lord Mountjoy, and comprehensively turns the tables on him.[2] Modern editors note that an abbreviated version of the anecdote appears in Erasmus' letter of 1515 to Martin Dorp, where it supports the case for a restored theology informed by the study of *bonae litterae* (Allen Ep 337: 676–84).

Here as elsewhere, comparison between the situations and strategies of Jerome and Erasmus is instructive. Where Jerome pilloried those 'like himself' who came to Scripture with a prior mastery of secular letters but who, unlike himself in his own estimation, mistook their own eloquence for the Word of God,[3] Erasmus seeks to resuscitate a literary and linguistic competence that could no longer be taken for granted, the loss of which had resulted, in his opinion, in the obscuring of gospel truths. Despite the contextual difference, their polemical and apologetic devices are interestingly similar. By caricaturing the would-be interpreter carried away by his (or her) own verbosity, each stresses the demands of an exegetical discipline that he himself seeks to embody and that Jerome, playing on Horace's prescriptions for an *ars poetica*, calls the *ars scripturarum*. Both writers are concerned to distance themselves from what might seem their natural company, but in neither case are the grounds for that distinction entirely clear. Jerome, whose own writings show him lionized by a group of aristocratic Roman women, affects scorn for those who debate Holy Scripture *inter mulierculas*. Erasmus, whose ideal of a Christian life-in-language was one of convivial discourse,[4] first makes his opponent the animator of a symposium in which he, Erasmus, is a talking partner, then lays a place for him at a banquet of his own noble and learned friends. On another occasion, presumably, Erasmus would have been there in his stead. If there is a difference between the situations of satirist and satirical object, it lies in the primary media of their exegetical activity, rather than in the social milieux in which they are seen to move. Several of Jerome's victims have 'stroked the public ear' (*aurem populi mulserint*), while Erasmus' hapless Franciscan is counted among the 'public preachers' (*qui declamant apud populum*).[5] Neither description is meant to flatter the orator. For their part, and in sharp contrast to such crowd-pleasers, Jerome and Erasmus write and publish books, many of them on the Bible. For one as for the other, the 'art of scripture' is also an *ars scribendi*, an art of writing. Without calling in question the status of the *ars dicendi* of rhetoric, which was traditionally understood to comprise the techniques of written composition as well as those of oral performance, this new or renewed emphasis on a doubly 'scriptural' mode of communication attests in each case to a distinct *prise de position* within the contemporary field of cultural production.[6]

Erasmus' *Paraphrases* on the Gospels, Acts, and Epistles provide a compelling instance of his scriptural art. 'Here,' he reportedly said of his first paraphrases of St Paul, 'I am in my own field.'[7] In saying this, suggests John Bateman, 'he meant that the activity of paraphrasing was part of the art of rhetoric' (CWE 50: xii), an inference that is encouraged, if not absolutely confirmed, by the technical history of paraphrase in the Latin tradition, with which Erasmus was thoroughly familiar,[8] and by his own practice of it in other contexts, including epistolography. Consequently, says Bateman, it should be possible in any given case to analyse 'the literary and rhetorical devices and other procedures which [he] employed to develop his paraphrase' (CWE 44: xvi), that is, to supply an *artis annotatio* or rhetorical commentary of the kind Erasmus himself furnishes (exceptionally) for Jerome's letter to Heliodorus (CWE 61: 123–31). Examples of such analysis are provided by other essays in this volume. As Bateman's careful phrasing already makes clear, however, the classical or Renaissance *ars rhetorica* may not by itself fully account for the texture of an Erasmian paraphrase on the New Testament. For while paraphrase falls naturally within the province of rhetoric as a technical discipline, *biblical* paraphrase is subject to 'genre'-specific rules of its own. In so far as those rules depend in Erasmus' case on a larger theory-and-practice of the *enarratio divinarum litterarum* or 'explication of divine literature,' considered as the primary function of the theologian,[9] they may be said to belong to a distinctively *scriptural* rhetoric. Alternatively, expanding Jerome's Horatian conceit of an *ars scripturistica* and slightly revising the traditional account of Erasmus' conversion 'from poet to theologian,'[10] we might regard them as part of a *scriptural poetics*.

Poetic considerations have a special relevance to biblical paraphrase, since, as Erasmus knew, the oldest and best precedents for his own activity in that kind were works of versification, beginning with Juvencus' Virgilian rendering of the gospel narrative in the time of Constantine.[11] 'What would my critics say,' Erasmus wrote of his recension of the Greek New Testament in 1516, 'were I to elucidate all the divine books by paraphrase ...? For Juvencus has been praised for daring to set the evangelical history in verse' (Allen Ep 456: 83–6). Later, when the *Paraphrases* themselves came under attack, he repeatedly allied himself with the fourth-century Christian poet (CWE 42: xvii, with references). The emphasis on Juvencus' boldness Erasmus found already in Jerome.[12] It is uncertain, however, how fully the author of the Vulgate approved the translation policy of his predecessor.[13] Whereas Jerome was once credited with encouraging the florescence of Latin biblical verse-paraphrase in late antiquity,[14] recent commentators are more circumspect.[15] It now seems likely that his Letter 53 to Paulinus was designed to dissuade the latter from experimenting in the Christian genre of biblical verse-paraphrase pioneered by Juvencus. Jerome was certainly hostile to the extreme form of Virgilian-Christian paraphrase in which biblical narratives were rewritten as *centones* or 'patchworks' of lines and half-lines lifted directly from the writings of the pagan poet.[16] Among practitioners in that sub-genre whose work Paulinus could have known was the poetess Proba, sometimes identified with the *garrula anus* in Jerome's catalogue of bogus biblicists.[17] It is with a swipe at their kind of 'childish and tricksterish' nonsense that Jerome concludes the excursus begun with the quotation from Horace, and launches on a book-by-book epitome of the Bible, displaying the 'world of Holy Scripture,' Erasmus says, 'as if through a lattice-work window,' *veluti per transennam* (CWE 61: 207).[18] The effect, as he suggests, may indeed have been to confirm Paulinus in his study of those books. In combination with a subsequent letter (number 58), this one should also have impressed upon him the vital importance of works of biblical *commentary* such as Jerome himself was already producing. It would have provided at best a very doubtful charter for the activity of continuous biblical *paraphrase*, whether in verse or prose. (Perhaps not surprisingly, Paulinus seems to have made no further essays in this still largely unexplored field.)

If Erasmus was sensitive to the ambiguities of Jerome's attitude to biblical paraphrase, he gives no sign of the fact. A more visible index of fellow-feeling with his precursor in the *ars scripturarum* is to be found in his strategic deployment of figures from a rogues' gallery like that in the first letter to Paulinus. Unlike Jerome, however, Erasmus is not content simply to silence the voices that deceive the public ear. Instead, as satirist and biblicist he endeavours to make that unruly member, the human tongue, into an instrument of scriptural truth. In doing so, I shall suggest, he inscribes a highly equivocal relationship between the imagined disorders of (feminine) speech and the (masculine) disciplines of writing on the Bible.

THE PARAPHRASE OF FOLLY

The *garrula anus* or tale-telling old woman has a loud inglorious career in ancient and medieval literature, enlivened from time to time by scenes in which she almost steps out of character.[19] If the strictures of the Apostle (1 Cor. 14: 34, 1 Tim. 2: 11) ensured that she would always have a place of honour in ecclesiastical satire,[20] instances of her direct interference in the male arts of Scripture – at least until the Reformation – are few and far between. Not coincidentally, it is Jerome's treatise *Against Jovinian* that supplies the materials for the most comically daring as well as romantic of all female paraphrasts of St Paul, the Wife of Bath. But it is Chaucer, not Jerome, who makes this verbally and venereally 'loose' woman into a biblicist. If Proba is attacked in Jerome's Letter 53, she is in a class of her own among that church father's *bêtes noires*. Never likely to be threatened by women exponents of the *ars scripturarum*, Jerome inverts and spiritualizes the topos of the *garrula anus* to create a select cast of essentially silent women: women who speak only when spoken for; widows like Paula and Marcella, young virgins already dead to the world like Eustochium; women who are heard in writing only when he, Jerome, throws their voices in his letters and prefaces, yet who also bespeak his works as a biblical writer. Jerome's launching of a literary career on the strength of this carefully assembled female claque may be one of the more successful confidence tricks in the history of Latin letters. Erasmus, for all his resourceful hieronymizing, never attempts anything like it. Nevertheless, in the *Praise of Folly* he gives the *garrula anus* her best outing since the *Canterbury Tales*, and claims the example of Jerome's satirical portraiture as his licence to do so.[21] When Dame Folly recalls the behaviour of those who profess themselves theologians, accusing them of 'fashioning and refashioning the Holy Scriptures at will, as if these were made of wax' and mocking their observance of what they take to be the rules of good rhetoric (CWE 27: 129, 132),[22] her satirical accent is recognizably that of an earlier female impersonator, equally zealous for the true art of Scripture, the author of the Vulgate.

Among Folly's false theologians, indeed probably the majority of them, are those 'so happy in their self-satisfaction and self-congratulation ... that they haven't even a spare moment in which to read the Gospel or the letters of Paul even once through' (CWE 27: 129). With such persons and their ill-served audiences in mind, Erasmus devised the *Paraphrases*. In doing so, moreover, he retained the mask or persona of Folly. 'Whatever reflections may have led to the decision to experiment with a paraphrase,' John Bateman writes, 'the fact is that the Paraphrases on the Pauline epistles [i.e., the first series undertaken by Erasmus] more closely resemble in their rhetorical structure and style the *Praise of Folly* than any other of his earlier writings or any extant paraphrase which he might have read.' In order to make the apostolic teaching dramatically present and 'applaudible' to an otherwise unreceptive audience, Erasmus would 'play the fool for Christ' as Paul had done. That meant acting the Apostle, speaking as if with his voice, so that nothing and nobody – no (other) book or expositor – should seem to come between the reader and the Word of God. 'Erasmus apparently believed that biblical exegesis, which is not to be confused with writing annotations, should be executed in such a way that the divine mysterium and, we may add, the power of the spirit, reveal themselves directly to the reader or listener in an oral context through the language of the exposition.' It is in the light of such a belief, Bateman argues, that we should seek to understand the 'rhetorical principles at work in his [paraphrastic] discourse.'[23] Thus, to picture Erasmus the biblical paraphrast, we might look first at Holbein's illustration of Folly in the pulpit. In her latest and most startling transformation, the well-travelled *garrula anus* has become the public voice of Scripture. Instead of 'Folly speaks,' the initial stage direction of the *Moria*, the first series of New Testament *Paraphrases* opens with a tacit declaration of the very principle that Michel de Certeau takes to have been subverted by textual-historical scholarship of the Erasmian kind: 'Holy Scripture speaks.'[24]

Readers wishing to test Bateman's sense of Erasmus' performance as biblical paraphrast can do so on the basis of his own translation of the paraphrases of the Pastoral and Catholic Epistles and of Hebrews (CWE 44, with his edition of the Latin text in ASD VII-6). And they will surely agree with him. On almost any page are to be found passages reminiscent of Folly's sermonizing. Here is 'Erasmus' at his most inventive, insinuating and affectively urgent, preaching apostolic doctrine as if from within the community of the apostles. The Pastoral Epistles, in particular, provide numerous hints for developing and specifying the ideal 'oral context' of biblical teaching. As instructions for the performance of the *evangelica functio* or 'service of the gospel,'[25] they have obvious metadiscursive appeal. Thus, for example, where the Vulgate text of 1 Timothy 3: 16 has the mystery of Christ preached and believed (*praedicatum est gentibus, creditum est in mundo*), Erasmus' apostle declares more roundly: 'Our mystery has been proclaimed to both Jews and Gentiles. Nor was this proclamation ineffective. The simple speech of the gospel, supported by the evidence of miracles, has persuaded the whole world, as no philosophy or human eloquence could have done, of something which would otherwise seem completely contrary to the order of nature' (CWE 44: 23). The application of 2 Timothy 4:5 (*opus fac evangelistae, ministerium tuum imple*) is clearer still: 'Make yourself truly a herald of the gospel. For those who teach their own views, though they may be called evangelists, certainly are not. But you, in the ministry which you are performing in my place, be sure to conduct yourself in such a way that what you teach is completely persuasive and deeply planted in people's minds, so that they are not easily shaken by those who will endeavour to teach a contrary doctrine' (CWE 44: 52). It would be hard to find a more concise rationale for the *Paraphrases* themselves.

In the same spirit, 1 Peter 4: 11 (*Si quis loquitur, quasi sermones Dei*), a text already favoured by patristic commentators, is subtly contaminated with Pauline (and Erasmian) notions of the teaching charism: 'If it falls to a person's lot to receive sacred doctrine or the gift of a learned tongue, he is not to use it for personal gain or empty glory but for the salvation of his neighbour and the glory of Christ, and his audience should perceive that the words they hear are from God, not from men, and that the one who speaks them is but *an instrument of the divine voice*' (CWE 44: 103; emphasis added).[26] Bateman points out that the image of the Christian as herald or proclaimer of the gospel, though not present in the Johannine epistles, is inserted there as well by the paraphrast (CWE 44: 174 n. 4). Another note clarifies an otherwise hard-to-follow rendering of 2 Tim. 2:15 (*Sollicite cura te ipsum probabilem exhibere Deo ... recte tractantem verbum veritatis*), in which Erasmus doubles the Vulgate's *recte tractantem* with his own more literal *recte secantem* (for the Greek *orthotomounta*): 'Conduct yourself in the work of the gospel in such a way that you need feel no shame before God who selected you. You will do this if you cut away all superfluous disputations and keep the teaching of the gospel on the direct road of faith and if, once you have cleared away the thicket of perplexing questions, you divide and handle the word of God with right judgment, *presenting to the people* only those matters which are properly relevant to the work of godliness and salvation' (CWE 44: 46 and n. 7; emphasis added). Here, as often in these *Paraphrases*, the evangelical teacher is envisaged as a preacher *ad populum*, or more specifically as a bishop (e.g., CWE 44: 154 n. 1 on James 1: 1). The significance of this fact cannot be too much emphasized. In taking up the scripts dictated by Paul (or 'Paul') and other evangelical writers, the evangelical actor-writer Erasmus not only offers instruction to those with a pastoral charge; he takes that charge upon himself.[27] Herein the biblical paraphrast is bolder than his hero Jerome, for whom the occupation of biblical commentator seems always to have been an alibi rather than an alias for that of public preacher.

Scarcely less marked than the Apostle's zeal for the *sermo evangelicus*, in this rendering, is his distaste for mere 'empty talk,' *inani-* or *vaniloquium* in the Vulgate for the Greek *kenophonia* or *mataeologia*, the latter a term to which Erasmus punningly opposes the true speech of *theologia* (CWE 44: 8 n. 21 on 1 Tim. 1: 6). *Ineptas autem et aniles fabulas devita, exerce te ipsum ad pietatem*, Paul urges Timothy (1 Tim. 4: 7), or as he is now made to say, considerately glossing a discrepancy in the transmitted texts of his own letter: 'Reject the frivolous old wives' tales of others. It would be more accurate to call these tales profane [Greek *bebelous*, misrepresented by the Vulgate's *ineptas*], alien as they are to the mysteries of evangelical faith. Let your object be to train yourself for genuine godliness rather than for verbal duels with a class of people whose garrulity is matched only by their obstinacy' (CWE 44: 25 with n. 4). This instance of 'double paraphrase,' as the annotator calls it, captures the two main classes of inane or garrulous speech in the Pauline-Erasmian taxonomy, the profane and the anile. The first kind is associated with the disputatiousness of false teachers, as at 2 Timothy 2: 16 which Erasmus develops at length (CWE 44: 46–7 with n. 8), the second primarily with Jews or judaizers (e.g., CWE 44: 59, on Titus 1: 10), but without precluding a wider range of reference. Once, gratuitously, Erasmus restores the *anilia* to their natural authors. *Anus ... in habitu sancto, non criminatrices, non vino multo servientes, bene docentes* is Paul's instruction in the Vulgate (Titus 2: 3). His more long-winded counterpart makes a further stipulation: 'You will admonish the older women ... not to tell malicious stories about other people's lives, a disease that is especially typical of that sex and time of life' (CWE 44: 61).

Perhaps the most pathetic passage in the Pastorals as paraphrased by Erasmus is 2 Timothy 2: 9, where Paul writes of his imprisonment.[28] In the Vulgate version we are reminded of the gospel he has preached, *evangelium meum, in quo laboro usque ad vincula, quasi male operans: sed verbum dei non est alligatum*. The paraphrase is pitched more heroically:

> For the sake of this gospel I suffer many evils ... even being imprisoned and shackled like some common criminal. But I do not desist from the preaching of the gospel even in these circumstances. The body has been chained; *the tongue that is a preacher of Christ cannot be chained*. Though a prisoner, I entice to Christ as far as possible whomever I can. What I suffer is of no concern to me provided that I make some additional gain for the gospel of Christ. (CWE 44: 45, modified)

Lingua Christi praedicatrix alligari non potuit. A rhetorical analysis of this sentence would note that Erasmus substitutes the unfettered tongue of the apostle for the unfettered *logos tou theou* of the biblical text, replacing an abstract metaphorical image of the unconfinability of the divine Word with a graphically literal one of the human instrument of the gospel, indomitable in virtue of what it preaches. The passage also invites two less technical comments. First, the literal 'looseness' of the apostle's tongue is an apt figure for the general loosing or loosening of his, Paul's, epistolary *phrasis* by and in Erasmian *paraphrasis*. Second, Erasmus' theology of the Word can be seen making a virtue of a property of the human tongue that he, with generations of moralists before him, habitually represented as a vice, especially of women. (Note also the unusual feminine substantive, *praedicatrix*.) Together, these observations frame an issue that forces itself on every reader of the *Paraphrases* who is reminded by them of Dame Folly. How can the copious utterance of the biblical paraphrast finally, or ever, be told apart from an old woman's garrulity?[29]

We should not, of course, expect Erasmus to address this issue directly, any more than we should expect to find him airing Jerome's doubts about the legitimacy of biblical paraphrase. Nor need we make a scandal of it, as if it pointed to some flaw or disabling paradox at the heart of the biblical-humanist project. The author of the *Moria* was a connoisseur of paradox, and it is a wise critic who can deconstruct his texts without appearing at once foolish and over-solemn. That said, an alertness to the opposition between evangelical and other, less desirable kinds of looseness-of-tongue may help us to appreciate what was at stake for Erasmus in the elaboration of a new scriptural rhetoric or poetics. The paraphrase on a passage from one of the Catholic Epistles offers us a point of special vantage.

'INSTRUMENTS OF THE DEVIL': ERASMUS AND HIS CRITICS

If the experience of adapting the epistles of Peter and Jude prompted Erasmus to reflect on the stylistic differences between their texts and Paul's, and so upon the variety of ends that a paraphrase might serve, he was even more self-conscious about the remaining paraphrases that would go to make up the *Tomus secundus* of the completed work, namely those on the Epistle of James, the Johannine epistles, and Hebrews, published in 1520 and 1521.[30] Dedicating the *Paraphrase on James* to Matthäus Schiner, cardinal-bishop of Sion, Erasmus explains that he never meant to expound these texts, considering them already sufficiently intelligible to most readers. Hebrews is in a simpler style than the genuine letters of Paul. 'The same is true of [the letters] ascribed to

James and John. John writes with such fullness that he virtually explains himself, and James almost confines himself to commonplaces' (CWE 44: 132). Why then bother to paraphrase them? Because, says Erasmus, the bishop had asked him to – and besides, unlike his *Novum Testamentum*, the *Paraphrases* on the Pauline and other epistles had so far escaped slander. Why do his critics harrass him so, 'at the risk of their own reputation and authority and to the detriment even of their sacred duty of preaching?' (CWE 44: 133 = CWE 8: 127). It was partly to spite these detractors, it seems, that he was willing to paraphrase even such Jacobean commonplaces as 'That religion is empty which is combined with lack of control of the tongue,' 'No man should take up the task of teaching unadvisedly,' and 'The chief plague of life springs from an unbridled tongue, just as on the other hand nothing is more useful than than a good and well-governed tongue' (CWE 44: 132 = CWE 8: 126). Trite as these topics were, Erasmus' handling of them is richly abusive of those whom he considered to be abusers of speech. As a result, the *Paraphrase on James* makes a fascinating prelude to one of the most unbridled of his own effusions, a work provoked by criticism of the *Annotations* and *Paraphrases*, the *Lingua* of 1525.[31]

'The tongue is a little member and boasteth great things,' writes the apostle, as he warns off dissident preachers of the gospel: 'My brethren, be not many masters, knowing that we shall receive the greater condemnation' (James 3: 5a, 1). Modern interpreters of this epistle advise against reading the whole of the ensuing diatribe on the vices of the tongue as though it were directed at would-be teachers. Bede, however, had taken it in just that sense and Erasmus, trailing the Anglo-Saxon monk closely here as throughout this book, follows suit. 'The human tongue has great utility whenever someone is teaching the elements of true godliness,' he begins, 'but to assume the task of teacher is to assume an office encumbered with risk.' He drives the point home:

> [L]et the man who aspires to the position of bishop and teacher examine and re-examine himself to see if he is equal to undertaking the burden. Let him above all reflect on the fact that he is assuming a responsibility that is subject to immense risk, since he will be rendering the most exact account to the supreme judge if he should teach otherwise than he ought. Because the speech of a person with author-

> ity has very great weight, its poison can spread more widely and dangerously. (CWE 44: 154)

This is the paraphrase on the first verse of the chapter. As he often does, Erasmus already inserts material suggested by what follows. At James 3: 2b–5 the biblical text introduces two images of control, those of a horse bit-in-mouth and a ruddered ship. In each case, the goverment of a large and potentially wayward body is assured by the discipline of one of its smallest members. The same rule, the apostle implies, should hold of the tongue as a member of the human body. While the image of bridling and hence the idea of 'oral' control are present as early as verse 2b, James does not mention the tongue itself until verse 5. Thus Erasmus is ahead of his text when, in the context given above, he expands on the risks attending over-ready teachers of the gospel by focusing on that unruly member. Verse 2 in the Vulgate reads: 'For in many things we offend all. If any man offend not in word, the same is a perfect man, and able also to bridle the whole body' (KJV). Here is Erasmus:

> Nothing, however, is more difficult than to exercise such control over *the tongue* in every respect that it never makes a slip. The weakness of our human nature makes everyone slip every day in many things. Therefore, if someone can avoid *every slip of the tongue*, this man might seem to be perfect and capable of controlling his whole body by the bridle of reason once he has *prevented that most slippery of the members* from committing any sin. (CWE 44: 154)

Not only is the paraphrast quicker than the apostle to fix on the misdemeanours of the tongue, unlike James he returns as soon as he can (in the next sentence) to the role of the teacher in the community, although the reference of the biblical text is by now more general: 'The one who prefers to play the role of pupil to that of teacher is farther away from the risk' (CWE 44: 154). Bede had noted the apostle's inclusion of himself in the first-person plural of verse 2,[32] but for Erasmus it is the tongue's capacity to do harm, rather than the fallibility of apostolic teachers, that needs to be stressed. His theme, a familiar one in his writings at all periods but here newly accented, is the power of language to act on human hearts and minds for good or ill:

> The tongue is a tiny part of the body, but all of the rest is virtually dependent upon it. Human speech is an effective and powerful force for either the benefit or the ruin of the multitude. It penetrates the minds of its hearers; it implants or weeds out pestilent beliefs; it arouses or calms passionate hatreds; it moves people to war or disposes them to peace. In sum, the tongue can propel a hearer in any direction at all. (CWE 44: 154)

Had this sixteenth-century apostle spoken with the voice heard earlier by Bede, his reader would have acquired a more collegial sense of Christian linguistic praxis. In the event, the 'we' of verse 2 disappears without trace as Erasmus hastens to turn a series of biblical commonplaces into a diatribe 'on evil teachers.'

The climax of this very Erasmian performance occurs in the paraphrase on verse 10 ('Out of the same mouth proceedeth blessing and cursing. My brethren, these things ought not to be so'). At first the application is general: 'You have learned to love God in your neighbour and your neighbour in God. You have learned not only that you must not injure anyone with the wantonness of your tongue but also that you have in fact a mandate to follow the example of Christ and to bless those who heap insults upon you' (CWE 44: 156). Then, within a few sentences, the fraternal 'you' has become an accusatory 'they,' the apostle a satirist. A voice like Folly's can be heard:

> They have in their mouth 'Lord, be merciful,' even as they cruelly rage against a brother with their tongue. They have on their lips, 'Our Father,' even as they pierce again and again with the lance of their tongue the neighbour for whose salvation Christ was pierced. They preach the goodness of God who saved mankind by his mercy while they themselves are quick to destroy it with the poison of their tongue. They preach of Christ's goodness to the human race while contrary to Christ's example they themselves sharpen their tongue against a fellow Christian. They pour out praise for the gentleness of Christ, who answered his slanderers calmly, *while they themselves assail with lies even the one who benefits them*. They proclaim themselves angels and heralds of Christ while they are the instruments of the devil. They promise the seed of heavenly doctrine while they sow pure aconite.

> They not only do such opposite things with the same tongue but even from the same pulpit they begin with the praises of God and then launch into denigration of a neighbour. The ruin with which they infect the minds of the audience is all the greater because under the fictitious appearance of religion they cover and disguise the deadly poison which they draw forth from their infected heart through the organ of the tongue. I ask you, brothers, does this not remind you of some kind of monster? (CWE 44: 157; emphasis added)

The translator's note on the italicized passage makes the essential point: 'The slandered benefactor is Erasmus himself.' In fact, the whole passage has a personal slant that marks it as apologetic. Where Bede had made a tiny breach in the apostle's text to admit mention of preaching,[33] Erasmus restates his view of the *evangelica functio*, now defined more sharply against its dysfunctional counterpart, the monstrously or diabolically split-tongued teaching of contemporary pulpit-preachers who 'proclaim themselves angels and heralds of Christ while they are instruments of the devil.'[34] If we take this hint and turn back from the paraphrase on James 3 to the author's complaints against critics of his *Novum Testamentum* in the dedicatory letter to Matthäus Schiner, we discover further evidence of a contrived affinity between apostolic linguistics and the theory-and-practice of Erasmian biblical scholarship.

His critics, Erasmus insinuates, were bringing sacred oratory into disrepute.[35] Yet he would not be thought to be mounting a challenge to their preaching prerogative. Glossing James 3: 1–2, Bede had been in no doubt that the apostle's intent was to remove from office those preachers of the Word who were inadequate to the task.[36] Erasmus' paraphrase is at once tactfully less clear on this point and, as we have seen, much fiercer against offending teachers. He now insists that the work of his scholarly seclusion (*nostris lucubrationibus*) is designed to support, not supplant, the evangelical labour of others. Let his position be clearly understood: 'I stand in the way of no man's reputation; I chase no man from his professorial chair, I interrupt no man's researches; I seek no promotion; I do not hunt for gain, but what little talent I have, I contribute to the common good' (CWE 44: 133 = CWE 8: 127).

Allowance made for the genre, this protestation is not far from an accurate report of Erasmus' situation at the time of writing. Whatever hopes he may once have had of regular patronage and promotion, by 1520 he had set a course for himself apart from the common ecclesiastical, civil, and academic careers. He had become a new-style Christian 'man of letters,' a freelance evangelist working through the press. He could therefore fairly claim not to be a competitor for positions or prestige held or sought by others. And yet his writings, notably those on the New Testament, were now being perceived – at least by some – as a dangerous threat to vested interests. The letter to Schiner, with the *Paraphrase* it introduces, belongs to a larger dossier on Erasmus' reaction to this changing state of affairs.

By late 1520, when he finished the *Paraphrase on James* in Louvain, Erasmus was contending with several kinds of critical opposition and detraction. There were those in that city and elsewhere who resented the efforts that he and his associates at the Collegium Trilingue were making to instal *bonae litterae* as the handmaiden of theology. There were those who objected to his revision of the Latin text of the New Testament and to the reformist tenor of certain of the *Annotations*. Since 1519 he had been open to charges of complicity with Luther. Heartened by these new manifestations of anti-Erasmian feeling, not a few individuals now took the chance to vent their longstanding annoyance with the author of the *Moria*. The boundaries between the different groups of opponents were not clear-cut. Erasmus himself complains of 'old-style theologians joining forces with [the mendicant, preaching orders of] Dominicans and Carmelites,'[37] and the majority of adversaries named or otherwise identifiable in his letters of this period can be put in one or both of those camps. It is a relatively simple matter, in any case, to locate some of the originals for the class of disreputable preachers described in the letter to Schiner. Beginning with letters of February 1520 to Archbishop Wolsey and Cardinal Campeggi, in both of which he announces completion of his *Paraphrases* on the Pauline epistles, Erasmus' correspondence of that year is full of references to preachers who use their access to the general ear in order to slander him. The letters consistently contrast the anti-evangelical utterance of such public preachers (*apud populum, apud imperitam multitudinem*) with the arduous and solitary labour of the expert biblicist (*lucubrationes, vigiliae, studia*).[38] By spreading hate and dissension where they should be proclaiming love and fellowship, these men betray their office. They are the prototypes of the twin- or split-tongued teachers of the paraphrase on James 3.

Two offenders receive special mention. The first is an English Francisan, Henry Standish, bishop of St Asaph's. In a deliciously comic narrative that but for its length would make a natural doublet to the earlier anecdote in the edition of Jerome, Erasmus relates how Standish had impugned his translation of John 1: 1 in a public sermon at St Paul's, only to be humiliated afterwards by two of the translator's allies during a court banquet. On being bested by one of these, Standish is said to have challenged his opponent to preach against him from the pulpit, to which invitation the latter cannily replied: 'I am not so foolish as to wish to pour out stuff like this in front of foolish women or an ignorant mob.'[39] In the same class as Standish but a nearer threat to Erasmus was the prior of the Carmelites at Louvain, Nicolaas Baechem of Egmond (Egmondanus), who on first seeing the *Novum Instrumentum* reportedly took it as a sign of the coming of Antichrist.[40] In late October of 1520, Erasmus and Baechem came before the rector of the university, who asked them to settle their differences. Why, asks Erasmus, does the Carmelite not set down his criticisms in writing, instead of defaming him before the common people?

> Whereupon [Erasmus relates in a letter to Sir Thomas More], being gravelled for an answer, he tried, as usual, a new tack. 'Ah,' he says, 'don't you wish you enjoyed a position of such authority?' 'What position?' I replied, 'the right to preach?' He nodded. 'Well,' said I, 'I have preached before now, and I think I could still say things more worth hearing than what I hear you sometimes produce.' 'Then why don't you?' he asked. 'Because,' I replied, 'I think I make a better use of my time by writing books; though I would not undervalue the work you put into your sermons, if only you would teach what contributes to amendment of life.' (CWE Ep 1162: 68–76)

The same terms of opposition appear in the dedicatory letter to Schiner:

> In every age [Erasmus writes], however blessed, the best things have always appealed to a minority. But was there ever a generation that gave more scope to ignorance, effrontery, shamelessness, stupidity, and abusive language [*linguae-*

> *que petulantiae*]? Write books they dare not, for these must undergo the silent criticism of educated men [*tacita doctorum hominum iudicia*]; their weapons are tongues steeped in venom, and their audience the unlettered multitude of poor and credulous women. This innocent credulity offers them their only hope of winning. What heroes! – these doughty performers with one single weapon, which they share with buffoons. (CWE 44: 134, modified; ASD VII-6: 119)

We are now close to the heart of matter. Erasmus, who chose the printed page as the scene of his evangelical activity, had fallen foul of men whose power was all in the tongue. Or that is how he himself represents his predicament, at the instant of paraphrasing the Epistle of James. 'You have a pen,' he has the diabolical Egmondanus say, 'we have a tongue.'[41]

The image of the tongue that begins to wag in Erasmus' writings around this time is an index of turf wars between rival groups of theologians. 'The violence and rancour of such reactions to the New Testament [as Baechem's],' writes R.J. Schoeck, 'can only be interpreted as stemming from resentment and fear. Such a world of new readings derived from intimate knowledge of the Greek was, for professional theologians who knew little or no Greek, beyond their philological reach: it was a threat.'[42] Erasmus seems not to have made much play with the tongue in this negative sense before 1520.[43] As one of the founders of the new Trilingual College at Louvain, an institution corresponding to his own Hieronymian ideal of biblical scholarship, he could be expected to take a positive view of this *membrum modicum*, until given reason to do otherwise. It is tempting to link the sudden proliferation of linguistic allusions in his work after 1519 to the scurrilous *Dialogus bilinguium et trilinguium* ('Dialogue of the Two- and Three-Tongued'), a satire on the opponents of the Collegium Trilingue first published in that year under the name of Konrad Nesen, for which Erasmus himself may have been in some measure responsible.[44] The 'two-tongued' persons of the title are theologians and monks opposed to the new Christian learning and closely connected – in some cases probably identical – with those satirized in the Paraphrase on James 3.[45] In the *Dialogue* they appear as votaries of the divine Até, a grotesque female figure with a lethally venomous tongue, as it were the apotheosis of the *garrula anus*.[46] Whatever the nature of Erasmus' involvement in this academic lampoon, a contextual study of the themes and images that culminate in the *Lingua* of 1525 would begin here. We have already seen that the new Erasmian linguistics has a special resonance in the *Paraphrases*. If we suppose that the trope of the tongue owed its currency to professional rivalries between exponents and opponents of 'new readings' in theology, what may its incidence in Erasmus' texts tell us about his perception of his own manner of preaching the gospel?

A clue can be detected in the passage about venomous tongues in the dedication to Schiner. Critics of Erasmus' *Annotations on the New Testament* were complaining that he had slighted such approved Catholic authors as Thomas Aquinas, Nicholas of Lyra, and Hugh of St Cher. 'In every age,' he retorts, 'it has been permissible to dissent now and again from the most eminent authorities' (CWE 44: 134 = CWE 8: 127). Indeed, he has disagreed on occasion with the likes of Ambrose, Jerome, and Augustine, writers due more respect than any Thomas, Hugh, or Nicholas![47] Then follows the passage quoted and discussed above: 'In every age, however blessed, the best things have always appealed to a minority ...' Twice in these parallel statements Erasmus appeals to history to legitimate and dignify his own proceeding. Twice he lays the emphasis on discrimination – between different authorities (or kinds of authority) in biblical interpretation, between the 'best' and the less good among contemporary productions. To have discriminated effectively in the first regard, he implies, is to have made oneself a victim – or, in the long perspective now recommended, the beneficiary – of discrimination of the second kind.

By choosing carefully between the opinions of earlier writers on the Bible, Erasmus has ensured that his own published output will attract only the minority of right-discerning persons. In other words, the position he has taken in the *Annotations* with respect to the (textual) company of prior interpreters has determined his present position with respect to the (real) community of readers and non-readers. In linking these two principles of discernment by a repeated appeal to history (*Nullo seculo ... Nullum fuit seculum ...*), Erasmus takes his stand on the same textual ground to which, always according to his own account, adversaries like Baechem already sought to confine him. The present is made to conform to the rule of the past, a past made available principally through the medium of writing. History will judge Erasmus as he judges Lyra, on the basis of what he has written or committed to print. And that is so because the verdict of 'history,' in this case, is the cumulative and consensual judgment of the learned, *tacita doctorum hominum iudicia*.[48]

What is perhaps most striking about this defence of the *Novum Testamentum* is how much more it appears to concede than the author of the *Paraphrases* can afford. How can a writer who stakes his reputation so exclusively on the silent judgment of learned posterity expect to be an effective preacher of the gospel in his own century? Unless Erasmus is at cross-purposes with himself, a less naive reading of these texts is called for. Is it possible that, in insisting as he does on the critical basis of his own productions and their textual solidarity with the writings of the church fathers, he was already defending himself against the accusation of possessing, as a writer, a dangerously, if not effeminately, loose tongue – an accusation which his performance *in the particular and novel genre of the biblical paraphrase* would have made only too plausible?[49] On that hypothesis, much of the rest of his polemic against preachers like Standish and Baechem can be construed as prophylaxis. As Jerome pilloried those 'like himself,' meaning the classically eloquent, in order to justify an idiosyncratically silent art of scriptural exegesis, so Erasmus may have needed – and in part created with his own doughty pen – a class of theologasters whose womanish babbling would legitimate, as if by contrast, his own evangelically motivated, textually disciplined, but none the less egregious loquacity. Granting as much, and following the lead of Erasmus himself in his commentary on Jerome's Letter 53 to Paulinus, we might care less in the end for the identities of his caricatural opponents than for the rhetorical force of the caricature.

THE TONGUE OF THE BOOK

According to Richard Waswo, writing on the *Paraphrases*, 'Erasmus always preferred the translating Ciceronian, Jerome, to the rhetorician of silence, Augustine.'[50] This appealing definition by opposites needs to be restructured if it is to answer the case. Much as Jerome admired Cicero the orator, in electing to follow the example of Cicero the translator he took a vow of silence. As a monastic writer on the Bible, translator, and commentator, he made a virtue of the fact that he, unlike contemporaries of his such as

Ambrose or Augustine, was *not* required to perform as a Christian *declamator apud populum*. Contrastingly, Augustine, despite his fervent desire for inward dialogue with God, committed himself from the mid-390s onwards to an oral ministry of the Word. Where Augustine gave precepts and examples for the public preaching of Scripture in the *De doctrina christiana* and other works, it was Jerome, more than any other Latin writer of the patristic age, who saw to it that the energies of generations of Christian intellectuals would henceforth be devoted to an art of Scripture as *ars legendi et scribendi*.[51] Emulator of Jerome in his edition of the New Testament, Erasmus brought this doubly scriptural art to the printed page, at the same time enhancing its textuality by the more or less systematic citation and critical review (in the *Annotations*) of the written opinions of 'approved authorities.' Had he stopped there, say in 1519 with the publication of the revised *Novum Testamentum*, he would already have outdone Jerome with respect to that part of the Bible. Erasmus, however, instinctively recognized that the mute letters of this immaculately printed Scripture (the ensemble of Greek text, Latin translation, and notes) would not by themselves infuse the hearts and minds of Christian men and women with a love like Christ's, even if those men and women were literate in Latin. Superior as it might be from a scholarly point of view to that earlier annotated edition of the Bible comprising the *Glossa ordinaria* and the highly regarded *Postillae* of Nicholas of Lyra (both products of a broadly 'Hieronymian' tradition in Christian Latin letters), the Erasmian Scripture had as yet no more active a presence. Unless the gospel message that it elucidated were now given voice by the theologians and preachers of the time, it would fail of its purpose. Since the theologians and preachers, in Erasmus' dim view of them, were not to be relied upon, he embarked on the *Paraphrases*, a work designed to give rhetorical force to the scriptural truth that he had already made plain. At that moment, if not before, he parted company with Jerome.

The ultimate expression of their author's intent to preach the gospel in print, the *Paraphrases* disclose more clearly than any other work of Erasmus the tension that both sustains and threatens his evangelical project. As John Bateman suggested several years ago, and as I have argued above, the speaking voice that Erasmus gives to the Pauline and – so far as he is able – other New Testament epistles is very like Dame Folly's: declamatory, cajoling, long-winded. It is as if, denied the right of public speech by the terms of his self-made vocation, he chose for his surrogate the most proverbially vocal of all possible personae, the *garrula anus*. Considered against the backdrop of preferred (male) discourses on Scripture from the time of Jerome, the choice was certainly startling. Yet there are few signs, if any, of unease on Erasmus' part during the period 1517–1519. Embarking on the Pastoral Epistles in the latter year, he gave predictably free rein to his paraphrase on the functions of the Christian teacher, inviting comparisons between the performance of bishops or others with a public duty of instruction and his own freelance activity. It is only with the publication of the *Paraphrase on James* at the end of 1520 that we detect any sensitivity to the potential conflict between his voicing of the gospel and that of other theologians and preachers. And even when it comes, the conflict does not relate directly to the form of the *Paraphrases*. Rather, I have suggested, the *Paraphrase on James* and its prefatory dedication register a more generalized, if intensely local, concern about the respective roles of writing and public speaking in Christian society. The most graphic index of that concern is the trope of the loose or poisonous tongue, a figure that now for the first time acquires a life in Erasmus' writings.

Tu stilum habes, nos linguam habemus ('You have a pen, we have a tongue') is the plea (or taunt?) that Erasmus puts in the mouths of his opponents. For him there could be no such simple separation of faculties. His theology of the divine Word dictated a scriptural rhetoric that, unlike Jerome's, obliged him to give tongue, albeit in print, to the gospel texts he had already so painstakingly edited.

In practice, of course, the 'voice' and 'tongue' of the Erasmian text would always be those of a reader or a reader's oral-aural imagination. Bateman notes that '[b]eginning in 1522, Froben issued the *Paraphrases* in two formats: a folio edition comparable in design and size to Erasmus' *Novum Testamentum* ... and a smaller octavo edition, divided into sections for separate binding if the purchaser so wished. Froben was in effect issuing a study edition to be read side by side with the New Testament and a "pocket-book" edition for private reading' (CWE 44: xiii).[52] Even these arrangements would do little to assist the non-Latinate to 'hear' the repristinated gospel text, until men (and some women) set about the task of translating the *Paraphrases* into the vernacular.[53]

NOTES

1 Jerome, Ep 53.7.1 (CSEL 54: 453): 'Sola scripturarum ars est, quam sibi omnes passim vindicent: "scribimus indocti doctique poemata passim." Hanc garrula anus, hanc delirus senex, hanc soloecista verbosus, hanc uniuersi praesumunt, lacerant, docent, antequam discant.' Jerome continues: 'Alii adducto supercilio grandia verba trutinantes *inter mulierculas* de sacris litteris philosophantur, alii discunt – pro pudor! – a feminis, quod viros doceant, et, ne parum hoc sit, quadam facilitate verborum, immo audacia, disserunt aliis, quod ipsi non intellegunt' ('Some with contracted brows weigh out their high-sounding word *among silly women*, philosophizing on the sacred writings, while others – for shame! – learn from women what they teach to men and, as if that were not enough, employ a certain facility, not to say boldness of speech to expound to others what they themselves do not understand'). Translations from Jerome's letters are my own. Erasmus places this one at the head of the fourth tome of his 1516 edition of Jerome's letters and opuscula (note 2 below), which is devoted to the *EXEGEMATICA*, 'hoc est, quae ad enarrationem divinae scripturae faciunt' ('that is, those things pertaining to the interpretation of divine scripture') (fol. 1v). For Erasmus' appeals to a textual and iconic 'Jerome' as a model for his own literary activity, see Jardine, *Erasmus, Man of Letters: The Construction of Charisma in Print*, esp. ch. 3, and for his general indebtedness to Jerome's biblical scholarship, Rummel, *Erasmus' Annotations on the New Testament: From Philologist to Theologian*. A selection of texts from the Jerome edition, including Erasmus' annotations on the letter here quoted, appears in CWE 61; for discussion, see my 'Erasmus' Jerome: The Publishing of a Christian Author.' The important work of Benedetto Clausi, *Ridar voce all'antico Padre: L'edizione erasmiana delle 'Lettere' di Gerolamo* appeared too late for me to take account of it here.

2 *Epistolarum sive librorum epistolarium divi Eusebii Hieronymi tomus quartus* (Basel: J. Froben, 1516), fol. 4v; CWE 61: 218–19.

3 Jerome, Ep 53.7.2 (CSEL 54: 453): 'Taceo de meis similibus, qui si forte ad scripturas sanctas post saeculares litteras venerint et sermone conposito aurem populi mulserint, quicquid dixerint, hoc legem dei putant nec scire dignantur, quid prophetae, quid apostoli senserint, sed ad sensum suum incongrua aptant testimonia, quasi grande sit et non vitiosissimum dicendi genus depravare sententias et ad voluntatem suam scripturam trahere repugnantem' ('I say nothing of persons like myself, who, if by chance they have come to the sacred writings after studying secular literature and are used to stroking the public ear with well-ordered speech, believe that what-

ever they say is the law of God, and, not deigning to find out what the prophets or apostles may have meant, adapt unsuitable passages to their own meaning – as if this were a high kind of rhetorical art, and not the most faulty, to misconstrue the sense of a text and make it, despite itself, obey their own will').

4 Marjorie O'Rourke Boyle, *Erasmus on Language and Method in Theology*, 135–40. For further nuances in a scriptural context, see Jane E. Phillips, 'Food and Drink in Erasmus' Gospel Paraphrases.'

5 Erika Rummel, *Erasmus and His Catholic Critics*, 1: 118, 122, identifies the preacher as Francis Birkhead ('Bricotus'), bishop of St Asaph's. In the past he has been taken for Birkhead's fellow Franciscan and successor in that see, Henry Standish. See the notice on Standish by R.J. Schoeck in COE 3: 279–80.

6 The terminology of 'field' and *prises de position* is Pierre Bourdieu's. See, e.g., his *The Field of Cultural Production: Essays on Art and Literature* and *The Rules of Art: Genesis and Structure of the Literary Field.*

7 Beatus Rhenanus in Allen 1: 64: '"Hic sum" inquit "in meo campo." Et sic erat. Inspiciebat veteres maxime interpretes, ex nostris Ambrosium, Hieronymum, Augustinum, Hilarium, ex Graecis Chrysostomum et huius imitatorem Theophylactum; ipse stilum accommodabat tantum' ('"Here," says he, "I am in my own field." And so he was. He consulted, above all, the ancient exegetes – Ambrose, Jerome, Augustine and Hilary among those of our language, Chrysostom and his imitator Theophylact among the Greeks. His own role was simply to apply a suitable style').

8 John B. Payne, Albert Rabil Jr and Warren S. Smith Jr, 'The Paraphrases of Erasmus: Origin and Character,' CWE 42: xi–xix, esp. xi–xiii.

9 *Ratio verae theologiae* (LB 5: 83F): 'At praecipuus theologorum scopus est sapienter enarrare divinas litteras.' Compare the description of the contents of the fourth tome of Erasmus' edition of Jerome ('quae ad enarrationem divinae scripturae faciunt'). In classical usage the *enarratio* is a grammatical genre applied principally to poetic texts. The generic title under which we now read the series of Augustine's (partly) preached discourses on a poetical text of Scripture, the *'Enarrationes' in Psalmos*, was assigned to it by Erasmus, himself the author of a similarly titled but unpreached series (CWE 63–5). On Erasmus' definition of the theologian's task, see Manfred Hoffmann, *Rhetoric and Theology: The Hermeneutic of Erasmus*, passim.

10 Cf. Jozef IJsewijn, 'Erasmus ex poeta theologus sive de literarum instauratarum apud Hollandos incunabulis,' 1: 375–84. The scheme is adopted, with modifications, by Rummel, *Erasmus' 'Annotations,'* 3–18. It originates with Jerome, who forged the distinction between secular and sacred letters that Erasmus and his contemporaries

inherited. For discussion of the 'poetic' quality of Erasmus' scriptural rhetoric, linking it to later theories of poetic affect such as that of Philip Sidney, see Richard Waswo, *Language and Meaning in the Renaissance*, 221f., with reference to the *Paraphrases*. One of Erasmus' conservative critics, Nicolaas Baechem, referred dismissively to his biblical scholarship as *poetria* (Allen Eps 1153: 215; 1126: 335). On Baechem and Erasmus, see note 40 below.

11 See Michael Roberts, *Biblical Epic and Rhetorical Paraphrase in Late Antiquity*, 67–76.

12 See Jerome's letter to the Roman orator Magnus, Ep 70.5.3 (CSEL 54: 707): 'Iuvencus presbyter sub Constantino historiam Domini salvatoris versibus explicavit, *nec pertimuit* evangelii maiestatem sub metri leges mittere' ('In the reign of Constantine the presbyter Juvencus set forth in verse the story of our Lord and Saviour, and *did not shrink* from forcing into metre the majestic phrases of the gospel' [trans. W.H. Fremantle, as repr. in CWE 61: 204; emphasis added]). Critical edition of Juvencus' poem in CSEL 24.

13 Before praising Juvencus as an *explicator evangelii* in his Ep 70, Jerome described him in *De viris illustribus* 84 as 'evangelia ... paene ad verbum transferens' ['rendering the Gospels almost word for word']. For Jerome, it seems, Juvencus' work came to represent an untenable middle way between his own elected roles of biblical translator and biblical commentator.

14 E.g., Ernst Robert Curtius, *European Literature and the Latin Middle Ages*, 446–8.

15 Jean-Michel Poinsotte, 'Jérôme et la poésie chrétienne' and esp. Yves-Marie Duval, 'Les premiers rapports de Paulin de Nole avec Jérôme: Moine et philosophe? Poète ou exégète?'

16 Jerome, Ep 53.7.3 (continuous with the passages quoted above, notes 1 and 3): 'Quasi non legerimus Homerocentonas et Vergiliocentonas ac non sic etiam Maronem sine Christo possimus dicere Christianum ...' ('As if we have not read Homeric and Virgilian centos, and thus found a way of calling even Maro a Christian without Christ'). Jerome then quotes a number of Virgilian lines that were capable of being construed in a Christian sense, several of which recur in extant biblical centos of the period.

17 Without pressing this interpretation of the phrase, Duval (n. 15 above) argues convincingly that this section of Letter 53 contains pointed allusions to the literary work of Paulinus himself, 'émule de Proba et de Juvencus' (214). Erasmus' note on the text shows only that he knew of the existence of Proba's poem. The latter has been published with a facing English translation by Elizabeth A. Clark and Diane Hatch, *The Golden Bough, the Oaken Cross: The Virgilian Cento of Faltonia Betitia Proba*.

18 CWE 61: 207. The image of the *transenna* or lattice-window is adapted from Cicero, *De oratore* 1.162, where Cotta is said to have caught a glimpse, in passing, of the riches of Crassus' eloquence. Terence Cave, *The Cornucopian Text: Problems of Writing in the French Renaissance*, 106–23 argues that in Erasmus' writings '[t]he rhetorical model which makes *brevitas* and *copia* mutually dependent is directly comparable, even interchangeable, with the hermeneutic model [associated with the image of the *transenna*] which links obscure places to clear places, allegories and enigmas to paraphrastic explication' (123). Thus interpreted, Erasmus' note on Jerome's Letter 53 would construe that text as an invitation to Paulinus to make a *paraphrase* of the scriptural books there condensed by Jerome. This is almost certainly a misreading of Jerome – a highly productive one for Erasmus.
19 Jan Ziolkowski, 'Old Wives' Tales': Jerome contributes the lion's share of late antique examples. See also Ziolkowski, 'The Obscenities of Old Women: Vetularity and Vernacularity.'
20 On the second-century context for the (pseudo-)Pauline caution against 'old wives' fables' at 1 Tim. 4: 7 and cognate passages in the Pastorals, see Dennis Ronald MacDonald, *The Legend and the Apostle: The Battle for Paul in Story and Canon*, ch. 3.
21 CWE 27: 84: 'St Jerome amused himself in this way with more freedom and sarcasm, sometimes even mentioning names.'
22 The second passage is followed by a rhetorical analysis of some typical performances by such teachers, all notable for their lack of purchase on the text of Scripture itself.
23 John J. Bateman, 'From Soul to Soul: Persuasion in Erasmus' Paraphrases on the New Testament,' 12–13.
24 See above, 3f.
25 See the editor's comment on Phil. 1: 1–3 at CWE 44: 294 n. 4.
26 The idea of the human speaker as an instrument played upon by God appears more explicitly elsewhere in Erasmus' writings: Bateman, 'From Soul to Soul,' 13 n. 56, with references. It is found in connection with 1 Pet. 4: 11 in Hilary of Poitiers, *Tractatus in psalmum*, 13.1 (CSEL 22: 79), probably derived from Origen; see Jacques Fontaine, 'L'apport d'Hilaire à une théorie chrétienne de l'esthétique du style (remarques sur In psalmos 13).'
27 Jane E. Phillips, 'The Gospel, the Clergy, and the Laity in Erasmus' *Paraphrase on the Gospel of John*'; Hilmar M. Pabel, 'Promoting the Business of the Gospel: Erasmus' Contribution to Pastoral Ministry,' with reference to the *Paraphrases* at 53–6, 59, 62.
28 Discussed further by Robert D. Sider, below 94–5.
29 I develop here a line of argument opened up by Patricia Parker, 'On the Tongue: Cross Gendering, Effeminacy and the Art of Words.'

Working between Erasmus' *Lingua* and his *De copia*, Parker aims to expose 'the intimate links between a male *copia* of style and the proverbial *copia* of the female tongue.' Of the dedicatory epistle to the former work, she remarks: 'Not only does Erasmus draw a clear connection between copiousness of style and a *loquacitas* gendered as effeminating; he also calls attention to the fact that his own often rambling discourse is infected by the diseases of the tongue of which it treats' (449). In the introduction to CWE 50, Bateman notes the occurrence of earlier Erasmian declamations *de lingua* in the paraphrases on James 3 (discussed below) and Acts 2: 3.

30 For a detailed history of the processes of composition and publication, see John J. Bateman's narrative below, 228–9.

31 On the circumstances of composition of the *Lingua*, see Elaine Fantham's introduction in CWE 29: 25–56, which notes in particular the impact of Noël Béda's criticisms of the *Paraphrases*. For the latter, see the essay by Erika Rummel in this volume.

32 Bede, *Commentary on the Seven Catholic Epistles*, trans. David Hurst, ad loc.: 'He did not say, "you offend" ... No, he said *we offend*, although a very great apostle of Christ was speaking, and he appended, *in many things*, and added, [we] *all*, that all might more carefully acknowledge themselves imperfect in acting or speaking the more they know most definitely that not even the perfectly good and those who proceed under the guidance of the grace of the Holy Spirit are able to pass along the way of this life without committing some offense.' Subsequent translations from Bede's *Commentary on James* are Hurst's. Latin text in CCSL 121.

33 Bede, *Commentary on James* ad loc.: 'so blessing and cursing are in no wise able to come together in one mouth; but [in] anyone who is accustomed to bless God in praying or in preaching the word [*vel verbum eius praedicando*] without avoiding also cursing people, it is clear that the bitterness of cursing destroys the sweetness of that person's blessing.'

34 Bateman renders *organa diaboli* as 'the organ of the devil.' I prefer 'instruments of the devil' for the echo in English of Erasmus' descriptions of the evangelical preacher as an 'instrument of the divine voice' (n. 26 above). The paraphrase on verses 11–13 develops the theme of the divided tongue, before returning to the more familiar topic of linguistic looseness as a kind of profanity: 'But how can it be that speech, though it originates in the same heart and comes bubbling out through the same tongue, is so inconsistent, while among so many different kinds of springs none is found which simultaneously produces sweet and bitter water from the same mouth? ... Does it not then seem to be somehow monstrous for the same person to be producing from the same heart through the same tongue

godliness and ungodliness, truth and falsehood, salvation and perdition? Therefore, since nothing is more destructive than a wicked tongue, nothing more wholesome than a good and well-instructed one, and since it is rare to find anyone able to control this member in every respect, the person who is to assume the position of teacher must be carefully selected from among a number of candidates ... Among the philosophers of this world the person who is the most obstinate debater and is second to none in the volubility of his tongue holds first place. They do not take this approach so that the listener may go away a better person but to make the winner feel prouder and the loser more downcast. Meanwhile the crowd is distracted every which way by different interests so that there is no solid benefit for either speaker or hearer' (CWE 44: 159–60). It is remarkable how long Erasmus clings to the image of the tongue after the biblical text has let go of it.

35 CWE 44: 133 = CWE 8: 127: 'What spirit hounds them on, those men who, at the risk of their own reputation and authority and to the detriment even of their sacred duty of preaching [*cum iniuria sacrarum etiam concionum*], endeavour so persistently to reduce the profit that the studious may hope to find in my work? This question only they can answer.'

36 Bede, *Commentary on James* ad loc.: 'Blessed James, therefore, removed them and teachers of their kind from the responsibility of [preaching] the word lest they be an obstacle to those able to carry it out properly.'

37 Allen Ep 1166: 18.

38 CWE Ep 1060: 21–38, to Wolsey: 'Many leading scholars all over the world express their thanks to me for my New Testament ... Yet these men shamelessly blacken my name in front of the public [*apud populum*] with their seditious clamour before they even read my book, though I have done them service. Here too some men of that kidney have raised their heads, and in your country I hear tell of a man who protested noisily before a crowded congregation that I wished to correct the Gospel of St John ... Before a learned audience could anything be more foolish? And before the unlettered multitude [*apud imperitam multitudinem*] could anything be more inflammatory? And meanwhile where is that sweet reasonableness of scholarship of which Jerome speaks? Where is that cheerful exercise in the field of Scripture [*in campo scripturarum*] without risk of hurt?' (= Jerome, Ep 115.1, to Augustine); Ep 1062: 97–110, to Campeggi: 'If words like these are used before the inexperienced public [*apud imperitam multitudinem*], what can be imagined more subversive? If before people of education and intelligence, what could be more crazy? And yet the men who do this in public [*publice*] wish to pass for

pillars of the Christian religion. They do not stop to reflect that, while they profess Christ's teaching, as they do, their attacks on the reputation of those who do them good service, or who at least strive to do so, are diametrically opposed to their professions. Besides which, they forget that all the time a great part of their efforts is wasted, both for them and for the common people [*cum ipsis tum populo*], as long as this behaviour loses them all their credit with their audience ... And on the other side, the works of those who are keen that their laborious nights should advance both learning and true religion to the best of their power [*lucubrationes eorum qui suis vigiliis et studiis et verae pietati pro sua virili consulere student*] are less profitable when such men read them.' See also, e.g., Ep 1153 and other texts cited below. Rummel, *Erasmus and His Catholic Critics*, 1: 121ff. provides a richly informed chronicle of these protests.

39 Allen Ep 1126: 82–3: 'Non sum ... tam stultus ut haec *apud stultas mulierculas et indoctam plebeculum* velim effutire'; Rummel, *Erasmus and His Catholic Critics*, 1: 123–7, with further references. In a letter of October 1520 to a well-wisher (Allen Ep 1147: 75–7) Erasmus stigmatizes Carmelites and Dominicans in general as the sort who spout dangerous nonsense 'apud stultas mulierculas, apud deliros senes, apud superstitiosas idiotas, apud simplices adolescentulos' ('in front of silly women, doting old men, superstitious people of no education, and simple-minded youths' [CWE 8: 60]). Once again, this is the language of Jerome's Horatian satire on rogue biblicists, only now there are madmen in the audience as well as in the pulpits!

40 See Rummel, *Erasmus and His Catholic Critics*, 1: 135–42, and the notice on Baechem by Marjorie O'Rourke Boyle in COE 1: 81–3. The latter quotes an epitaph on him, attributed to Erasmus, containing the line 'Dilexit rabiem, non habeat requiem' ['He loved strife, may he not have rest'], and another, set up by his fellow Carmelites, which asks, 'Quid fert sarcasmo? Stylus est consuetus Erasmo' ['What should he suffer by sarcasm? That is how Erasmus writes']. See also CWE 85: 374–5.

41 Allen Ep 1162: 205–6: 'Tu stilum habes, nos linguam habemus.' Cf. Ep 1166: 35–6: 'Sic cogitant secum. "Scribat ille doctis, qui pauci sunt; nos latrabimus apud populum"' ('I know what they think: "Let him write for the learned; there are not many of them. And we will bluster away before the public"' [CWE 8: 106]); the targets of this letter are Baechem and certain Dominicans.

42 R.J. Shoeck, *Erasmus of Europe: The Prince of Humanists, 1501–1536*, 223.

43 Allen Ep 1042: 1–6, 'to a certain detractor,' from late in 1519, may be the first significant example: 'Quomodo sis abusus lingua tua ... non me clam fuit,' Erasmus begins, adding: 'non ignoras quam foedum

sit ulcisci sese obtrectatrice lingua, idque in conviviis' ('The way in which you misused your powers of speech ... did not escape my notice ... [Y]ou know very well how disgraceful it is to seek your revenge in abusive remarks' [CWE 7: 130–1]).

44 See the introductory note by Peter G. Bietenholz to the translation of the dialogue in CWE 7: 330–3. Latin text ed. Ferguson, *Opuscula*, 206–24.

45 For an echo of the controversy with Baechem in the mention of 'a poisoned tongue' in the *Paraphrase on 1 John*, see CWE 44: 190 n. 17.

46 See esp. CWE 7: 339, where Mercury dialogues with the trilinguist Baramia. '*Mercury*: Indeed the whole of her is nothing but venom ... What the juice of ambrosia is to us, what blood and gastric juices are to you, that's what pure poison is to her. It is distributed through her whole body, as with a viper; but its power is particularly in her tongue. *Baramia*: I wish I had that tongue. *Mercury*: What would you do with it? *Baramia*: Wipe my arse. *Mercury*: To my mind you would be better off wiping it with a nettle than with such poison as that.' The name Até points to the vice-chancellor of the University of Louvain, Jan Briart of Ath.

47 Allen Ep 1171: 72–8: 'Nullo seculo non licuit alicubi dissentire a quamlibet probatis autoribus. Si a solo Thoma dissentirem, videri possem in illum iniquior. Nunc et ab Ambrosio et ab Hieronymo et ab Augustino non raro dissentio, sed reverenter; in Thomam etiam candidior quam ut multis bonis et eruditis viris gratum sit. Sed hanc reverentiam non opinor me debere Hugonibus aut Lyranis omnibus, etiam si Lyrano non nihil debemus.' For Erasmus' continuing reliance on the scholastic commentators here named in his *Paraphrases* of 1519–21, see CWE 44: xv and the index to that volume.

48 Cf. Ep 1155 to John Reuchlin, 8 November 1520: 'You are too deeply seated in the affections of all men of good will [*bonorum virorum*] to be torn thence by any insinuations on the part of the Jacobites [i.e., the Dominicans]. The truth must win. And the unspoken judgments of men of good will [*tacita bonorum iudicia*] will acquire an authority which will retain its force even among posterity' (CWE 8: 79). The significance of this turn of thought in Erasmus' writing at the time is underscored by P.G. Bietenholz in CWE 8: xiii. The emphasis on *boni viri* in the letter to Reuchlin makes explicit a gendering of the 'silent judgments of posterity' that is elsewhere less marked but always implicit. The (virile) writer appeals to 'learned men' while the (effeminate) babbler puts his trust in 'silly women.'

49 This charge, without the gender slur, would later be levelled at Erasmus by Béda, in the context of his criticisms of the *Paraphrase on Luke*: 'In the first place, it cannot pass without suspicion of a danger that you continuously seek the good of others, as you think, by

relentlessly writing new books of which the Church has no need ... For the teaching of the Apostle is to be observed, when he says, "Though I speak with the tongues of men, etc." and "Though I have all knowledge, etc." and "Thou therefore which teachest another, teachest thou not thyself?"' (Allen Ep 1579: 41–8). Replying to Béda's insinuation that he was publishing books out of a desire for popular adulation, Erasmus again appeals to the judgment of the learned (Allen Ep 1581: 639ff.) The correspondence dates from mid-1525, when he was composing the *Lingua*. See also below, 272 n. 26.

50 Waswo, *Language and Meaning in the Renaissance*, 220 n. 21, previously cited by Parker, 'On the Tongue,' 449 n. 7.

51 For these distinctions, see my 'Conference and Confession: Literary Pragmatics in Augustine's "Apologia contra Hieronymum."'

52 For a fuller development of this theme, see Bateman's remarks below, 221, 229–30.

53 On the abiding tension in Erasmus' evangelical thought and practice between the requirement of general persuasiveness and the commitment to good Latinity, see the comments of Jacques Chomarat in his introduction to the *Ecclesiastes*, a work of 'theory' that complements the practice of the *Paraphrases* (ASD V-4: 5–7), and John W. O'Malley, 'Erasmus and the History of Sacred Rhetoric: The *Ecclesiastes* of 1535.'

TWO

Exegetical Fictions? Biblical Paraphrases of the Sixteenth and Seventeenth Centuries

Bernard Roussel

Erasmus began composing paraphrases on the Pauline epistles in 1517. At the time, he considered this to be a novel undertaking, but less onerous than the preparation of a critical edition of the New Testament.[1] Are we then witnessing the invention of a literary genre? In his *Bibliotheca sancta* (1566), Sixtus of Siena answers the question in the negative. Sixtus names ten *paraphrastae*, including Philo (20 BCE–50 CE), Hegesippus (second century) and Gregory Thaumaturgus (c.213–c.270) among the ancients, Peter Comestor (twelfth century), and, of his contemporaries, Francis Titelmans, apparently 'forgetting' Erasmus.[2] One might also recall the *Paraphrasis sancti Evangelii secundum Ioannem*, in verse, of Nonnus of Panopolis (c.400),[3] and consider that the *intelligentia ex graeco* of the Pauline epistles provided by Jacques Lefèvre d'Étaples[4] occasionally has the air of a paraphrase. It is possible, nonetheless, to take Erasmus as the 'inventor,' at the beginning of the sixteenth century, of a model that was to be claimed by other authors in their turn, as each in his own way set about composing paraphrases of biblical texts.

In the following pages, we shall be concerned with four authors of paraphrases on the Pauline epistles. For the sake of brevity and coherence, our examples are taken from their paraphrases on the Epistle to the Ephesians. There is another reason for this choice: exegesis of this late letter, which we now know to be non-

Pauline, demands a knowledge of Hellenistic Christianity that was beyond the range of sixteenth- and seventeenth-century scholars. The study and translation of this epistle thus brought them up against the limits of their erudition. Grappling with the words, expressions, and rhetorical forms of the Greek and Latin texts on the one hand, interrogating the patristic and medieval tradition of interpretation on the other, they were forced to make sense of a discourse that remained strange to them, and, for that purpose, to draw on resources outside their scholarship. The modern student of these texts must resist the temptation to make anachronistic judgments of the value of such interpretations from the Ancien Régime by comparing them with the fruits of contemporary biblical science.

We have selected four authors posterior to Erasmus, so as to evoke the *longue durée* of this form of exegesis while also including writings representative of diverse religious communities. The paraphrasts are as follows.

Francis Titelmans (1502–37). As professor at Louvain (before 1535), he displayed his competence as a biblicist by publishing an *Elucidatio in omnes Epistolas apostolicas* (1532). This is, in fact, a paraphrase.[5] He was both a contemporary and a tenacious opponent of Erasmus.

Pierre de Launay (1573–1661). A Protestant scholar of the generation of the French Reformed that benefited most fully from the Edict of Nantes. He was not a 'minister of the word,' but then had not Erasmus written that *nulli non licet esse theologum*? His *Paraphrase et exposition*[6] might usefully be compared with that of Moïse Amyraut,[7] with whom he was allied before entering into controversy with him. The comparison is not, however, pursued here.

Antoine Godeau (1605–72). Bishop of Grasse and Vence, and a member of the Academy. He was a witness and party to the tensions that wracked French Catholicism in the second third of the seventeenth century.[8]

Henry Hammond (1605–60). An Anglican minister during the troubles in England.[9]

One point must be conceded at the outset: it is not possible to prove that all these men were attentive readers of Erasmus' *Paraphrases*. Robert D. Sider already says as much in the preface to the first volume of paraphrases in the Collected Works of Erasmus in English: 'We are not yet in a position,' he writes, 'to determine precisely the influence of the *Paraphrases* on the life and literature of Britain and the continent ... In the final analysis, it may be very difficult to distinguish echoes from the *Paraphrases* and those from the Bible' (CWE 42: x). Several arguments can be advanced in support of this statement. The *Paraphrases* cannot be cited as concisely as the *Annotations*. For reasons both of style and of the proximity of source-text, borrowings from the Erasmian *Paraphrases* are not identified as such by later authors. These authors all refer to the same patristic texts, even when they do not do so explicitly. Finally, all participate in the same biblical culture and are therefore disposed to read the Epistle to the Ephesians as though it were a Pauline text. This fact accounts for the multiplication of references and allusions to authentically Pauline letters. Like Erasmus, but not necessarily because of him, the paraphrasts discover Pauline themes in the epistle – the respective relations of the Jews and gentiles to the Church, the Law and the Gospel, eschatology, etc. The effect of this convergence is to obscure the traces of any reading of Erasmus's *Paraphrases*, be it sympathetic or adversarial. Hence, there is no possibility of fixing the measure of these authors' reception (in the strict sense) of Erasmus. Instead, on the basis of a few selected pages, we shall here endeavour to establish certain points of analogy and comparison. A recognition of the originality of each paraphrase will prepare the way for our conclusions on the placing of these works in the history of the literature generated by the Bible.[10]

I

First analogy: a careful study of the source-texts – here, Greek and Latin – precedes the composition of the paraphrase. The notion that these paraphrases were an effusion of the pen or of their author's humours, as a first glance might lead one to believe, must be abandoned. We know that Erasmus published a 'critical' edition of the Greek text of the New Testament and a Latin translation, clarified and justified by the *Annotations*, in 1516, followed later by paraphrases; those on Ephesians date from February–March 1520 and are thus posterior to the second edition (1519) of the New Testament and *Annotations*.[11] It must also be recognized, however, that the paraphrases – whether of Erasmus himself or other authors – do not always accurately incorporate the critical and philological comments presented by the *Annotations* and 'translated' in the Latin version.

As an example, consider the expression found in Ephesians 2: 5: *sunezoopoiese toi Christoi*. An annotation reveals that Erasmus noticed the oddness of the locution. He suggests a literal translation of it (*convivificavit Christo*) and criticizes the transmitted Latin text (*convivificavit nos in Christo*), pointing out that *nos* and *in* have no equivalents in Greek. His own Latin translation of 1516 (*nos una cum Christo revixisse*) seems to be a compromise between philological rigour and intelligibility; *nos* reappears there, but is not repeated in the parallel constructions of verse 6 (*simulque cum eo resuscitavit, & simul cum eo sedere fecit inter coelestes, in Christo Iesu*), which are closely coordinated (*simulque*) with what precedes them; finally, the Greek dative is explained by reference to the *sun-* prefix of the verbs.[12]

Erasmus' paraphrase on verses 5 and 6 takes the form of a response to the question posed in verse 4: *unde vita, unde salus*? The answer is clear: salvation does not follow from personal merits or from observance of the Mosaic law, but has its source in the unmeasurable free benevolence of God. The French translation published at Basel in 1563 preserves the shape of the original:

> Mais d'où attendons nous vie? d'où nous viendra salut? Nullement de noz merites, ny par le moyen de la loy Mosaique. D'où donc? Sans doute de la pure largesse de Dieu le pere, duquel la benignité est si plantureuse, & la charité envers le genre humain si grande, que non seulement il ne nous punit point ainsi qu'avions bien deservy, mais aussi alors qu'estions morts à cause de noz pechés, il nous a ensemble avec Christ remis en vie: *Qui n'estoit, di-ie, de nostre merite, mais ce qu'il donne est de pure grace.* Et non seulement nous a remis en vie avec le fils, ainçois nous a eslevés, de ces choses basses aux hautes, & nous a la posés par Iesus Christ, par le moyen duquel nous avons communement, tout ce qu'il a, luy qui est nostre chef: & si possederons maintenant en esperance, ce que bien tost nous possederons de faict.[13]

In the clause translated 'Qui n'estoit, di-ie, de nostre merite ...,' which is in parentheses in the Latin text of the paraphrase, the possessive adjective is in the first person (*meriti nostri*), whereas the Greek (and Latin) text of the Bible has the second-person form. Erasmus is writing of the salvation of every Jew who turns to Christ and is joined with him (*una cum Christo*). One also notes the gradation produced by the double use of a 'not only ... but also' construction (in which *non solum* in the first instance is followed by *neque tantum* in the second) and by the passage from *cum* to *per* with reference to Christ. The close of the paraphrase reveals the influence of Pauline texts on the interpretation of an epistle that Erasmus took to be also Pauline. Here he picks up the themes of the union of head and body, and of a salvation that is 'already ... but not yet.' Christians now possess in hope what they will shortly possess in reality – that is, after death. The author of the Epistle to the Ephesians does not speak in such terms. The paraphrase is much richer in theological harmonics than the translation, which is itself slightly at odds with the annotation. In his paraphrase Erasmus is writing a kind of chronicle of Christian existence: the story of a return to life by an act of faith in Christ and of gradual sanctifying spiritualization, in the perspective of a total history of salvation. He does not strictly mark the aorists of verses 5 and 6; *nos* is restored; the prefixes of the Greek verbs give way to the *in* of the transmitted Latin text. Erasmus the paraphrast plays false with Erasmus the grammarian. Pierre de Launay, who had read Theodore Beza,[14] would likewise accentuate the theme of the union of Christians with Christ, 'nostre chef, avantcoureur pour nous,' but take the *sun-* prefixes to express the common destiny of Jews and Gentiles.[15]

Such examples could be multiplied. The paraphrases were only composed after prior study of the source-text and versions, their vocabulary, grammar, and rhetoric, but the fruits of this preliminary work were not all included in the final text. Scholarly abilities similar to Erasmus,' perhaps nourished by his work, were brought to bear by other authors. And they were sufficient to the task. Titelmans was an eminent biblicist as well as a conservative theologian. Pierre de Launay was an accomplished scholar; in all probability he used the *Annotations* of Theodore Beza as well as the French Bible of Geneva which, in its 1588 edition, incorporated an impressive digest of biblical science and whose text he had printed on the page facing his paraphrase. Antoine Godeau writes of having consulted the Greek text and the Fathers;[16] he also seems to have had an eye on the commentary on the Epistles by Cornelius a Lapide (1567–1637), published in 1627. Henry Hammond collaborated on the Polyglott of Walton (1654–7); a fine specimen of his erudition is elicited by Ephesians 2: 9, where he cites one of the most learned Christian Hebraists of the sixteenth century, Paul Fagius, for a reference to the Targum by which to explain how Christ descended into the womb of the Virgin as if into the lowest parts of the earth.

The typographical presentation of the paraphrases confirms the hypothesis of scholarly seriousness. The source-text, in Latin or in vernacular translation (Titelmans, de Launay), is printed opposite the paraphrase, sometimes with explanatory notes (de Launay, Hammond). The paraphrase appears as a text for study. Its layout renders the reader both a service and a guarantee.

We have so far dealt with the first stage of the work, one of undoubted importance and perfectly in line with Erasmus' own conception of the paraphrase. The task of learned exegesis is compounded by the need to produce a plain text. As Erasmus put it, one must conceal the fact that the Epistle to the Ephesians is more encumbered than others with hyperbata and other causes of obscurity.[17] These potentially disastrous obstacles to understanding are to be removed. That is also the opinion of Antoine Godeau, who remarks that '[on] bannit l'Escriture des cabinets où règne la Politesse, et tout ce qu'elle peut obtenir de ces grands génies qui s'en sont rendus Maîtres [viz. Academicians], c'est d'estre reléguée dans les Cloistres ou parmy les Mélancholiques.'[18]

The composition of a paraphrase must observe certain rules of art, and Jacques Chomarat has described at length those to which Erasmus bound himself.[19] An elegantly simple example is provided by his paraphrase of Ephesians 1: 1 (see appendix 1). In the source, Paul's name is associated with an expression that combines a technical term with a genitive construction: *apostolus Iesu Christi*. The translation that defines the technical term (*legatus*, 'ambassador') suggests an amplification based on an opposition (*non ... aut / sed ...*), which is then reproduced for the source-phrase *per voluntatem dei*. The second part of the paraphrase of verse 1 is accounted for by a notable modification of the order of terms in the expression *sanctis qui agunt Ephesi, et fidelibus in Christo Iesu*. The word *omnibus*, attested only in the Latin text of the epistle, resurfaces to create a striking contrast with the more restrictive definition now given of what it is to be 'saints' and 'faithful': *omnibus qui vivunt Ephesi ... & ita vivunt, ut ... et syncero pectore credunt ... non aliunde ... nec ...*

Erasmus hierarchizes the elements of a paraphrase, clarifies statements by playing on alternative or contradictory expressions, and makes use of symmetrical formulas (*quam unde sumpserit exemplum / quam unde profectus est exordium*). Needless to say, the chosen rhetorical form matches the learned interpretation proposed. Given that Erasmus takes this epistle to be Pauline, it is no surprise to see him introduce the 'Paul of history' through an allusion to the call he received on the road to Damascus (Acts 9). This is the Paul whose preaching, as now reiterated in the Epistle to the Ephesians, has opened the Church to gentiles as well as Jews (*omnibus*), provided they respond to the divine offer: *ita vivunt, ut* ... 'Erasmian religion' can thus be seen to dictate the recomposition of the source-text. Its keynotes are the break with Judaism, moral living, and sincerity of faith. Others, after Erasmus, would likewise follow rules of writing favourable to their respective religious affiliations.

Titelmans (appendix 2) intercalates segments of the contemporary Vulgate with additions that contain many liturgical and doctrinal expressions. This fusion of traditional and more personal elements is a means of appropriating the authority of the source-text and inserting oneself into the flux of tradition.

Henry Hammond, seizing the didactic opportunity, develops a dramatic exposition of Ephesians 1: 9–10 (appendix 5). The revelation of the secret of the divine plan, which consists of the gratuitously merciful preaching of salvation to the gentiles, intervenes at the very moment when human depravity has reached its height and catastrophe looms. An old question is evoked, to which Erasmus had given a different reply: Why did God wait so long?[20] Hammond, moreover, proves himself more 'ecclesiastical' than Erasmus: the mystery is revealed 'by the *preaching* of the Gospel' and the recapitulation is said to be an integration of all believers in the Church.

Pierre de Launay introduces a note of pathos into the epistle by multiplying the instances of a Pauline 'I' in verses 8 to 10: 'De laquelle grace, ie puis dire veritablement, qu'il a largement fait decouler sur moi les ruisseaux, me retirant de l'erreur & de l'aveuglement pharisaïque ... En m'illuminant en la vraie et droite connoissance ... Et me reuelant & manifestant sa bonne volonté ... Laquelle bonne volonté il m'a reuelée & manifestée ...' Then he develops a grand vision of the Church visible and invisible: '... afin qu'en ces derniers temps, ausquels sa divine providence auoit reserué le plein accomplissement de ses promesses, il recueillist & r'assemblast en un, tout son Israel, asçavoir tant celui qui est desia és cieux, que celui qui est encores sur la terre, & qui reste à venir: & que des uns & des autres, c'est asçavoir des Iuifs & des Gentils, il fist un seul corps, duquel Iesus Christ soit le chef.'[21]

Antoine Godeau observes one of the functions of the paraphrase, which is to make it easier for readers or auditors to take possession of an ancient and difficult text. To this end he now and again adopts a style of pastoral exhortation: 'Mes frères, élevons nos mains vers le ciel, et célébrons continuellement les merveilles de la bonté du Père Éternel, qui nous donnant Iesus-Christ son Fils, nous a donné par ses mérites des benedictions & des graces mille fois plus excellentes que les Israëlites ont autrefois receues.'[22] Paul goes up into the episcopal chair of the cathedral of Grasse! (We may note in passing that such flourishes of sacred oratory are at times even more pronounced in the writing of Moïse Amyraut.) A feature common to all these authors is their tendency to multiply expressions of Christian anti-Judaism through the expansion of Pauline tropes; here, perhaps, we may detect a lasting *effet de lecture.*

The composition of a paraphrase implies a transition from philology to the art of eloquence. Erasmus was the first to countenance the displacement that accompanies the production of statements designed to explain or embellish the source-text. At this moment, every author begins to imprint the 'epistle' with his own personal device, first stylistic, then doctrinal. To borrow a metaphor from Jerome: rising from the same source, biblical paraphrases are so many streams (*rivuli*) that diverge according to the accidents of time and terrain.

II

The project of composing a biblical paraphrase involving textual study *à la façon d'Érasme* places those who undertake it in a paradoxical position. On the one hand, they claim to efface themselves in favour of the biblical author: the 'subject' of a paraphrased epistle remains an apostle and the aim of the exegete, and then of the paraphrast, is to find a way into the *mens* or *intentio* of the author. In the sixteenth century, no one doubted that this could be done successfully. On the other hand, every paraphrase constitutes an individual literary creation on an assigned theme.

Adopting the terms of analysis proposed by Maurice Pergnier, we can say then that the paraphrastic project complicates the 'parameters of the message.'[23] In the first place, the 'issuer' – the Greek author of the epistle – can no longer be so clearly envisaged when the philological task is seen to include the detection and accumulation of textual variants, as it increasingly was after the publication of the works of Erasmus. Next, the paraphrast must eliminate a number of possible solutions, since he does not have the option of harbouring ambiguities or putting forward several alternatives. In his effort to grasp the 'sense' of the text and rewrite its message, he necessarily favours a particular class of 'addressees,' such as preachers, educated persons lacking biblical knowledge, or co-religionists in search of edification. Finally, the 'carrier' will vary: certain paraphrases are designed to be read with the eyes and then meditated upon, others appear destined for public recitation, while still others occupy a space mid-way between learned study of the text and composition of a sermon. This concept of 'carrier' can be extended to include consideration of the nature of the physical books (format, paper), typography, and page layout.

A revealing example is provided by Ephesians 4: 8,[24] since there the commentators were dealing with a commented 'citation' of Psalm 68: 19[25] (otherwise 68: 18 or 67: 19) and had to paraphrase a 'Pauline' paraphrase of the psalmist's verse. The problems posed by this verse are well known. The New Testament formula corresponds neither to the Massoretic text of the psalm nor – because of the substitution of persons between 'he gave gifts' and 'you received gifts' – to the Greek version of the Septuagint. Here are the texts as they appear in the 1560 English Genevan translation:

> Ephesians 4: 8: Wherefore he saith, When he ascended vp on hie, he led captiuitie captiue, and gaue giftes vnto men.
> Psalm 68: 19[18]: Though art gone vp on high: thou hast led captiuitie captiue, and receiued giftes for men: yea, euen the rebellious hast thou led, that the Lord God might dwell there.

Erasmus and our other four authors resolve the problems in their different ways. There is no question for them that the Pauline verse contains a citation of a psalm of David. But is it a prediction or a prophecy? And does the transition from 'you received' to 'he gave' arise from the decoding of a Hebraism (as Beza thought) or from an interpretation that anticipates the following two verses?

For brevity's sake, we confine ourselves to the treatments of Pierre de Launay and Antoine Godeau.

De Launay (appendix 3) attributes 'He said ...' to David predicting the resurrection of Jesus Christ. This learned reformer then develops the metaphor of a victorious general leading his captives in triumph. A note identifies those captives as including, notably, Satan and the fallen angels. Next de Launay hints – without clearly stating – that it is from the booty seized from his enemies that the victor draws the gifts that he distributes to humanity. The paraphrase on verse 10 further specifies that only members of the Church are here envisaged and that the 'gifts' are not just those of ministry. Theodore Beza had already resorted to a Hebraism to explain that 'receive' can mean 'give': this is the effect of attending only to the end result of what is initially an act of seizure.[26]

Antoine Godeau (appendix 4) sees here a prophecy made by David: 'David, voyant en esprit cette liberalité de laquelle il devait user envers nous, dit que "Montant dans le Ciel, il a mené la captivité en triomphe," c'est à dire, les hommes qu'il avait retirez de l'Empire de la mort.' De Launay has a different understanding of the metaphor: for him the 'captivity' refers to human beings formerly captive but henceforth freed. 'Et il [le Christ] leur fait ses largesses, leur distribue les biens qu'il n'avoit receus que pour leur en faire part.' On this point, Godeau remains close to Erasmus. Among the number of the vanquished, the latter had identified both 'sin' and 'the devil,' despite the fact that the term for 'devil' appears nowhere in the Epistle to the Ephesians. Most importantly, Erasmus had combined a rewriting of the pseudo-citation with elements of his interpretation to come:

> Car Christ ayant vaincu les enfers & estans ressuscité, est monté au regne celeste du Pere, menant avec soy l'enseigne de sa victoire, une trouppe de captifs delivrés de la tyrannie du peché & du diable: Et d'enhaut de la pure largesse du pere, il donne par l'esprit celeste diverses sortes de dons, les distribuant entre les hommes à la façon des victorieux, qui au milieu de leurs triomphes ont accoustumé espandre de quelque lieu haut, d'or et argent à poignées parmy le peuple.[27]

From the point of view of the 'addressees,' both solutions are elegant.

But what displacements are now entailed for the verses that follow the Old Testament citation? None of these paraphrasts echoes the reluctance of Jacques Lefèvre d'Étaples to understand the theme of a journey other than metaphorically.[28] For Erasmus, the descent 'to the lowest place' is the Descent into Hell mentioned in the Apostles' Creed. It is the demonstration of a voluntary abasement that earns Christ the distinction of unequalled 'merit.' The 'most high place' denotes this condition of the elevated Christ in which – an Erasmian trait par excellence – he is more nearly and more effectively one of us than he was during his time on earth. Now he is present through the Spirit.[29] In the introductory treatises of Erasmus' New Testament, the possession and reading of the Gospels are said to compensate advantageously for the 'physical' absence of Jesus Christ.[30]

Strictly 'Calvinist' on this point, de Launay evokes the incarnation of Jesus Christ and his death on the cross. The implicit reference to the Epistle to the Philippians (2: 6ff.) is accompanied by a particular interpretation of the formula *in inferiores partes terrae*. In the French Geneva Bible of 1588 one reads: 'les parties les plus basses de la terre.' Under de Launay's pen this becomes: 'cette terre, qui est la partie la plus basse de cette machine ronde.' The alteration in phrasing is most significant.[31]

Godeau prolongs another interpretative tradition. For him Christ's descent is into the limbo from which he rescues the patriarchs and prophets (see 1 Peter 3: 19). Then, according to a habitual procedure of this bishop-paraphrast, the Davidic vision prompts a summons to the 'imitation of Christ': 'C'est pourquoy, mes frères, si vous voulez vous eslever comme luy, il faut que vous vous abaissiez à son exemple, & entriez dans une profonde meditation de vostre neant, de vostre misere, & de la necessité de son secours.' This is a clear departure from the Erasmian reference to the sole merit of Christ. Godeau also offers a very inclusive interpretation of the *ut impleret* of verse 10: it refers to the verification of all the biblical prophecies of Christ, to the completion of the work of redemption through his reign over all human beings, and to the manifestation of his victory in all the places where he has triumphed and imposed his rule (appendix 4).

To summarize the results of this analysis: as the reader of a sort of 'Hellenistic Targum' that he is unable to identify as such, each of these authors draws on the hermeneutical or theological tradition closest to him in order to deal with a major exegetical difficulty. Typological or christological interpretation of the cited psalm? Descent to hell, to limbo, or from the cross? The paraphrase confirms ideas derived from different confessional and ecclesial affiliations. For each of these authors the biblical writings contain the 'norm' of doctrine. Some, for example, are concerned to corroborate the notion of limbo by means of a supposedly Pauline verse; others seek by the same means to refute that belief. Thus is the writing of paraphrase constantly tilted towards a more or less discreet polemic.

III

Should these Erasmian and post-Erasmian biblical paraphrases be regarded as so many exegetical fictions?

We have seen them to be the fruit of learned study: the critical establishment of a text and its annotation are their preconditions. Whether composed in Latin or in a vernacular language, they look like the outgrowth of 'translations' whose authors have been moved to attempt a dynamic equivalence between texts. The rhetoric of whole discourses, the syntax of particular constructions, the lexical value of individual terms are first brought to light. Then attention turns from the source-text towards a public to whom the 'message' must be addressed in a manner that will make it intelligible, leaving aside everything that could give the impression that the biblical writings are merely old, cold texts, inviting no response on the reader's part. Erasmus and his imitators had no doubt that it was possible to discern the 'sense' intended by the original author of the text, which they take to be (as it were) buried inside it. Nor did the process of transfer from one language to another seem to them to entail any transformation of the 'message' that they were delivering – in the strict sense of that word – for the profit of their readers. Erasmus, indeed, nourished an ambition to compose a *paraphrasis* that would not be a *paraphronesis*, to say things 'otherwise than Paul had, but without saying anything other than he did.'[32]

Titelmans displays the same hermeneutical naivety in the instructions placed at the beginning of his work, which recall orthoptical exercises used for the correction of squints. In this case, rather than have the patient bring two separate images into a single focus, the aim is to persuade the reader that the paraphrase can be substituted, without loss, for the source-text. First the reader is to fix the Latin version of the biblical passage firmly in mind. Then he or she is to consider the *elucidatio paraphrastica* by itself. The third stage of the exercise requires the mental superimposition of the two texts, such that the meaning (*sententia*) of the source-text is disclosed by the *elucidatio*.[33]

Considered in the light of a reading of the paraphrases themselves, these directions only serve to underline their complexity. On the one hand, the fiction is maintained – for the Epistles – of an apostle who expresses himself in the first person. On the other hand, every paraphrase reflects choices made by its author, and thus becomes an apocryphon whose fictional attribution fools no one.

It is said that one day St Columba sat down on the top of a hill on the island of Iona and, realizing that he could no longer see his native Ireland, decided to remain there. *Mutatis mutandis*, the authors of biblical paraphrases follow the example of St Columba. They invite their readers to situate themselves at a distance from the source-text, 'in' the paraphrase that they have composed. Even if they see the mote in the eye of their competitors' work, they are incapable of any critique of their own, both because they lack adequate tools for hermeneutical and critical reflection and because they have internalized powerful theological and confessional interests.

To persuade ourselves that this is so, we need only look again at Ephesians 1: 1: 'Paul, apostle of Jesus Christ by the will of God.' Erasmus finds here a pretext for expounding one of his main convictions: Paul is the divine agent of the providential merger of Jews and gentiles in a single Church, beyond anything that the Law of Moses or philosophy could bring about (appendix 1). De Launay, for his part, emphasizes that Paul '[est] éleu & establi Apostre de Iesus Christ, par la volonté & puissance de Dieu': the vocation of Paul is thus exemplary for the one that founds the ministries of the Church, a point on which Theodore Beza had also insisted.[34] Each paraphrase develops a distinctive discourse that cannot be reconciled with those of other authors.

The historian of these paraphrases may therefore be inclined, at the risk of a slight anachronism, to adopt the position taken by exponents of a 'postmodern' approach to the Bible: 'we must say what reading we are guilty of.'[35]

Let us consider this matter in a little more detail. Erasmian and post-Erasmian paraphrase enriches the abundant body of literature generated by the biblical writings. Two salient features of biblical paraphrase distinguish it from biblical translation. First, paraphrase provides a clarification of the *adunata* – the textual obscurities that Origen believed were there to stimulate the reader's intellect. Idiomatic usages are explained, hyperbata resolved, coordinations restored, terms defined; every ambiguity or polysemy is expunged. Second, in paraphrase the literal and 'spiritual' senses of the biblical text are fused, whatever method may be employed for this purpose. Paraphrase thus nicely illustrates a principle of Gregory the Great around which Pier Cesare Bori has constructed a whole book, namely that 'Scripture grows with its reader.'[36] (To which we should add that no tradition is strong enough to regulate the growth.) Gregorian metaphors are explicitly recycled by Antoine Godeau: 'L'Écriture est une manne qui a plusieurs goûts et une manière capable de recevoir plusieurs formes.'[37] The same writer identifies the various functions of paraphrase in the Catholic tradition after Trent. The object may be to render the biblical writings congenial to cultivated persons: 'J'ay donc voulu essayer de confondre ces esprits prophanes, & les engager à sa lecture [i.e., of Paul], le présentant à leurs yeux tendres et délicats sous une forme un peu moins austère, que n'est celle qu'il porte dans la version de nos Bibles.'[38] Or it may be to avoid any direct contact with the Bible on the part of the ordinary believer, by the substitution of one text for another:

> Ce n'est pas que je veuille mettre l'Escriture entre les mains de toutes sortes de personnes indifferemment. L'Eglise, qui est conduite par le sainct Esprit, s'est avec beaucoup de raison reservé le pouvoir d'en permettre la lecture, ou de l'interdire. Et j'estime qu'il n'y a rien de plus ridicule que l'arrogance de nos nouveaux Docteurs, qui croyent qu'à l'ouverture du livre, le sainct Esprit descend sur eux pour leur en donner l'intelligence, qu'à leur abord les ombres se retirent, & que la Verité est si amoureuse de leurs entendements que c'est à eux seuls qu'elle se montre toute nue ... L'humilité donc est la première disposition que je souhaitte à ceux qui liront ces Paraphrases.[39]

Among authors of the Protestant tradition, the motivation for paraphrase is more obviously a desire to elucidate the received biblical writings as *source* of religious knowledge, *norm* of doctrines, and *code* for moral and liturgical life.

As exegetical fictions, these paraphrases are excellent documents for the history of the reception of biblical writings in different 'communities of reading and interpretation.'[40] The authority of the text and the partiality of its interpretation are both affirmed, in a way that is at once coherent and premeditated. These are strong inducements for a reading of biblical paraphrases as sources for the history of theologies and of culture.

In conclusion, we may be permitted to recall the *locus* of our own research[41] and to make one pertinent observation. Biblical paraphrase, since at least the beginning of the sixteenth century, has been a familiar genre in Christian milieux. At the present day, though perhaps with less 'science' to their credit than sixteenth- and seventeenth-century authors possessed for that time, many Christians are being encouraged to contribute to a 'pluralist reading' of the Bible – that is, to compose their own paraphrases. In ancient Judaism, by contrast, we know that Targums did not proliferate. And the publication of a paraphrase on the Koran would today be badly received in Islam. The question of the status and use of writings designated as 'canonical' because held to be 'revealed' is thus posed anew. Pursuing comparisons such as these, one might begin an interesting debate on a literary genre first made prominent in the modern period by Erasmus and subsequently adopted by many other Christian authors.

Translated by Mark Vessey

APPENDICES

1. Erasmus, Ephesians 1: 1

Latin translation
Paulus Apostolus Iesu Christi per voluntatem dei, sanctis qui agunt Ephesi, & fidelibus in Christo Iesu.

Paraphrase
Paulus legatus non Mosi, aut ullius hominis, sed Iesu Christi,

cuius ago negotium, legatus autem non meapte occupatione, aut hominum legatione, sed autoritate iussuque dei patris, qui me per filium suum iussit evangelicae doctrinae inter gentes esse praeconem, hanc epistulam scribo omnibus qui vivunt Ephesi, & ita vivunt, ut & ab hujus mundi vitiis ac sordibus sese tueri studeant immunes & syncero pectore credunt evangelio Iesu Christi, non aliunde sperantes innocentiae sanctimoniaeque praemium, quam unde sumpserunt exemplum, nec ab alio praestolantes felicitatis suae summam quam unde profectum est exordium.

[*Hierarchical arrangement of elements of the paraphrase*]
Paulus
legatus
    non Mosi,
        aut ullius hominis
    sed Iesu Christi,
        cuius ago negotium
legatus autem
    non meapte occupatione,
        aut hominum legatione,
    sed autoritate iussuque dei patris,
        qui me per filium suum iussit evangelicae doctrinae inter gentes esse praeconem,
hanc epistulam scribo
omnibus qui vivunt Ephesi,
    & ita vivunt, ut
        & ab hujus mundi vitiis ac sordibus sese tueri studeant immunes
        & syncero pectore credunt evangelio Iesu Christi,
            non aliunde sperantes innocentiae sanctimoniaeque praemium,
                quam unde sumpserunt exemplum,
            nec ab alio praestolantes felicitatis suae summam
                quam unde profectum est exordium.

2. Francis Titelmans, Ephesians 1: 1–6

[Each verse of Titelmans' paraphrase is preceded by the same verse as it appeared in a 'Vulgate' of the 1530s. **Bold**: material specific to Titelmans. Without emphasis: words and expressions common to the 'Vulgate,' Erasmus, and Titelmans. *Italic*: words and expressions common to the 'Vulgate' and Titelmans. Underlined: words common to Erasmus' Latin translation and Titelmans.]

[1] Paulus apostolus Iesu Christi per voluntatem Dei,
omnibus sanctis qui sunt Ephesi, & fidelibus in Christo Iesu.

[1] Paulus **secundum** voluntatem Dei **patris** apostolus Iesu Christi **filii eius, scribit salutemque dicit** *omnibus* fidelibus qui *sunt* Ephesi, **atqui etiam omnibus qui credunt in Christum, ubicunque locorum consistunt aut cuiuscumque conditionis statusve existunt.**

[2] Gratia vobis & pax a Deo patre nostro &
Domino Iesu Christo.

[2] Gratia **sit** vobis **Spiritus sancti, & vera** pax **cordis** a Deo **qui est pater noster, & a** Domino Iesu Christo.

[3] Benedictus Deus & pater Domini nostri Iesu Christi,
qui benedixit nos in omni benedictione spirituali,
in caelestibus, in Christo.

[3] Laudandus atque magnificandus cum gratiarum actione est Dominus Deus, qui beneficentiam suam erga nos ostendit, in donatione spiritalium bonorum, quae in coelo possidebimus, per Christum Iesum.

[4] Sicut elegit nos in ipso ante mundi constitutionem,
ut essemus sancti & immaculati in conspectu eius in charitate.

[4] **Iuxta quod** elegit nos **pater ab aeterno, in filio suo,** antequam iacerentur fundamenta **orbis, id est,** ante **creationem mundi. Elegit (inquam)** ut essemus sancti **per fidem veram** et *immaculati* **in operibus bonis, in veritate,** coram **eo, idque in amore et libertate, non in timore atque servitute.**

[5] Qui praedestinavit nos in adoptionem filiorum,
per Iesum Christum,
in ipsum, secundum propositum voluntatis suae,

[6] in laudem gloriae gratiae suae, in qua gratificavit nos in dilecto ...

[5] Qui **pater, praeordinavit ab aeterno facere** nos filios suos adoptivos, per **mediatorem** Christum, **ut nos sic unum faceret cum seipso. Neque hoc ulla fecit, aut necessitate compulsus, aut utilitate inductus, sed** *secundum propositum* **benignae** voluntatis suae **[6] et magnificentia** gratiae suae, **per quam** nos, **qui ante eramus abominabiles & sordidi honestavit, ornavit, gratosque fecit & amabiles,** *in dilecto* **filio suo, quem pro nobis cohonestandis, fecit esse opprobrium hominum.**

3. Pierre de Launay, Ephesians 4: 8–10

Geneva 1588	de Launay
([7] *Mais la grace est donnée à chacun de nous, selon la mesure du don de Christ.*)	(Mais les graces de cet Esprit, nous sont données & dispensées, selon la mesure qu'il plaist à Iesus Christ, lequel nous les a meritées par son anéantissement & par ses souffrances, & qui les eslargit à chacun de nous, selon qu'il le juge expedient.)
[8] *Pour laquelle chose*	Et pour preuve que c'est Iesus Christ qui nous les a meritées par son anéantissement, & qui ensuite nous les distribue selon son bon plaisir,
il dit,	Le Prophete Royal parlant de lui,
estant monté en haut,	dit qu'estant monté au Ciel,
il a mené captive grande multitude de captifs,	il a emmené captive une grande multitude d'ennemis par lui pris prisonniers,
& a donné des dons aux hommes.	& a ensuite donné et distribué divers dons aux hommes.

[9] *Or ce qu'il est monté,*

qu'est-ce autre chose,
sinon que premierement il
estoit descendu
és les parties les plus basses de la
terre?

Or ce qui est dit, qu'il est
monté,
denote certainement, qu'il
estoit auparavant
descendu en cette terre,
qui est la partie la plus basse
de cette machine ronde.

[10] *Celui qui est descendu,*

Ce mesme Iesus donc, qui
s'est abaissé & anéanti
iusques à la mort de la Croix,
& qui par son anéantissement
nous a mérité & acquis la vie
et la gloire,

c'est le mesme qui est monté
sur tous les Cieux,
afin qu'il remplist toutes choses.

c'est celui là mesme, qui est
monté au dessus de tous les
Cieux, afin qu'en suite il
épandit sur son corps, qui est
l'Eglise, toutes les graces &
benedictions qu'il luy avoyt
aquises, & qu'il vivifiast
chacun de ses membres, & les
remplist de vie, de force, &
de vigueur spirituelle.

4. Antoine Godeau, Ephesians 4: 8–10

[Jesus Christ's distribution of graces is full of justice.]

[8] David, voyant en esprit cette liberalité de laquelle il devait user envers nous, dit que

> montant dans le Ciel, il a mené la captivité en triomphe, c'est à dire, les hommes qu'il avait retirez de l'Empire de la mort, & qu'il leur a fait ses largesses, qu'il leur a distribués les biens qu'il n'avait receus que pour leur en faire part.

[9–10] Certes, de ce qu'il est monté, nous devons inférer qu'auparavant il est descendu dans les plus basses parties de la terre, où tant de Patriarches et de Prophètes attendaient sa venue avec impatience.

C'est pourquoy, mes Frères, si vous voulez vous eslever comme luy, il faut que vous vous abaissiez à son exemple, & entriez dans une profonde meditation de vostre neant, de vostre misere, & de la necessité de son secours. Ce n'est pas sans raison qu'il est descendu auparavant que de monter par dessus tous les Cieux, pour y établir son Throsne, & de là considérer la Cour des Anges, & des hommes bien-heureux, qui ne peuvent se lasser de le contempler.

Car il a tenu cet ordre afin de vérifier tous les Oracles de l'Escriture qui l'avaient prédit, & pour achever l'oeuvre de nostre rédemption, de laquelle son Ascension est l'accomplissement, pour faire sentir le mérite de son Sang sous la terre, sur la terre, & dans le Ciel, nous envoyer de là la grâce de son saint Esprit, régner sur tous les hommes par son Évangile, & comme un Monarque triomphant, se faire voir avec les marques de sa victoire & de sa puissance dans tous les lieux de ses conquestes & de son obéissance.

5. Henry Hammond, Ephesians 1: 9–10

[Trans. Ernest Best, 104: 'making known to us the mystery of his will, according to his good pleasure which he purposed in him, for the administration of the fullness of times, / to sum up all things in Christ, the things in heaven and on earth.']

Having now by the preaching of the Gospel to the Gentiles also manifested to us that secret will of his, of which there can be no cause or motive rendred, but his own free mercy and purposed resolution, which till now hath been kept as a mystery (no man imagining that God ever intended any such thing,) but which he had long since proposed to himself, and reserved in his wise dispensation to be performed and delivered out at his season, in these last and worst times, when the sins of men being advanced to such an height, it might rather have been expected that God should proceed to execute vengeance on them. This, I say, which was the just time that God had resolved on for this purpose, to gather together his dispersions, as it were, and to unite all in Christ, to bring into the pale of the Church a whole world of believers, the very Gentiles, all discrimination being removed by Christ through his death and resurrection ...

[Latin version]
Praedicatione Evangelii apud Ethnicos, aperuit nobis arcanum illud suum consilium, cuius causa nulla proferri potest, praeter liberam ipsius misericordiam; quod consilium hactenus occultum fuerat, veluti mysterium quoddam, (cum nemo posset suspicari Deum tale quidquam facturum), sed id jamdudum apud se ceperat, donec, pro sapientissima administratione providentiae divinae, suo tempore revelaretur, postrema hacce & corruptissima aetate, qua usque aucta erant peccata, ut potius ultio divina esset expect-anda.

Hoc erat tempus, quo Deus constitueret dispersos suos liberos congregare, omnesque adjungere Christo & intra ecclesiae christianae terminos mundum integrum credentium adducere, ne Ethnicis quidem exclusis, cum omne gentium discrimen, morte et resurrectione Christi, sit sublatum.

NOTES

1 See Jacques Chomarat, *Grammaire et rhétorique chez Érasme*, 587 n. 2.

2 *Bibliotheca Sancta a F. Sixto Senensi ... collecta*, 2d ed. (Frankfurt, 1585), Liber Quartus, 'Catalogus alter, in quo divinae Scripturae expositores in varias distribuuntur classes,' 346: 'Paraphrastae.'

3 The Greek title is *metabole* (see PG 43: 671ff., 749ff.). It was published at the beginning of the sixteenth century by Aldus Manutius, then at Haguenau in 1527. Martin Bucer refers to it in his commentary on the Fourth Gospel: Irena Backus, 'Ulrich Zwingli, Martin Bucer and the Church Fathers,' 650, citing her edition of the *Enarratio in Evangelion Iohannis* (Leiden: E.J. Brill, 1988).

4 Cited below, n. 28.

5 Francis Titelmans, *Elucidatio in omnes Epistolas apostolicas ... una cum textu ad marginem adiecto & ita commode distributo, ut unaquaeque textus particula suae elucidationi ex adverso respondeat, iuxta veritatem veteris & vulgatae aeditionis, additis argumentis, quae et Epitomatum vice esse possint, totam Epistolarum substantiam iuxta ordinem singulorum capitulorum, summatim complectentibus. Per fratrem Franciscum Titelmannum Hasselensem, ordinis Fratrum minorum, sacrarum scripturarum apud Lovanienses praelectorem, ex ipsa authoris recognitione iam denuo typis excusa* ... Parisiis, apud Ioannem Parvum (1532).

6 Pierre de Launay, *Paraphrase et exposition sur les Epistres de Saint Paul* ... Se vend à Charenton, Par Louis Vendosme, demeurant sur le Quay de Gèvre, à l'Enseigne de la Caille, & au Sacrifice d'Abraham (1650). For the Epistle to the Ephesians, see the *Seconde partie*.

7 Moïse Amyraut, *Paraphrase sur l'Epistre de l'Apostre S. Paul aux Galates, sur l'Epistre aux Éphésiens, sur l'Epistre aux Philippiens* (Saumur: Jean Lesnier, 1645).

8 Antoine Godeau, [vol. 1] *Paraphrase sur les deux Epistres de St Paul aux Corinthiens par A. Godeau, evesque de Grasse* (Paris: Jean Camusat, 1637), 1–35: 'Discours sur la Paraphrase des Epistres de S. Paul'; [vol. 2] *Paraphrase sur les Epistres de Sainct Paul aux Galates, Ephesiens* [386ff.], *Philippiens, Colossiens.*

9 Henry Hammond, *A Paraphrase, and Annotations upon all the books of the New Testament* (London: J. Flesher for Richard Royston, 1653). The English text in appendix 5 below is taken from the third edition (London: J.F. and E.T. for Richard Royston, 1671) and the Latin from *Novum Testamentum Domini nostri Iesu Christi ex versione Vulga-ta cum Paraphrasi et Adnotationibus Henrici Hammondi, ex Anglica Lingua in Latinam transtulit ... Iohannes Clericus ...* (Amstelodami, apud Georgium Galletum, 1698). The paraphrase on Ephesians is at 187–206 of the *Tomus secundus.*

10 A study of the paraphrases on the Psalms would almost certainly lead to different observations and conclusions, on account of the particular status of those texts and their liturgical and devotional uses.

11 On Erasmus' special intent to produce a good Latin translation, clarified by the *Annotations*, see H.J. de Jonge, 'Novum Testamentum a nobis versum: The Essence of Erasmus' Edition of the New Testament.'

12 *Erasmus' Annotations on the New Testament: Galatians to the Apocalypse*, ed. A. Reeve, 597. For the problems in the interpretation of this expression, see Ernest Best, *A Critical and Exegetical Commentary on Ephesians*, 214ff.

13 Eph. 2: 4–6 in *Les Paraphrases d'Erasme divisées en deux Tomes, dont le premier contient l'Exposition des quatre Evangiles et des actes des Apostres. Nouvellement translatées de Latin en Françoys* ... A Basle, de l'Imprimerie des Frobenn [*sic*!]. Avec privilege de la maiesté imperiale (1563). Ephesians appears at 778–93 of *Le second Tome de la Paraphrase de Didier Erasme de Roterodame, sur la reste du nouveau Testament, c'est assavoir sur toutes les Epistres des Apostres*, the passage cited here at 782 (emphasis added). For the history of the early French versions, see the essay by Guy Bedouelle in the present volume. The Latin text of LB 7: 976D–E, given below, has been checked against editions published in Erasmus' life time: 'sed unde vita, unde salus? Haud quaquam ex nostris meritis, nec ex legis Mosaicae beneficio. Unde igitur? Nimirum ex gratuita largitate dei patris, cuius tam opulenta est benignitas, tantaque pietas erga genus humanum, ut non solum non animadverterit in nos, sicut eramus commeriti, verumtamen

cum essemus mortui propter peccata nostra, una cum Christo revocarit nos ad vitam (non erat, inquam, hoc meriti nostri, gratuitum est quod donat) neque tantum revocavit ad vitam cum filio, verumetiam revexit nos ab his humilibus rebus ad coelestia, atque ibi nos collocavit per Christum Iesum, per quem habemus communiter, quicquid habet ille caput nostrum, ac nunc spe possidemus, quicquid mox sumus re ipsa possessuri.'

14 See *Iesu Christi Nostri Novum Testamentum ... cuius Graeco contextui respondent interpretationes duae: una, vetus, altera Thedori Bezae. Eiusdem Theodori Bezae Annotationes* ... Sumptibus Haered. Eust. Vignon (1598) 2: 267f.

15 De Launay, *Paraphrase et exposition*, 18: '[4–5] Mais lors que nous tant Iuifs que gentils, estions ainsi gisans & morts en nos fautes & pechez, Dieu ... nous a par cette sienne immense charité, dont il a esté touché et porté envers nous, viuifiez conjointement auec Iesus Christ, lequel il nous a donné pour nostre chef, & par la grace & communion duquel, & vous gentils, & nous Iuifs, obtenons le salut. [6] Et nous a conjointement avec Christ, ressuscitez & fait asseoir avec lui ès cieux les plus hauts, esquels il est monté & entré en nostre nom, & comme avant coureur pour nous.'

16 Godeau, *Paraphrase sur les deux Epistres*, 16 (from the 'Discours sur la Paraphrase des Epistres de S. Paul'): 'J'ay consulté les plus renommez, et je ne donne aucune explication sans autorité. Ceux que j'ay principalement suivi sont sainct Chrysostome, Oecumenius, sainct Ambroise, Primasius, sainct Thomas, Denys le Chartreux, apres lesquels je pense qu'on ne sçauroit faillir.'

17 See his introduction to the annotations on the Epistle to the Ephesians in *Erasmus' Annotations on the New Testament: Galatians to the Apocalypse*, ed. Reeve, 591.

18 Godeau, *Paraphrase sur les deux Epistres*, 2.

19 Chomarat, *Grammaire et rhétorique chez Érasme*, 587f.

20 In fact, Erasmus admits to having no reply: 'Que si quelqu'un demande pourquoy c'est quayant esté si long temps caché, il a orprimes reuelé (*nunc demum aperiat*): Ie n'ay que luy respondre sinon que ce bon Dieu l'a ainsi voulu, lequel ne peut rien vouloir qui ne soit tresbon, veu qu'il est la bonté mesme' (*Le second Tome de la Paraphrase*, 780).

21 De Launay, *Paraphrase et exposition*, 2.

22 Godeau, *Paraphrase sur les Epistres*, 396, on Eph. 1: 3f. See also appendix 4 on Eph. 4: 8–10.

23 Maurice Pergnier, *Les fondements socio-linguistiques de la traduction*, 41ff.

24 Erasmus, *Novum Instrumentum* (1516): '[8] *dio legei. Anabas eis hupsos eichmaloteusen aichmalosian, edoken domata tois anthropois.* [9] *to de*

anebe, ti estin, ei me oti kai katebe proton eis ta katotera mere tes ges; [10] *ho katabas autos estin kai ho anabas huperano panton ton ouranon, ina plerosei ta panta.'* Robert Estienne's edition of the Vulgate (Paris, 1532): '[8] Propter quod dicit. Ascendens in altum captivam duxit captivitatem dedit dona hominibus. [9] Quod autem ascendit quid est, nisi quia & descendit primum in inferiores partes terrae? [10] Qui descendit, ipse est & qui ascendit super omnes caelos ut impleret omnia.'

25 The history of the tradition and interpretation of this text was beyond the scholarly powers of sixteenth- and seventeenth-century exegetes. It may be noted, however, that John Calvin did not see a citation of the Psalms in the verse: 'Quanquam ego in diversam sententiam magis inclino: Paulum data opera verbum mutasse nec adduxisse tamquam ex psalmo sumptum, sed potius ex seipso protulisse, quod praesenti instituto aptum erat': *Commentarii in Pauli Epistolas ad Galatas, ad Ephesios, ad Philippenses, ad Colossenses,* in *Ioannis Calvini opera omnia,* series 2: *Opera exegetica Veteris et Novi Testamenti,* vol. 16, ed. Helmut Feld (Geneva: Droz, 1992), 224, lines 29ff. He was not followed in this interpretation.

26 Beza, *Iesu Christi* ... (n. 14), 2: 275, ad Annot. 8, lines 36ff., with references to Gen. 32: 13 and Acts 7: 9.

27 Erasmus, *Le second Tome de la Paraphrase,* 786.

28 Lefèvre, *S. Pauli epistolae XIV ex Vulgata, adiecta intelligentia ex graeco, cum commentariis,* facsimile reprint of 1512 Paris edition (Stuttgart: Frommann, 1978) fol. 164v.

29 Erasmus, *Le second Tome de la Paraphrase,* 786: 'Aussi n'y a-t-il point de descente que d'enhaut. Descendre est premier que monter: Car rien ne merite hautesse, que humilité & abaissance de soy. Or de grande abaissance, s'ensuit une tres-grande hautesse. Christ du plus haut ciel qui est par dessus tout, s'est abaissé iusqu'aux enfers par dessous toutes choses. Et par cela a merité d'estre derechef esleué par dessus le plus haut de tous les cieux, retirant ainsi de nous la presence de son corps, à fin d'emplir tout d'enhaut de dons celestes, & nous assister par un autre certain moyen, & avec plus grande efficace qu'il ne fit oncques, lors qu'il conversoit avec nous en terre.'

30 See the *Paraclesis* in *Érasme: Les Préfaces au Novum Testamentum,* ed. Yves Delègue, 89, and above, 14 n. 11.

31 See Beza, *Iesu Christi* ... 2: 275, ad Annot. 9: '... id est in terram, quae pars est mundi infima, ut idonei interpretes explicant.' There is a clear allusion to Calvin: 'Comparatur enim non una pars terrae cum altera, sed tota terra cum coelo: ac si diceret, ex sede tam excelsa, in hoc nostrum profundum barathrum descendisse' (Calvin, *Commentarii in Pauli Epistolas* 226). De Launay places himself squarely within an interpretative tradition.

32 See the dedication of the paraphrase on the Epistle to the Romans to Cardinal Grimani (LB 7: 773).
33 Titelmans, *Elucidatio in omnes Epistolas apostolicas*, fol. Ai v. The reader is to read and reread the text 'etiam si non intelligas.' 'Deinde, cum ipsa textus verba simpliciter sic considerata, menti leniter impresseris, ad Elucidationem transiens, & ipsam per se legas attente, sine textus collatione, ac in simplici eius lectione tantisper immorare, usque dum eius vim atque sententiam pro tuo captu, plene comprehenderis. Tum demum ad collationem accedens, textus verba cum Elucidationis sententiam conferas. Ubi perpendum erit exacto iudicio, quo nam modo Elucidatio idem habeat quod textus, iterumque textus, quibus sub verbis dicat, quod secundum sententiam verbis aliis habet Elucidatio ...'
34 Beza, *Iesu Christi ...*, 2: 1 on Rom. 1: 1; 2: 228 on Gal. 1: 1.
35 George Aichele et al. (The Bible and Culture Collective), *The Postmodern Bible* 5, quoting L. Althusser.
36 Pier Cesare Bori, *L'interprétation infinie: L'herméneutique chrétienne ancienne et ses transformations*, 11–62.
37 Godeau, *Paraphrase sur les deux Epistres*, 16.
38 Ibid., 13.
39 Ibid., 5, 11.
40 See André Lacoque and Paul Ricoeur, *Penser la Bible*, 15.
41 A Centre d'Études des Religions du Livre that groups together a number of Directeurs d'Études from the Section des Sciences Religieuses of the École Pratique des Hautes Études and members of the Centre National de la Recherche Scientifique.

THREE

Historical Imagination and the Representation of Paul in Erasmus' Paraphrases on the Pauline Epistles

Robert D. Sider

Erasmus' interest in Paul can be traced back at least as far as the autumn of 1499, when he met in Oxford a relatively young John Colet, whose lectures on the letters of the Apostle were widely admired. After Erasmus' return to Paris in 1500, an unsuccessful attempt to write his own commentary on the Pauline epistles was replaced in subsequent years by a recurrent resolve to do so. A mishap while riding his horse in Ghent in the summer of 1514 transformed resolve into vow, a vow to the Apostle himself (CWE Ep 301: 20–2); and it was to the Apostle (and to God) that he returned thanks upon his recovery (CWE Ep 301: 34). Though Erasmus never realized his resolve or fulfilled his vow, his writings suggest that throughout his life he tended to think of Paul in superlatives. He urged John Poppenruyter, to whom he dedicated the *Enchiridion*, published in 1503, to 'make Paul your special friend, him you should learn by heart' (CWE Ep 164: 39–42). A 1520 addition to the *Ratio verae theologiae* declares that 'no one resembled more precisely our teacher Christ than Paul,'[1] and in a 1527 addition to the *Annotations on Romans*, Erasmus claims that Paul, when moved by emotion, surpassed even Cicero in effecting the grand manner (CWE 56: 234). Yet perhaps nowhere do we have a more significant indication of the special place of Paul in Erasmus' life than in a very subtle hint hidden in the *Paraphrase on Romans* (published November 1517), where the words of Paul in paraphrase – *nulli concedam* – echo those on Erasmus' seal.[2] Here it would seem Erasmus wished to make Paul his own. Hieronymus Emser, at least, apparently thought such an identification appropriate, and anticipated the equation suggested in the paraphrase. Writing to Erasmus from Dresden on the Ides of March, 1517, Emser begins: 'Greetings, Erasmus, chosen vessel, and next after Paul as teacher of the Gentiles' (CWE Ep 553: 1–2).

This short account of Erasmus' attachment to Paul offers a sufficient justification to undertake a search for the figure of Paul in the paraphrases on the Pauline epistles. I propose to proceed in four steps. First I shall assume, as no doubt Erasmus did, that the book of Acts provides an appropriate narrative structure for an account of the life of Paul, and I shall attempt to elicit in sequence Erasmus' interpretation of the nodal events of the Apostle's life – the conversion, the missionary endeavours, the imprisonment – as these appear in the paraphrases on the Pauline epistles. Second, I shall look for the special features that characterize the apostleship in these paraphrases, for it is primarily as an apostle that Paul comes before us in the New Testament; we shall want to know, then, how in the paraphrases Erasmus envisions the apostolate. Third, I shall make some more general, if still necessarily tentative, inferences about the mode and motives of Erasmus' portrayal of Paul. Finally, in order to set in perspective the portrait of Paul that emerges from our primary study of the epistles I shall, in conclusion, cast a brief and very summary glance at remarks gathered from a broader range of Erasmus' writings that point to the apostolic figure in images that should prove instructive through comparison and contrast with those in the paraphrases on the thirteen epistles.

It will be advantageous to note here a pair of considerations that will circumscribe our study. On the one hand, we shall understand as the 'Pauline epistles' the letters Erasmus himself ascribed to Paul, without the maverick Hebrews.[3] By limiting our central study to the epistles we shall be able to observe the Erasmian construct of the Apostle as it emerges from documents that can function as primary historical sources. On the other hand, there can be no question of eliciting a 'biography' of Paul from the paraphrases on the epistles. The paraphrases are a clarification of the text;[4] and while clarification offered opportunities to add details to the biblical narrative, to highlight or, it may be, shift biblical emphases, to give rhetorical colour to statements articulated and deeds narrated in the original, the necessity to follow the biblical text nevertheless limited the paraphrast's freedom. Through the added details, the emphases, the rhetorical colour in the paraphrases, we can seek Erasmus' interpretation of the great events that seem to lie at the centre of Paul's life, but we are not likely to find in the *Paraphrases* a holistic portrait of a character in the process of change and development.[5]

ASPECTS OF THE LIFE OF PAUL

1. *Conversion: Continuity and Change*

In the paraphrases on the Pauline epistles Erasmus shows very little interest in the typically biographical details of Paul's life before his conversion. He uniformly refrains, for example, from filling in the story of Paul's past by allusion to his birth at Tarsus, his Roman citizenship, his education under Gamaliel. For Erasmus, it is only in the event of conversion that Paul's prior life finds significance. He apparently recognized that conversion invites one to attempt to account for both continuity and change in an individual's life, while such an accounting demands a consideration of the past. In the paraphrases on Galatians 1: 13–14 Erasmus builds on the biblical text to appeal to divine destiny, hence, ultimately, to mystery, to explicate the change.[6] At the same time, the paraphrases point to aspects of continuity between past and present, between the unconverted Paul and the future apostle: his zeal, his endeavour to maintain a good conscience, to perform an honourable and pleasing service to God. 'You know how I abhorred the gospel of Christ ... I ravaged [the church] with an utterly hostile mind, thinking that I was performing an honourable and pleasing service to God ... I erred in judgment, not in heart, and I opposed the author of the Law out of zeal for the Law. And God allowed this for a time by some secret plan of his ... Accordingly, when he called me by his own gracious goodness ... did I hesitate?' (CWE 42: 100–1). There are visible here lines of continuity, while the transformation is credited to the 'secret plan' and the 'gracious goodness' of God.

The paraphrase on Romans 1: 1 likewise attempts to draw the lines of continuity in the life of Paul before and after conversion: always a servant, always a Pharisee. In this paraphrase, however, the emphasis falls upon the transformation brought by conversion. Playing upon the change of names from Saul to Paul, Erasmus hints at a change in character, but the change brought by conversion is predominantly a change in the direction of life: 'I am Paul, though formerly Saul ... peaceful though formerly restless, until recently subject to Moses ... I have been made a servant of Jesus Christ. Not ... a deserter ... of my former tradition ... I am now more happily separated than I was before ... truly worthy of the name of Pharisee' (CWE 42: 15).

Paul's conversion as a new orientation thus articulated in the paraphrase on Romans 1: 1 finds its most persistent representation throughout the *Paraphrases* in a new identity that entailed the virtual renunciation of ethnicity. In the paraphrase on Galatians 2: 19–20 Paul points to his past: 'As a Jew,' he says, 'I had to do with the Law' – he points also to the change brought by conversion: 'But ... I died to the burdensome Law ... Saul, that champion of the Law and persecutor of the gospel, has died' (CWE 42: 106–7). The paraphrase on Philippians 3: 3–9 abjures race even more explicitly: 'At that time, since I had not yet learned Christ, I thought myself enviably fortunate in my nobility of race ... but when through the gospel of Christ I learned wherein true righteousness lay ... I cast aside and abandoned what I had so greatly admired' (LB 7: 999D–E). We may find the theological basis for the rejection of ethnicity in the paraphrase on 2 Corinthians 5: 17, where the simple text of Scripture, 'If anyone is in Christ he is a new creation, old things have passed away,' in paraphrase finds illustration in ethnic and social distinctions: 'Accordingly, whoever is grafted into Christ through baptism puts aside the old dispositions. He does not think, "This man is a Jew, that one a Greek; here is a slave, there a free man" ... Have nothing to do with such expressions of a strictly human provenance – like "here is a Greek ... there is a Jew." A person has ceased to be what he was, and through the workmanship of Christ has been turned into a new creation, a person as different from his former self as a human being is from an animal' (LB 7: 925A–B).[7]

The theory was fine; in practice the biblical text forced some qualification. The problem can be illustrated from the *Paraphrase on Romans*. In the biblical text Paul speaks of the Jews as 'they' or 'them'; he also speaks of 'we Jews' (3: 9) and of 'Abraham, our father' (4: 1, 12); and to the question 'Has God rejected his people?' he exclaims in response, 'By no means! I myself am an Israelite' (11: 1). Throughout Romans (and, I believe, elsewhere)

Erasmus in paraphrase generally adopts the personal pronouns and possessive adjectives of the biblical text, though not quite always. In the case of Romans, whether he does so or not appears to depend on the dramatic needs of the narrative. Thus in Romans 4, where the argument seeks to demonstrate, as it moves from humanity's past to the Christians' present, that Abraham is the father of Jews and gentiles alike, the possessive adjective 'our [father Abraham]' is twice omitted from the paraphrase (cf. Rom. 4: 1 and 12), so that Abraham can be understood more clearly as the father of all in Christ; here Paul disregards his Jewish identity. By contrast, in chapter 11, where Paul is about to reveal the divine secret that in the grand finale of history the Jews will acknowledge Christ, the Paul of the paraphrases speaks frankly of his relation to both Jews and gentiles, affirming his Jewishness, but not without qualification: 'I address you gentiles ... the apostle of the gentiles, though a Jew by birth ... I will strive to reveal you as worthy of Christ if somehow in this way I might challenge my own people – for they are my people by blood relationship, but strangers in the matter of faith' (CWE 42: 64–5). Thus, in the *Paraphrases* Erasmus appears to suggest that Paul, through his conversion, realized in himself the goal of Saving History, understood as the elimination of ethnic distinctions, but that as an actor in a Saving History still uncompleted and extending beyond himself, the Apostle acknowledges reluctantly his identity as a Jew.

2. *The Missionary Journeys*

(a) The Call: We shall presently observe that, according to Acts, Paul's great missionary journeys were begun with a commission from the church. Yet in both Acts and the epistles Paul's call to preach is closely associated with the conversion. In the biblical text the precise relationship between conversion and call is ambiguous. In Acts 26 the two are represented as simultaneous. In Acts 22 call follows conversion, though Ananias foretells the call at the time of baptism. In Acts 9 the divine voice reveals the call to Ananias but not to Paul. In the paraphrases on the epistles Erasmus makes no attempt to clarify the relation of conversion to call. Nevertheless, if one regards the two as a single event with two foci, Erasmus radically privileges the call. At the one point in the paraphrases on all the epistles where, for the conversion narrative, Erasmus recalls a detail from Acts, it is the image of Ananias as prophet of the call that he evokes: the Paul of the paraphrases tells the Ephesians that they can read in his other epistles about the secret revealed to him – how Christ foretold to Ananias that the apostle would carry his name to the gentiles, a command given also to Paul himself.[8] In the paraphrase on Galatians 1: 15–16 Erasmus appears to eliminate the ambiguity of the biblical text, which suggests an allusion to both conversion and call: 'But when God was pleased to reveal his Son to me, so that I might proclaim him among the gentiles ...' (NRSV). Here Erasmus follows his own translation, which forces an allusion strictly to the call by interpreting the 'in me' or 'to me' of the Greek[9] as 'through me': 'to reveal his Son through me.'[10] The paraphrases on Galatians 1: 6–17 emphasize the allusion to the call by a series of rhetorical questions intended to suggest its compelling power: 'Did I hesitate to undertake the duty ...? did I distrust this oracular command ...?' (CWE 42: 101). We may note here that elsewhere, also, the paraphrases stress even more abruptly the sense of compulsion felt by the neophyte as he heard the call.[11] For Erasmus, as we shall see, the nerve centre of Paul's life as a Christian was the proclamation of the Word.

(b) The Early Years: In the biblical record, Paul begins to preach shortly after his conversion,[12] but the narratives generally make little of his early missionary work. Indeed, the narrative of Acts creates the impression that the great period of Paul's missionary activity began with the first missionary journey commissioned by the church of Antioch (Acts 13: 2–3). In the *Paraphrase on Galatians* Erasmus challenges the impression derived from Acts. The epistle itself informs us of Paul's presence in Damascus and Arabia (1: 17), but tells us nothing about his activity in these places, and there is only a passing mention of Paul's work in the 'regions of Syria and Cilicia' (1: 22). For Erasmus the paraphrast, however, the compelling power of a call directly from God such as Paul's, and of the Apostle's unhesitating obedience to it, evidently could only mean that Paul's missionary journeys – or, at the very least, his unabated missionary activity – must have begun in earnest immediately upon his conversion and call. Erasmus follows the tradition represented by the *Glossa ordinaria* in assuming that Paul preached in Arabia,[13] but he gives to the tradition the romantic details that construct the event as a missionary journey: 'I went without delay to Arabia, and did not shrink from presenting the name of Christ ... to wild and barbarian races' (CWE 42: 101). Paul returned to Damascus, Erasmus notes, where 'he had first begun to preach' (ibid). After three years he went to Jerusalem, but only to make a 'courtesy call' on Peter and James; he was not, the paraphrase emphatically says, seeking their authorization for a ministry that had already been commissioned by God himself. Thence a further, obviously extended, journey to Syria and Cilicia, 'proclaiming everywhere the name of Christ (ibid).[14] Thus, according to the paraphrase on 2:1, Paul had 'preached the doctrine of the gospel for fourteen years, chiefly to the gentiles,' before he went up again to Jerusalem (CWE 42: 102).[15]

(c) The Major Journeys: That a passionate desire to preach drove Paul through Asia and Europe on his 'missionary journeys' is attested by his own words in his letters, perhaps nowhere more decisively than in Romans 15: 15–24. Since Erasmus envisions the Apostle as, above all, a preacher, we are not surprised to find that in the paraphrases on these verses images of preaching culminate in words that, as we have seen, echo the motto on Erasmus' seal[16] to point to a portrait of an Apostle who, as preacher, is second to none: 'I zealously perform [the will of Christ] with all my strength ... bringing the gospel of God to light among you gentiles ... to some extent I can be proud ... rejoicing before God for the happy outcome of my preaching ... I attribute this ... to Jesus Christ ... with whose help I perform the duty of preaching ... I am nothing other than an instrument and a minister. Therefore, while I boast about the success of my preaching, I preach the glory of Christ, not my own. And in this way, it is certainly right for me to boast, inasmuch as I attribute praise of my service to God in such a way that nevertheless I yield to no man' (CWE 42: 85–6).

However much Paul might have understood his missionary years from the perspective of his preaching, his letters assure us that the context of his preaching was almost constant struggle. Indeed, for modern readers, much of the interest of the letters lies in the possibilities they offer to reconstruct the events and circumstances of Paul's life during these years. It is clear that Erasmus also undertook to construct in his imagination a 'staging' for those apostolic encounters that induced Paul to write his letters.

Needless to say, Erasmus did not bring to his reconstruction the sophistication of modern scholarship. In the first place, the paraphrases show little interest in establishing a precise temporal sequence for the letters that could then be carefully correlated with the events of Paul's life. Notes on time and place in the Arguments that prefaced the paraphrases on the epistles strike the modern reader as essentially archival: we are told that Paul spent 'quite a few days' at Philippi (LB 7: 991–2), that he laboured for a year and a half to convert the Corinthians (LB 7: 855–6), and for three years to make Christians of the Ephesians (LB 7: 971–2); but there is no indication that Erasmus sees in these time periods the opportunity they offer to add perspective to the biography of the Apostle. He recognizes that Colossians is a prison epistle, but he is content to say that it was written either during an earlier imprisonment in Ephesus or a later one in Rome. Erasmus acknowledges Ambrosiaster's observation that there were three letters to the Corinthians (LB 7: 857–8),[17] but he notes that 'Greek interpreters' disagree, and he resorts to ambiguity in 1 Corinthians 5: 9 when he paraphrases, 'I bade you a little earlier' (LB 7: 874B). He believes the Epistle to Titus was written from Nicopolis 'before the troubles' – that is, before Paul's afflictions – presumably, therefore, at an earlier point in Paul's missionary career, but the comment passes without any suggestion of its historiographical significance (CWE 44: 56). Indeed, of the Arguments to the epistles only that to Romans places the epistle within the context of a significant portion of Paul's life. Second, the modern scholar is likely to find the context proposed for the individual letters insufficiently nuanced.[18] Erasmus postulates Judaizers as the ubiquitous enemy of the Apostle, but it is unlikely that the first letter to the Thessalonians, for example, presupposes that the troublemakers there were Judaizers.[19]

It is possible, however, to observe Erasmus' imagination at work as he attempts to reconstruct from the epistles Paul's reaction to the turbulent events his preaching evoked. Erasmus appears to read the epistles under the fundamental assumption that Paul's statements, at least his more pressing statements, presuppose a target. Thus his repetitive claim that he glories only in Christ and his cross (1 Cor. 1: 31; Gal. 6: 14) implies enemies who sought self-glorification. That the Apostle should so insistently defend his practice of self-employment (1 Cor. 9) could only mean that his enemies strove for financial gain from preaching their gospel. He boasted in the visions he was granted (2 Cor. 12: 1–5) because his enemies validated their mission by appealing to the visions they had been granted. It appears, then, that to a considerable degree Erasmus found his Paul defined in the epistles in the terms established by his opponents; hence, in the *Paraphrases* the figure of the preacher became particularized and acquired individuality against the portrait of his enemies. These are most fully described in the paraphrases on the letters to the Galatians and the Corinthians.

Paul's enemies receive a brief generalizing description in the Argument to Galatians. They are 'pseudo-apostles ... supposedly sent by Peter and James, the leading apostles ... They disparage the authority of Paul ... claiming that he was inconsistent' (CWE 42: 98–9). The paraphrase itself develops the picture much more fully. These men are 'more truly preachers of Moses than of Christ,' who impose upon the simplicity of the Galatians, confusing them with the 'splendid titles of the highest apostles,' and misusing the names of Peter, James, and John to ensnare them in the burdens of the Law (CWE 42: 98–9). They themselves are Jews (CWE 42: 129) and are 'Jew-pleasers' – they both seek the favour of the Jews (CWE 42: 99) and fear persecution from the Jews (CWE 42: 129). In contrast to Paul, they preach from motives of profit and pride, to ensure their own gain and glory (CWE 42: 118, 123). Because Paul's own apparent vacillation over Jewish practices provides a handle for the pseudo-apostles to arouse mistrust, Paul defines himself as the apostle of 'accommodation' for the sake of the gospel (CWE 42: 100, 103, 123–4). Because they compare him disparagingly with the 'highest apostles,' he asserts his independence from these revered figures (CWE 42: 105) and affirms the superiority of his own apostolic vocation (CWE 42: 97), but at the same time suggests that the straightforward truth of the gospel he preached was reflected in his outward appearance as a humble and insignificant man (CWE 42: 105).

As the Argument to 1 Corinthians indicates, Paul's enemies in Corinth also are Judaizers, who perform their unwelcome mission as a means to achieve gain and glory (LB 7: 855–8). But Erasmus finds in the Corinthian context details that refine the construct. He imagines Corinth as a city whose wealth and pride, knowledge and eloquence are esteemed, and these are values to which the Corinthian converts are still lamentably alive. The pseudo-apostles catch their prey, therefore, by vaunting their Law, their wealth, and their wisdom (LB 7: 864B on 1 Cor. 2: 1). They categorize apostles: they think Peter and James the most distinguished (LB 7: 860C on 1 Cor. 1: 7); and they proudly claim to be instructed by the chief apostles, those indeed that gloried in the fact that they shared race, even family kinship, and just a few years ago daily association with the Lord (LB 7: 924B–C, F on 2 Cor. 5: 12, 16) – indeed at this point the paraphrase hints at a sort of collusion between the *praecipui apostoli*, 'the chief apostles,' and the pseudo-apostles. Further, the wisdom and authority of these pseudo-apostles derives not only from their most distinguished teachers, but also from the visions they claim to have been granted (LB 7: 937F on 2 Cor. 12: 1). They boast that they are Jews (LB 7: 936C–E on 2 Cor. 11: 18–22); and they themselves assume the name of apostle, seeking to satisfy their belly (LB 7: 935D–F on 2 Cor. 11: 11–13; cf. 936C on 2 Cor. 11: 18).

Seen against a background thus constructed in the *Paraphrases*, Paul's own declarations in the biblical text appear as a self-portrait designed to counter the claims and pretensions of his opponents. He is a man proud of his intellectual simplicity and his lack of eloquence (1 Cor. 2: 1–4), he acknowledges his unpretentious presence (1 Cor. 4; 2 Cor. 10: 1–11), and he feels no shame in earning his living by the work of his own hands (1 Cor. 9); at the same time, he claims an acquaintance with Christ (2 Cor. 5: 16), he boasts a purebred pedigree, a unique apostolic call, and gifts of visions and tongues (2 Cor. 11–12; 1 Cor. 14: 18). It is the image of a man who defines himself in reference to the turbulent historical situation in which he is embroiled. Erasmus' Paul is not a timeless icon of divine wisdom!

3. *The Final Years*

(a) The Double Imprisonment: Erasmus follows the view well-attested already in early Christianity that Paul was twice imprisoned in Rome.[20] This view accommodated the inference from 2 Timothy 4: 17 that Paul undertook a vigorous preaching campaign between the two incarcerations.[21] The argument to 2 Timothy places the writing of the letter at the time when Paul was appearing for the second time before Nero's court (CWE 44: 40), and the paraphrases on 2 Timothy 4: 9–17 (CWE 44: 53) imply as much. The paraphrases on these verses go well beyond the details of the biblical text strictly interpreted, and we note in particular their stress upon Paul's devotion to the task of preaching. He is not, in these paraphrases, free to teach quite openly and without hindrance as he is in the first imprisonment recorded in

Acts 28: 30–1. Hence, he calls for Timothy to help him, for 'imprisonment prevents me from walking here and there at will to carry out the work of the gospel' (CWE 44: 53). He recalls his first trial before 'Caesar's courts,' when all, terrified by fear, forsook him, but he was 'delivered from the jaws of the most savage lion' with the help of God, who drove him hither and yon through different lands' to preach the gospel, in the midst of which service he was finally carried to Rome (CWE 44: 53).

(b) Preacher to the End: We have just seen that Paul calls Timothy to Rome to enable the preaching of the gospel while he suffers imprisonment there. Paul's burning zeal for the preaching of the gospel finds what is perhaps its ultimate exemplification in the paraphrases on Philippians 1: 14–17, where the Apostle expresses a careless, even rapturous, joy that the gospel is being preached, even though by others. Erasmus eliminates the ambiguity of the biblical text by defining three groups who are engaged in proclaiming the gospel.[22] Some give out the message[23] in a malicious spirit, endeavouring to fan the flame of Nero's hatred against the Christians: they believe that if he sees the sect growing, a sect he believes is destructive to the state, he will more quickly put to death a staunch leader like Paul.[24] A second group, good Christians, are merely jealous of Paul, and see his imprisonment as their opportunity to surpass the Apostle in evangelical fervour, and so put his fame into the shade by their success. A third group, both Christians and good friends of the Apostle, preach the gospel because they love him and wish to help him, even in prison, to carry out his ministry. Paul welcomes all groups: only let the gospel be preached![25] Thus, even in prison the commission to preach, received in the call, still dominated the Apostle's life.[26] In the paraphrases on the epistles, Paul is the prince of preachers rather than the first of theologians.

THE APOSTOLATE OF PAUL IN THE *PARAPHRASES ON THE PAULINE EPISTLES*

Though preaching lies at the heart of Paul's apostolate in the *Paraphrases*, Erasmus nevertheless seizes numerous opportunities provided by the biblical text to explore the implications of the apostolate, and in doing so greatly enriches the portrait of Paul he otherwise presents. Four aspects of the apostolate find noteworthy explication in the *Paraphrases*: the excellence of the call, the revelation of the mystery, the labours, and the apostolic identification with Christ.

1. *The Apostle Uniquely Called*

The position of Paul in relation to the other apostles has been a matter for discussion from the earliest days of the church. Paul's own letters show that some of his contemporaries not only belittled his apostolate, but questioned its validity altogether.[27] Faced by the challenge of Marcion, some early Christian authors attempted to reduce the stature of Paul in relation to the other apostles.[28] Quite the contrary is the case in the *Paraphrases* of Erasmus, where Paul is represented as the superior apostle. His superiority is grounded first in the special circumstances of his call. To the Corinthians who may be tempted to lament that they received an 'inferior apostle' the paraphrastic Paul admits that he did not see the Lord in the flesh, but he retorts that he did see the immortal Lord (LB 7: 924C on 2 Cor. 5 :12). The point finds greater elaboration in the paraphrase on Galatians 1: 1: he was not called as the others were, by the still mortal Christ, but rather by the Christ risen and ascended, the Christ from heaven, now the immortal Son of God; he was the only one to be called after Christ had put aside every weakness of the human condition, and was no longer acting as a man but as God' (CWE 42: 97).

2. *The Apostle of the Mystery*

Perhaps the most distinguishing mark of Paul's call to apostleship is the disclosure of the divine mystery that accompanied it. In Galatians 1: 11–12 Paul affirms that 'the gospel proclaimed by me ... came through a revelation' (NRSV). For Erasmus, divine revelation is 'mystery,'[29] and the paraphrases define a disclosure centred in Paul: 'Christ himself deigned to disclose to me the mystery of the abolition of the old law and the introduction of the new' (cf. CWE 42: 100). The mystery was centred in Paul not only because it was revealed to him, but also because his apostolate was a commission to disclose it to others. Thus, at the conclusion of Romans, the 'mystery now disclosed, and through the prophetic writings ... made known to all' (16: 25–6 NRSV) is, in paraphrase, emphatically located in the apostolate of Paul, the biblical text becoming 'the mystery revealed according to the oracles of the ancient prophets and made known by the radiant gospel' – with an explanation added: 'This has happened by the decree and order of God who delegated to us the duty of preaching and the task of making his secret known' (CWE 42: 90). In the paraphrase on Colossians 1: 25–6 the role of Paul in the disclosure of the mystery is so heightened that the two, Paul's ministry and the mystery revealed, seem to be virtually equated: 'I perform the duty assigned ... especially the evangelization of the gentiles – that I might supply by my efforts what seemed to be lacking in his ... and that I might spread abroad ... [the good news] that a path to gospel salvation lies open to the gentiles through faith. It is by my preaching especially that [this] has been revealed to them' (LB 7: 1008C–D). Nowhere do the paraphrases more emphatically, almost exclusively, associate the mystery with Paul's call and ministry than in Ephesians 3: 3–4, where the revelation of the mystery decisively distinguishes him from the other apostles: 'This secret [*arcanum*], formerly concealed from other apostles, Christ has disclosed especially to me ... To me Christ's secret plan was not unknown, for Christ both foretold to Ananias that I would bear his name among the gentiles and he himself bade me go to the nations far off to serve as his envoy' (LB 7: 978F–9A). Thus, in the *Paraphrases* Erasmus marks Paul by accentuating his unique role in the revelation of the mystery.

3. *The Apostle of Labours Unsurpassed*

If Paul's superiority to the other apostles is attested by his extraordinary call and the disclosure of the mystery attendant upon it, it is in his labours that he demonstrates his special excellence. He reminds the Corinthians that if it is the mark of an apostle to found a church, he, and he alone, founded the church at Corinth. They need not think that in Paul they received an inferior apostle, they need not long for Peter and James whom some regard as the chief apostles; rather, it is precisely the Corinthians' conversion under Paul that proves his apostolicity. They are, he says, the *diploma* ('certificate') that signifies to all the apostolic ministry committed to him (LB 7: 888B–C on 1 Cor. 9: 2). They have, moreover, received from him everything that other churches, founded by revered apostles, have received: miracles added force to his preaching, while prodigies and powerful deeds seen in their midst are indisputable evidence that Paul is an apostolic man.[30] In fact, the Paul of the *Paraphrases* repeatedly boasts that in his labours he is superior to the other apostles: how, he asks, is he less than the other apostles when he is their equal, or perhaps their superior, in labours (LB 7: 888C–D on 1 Cor. 9: 4)? He grants that he, as the persecutor of the Christians, was unworthy to be chosen apostle, even if last of all; 'nevertheless,' he says, 'in performing the gospel ministry, I have not shown myself to be last, but I have carried through more labours than any other apostle – just in case anyone is inclined to attribute less authority to me because I was named apostle last' (LB 7: 906F–7A on 1 Cor. 15: 10). He scorns those who take pride in their ethnic blood, and turns to the evidence that truly attests to an apostolic heart: 'I,' he says, 'have carried through more labours than they' (LB 7: 936F–7A on 2 Cor. 11: 23). If labours verify the apostolate, as indeed they do, then Paul is the supreme apostle. In the *Paraphrases* Erasmus' representation of Paul as the apostle of evangelical labours might well appear as an extended exposition on the Apostle's words in Romans 15: 18–19: 'I will not venture to speak of anything except what Christ has accomplished through me ... by word and deed, by the power of signs and wonders ... so that from Jerusalem and as far around as Illyricum I have fully proclaimed the good news of Christ' (NRSV). We may recall that Erasmus concluded the paraphrases on these verses with a declaration by Paul that he can truly boast in these labours, attributing praise to God, 'but in such a way that I yield to no one [*ut ... nulli concedam*]' (LB 7: 828C–D).

4. *The Apostolic Identification with Christ*

While the words just quoted from Romans proudly point to Paul's labours, they indicate also the Apostle's special relationship to Christ, for they are labours Christ has wrought through Paul. The *Paraphrases* accentuate the close identity between Paul and Christ apparent in the biblical text. First, the *Paraphrases* equate the commission of Paul with the commission of Christ: both are ambassadors sent from God. Thus the paraphrase on 1 Timothy 1: 1: 'Paul, the apostle and emissary of Jesus Christ ... He too once carried out a mission as the representative of the Father ... I was called to [my mission] by the will of the Eternal Power ... For in my view whatever the Son imposed upon us at the Father's command has been imposed by the Father himself' (CWE 44: 5). The same point is made more briefly when the Apostle introduces himself in 2 Corinthians: 'Paul, who is undertaking a mission in the name of Christ on the authority of God the Father ...' (LB 7: 915A on 2 Cor. 1: 1); and the identity is yet more strongly expressed in the paraphrase on 2 Cor. 5: 18–20: 'The Father has committed to us the preaching of reconciliation, so that just as the Son undertook on the Father's behalf a mission among human beings, so we fulfill our mission on behalf of Christ ... We fulfill this mission in the place of Christ [*vice Christi*] who committed it to us, and so in the name of Christ we beg you – as though God were exhorting you through us – that you put away your former sins, and be reconciled to God' (LB 7: 925B–C). In the paraphrase, just as God has spoken in Christ, so God and Christ speak through Paul.

It is, however, in the act of suffering that the Paul of the *Paraphrases* is most insistently identified with Christ. In the paraphrase on Galatians 4: 12–14 Erasmus understands Paul's 'physical infirmity' (NRSV) as 'the outward appearance of a humble and lowly man, subject to troubles, hateful ... on account of the name of Christ.' In preaching the gospel to the Galatians he 'lowered himself to their weakness' – the idiom belongs to the theology of the Incarnation – and the Galatians in turn received Paul as Christ, even worshipped Christ in Paul (CWE 42: 117). At the end of the letter (6: 17) the paraphrase interprets the famous *stigmata* as Paul's sufferings – the marks of Christ branded on his body, demonstrating that he was deemed worthy to represent (*imitari*) the cross of Christ (CWE 42: 130; cf. CWE 42: 130 n. 7 and LB 7: 968A). In 1 Thessalonians 2: 14–16 the similarities drawn between the sufferings of the Thessalonians and those of the Judaean Christians are sharpened by paraphrase into an implied identity of Christ and his Apostle, and, indeed, of other Christians who suffer: 'What Christ, what we, what the other Jews have suffered ... you also have suffered at the hands of your own race, for just as they killed the Lord Jesus, and before him had slain the prophets, so they persecute us, the heralds of gospel truth ... as though it was not enough for them ... unless we too suffer and perish at their hands' (LB 7: 1020D–E). In the next chapter the paraphrase goes beyond the warrant of the text to compare again the sufferings of Christ and his Apostle: 'It should not seem strange to you if the preachers of the gospel should meet with such sufferings, since you have known now for some time that I was chosen by God to glorify the name of Christ by my bodily sufferings, reflecting in this way my teacher and Lord' (LB 7: 1021E on 1 Thess. 3: 3). Nor did Erasmus lose the opportunity afforded by 2 Corinthians 4: 8–12. Twice the word *imitari* is repeated in the paraphrases on these verses: in his sufferings the apostle imitates as best he can the Lord Jesus whom he preaches. In his sufferings, through which he dies, as it were, for the Corinthians, he imitates the death of Christ, who died for all (LB 7: 922B–D). With his Lord, the Apostle, too, is the 'suffering servant.'

This view, that the Apostle suffers with Christ on behalf of others, finds such an uncompromising expression in the biblical text of Colossians 1: 24 that Erasmus evidently felt obliged in paraphrase to explicate the theology of apostolic suffering. Erasmus first sharpens the biblical text ('I am now rejoicing in my sufferings *for your sake*' [NRSV; italics added]) to make the bold claim that his sufferings are for their salvation: 'I rejoice in the [sufferings] I bear *for your salvation*.' The paraphrase goes on to explain and defend the claim: 'Why should I not say that I am suffering for your salvation, for which Christ suffered? Why should an apostle be reluctant to do what our leader [*princeps*] did not hesitate to do? Not only did he suffer for us in his own body; he also suffers somehow in ours, as though making good through his vicars [*vicarii*] what might have seemed inadequate in his own sufferings – not because his death was in itself insufficient, but because the suffering of head and members, of the leader and his vicars is somehow one and the same. The more abundant it is, the more it redounds to the increase of your salvation, and not of yours only, but that of the whole body of Christ, the Church' (LB 7: 1008B-C).

ERASMUS AND PAUL IN THE *PARAPHRASES ON THE PAULINE EPISTLES*

The paraphrases on the epistles provide ample material to justify the apparently conflicting claims of both Noël Béda and Erasmus. Noël Béda complained that in the *Paraphrase on 1 and 2 Corinthians* the voice of Erasmus could easily be heard through the *persona* of Paul, which is, in effect, to say that the paraphrastic Paul spoke from an imaginary construct of the sixteenth century. Erasmus' representation of Paul's historical situation, particularly during the missionary years, as one largely dominated by a coterie of Judaizers determined to shackle Christians with regulations and stifle them with ceremonies, invited cogent analogies with ecclesiastical life in the sixteenth century. Moreover, Erasmus himself, at points, virtually forces the analogy. For example, in the paraphrase on 1 Corinthians 3: 4 Paul condemns the party spirit in Corinth by transparent allusions: 'If some Frangilius, or Benotius, or Argulius, or Carmilius – or anyone with whatever name, for I have mentioned these only as examples – should devise some human rule of life, will you, forthwith, preening yourselves on names like this, engage in ugly strife ...?' (LB 7: 867A). Allusions here to the Franciscan, Benedictine, Augustinian, and Carmelite monastic orders are blatantly evident. At the same time, our study has shown that Erasmus was not without some justification in his counter-claim that he created the Pauline *persona* with due attention to the life and times of the Apostle (cf., e.g., *Divinationes* and *Elenchus* LB 9: 474B–E and 507D–E).

We have seen that in the words *'nulli concedam'* assigned to Paul in the paraphrase on Rom 15: 19 Erasmus suggests, in part no doubt playfully, a certain identity between himself and the Apostle. I should not wish to go further to argue that in the Paul of the paraphrases on the epistles Erasmus created a reflection of himself.[31] At certain points, however, the portrait of Paul that has emerged from this study bears the distinctive marks of Erasmus' understanding of himself and of his world. Paul's conversion summoned the Apostle to a new orientation that led him to put ethnicity behind him, and to see himself rather as a member of the body of Christ. Erasmus expresses a personal view in the annotation on Romans 12: 16, '[feeling] the same thing in turn,' when he laments the social and ethnic distinctions that plague European society – 'the German hates the French, the Englishman hates the Scot' – and notes that Paul calls for a new way of thinking (CWE 56: 339). The passion of the paraphrastic Paul for preaching must have been a theme personally congenial to the satirist who deplored in the *Praise of Folly* the level to which some preaching had fallen in his day, and to the preceptor of preachers who wrote the *Ecclesiastes*.[32] Indeed, the portrait of Paul as preacher gains interest if we assume, with Jane Phillips, that Erasmus wrote the *Paraphrases* not only for the sake of the clergy, but so that the laity could participate 'in the practice of the clerical vocation.'[33] We may observe also that the notion of mystery so fundamental in the *Paraphrases* to the Apostle's understanding of truth fits well the presuppositions that lie at the heart of the Erasmian understanding of theology, and are reflected in the *Methodus* and the *Ratio verae theologiae*, where the revelation of truth is represented as a mystery.[34] Finally, the emphasis of the *Paraphrases* on the prodigious labours of Paul recall Erasmus' conceptualization of his own labours as 'herculean.'[35] Clearly, analogies and evocations do not constitute a reflected image of the Paul of the *Paraphrases*, but they suggest that Erasmus might well have recognized in the Paul of the *Paraphrases* a portrait of the Apostle that supported his own intellectual interests, and whose contour at points fit himself pleasingly well.

THE REPRESENTATION OF PAUL IN OTHER WRITINGS OF ERASMUS

The portrait of the Apostle that emerges from the paraphrases on the thirteen epistles is one to which modern scholars may readily grant authenticity in its main outlines – Paul's passion to preach, his perception of his unique role in the apostolic college, and his self-understanding as a central figure in salvation history. In paraphrasing these epistles Erasmus observed so sufficiently the demands, both linguistic and historical, of the biblical text and context that we can recognize in his representation the essential Paul. The figure that emerges from a wider range of Erasmus' writings has, perhaps, been drawn rather more freely, less decisively shaped by sensitive historical reflection, though the *Paraphrase on Acts* stands in part as an exception to this general tendency.

There is no indication that Erasmus felt severely the disjunction between Acts and the epistles of Paul. If Acts as a 'secondary source' allowed for greater imagination in the reconstruction of events than did the epistles, the epistles are nevertheless important to Erasmus in recreating the Paul of Acts. Accordingly, there are points at which the representation of Paul in the *Paraphrase on Acts* (the last of the paraphrases to be published) recalls emphases found in the paraphrases on the epistles. I have already noted the importance of the 'accommodating' Paul in the *Paraphrase on Galatians*. This characteristic of the Apostle is grounded in Paul's own words in 1 Corinthians 9: 19–23, in the paraphrases on which Erasmus had illuminated the image of accommodation with references to an exemplifying record drawn chiefly from Acts: vows made, Timothy circumcised, Athenians addressed in language suitably familiar to them. In the *Paraphrase on Acts* Paul's address to the Athenians becomes a carefully crafted effort intended to illustrate the text from Corinthians, and at the same time to exhibit one of the finest moments of Paul's adherence to the principle of accommodation. Erasmus labours the point: 'But God ... snares each person by taking advantage of the things each especially likes ... so Paul, who knew how to become all things to all people, and how to accommodate his eloquence to the character of any listener, found a theatre for himself in the midst of the Martian quarter' (CWE 50: 108). Further, we meet again, if only briefly in the paraphrases on Acts 20, the suffering apostle so starkly presented in the paraphrases on the epistles. Addressing the Ephesian elders, the paraphrastic Paul claims a close identity with Christ in suffering: 'I have followed in the footsteps of the one who cast himself down, who handed himself over to suffering and to death to cleanse and establish his church' (CWE 50: 122).

Yet by far the most persistent representation of Paul in the *Paraphrase on Acts* is that of God's conquering warrior. In this paraphrase Erasmus places Paul's missionary activity within the context of the mythic images of cosmic warfare. These images, too, are rooted in the Pauline epistles – for example, 2 Corinthians 10: 4–5 and Ephesians 6: 10–17 – but the paraphrases on these verses in the epistles go little beyond the biblical text in characterizing the Apostle. In the *Paraphrase on Acts*, however, the images of warring prince and military champion assume a prominent place. At the moment of Paul's conversion, the Lord assures Ananias, summoned to be the future apostle's baptizer, that Paul will be a 'sort of champion for my gospel ... armed with my Spirit, and girded with the sword of the gospel word, he will carry on a war against those who hate my name' (CWE 50: 65). Once converted, the Apostle immediately becomes an 'evangelical warrior,' 'cutting the throats of the Jews with the testimonies of their Law, as though with their own sword' (CWE 50: 66). 'Like ambitious kings intent upon extending the boundaries of their authority,' he chooses Timothy as a good administrator for the gospel kingdom (CWE 50: 101). The Philippian jailor is 'booty' taken for Christ (CWE 50: 105). Like a good general, Paul flees to fight again, or flees to fight in flight (CWE 50: 66, 106). Strikingly, the image of the warrior apostle is also elaborately traced out in the dedicatory letter to Erard de la Marck that prefaced the *Paraphrase on 1 and 2 Corinthians* (CWE Ep 916: 218–40).

When we move outside the *Paraphrases* we find a multitude of succinct and pithy descriptors applied to the Apostle, descriptors that do not so much seek justification from a biblical context as they seek to derive from the character of the Apostle authority for whatever argument may be in hand. Appropriately the warrior apostle makes his appearance in the *Enchiridion*, where he is the 'standard-bearer of the Christian forces' and 'incomparable defender of the spirit' (CWE 66: 26, 74). In the *Antibarbari*, that spirited defence of humanistic learning, Paul is 'most learned among the apostles' and 'most highly instructed in all branches of literature' (CWE 23: 71, 113), while in the *Institution of Christian Matrimony* he is 'the church's most eminent teacher' (CWE 69: 216). He holds by tradition the title of 'teacher of the gentiles,' a title appropriate enough in the *Paraphrase on Acts* (CWE 50: 84, 116), but one that Erasmus does not spare elsewhere (cf. CWE 28: 393, CWE 70: 129, CWE Ep 1381: 103). The bishop of Liege is invited to carry around the *Paraphrase on 1 and 2 Corinthians* so that he might have with him 'Paul, the supreme interpreter of our religion' – not so much a preacher as a theologian for the bishop, it would appear (CWE Ep 916: 48). With the aid, no doubt, of the marvellous images evoked by the Apostle in 1 Corinthians 13, Erasmus' Paul becomes the apostle of charity (CWE 66: 71, CWE 27: 299), and a mirror of perfect love (CWE 70: 16). Having given his life for others, he appears in *The Tongue* as the true emulator of Christ, though he has himself 'found no emulator' (CWE 29: 327; cf. the *Ratio*, Holborn, 241, lines 14–15). Nor does Erasmus forget the cachet the Apostle brings to rhetoric. Paul is the 'heavenly orator' in the *Paraphrase on Acts* (CWE 50: 86); he is the 'heavenly spokesman' of the Epistle to the Romans (CWE Ep 710: 34); while in *A Short Commentary on Prudentius' Hymn on Jesus' Epiphany* he is the 'able orator' whom God sent to the Greeks, 'well suited to take issue with philosophers' (CWE 29: 196).

Characterizing phrases of this sort find their sharpest formulation in the oxymoron, a rhetorical figure evidently cherished by Erasmus. The figure is used by Erasmus to convey a wide-ranging characterization of Paul in the dedicatory epistle to the *Paraphrase on 1 and 2 Corinthians*: 'Tent-maker and pontiff, off-scouring of the world and chosen instrument of Christ, who picked this sublime humility, this tongue-tied eloquence and stammering flow of words to spread the glory of his name' (CWE Ep 916: 240–3). Elsewhere also oxymora point to an unexpected combination of contrasting characteristics, two pairs especially – piety and cunning on the one hand, and modesty and arrogance on the other. Writing to John Colet in 1512 Erasmus observes that Paul 'for all his pronounced modesty ... turns boastful and vaunts himself with a kind of sanctified insolence' (CWE Ep 260: 14–16). In the *Annotations on Romans* he notes that Paul 'is a man boasting with the greatest modesty, and modest in his vaunting, proud in Christ, humble in himself' (CWE 56: 408). Earlier in the same work he noted Paul's ability to speak just the right words to his Roman audience: 'This,' Erasmus declares, 'is pious cunning and holy flattery' (CWE 56: 37). Such 'pious cunning' is a form of 'accommodation,' an aspect of the Apostle's character for the expression of which Erasmus has a seemingly inexhaustible stream of images: 'This apostle of ours is always skillful and slippery ... such a squid, such a chameleon – he plays the part of Proteus or Vertumnus' (CWE Ep 916: 408–10). The image of the chameleon appears again in the *Ratio* and added to it is that of the polypus (*Ratio*, Holborn, 223, lines 33–6 and 248, line 31). And yet it should be noted that for Erasmus accommodation was not simply a matter of cunning, but also of civility and courtesy, qualities, he repeatedly observed with admiration, that were possessed by the Apostle (cf. CWE 56: 36–7, 128, 416).

Just as the portrait of Paul drawn in the paraphrases on the thirteen epistles reflected partially and dimly Erasmus' own character, so it may be that Erasmus found in the holy cunning of the man of modest boasting, in the gentle civility of the man of accommodation, an image reassuring to himself. Still, as I have suggested, the representation of Paul in the broad range of Erasmus' writings outside the *Paraphrases* seems to have been created in large part rather from the demands of argument, apology, and defence. This Paul, a man of strength in humility, of modesty and civility, of courtesy and accommodation, of charity and learning, offered a salutary image especially for the potentates of this world, secular or ecclesiastical. Significantly, it is an image of this kind that Erasmus brings directly to bear on his discussions with Luther. In his first letter to the Reformer in May of 1518 he pointed out that 'one gets further by courtesy and moderation than by clamour ... That was how Paul did away with the Jewish law' (CWE Ep 980: 46–7). Later, when the debate between the two had become bitter, Erasmus offered a comparison between Luther and Paul. He condemned Luther's arrogance, 'so enormous that I have never seen its like in anyone,' and recommended that he imitate Paul, who 'became all things to all men' (*Hyperaspistes*, 2, CWE 77: 631–3).

NOTES

1 Holborn, *Desiderius Erasmus Roterodamus: Ausgewählte Werke*, 241, lines 14–15.

2 See Robert D. Sider, '*Concedo nulli*: Erasmus' Motto and the Figure of Paul in the Paraphrases.' I take this opportunity to correct the translation on page 9, col. 2: *tantum organum* is, clearly, 'only an instrument.' The general force of my argument in the article is not substantially affected by the correction.

3 Though for his paraphrases on the epistles Erasmus adopted a traditional view that ascribed Hebrews to Paul, he himself generally denied the Pauline authorship; cf. CWE 44: 212 n. 3.

4 But for an important qualification of this view see John J. Bateman, 'From Soul to Soul: Persuasion in Erasmus' Paraphrases on the New Testament.' Bateman shows that the ultimate goal of the paraphrases is persuasion and the transformation of the individual.

5 For Erasmus such a portrait might in any case have been difficult to imagine. Cf. n. 7, below.

6 Erasmus' efforts to address the problem of change through conversion gains perspective against the background of Peter Bietenholz's claim that Erasmus saw an individual as a personality with a fixed centre, with the result that fundamental change of character seemed inexplicable; cf. his *History and Biography in the Work of Erasmus of Rotterdam*, 69–89.

7 The transformation effected by baptism and the 'new birth,' whereby an individual is 'grafted into Christ' or 'adopted' into a new family, thus becoming a member of a new people, resulting in a new orientation in life, would seem to be a theme central to Erasmus' understanding of 'Pauline theology' in the *Paraphrases*. Cf., e.g., the paraphrases on Rom. 8: 15 (CWE 42: 47); 1 Cor. 1: 8–9 (LB 7: 860E–F); Eph. 1: 4–5, 13 (LB 7: 973B–D, 947C–D); Col. 1: 12–13 (LB 7: 1006D–F); and Col. 3: 11 (LB 7: 1013A). But a full and properly nuanced study of Erasmus' representation of Pauline theology in the *Paraphrases* is beyond the scope of this paper.

8 Cf., e.g., the paraphrase on Eph. 3: 3–4. Though there is some ambiguity in the text of the paraphrase, it may favour the narrative of Acts 22, which separates conversion and call, but the question of sequence is not at issue in the paraphrase.

9 Understood as 'to me' by such modern translations as NEB and

NRSV; so also J. Louis Martyn, *Galatians: A New Translation with Introduction and Commentary*, 158.

10 Erasmus follows his own translation from 1519; in 1516 Erasmus had accepted the Vulgate's *in me*. Erasmus frequently commented on the equivalence between the Greek *en* in the New Testament and the Latin *per*; cf., e.g., the annotation on Rom. 1: 4: 'in power' (CWE 56: 16).

11 Cf., e.g., the paraphrases on 1 Tim. 1: 1 and Titus 1: 3 (CWE 44: 5 and 58).

12 Cf. Gal. 1: 23, 2: 2; also Martyn, *Galatians*, 17.

13 See the interlinear comment on the verse in *Biblia latina cum glossa ordinaria* ... (Basel: Froben and Petri, 1498), *pars sexta*, mv.

14 The text of the paraphrases on Gal. 1: 21–3 significantly rewrites the biblical account, which indicates that Paul was unknown to the churches of Judaea. In the paraphrases it is the Jewish congregations in Syria and Cilicia that had not seen Paul's face. The *nam* introducing the paraphrastic statement in 1: 21, 'for in these regions also [i.e., Syria and Cilicia] some congregations of Jews had begun to unite in ... Christ' suggests that Paul's missionary activity in Syria and Cilicia is somehow related to the existence of these Jewish Christian congregations: does Erasmus wish to say that Paul deliberately avoided the Jewish Christians to go to the gentiles? or that he used them as launching pads for his ministry to the gentiles? – in which case the paraphrase, speaking of Jewish Christian ignorance of Paul, might refer to their ignorance of him in his earlier years in the region, before his return to his native land as a Christian. Possibly at this point the paraphrast was simply nodding!

15 From the Argument to the epistle we gather that Erasmus thought the fourteen years included only those while Paul was in Syria and Cilicia, and not all the time since his conversion (CWE 42: 95).

16 Cf. n. 2, above.

17 Cf. Henry Joseph Vogels, ed., *Ambrosiastri qui dicitur commentarius in epistulas Paulinas*, Pars II: *In epistulas ad Corinthios* (CSEL 81/2) 57, lines 5–9.

18 Our study fully supports the observation of Peter Bietenholz that Erasmus is remarkable for his 'ability to understand a literary composition as the document of a given historical situation' (Bietenholz, *History and Biography*, 31), for it is this ability that has enabled Erasmus to create a significant construct of Paul's central missionary years. Yet our study also shows Erasmus' limitations in catching the finer nuances of a historical situation reflected in documents regarded not only as historically conditioned, but also as sacred.

19 Cf., e.g., I. Howard Marshall, *1 and 2 Thessalonians*, 16. Marshall notes, however, that F.C. Baur and the Tübingen School of the nineteenth century adopted the view assumed by Erasmus.

20 Cf. Eusebius, *Ecclesiastical History* 2.22.2–3.
21 Cf. J.N.D. Kelly, *A Commentary on the Pastoral Epistles*, 217–18, and for Erasmus' representation here, CWE 44: 53 n. 11.
22 For the ambiguity of situation reflected by the biblical text cf. F.W. Beare, *The Epistle to the Philippians*, 59–60.
23 For Paul as preacher, the 'message' is, characteristically in the *Paraphrases*, left undefined or only vaguely defined as, e.g., 'the gospel' or 'the Lord Jesus'; cf., e.g., the paraphrase on Col. 1: 23 (LB 7: 1008A) where Paul urges the Colossians to let no one deflect them from Christ, from whom comes all that is promised by the gospel, 'of which I am preacher'; also the paraphrase on 2 Cor. 4: 9–10, 'Jesus whom we preach' (LB 7: 922B–C). For the representation of Pauline theology in the *Paraphrases*, cf. n. 7, above.
24 These are not precisely defined. Are they the 'enemies of the cross' of Phil. 3: 18–19, who, in the paraphrases on those verses, are clearly Judaizers?
25 Erasmus seems to suggest that Paul was able to preach the gospel vicariously through friend and foe alike.
26 For the sense of compulsion that accompanied the Apostle's call see 2(a) and n. 11, above. Still, it is instructive to observe the force of context, and Erasmus' fidelity to the historical construct imagined, when he paraphrases the golden text of gospel proclamation found in 1 Cor. 9: 16 ('Woe to me if I do not proclaim the gospel,' NRSV). In the paraphrase Paul responds in the first instance to the circumstances determined by the situation, in which the Apostle proudly insists that he has earned his keep: he must preach, for it was the commission given him, but if he goes beyond the obligation of his commission and preaches *gratis*, he in fact has something about which he can boast. The explanation of the boast – and not the affirmation of the commission – takes centre stage in the paraphrase at this point; the compelling power of the call as an Erasmian theme is not overlooked, but it has been subordinated to the contextual details that give coherence to the immediate historical construct.
27 Cf., e.g., 1 Cor. 9, 2 Cor. 11.
28 Cf. Robert D. Sider, 'Literary Artifice and the Figure of Paul in the Writings of Tertullian,' 104.
29 In his annotation on Gal. 1: 12 ('accepi illud neque didici') Erasmus recalls Jerome to validate his understanding of the biblical 'revelation' [*apocalypsis*] as 'mystery.' Cf. Jerome, *Commentarii in epistulam ad Galatas*, 1 (on 1: 11), PL 26: 323A–B, where Jerome notes that the word *apocalypsis* ('revelation') is not used by the Greek philosophers, but belongs to the idiom of Scripture to refer to something once hidden but now unveiled and brought into the light. According to Georges Chantraine, Erasmus attributed to Paul a creative role in

applying to the word 'mystery' the predominant sense of 'the disclosure of what was hitherto concealed'; cf. his 'Le musterion paulinien selon les *Annotations* d'Erasme.'

30 See the paraphrases on 1 Cor. 1: 6–7, 2: 4, 4: 8–9, and 2 Cor. 12: 12 (LB 7: 860B–C, 864D, 971A–C, 939B); also on 1 Thess. 1: 5 (LB 7: 1017F–18D).

31 Cf. the claim made by Jacques Chomarat, 'Grammar and Rhetoric in the Paraphrases of the Gospels by Erasmus,' 65: 'The Jesus of the *Paraphrases* obviously presents many features which are, admittedly, those of Erasmus himself.' For a criticism of this position see Bateman, 'From Soul to Soul,' 12, col. 3.

32 Cf. CWE 27: 182–5 for a satirical representation of preaching, and for an evaluation of *Ecclesiastes* see John W. O'Malley, 'Erasmus and the History of Sacred Rhetoric: The *Ecclesiastes* of 1535.'

33 Jane E. Phillips, 'The Gospel, the Clergy, and the Laity in Erasmus' *Paraphrase on the Gospel of John,*' 99.

34 Cf. Holborn, 150, line 23 – 151, line 24; 179, line 19 – 180, line 34.

35 Cf. CWE Ep 1330: 19–21; *Adagia* III.i.1.

FOUR

Triumphs, Trophies, and Spoils: Roman History in Some Paraphrases on Paul by Erasmus

Mechtilde O'Mara

In the massive undertaking represented by the *Paraphrases* as a whole and within each paraphrase, Erasmus approaches his task of paraphrasing by taking into account the tenor of a whole passage. Especially in the case of the paraphrases on the Pauline epistles, he communicates the content enriched by his reading and personal reflections in order to expand Paul's concentrated instruction. The general order of ideas in the Pauline text is preserved, but not at all with the neatness suggested by the format of LB, the eighteenth-century Leiden edition, which at times does violence to the sentence structure.[1] Three kinds of passages in the Pauline text are especially likely to receive extensive amplification in Erasmus' paraphrase: those that had suffered in the Vulgate from a mistranslation of the Greek or misrepresentation of the concepts presented; those that mentioned, or merely implied, excessive attachment to the externals of religion; and finally, those that had been the focus of quibbles in academic theology that he wished to recall to its sources in Holy Scripture (CWE Ep 1183: 38–44). Sometimes the amplification draws on classical texts that may have a somewhat tenuous relationship to the passage being amplified.[2]

As one illustration of this practice, consider the following passage, part of the paraphrase on Ephesians 4: 7:

> The fact that his gifts do not appear identical or equal in all, should not stand in the way of our harmony, any more, assuredly, than we see torn asunder the mutual consensus of the body's members because they all are not equally efficacious for the same end and do not feel the influence of the head in the same degree. Instead this very diversity ought rather to invite to harmony. For as long as no one of the members is independently, entirely self-sufficient, individual members stand in need of each other's service, and there is no reason for one to be able to despise another. (LB 7: 981D)[3]

Introduced between paragraphs more closely paraphrasing Ephesians 4: 6 and 4: 7, the sentences quoted are reminiscent of the famous fable of Menenius Agrippa narrated in Livy.[4] The insertion is not at all foreign to the Pauline teaching.[5] In his paraphrase on Romans 12: 4 (CWE 42: 70), while discussing the body of Christ, Erasmus had already introduced specific mention of particular members (the eyes, the feet, the stomach and hands), as Livy had done (the hand, the mouth, the teeth, and the stomach) to illustrate the destructive dissension of members within the civic body. Here, in the paraphrase on Ephesians, he reuses the image and so achieves his purpose of 'giving Hebrew turns of speech a Roman dress' (CWE Ep 710: 33–5 = CWE 42: 2).[6]

In the dedication of his *Paraphrase on Romans,* Erasmus acknowledges that his sixteenth-century readership, adult Christians educated in the Latin language, differs from the original audience of Paul, raw and recent converts to Christianity. It was appropriate that Paul provide for them indications of the Christian mysteries rather than full explanations of the faith. Yet Paul's content was often dense, his language at times obscure, his Greek intermixed with Hebrew idiom. Erasmus' role as a paraphrast is to elucidate Paul's teaching and make it more attractive and more intelligible to his contemporaries (CWE Ep 710: 12–53). To unfold the implications of Paul's texts and underscore its relevance to his own contemporaries Erasmus employs useful parallels and analogies from classical literature.

In what follows, I shall focus on Erasmus' *Paraphrases on the Epistles to the Ephesians, Philippians, Colossians, and 1 and 2 Thessalonians.* This group of paraphrases may be taken as a fair sample of Erasmus' work in the genre: it is varied in its addressees, it is neither the first nor last of its kind, and it comprises the series of texts with which I am most familiar. The collection was published together and dedicated to Cardinal Lorenzo Campeggi, papal legate to England, by a letter dated in all editions to 5 February 1519 (Ep 1062).[7] Both Campeggi and Domenico Grimani,[8] to whom the *Paraphrase on Romans* is dedicated, were scholarly cardinals whom Erasmus associated with Rome, the centre of Christendom, and fitting dedicatees for the works by which he hoped to obtain or maintain official papal support for his project of new learning based on the study of the ancient languages. The resultant rhetoric accommodates classical and biblical themes.

The dedicatory letter points towards the subject of ancient history in the *Paraphrases*. The first paragraph of the letter reflects Erasmus' interest in history when it illustrates a comment on the mutability of human fortunes by a sketch of the cycle of constitutional arrangements in ancient Rome.[9] In the letter's opening[10] we recognize an allegory adopted from Cicero's *Pro Murena* 35 and recommended by Quintilian as an excellent example of the effect to be achieved by combining simile, allegory, and metaphor.[11] Erasmus in his turn had endorsed Quintilian's praise by citing it in the *De duplici copia verborum ac rerum*, I.19 (CWE 24: 337, lines 8–15), by including 'Man's a Euripus' among the *Adages* (CWE 32: 215–16), and by employing the same image in the context of Roman history in the dedication of his edition of Suetonius (Allen Ep 586: 66–71, CWE Ep 586: 74–80). In *Pro Murena*, Cicero likens the unexpected changes in popular attitudes to the wide variations in the winds and currents of the Euripus (a narrow strait between Chalcis in Euboea and Aulis in Boeotia). This image in the dedicatory letter may imply a subtext associating Erasmus with Cicero in his defence of Murena against false accusations put forward by enemies internal to Rome who were eager for prosecution out of motives of personal hatred and self-aggrandizement. In *Pro Murena*, Cicero says that he is acting for the sake of friendship, for the protection of Murena's reputation, for the sake of peace, quiet, harmony, liberty, and, finally, for the life and safety of all.[12] *Pro Murena* was delivered late in 63 BC during the period in which Cicero, as consul, was dealing with the Catilinarian affair, a conspiracy to overthrow the government and to destroy Rome from within.

Erasmus, at the time of dedicating this collection of paraphrases, was suffering from what he considered to be false accusations made by such individuals as Lee, Standish, and Baechem, whose motives seemed far from pure and who were working against the peace and harmony necessary for serious study.[13] As Cicero had acted on behalf of the Roman Republic against enemies within the city, Erasmus saw himself as the champion of the Republic of Letters, defending not only the church but also the new scholarship that was based on the words of Sacred Scripture. His opponents were those within the church who were holding on doggedly to the old scholastic methods and emphasizing rules concerned with external actions. Danger to Erasmus was increasing as measures against Luther, with whom his name was being associated,[14] became increasingly violent. Erasmus honours Campeggi with this dedication. At the same time, he appeals for an intervention in defence of scholarship to one who is both a recognized patron of learning and a powerful diplomat of the highest rank within the church. As Cicero early in his speech defended his integrity in undertaking to defend Murena,[15] so Erasmus in his dedication strongly justifies his own approach to the study of Sacred Scripture. By implying an association with Cicero as an *exemplum* of the lover of peace and harmony working disinterestedly for the common good, the quotation effectively contributes to a graciously expanded fluency, while at the same time it functions as an instrument of persuasion.[16]

The dedication to Campeggi underwent a massive revision between its original publication and the version that appears in the 1521 editions. Not only did Erasmus expand and amplify the letter, employing many of the means that Chomarat discusses in his study of amplification in the paraphrases,[17] he also corrected, in the second version, the sketchy (and inaccurate) account of Roman history that had been included as an illustration of the fluctuations in human affairs:

> If one were to try to stand against the sea or to channel its course another way, one would never do it without putting all things in serious jeopardy and *immense* upheaval. It was thus that in old days the monarchy of the Romans gave way to a democracy *or at least an oligarchy*, which in its turn advanced to such a pitch of licence that there was need of *tribunes of the people and* dictators and after that even *of Emperors* whose power rose to enormous heights and provoked once more a desire for *the earlier forms of the republic.*[18]

The italicized words translate Erasmus' revisions introduced as corrections of the historical analogy.[19] There never was a democracy at Rome, though there were some early calls for concessions to the voting public, most notably in the period of internal strife in which the *plebs*, resentful of their impoverishment after fighting with distinction in Rome's wars, seceded from the city.[20] This resentment of the people against the governing senatorial class in 494 BC was alleviated by the famous fable of Menenius Agrippa that developed the analogy of the interdependence of the parts of the body and applied it to the body politic.[21] The glaring errors in basic constitutional history to be found in the earlier version of Erasmus' letter call for some explanation.[22] Nevertheless, there is, in his amplification of Paul's teaching, evidence of Erasmus' awareness of the historical realities of ancient Rome.

As three examples of these Roman realities let us consider some trophies, triumphs, and spoils that Erasmus has either embellished or imported into these paraphrases to make the text more accessible to his sixteenth-century readers. In paraphrasing the reference to Psalm 68: 18 at Ephesians 4: 8, 'When he ascended on high he led a host of captives and he gave gifts to men' (RSV), Erasmus writes:

> For when Christ had already vanquished the infernal powers in war, alive again, he ascended to the Father's realm on high, leading with him the *trophy* of his victory, the flock of captives freed from the tyranny of sin and the devil. And then, in keeping with the Father's generosity he gave various kinds of gifts through the heavenly Spirit, distributing them among men just as those who are celebrating a *triumph* normally scatter presents, tossing them among the people from on high. From heaven he sent the gifts and heavenly were the gifts he sent. (LB 7: 981E–F)

Here I have italicized both 'trophy' and 'triumph.' Both words are introduced without any comparable term appearing in the Greek text or the Latin translation. The Vulgate does use the verb 'to triumph,' *triumphare*, at 2 Corinthians 2: 14 and at Colossians 2: 15 and only there in the New Testament. 'Trophy' (Lat. *tropaeum*, Gk. *tropaion*) seems not to occur at all. When Erasmus introduces the concept of a triumph into his paraphrase on Ephesians 4: 8 or at 1 Thessalonians 2: 19, he is again pointedly giving the text of Paul a

Latin formulation, for the word 'triumph' used in its strict sense can apply only to a Roman phenomenon: the triumphal procession of a victorious general formally acknowledged as such by the Roman Senate. We cannot know how familiar with the triumph the original readers of Ephesians and Colossians were, but triumphs had been described in a variety of literary sources during the Republic and Principate. Officially sanctioned by the Senate, the parade followed a fixed route. The general, robed in the garb of Jupiter Optimus Maximus, rode in a four-horse, gilded chariot; his soldiers shared in his celebration and marched in the parade to the accompaniment of spontaneous songs; the captives were led in disgrace at the end of the parade, taken away for execution while the triumphing general ascended to the Capitol. The Arch of Titus, still standing in the Roman forum, depicts on its inner wall such a parade and one that took place within a few years of Paul's time in Rome. Versnel notes that many have seen in the ceremony a connection with a divine manifestation, a kind of epiphany.[23]

Erasmus, in using the term 'triumph' in his paraphrase on Ephesians 4: 8, is being faithful to the underlying meaning of the text and gives it a vivid and memorable expression. Yet in his further amplification he has strayed from the Roman understanding of triumph. When he writes of Christ as 'distributing them [gifts] among men, just as those who are celebrating a triumph *normally* (Lat. *solenne*) scatter presents, tossing them among the people from on high,' Erasmus has confused with the triumphal procession elements drawn from the biographies of the emperors Gaius Caligula and Nero. I have found no evidence in the literature to indicate that indiscriminate tossing of gifts was a normal part of the triumph. Suetonius, however, says that Gaius threw coins from the roof of the Basilica Julia to the people for several days in succession and that he scattered *missilia* of various kinds; Nero too scattered all sorts of things to the people in festival celebrations.[24] Erasmus' familiarity with Suetonius' *Lives of the Caesars* is evident, since in 1517 he had both edited the work (see its dedication, Ep 586) and had also reviewed an edition of Suetonius from the Aldine press (see Ep 648).

The laurel crown the *triumphator* wore, and the golden crown that was held over his head were also features of the triumph;[25] mere mention of the Thessalonians as Paul's 'crown of glory,' at 1 Thessalonians 2: 19, is enough to evoke the imagery of the triumph for Erasmus in his paraphrase:

> What hope, therefore, is ours, or what is our joy, or what is our crown? Is it not you also among the other Gentiles I have gained for Christ? If not in the eyes of the world, certainly in the eyes of the Lord Jesus Christ. After the foes of the Gospel have been defeated, when the *triumph* is openly celebrated at his coming, what *trophy* is there, what souvenirs of victory will I exhibit in that procession except you and others like you? (LB 7: 1021B–C)

In both paraphrases, Erasmus has linked the *triumph* with a *trophy* similarly introduced gratuitously. In both Greek and Latin literature the word 'trophy' refers originally to the monument set up at the point in a battle at which the tide turned and the enemy took flight. It was customary to set up at that point a marker, a tree-trunk or a pole or something more substantial, and to affix to it the shields and other armour of the vanquished enemy. In Suetonius' description of the funeral of Julius Caesar, we read of a trophy used as a symbol of the dead ruler.[26] In Erasmus' thinking the *trophy* is the 'host of captives' saved by Christ (Ephesians 4: 8) and the memorial of his victory (1 Thessalonians 2: 19).

My final instance of triumphal imagery is from Erasmus' paraphrase on Colossians 2: 14–15, which amplifies fourfold the passage it paraphrases. The RSV may represent the Greek text inasmuch as it is of comparable length and a straightforward translation:

> having cancelled the bond (Gk. *cheirographon*) which stood against us with its legal demands; this he set aside, nailing it to the cross. He disarmed the principalities and powers and made a public example of them triumphing (Gk. *thriambeusas*, Lat. *triumphans*) over them in him.

Erasmus' paraphrase reads:

> On the contrary, that long-standing, binding contract (Lat. *chirographum*) on account of which the devil was oppressing us, Christ has abrogated by the profession of gospel faith on account of which the offences of our former life are not being imputed to anyone. Whatever could be exacted from us on

> the terms of this binding contract (*chirographo*), Christ himself has paid on the cross on which the contract (*chirographum*) was torn to pieces and completely destroyed. Nor is there reason for us to fear the tyranny of Satan after Christ on the cross conquered, through his own death, death's source, by recovering us – *like glorious spoils* – snatched away from demonic principalities and powers that, conquered, occasioned a triumph. For then did he frankly and openly display them, vanquished and indeed despoiled, not only to men but also to angels when he carried them about *as if in triumph* and exhibited them ruined and shattered; not through the help of angels or men, but by his own power, such a magnificent *trophy* did he hang upon the cross that it was visible from high above to all. [27]

Erasmus' paraphrase develops the images of the original and even one of the words, *chirographum*, translated here as 'binding contract' or simply 'contract.' This transliteration of the Greek original is the word that the translator of the Vulgate also employed. Used nowhere else in the New Testament, *chirographum* is a word at home in Cicero, Suetonius, and Quintilian, where its prime meaning is a document written by one's own hand, or at least personally signed.[28] A chirograph may be used as evidence in legal cases, for example in the passages from Cicero's *Brutus* and in the Quintilian reference. In his annotation on Colossians 2: 14, *chirographum decreti*, Erasmus notes the binding force in law of a document personally signed, and he comments on the metaphorical use of the word in the passage (LB 6: 889E). Lest the reader miss the implications of the *chirographum*, Erasmus repeats the word twice more within this short section of his paraphrase.

Erasmus continues the legal language with *antiquavit*. Whereas the word he is paraphrasing (Gk. *exaleipsas*) has as its primary meaning 'to wash' or 'to plaster over' and, metaphorically, to wipe out one's previous understanding in order to begin afresh,[29] it is used in the Greek orators for striking out laws, or for striking a name from the register of citizens.[30] Erasmus' annotation *chirographum decreti* (LB 6: 889E) also describes the various ways by which a document might be invalidated or rescinded. With the verb *antiquavit* Erasmus has employed the image of a legal document and described its abrogation or annulment using a term that appears almost exclusively in legal contexts in Cicero and Livy.[31]

At this point, we should notice the epithet attached to the chirograph in the opening line of the excerpt. It is 'long-standing' or 'old' (Lat. *vetus*). Gratuitously added by Erasmus, the epithet exemplifies his elaboration of the passage's tacit meaning by amplification. At the same time, *vetus* prepares the way for the antithesis of old law and the gospel faith, which by implication is new. *Vetus* is confirmed by *antiquavit* and justifies Erasmus' addition in the words that follow.

Such antithesis is a feature of orality in that it functions as a means of reinforcing ideas that are important for the comprehension of the whole and that might be missed by one who hears the word as an evanescent sound rather than reads it in a fixed text. While the written word is intended to be read, elements from a largely oral culture were still prevalent in sixteenth-century Europe.[32] Like Paul's epistles, written documents meant to be read aloud,[33] the Latin *Paraphrases* of Erasmus belong to a genre that is particularly amenable to oral presentation: a written discourse, it preserves the features of oral structure. The opening word of the excerpt *imo*, 'on the contrary,' articulates the relationship of the paragraph to what has gone before. It signifies that the present sentence will correct, if not flatly deny, the previous statement. By means of such signposts Erasmus enters into a kind of dialogue with the reader, keeping the latter's attention focused, with the skill of an extraordinary story-teller.[34]

Erasmus' choice of *dependit* is interesting: the perfect form is common both to *dependo, -ere, dependi,* which means 'to pay (money, a price, a penalty)' and to *dependeo, -ere, dependi,* which means 'to hang down from.' While the latter, a second-conjugation verb, is intransitive (to hang down from) and so could not take the direct object *id* that stands first in the clause, Erasmus' word suggests the connection between Christ's hanging on the cross and his paying of our debt. The homonym is, in fact, a latent pun, the product of Erasmus' sensitivity to language and his ability to exploit ambiguity.

Two expressions italicized in this passage, 'like glorious spoils' (*velut opima spolia*) and 'as if in triumph' (*velut in triumpho*) contribute again to Erasmus' purpose of making Paul's Greek at home in Latin. Moreover, they bring us back to the language of spoils and triumphs. For both, *velut* signifies that Erasmus is using figurative language; his meaning, while close to the original, is very sharply focused for the reader who is familiar with

Latin idiom and with Roman history. Both phrases point to a military context. The *opima spolia* denote a military achievement recognized under that title in only three cases up to the end of the Roman Republic: Romulus, Cossus, and Marcellus.

Livy, our main (though not our only) source for the expression, explains its origin and significance in connection with a victory of Romulus.[35] In describing the triumph in which Cossus was the main ornament, in contradiction to all the previous historians on the subject, but on the authority of Augustus (who said that he had personally viewed the inscription), Livy tells us that Cossus was consul when he won the *opima spolia* and explains that those spoils are properly called *opima spolia* that a general (*dux*) takes from a general; and only a person under whose auspices a war is being waged is recognized as general.[36] Clearly in Livy's view, and to judge from the careful restrictions put around them by the Emperor Augustus, the *opima spolia* were a rare and special achievement, an honour far exceeding even the triumph itself. This is a conspicuous example of Livy's reconsideration of a subject concerning which he finds his sources in conflict. It is also an example of Erasmus' choosing to embellish his text with a concept that has given rise to second thoughts in the historian.

Against this background we can see the connotations that the expression *opima spolia* conveys with amazing economy in Erasmus' paraphrase. These two words underline the notion that Christ, commander in chief of the victorious army, engaged the opposing general (Satan), slew him, and personally stripped away the prize. The imagery of triumph and trophy that follows corresponds to the outline given above in connection with their use in the paraphrases on Ephesians 4: 8 and 1 Thessalonians 2: 19. If for the modern reader 'triumph' is a synonym for victory and a 'trophy' can be any symbol of victory, the objective reality signified by these words in Paul's day is enhanced by the vivid colours and expanded context provided by Erasmus' paraphrase.

Although it was printed with the 1520 versions of the paraphrases on Ephesians, Philippians, Colossians, and 1 and 2 Thessalonians, the address to Cardinal Campeggi was, it would seem, no more than a rough draft. It served as an outline for the gracious, amplified version that was first printed in 1521 and repeated in subsequent editions of the paraphrase collection. The letter itself, in both draft and finished form, and the paraphrases reflect the interest in history to be expected of Erasmus, who had read closely the *Historiae Augustae Scriptores* and Suetonius and recently written a preface to a new edition of Livy. Erasmus' correspondence indicates that he was engaged in reading the historians and Cicero within the period of his work on the paraphrases.[37]

Where a discussion about the factual details of an item in Livy has caught his eye, as is the case with the historian's description of both the Euripus and the *spolia opima*, Erasmus has noted the item. His manner of incorporating the detail into his paraphrase accomplishes the objective of making Paul's doctrine at home in the Latin language and rendering his teaching more attractive and more accessible to his readers.

The historical imagination with which Erasmus paraphrases the epistles enables him to appropriate the authority of the ancient historians to validate his interpretation. In a spirit of friendly rivalry with the evangelist, Erasmus provides for his sixteenth-century contemporaries a contextual understanding of the ancient text. At the same time, he suggests for the Pauline teaching a moral application to his own time. By using the terminology of triumphs, trophies, and spoils, relevant to antiquity, he appears to distance the text, making it less threatening to his contemporaries, less likely to evoke resistance. Although he is generally well informed on matters of ancient history, Erasmus uses history primarily as a model and source of elegant prose style. The historical detail with which he embellishes his paraphrases may not always be precisely accurate, as, for example in the description of the triumph in the paraphrase on Ephesians 4: 8. The exact historical parallel, however, is less important to Erasmus than the general tone of the passage and its accessibility to his sixteenth-century readers.

NOTES

1 LB begins each paragraph in the paraphrase with the number that indicates the Vulgate verse being paraphrased and quotes in the margin the relevant verse or two; at times the sentence structure of the scriptural text and/or of Erasmus' paraphrase on it is overridden by this arrangement, e.g., in *Paraphrase on Ephesians* 1, the paragraph whose beginning is indicated '18, 19' belongs syntactically to the preceding paragraph.

2 Erasmus provides explanations, defences of his interpretation, and

alternative readings for problem passages together with some patristic, classical, and medieval sources in the *Annotations*. For his annotations on Ephesians, see LB 6: 831–60; the prefatory material to CWE 56: ix–xviii provides a concise account of the annotations with special reference to those on the Epistle to the Romans.

3 'Nec illud officere debet nostrae concordiae, quod huius dotes, nec eaedem, nec pares eminent in omnibus, nihilo magis profecto, quam distrahi videmus membrorum inter ipsa consensum, quod nec ad usum eundem aeque valeant omnia, nec pariter sentiant capitis influxum. Imo haec ipsa varietas magis invitare debet ad concordiam. Etenim dum nulli cuipiam membrorum omnia sua praesidia constant ex sese, sit ut singula alterius egeant officio, nec sit quod aliud possit aliud contemnere.'

4 Livy (59 BC–17 AD), the Roman historian writing in Latin in the Augustan age, reports at 2.32.8–12 on the secession of the plebs from the city of Rome in 494 BC when Menenius Agrippus, an orator trusted by the people as one of their own, convinced them that harmony within the body politic was essential to civic life by telling a fable that drew the analogy of the parts of the state to the members of the human body. The resulting negotiations established 'tribunes of the people,' officials having personal inviolability and the responsibility to protect the interests of the common people against actions of consuls or other magistrates.

5 See Eph. 4: 4, 14–16, Rom. 12: 4–8, and 1 Cor. 12: 27–8 for Paul's teaching on the Church as Body of Christ.

6 Erasmus employs the fable again at CWE Ep 1191: 29–32. On the history of the fable and its parallel in Paul, see R.M. Ogilvie, *A Commentary on Livy: Books 1–5*, 312–13 (on Livy 2.32.8–12) and Andrew R. Dyck, *A Commentary on Cicero, De Officiis*, 2: 526–7 (on the image used at *De off.*, 3.22). Erasmus had edited and annotated *De officiis* in 1501 (Ep 152), and published a revised edition amplified by inclusion of other Ciceronian works and with a new preface in 1519 (Ep 1013).

7 See John F. D'Amico, 'Lorenzo Campeggi,' in COE 1: 253–5. On the dating of Ep 1062 see the introductions to the letter in Allen and CWE and the comments of John J. Bateman, below 223–4 and n. 31, who reads '1519' as 'evidently a mistake for 1520' and offers some explanations for the confusion.

8 See D.S. Chambers, 'Domenico Grimani,' in COE 2: 132–4.

9 For the articulation of the cyclic theory as applied to Rome's growth and development see Polybius, the Greek historian of Greek and Roman affairs, at 6.4.7–9.14; for a survey of political theories of cyclical government see F.W. Walbank, *A Historical Commentary on Polybius*, 1: 643–59.

10 According to the 1520 version: 'Quoties inconstantiam rerum

humanarum intueor, reverendissime pater, uideor mihi prorsus Euripum quempiam videre, adeo vicibus irrequietis, susque deque uoluuntur, nec possunt eodem in statu diu consistere' ('Whenever I survey the mutability of human affairs, most reverend Father, I seem to see precisely some Euripus, so incessant are the changes as they surge up and down, and cannot long continue in one stay'). Translation of the shorter version is adapted from CWE Ep 1062: 4–7, which translates Allen Ep 1062: 1–5. Translations of Erasmus' works will be from the CWE where such exist, for classical authors from the Loeb Classical Library unless otherwise indicated.

11 Cicero, *Pro Murena*, 35 is quoted with minor changes by Quintilian 8.6.49, which in turn is quoted by Erasmus. For other classical and patristic uses of the image see Arthur Stanley Pease, *M. Tulli Ciceronis De Natura Deorum*, 2: 1012–13.

12 Cicero, *Pro Murena*, 78

13 See Erika Rummel, *Erasmus and His Catholic Critics*, esp. 1: 95–120 (Lee), 1: 122–7 (Standish), 1: 135–43 (Baechem), and Erasmus' correspondence for the years 1518–21 (e.g., Ep 1053, CWE Ep 1060: 6–45).

14 For extensive justification against incriminations of collaboration with Luther see Erasmus' letter to Campeggi of 6 December 1520 (CWE Ep 1167: 87–504).

15 Cicero, *Pro Murena*, 2: 'Because in this fulfilment of my obligation I have been attacked by the prosecution for the vigour of my defence and even for the fact that I have taken on Murena's case at all, before I begin to speak in his defence, I shall say a few words on my own behalf.'

16 Erasmus venerated Cicero not only as a stylist but also as a good man (CWE Ep 1013: 40–90). On the literary and historical use of examples in the late Renaissance and early modern period, see the special issue of the *Journal of the History of Ideas* 68 (1998) devoted to 'The Crisis of Exemplarity,' especially François Cornilliat, 'Exemplarities: A Response to Timothy Hampton and Karlheinz Stierle,' 620–2, and Michel Jeanneret, 'The Vagaries of Exemplarity: Distortion or Dismissal?' 568–72.

17 Jacques Chomarat, *Grammaire et rhétorique chez Érasme*, 1: 587–710; also Chomarat, 'Grammar and Rhetoric in the Paraphrases of the Gospels by Erasmus.'

18 '[S]i quis mari conetur obsistere, aut huius cursum alio deriuare, numquam id fecerit sine graui discrimine rerum *ingentique* tumultu. Sic olim Romanorum monarchiam excepit democratia *aut certe oligarchia*, quae et ipsa tandem eo licentiae processit ut *tribunis plebis ac* dictatoribus foret opus, mox etiam *Imperatoribus*, quorum potestas in immensum euecta fecit, ut rursus *pristini reipublicae status* desiderarentur' (Froben octavo edition of 1521, sig. dd2). I have italicized here the significant changes, including added words and the

replacement of the second mention of 'kings' by 'Emperors' in the later, 1521, text.

19 Andrew Lintott discusses both the underlying theory and the development of Rome's constitution in *The Constitution of the Roman Republic*.

20 Livy narrates the secession of the *plebs* and the granting of tribunes at 2.32–3.

21 Livy describes the senatorial arrogance contributing to the revolt at 2.3–4, 23, 27, and the speech of Menenius Agrippa at 2.32.9–11.

22 The earlier dedication seems to have been composed in haste. See above, note 7.

23 For a collection of the evidence on the attire, carriage, and implications of the triumph see H.S. Versnel, *Triumphus: An Inquiry into the Origin, Development and Meaning of the Roman Triumph*, 56–93, 95–6. He writes: 'The exclamation *triumphe* proves that he [the triumphator] was looked upon as the god manifesting himself' (92).

24 Erasmus' diction here ('quemadmodum triumphantibus est solenne, *missilia in populum* e sublimi *spargere*') points to his source in Suetonius' 'e fastigio ... *sparsit*' ('he scattered [sums of money] from the gable') and especially the latter's '*sparsit* et *missilia*' ('he even threw about gifts') and '*sparsa* et *populo missilia*' ('presents were thrown to the people'): *Lives of the Caesars: Gaius Caligula*, 37.1, 18.2; *Nero*, 11.2. On gifts of money and goods from the emperor see also Fergus Millar, *The Emperor in the Roman World, 31 B.C.–A.D. 337*, 135–9.

25 Versnel, *Triumphus*, 76.

26 Suetonius, *Divus Iulius*, 84.1; Caesar's funeral is discussed by Stefan Weinstock, *Divus Julius*, 350–5.

27 'Imo vetus illud chirographum, per quod nos urgebat Diabolus, Christus antiquavit professione fidei Evangelicae, per quam non imputantur ulli vitae prioris commissa. Quidquid enim ex hoc chirographo poterat a nobis exigi, id ipse Christus dependit in cruce, in qua dilaceratum est chirographum, ac penitus sublatum est e medio. Nec est quod Satanae tyrannidem metuamus, posteaquam Christus in cruce sua morte mortis auctorem devicit, nos ereptos, *velut opima spolia*, referens a devictis ac triumphatis principatibus ac potestatibus Daemoniacis. Tunc enim illos libere palamque victos atque exsutos ostendit, cum hominibus, tum Angelis, circumferens *velut in triumpho*, et ostentans adversarios concisos fractosque, non Angelorum aut hominum praesidiis, sed sua ipsius virtute, tam magnificum *trophaeum* suspendit in cruce, ut esset omnibus e sublimi conspicuum' (LB 7: 1011A–B).

28 Cicero, *Brutus*, 80.277; *1 Phil.*, 7.16, 18; *2 Phil.*, 4.8, 38.97; *5 Phil.*, 4.12; *Ad Att.*, 2.20.5; *Ad fam.*, 10.21.1, 3; Suetonius, *Div. Iul.*, 17.2; Quintilian 5.13.8.

29 Plato, *Theaetetus*, 187B.
30 See Liddell and Scott, *A Greek-English Lexicon*, s.v. *exaleipho*.
31 E.g., Cicero, *Ad Att.*, 1.13.3, 1.14.5; both references are concerned with a bill proposed under a decree of the Senate that Piso is attempting to have rejected; Livy, too, uses the verb to mean the abrogation of proposed legislation, 5.30.7, 27.21.4.
32 See Jean-François Gilmont, 'En guise de conclusion ...,' 502.
33 As we can see from their address to collectives, 'To all God's beloved in Rome,' Rom. 1: 7; 'to the Church of God at Corinth,' 1 Cor. 1: 2 and 2 Cor. 1: 2; so also Gal. 1: 1, Eph. 1: 1.
34 Jean-Claude Margolin, 'L'art du récit et du conte chez Érasme.'
35 Livy 1.10.4–7; on the *opima spolia* and the rituals surrounding the presentation, see Versnel, *Triumphus*, 306–13.
36 Livy 4.20; for a convenient discussion of the problems associated with this passage see Ogilvie, *Commentary on Livy*, 563–7.
37 On 23 February 1519, Erasmus commended to the reader a new enlarged edition of Livy (Ep 919); he read Cicero's *De Officiis* during the summer of 1519 (CWE Ep 1013: 33–47); he had prepared in 1517 an edition of Suetonius and the *Historiae Augustae Scriptores* (dedication Ep 586), and for the 1518 publication of that edition by Froben he provided a preface that reviews a recent Aldine edition (Ep 648).

FIVE

Sub evangelistae persona: The Speaking Voice in Erasmus' *Paraphrase on Luke*

Jane E. Phillips

Erasmus' *Paraphrase on Luke* begins with a dedication to Henry VIII of England. Among the dedications of the various *Paraphrases* this one stands out because its careful composition centres on the tradition, a very ancient one, that the actual Luke was both a physician and a historian.[1] After courtesies explaining the fitness of dedicating paraphrases of the Gospels to kings, Erasmus touches first on Luke's character as a physician not only of bodies but, with the aid of the gospel's divine medicine, of souls as well. He then gives an account of Luke's life (drawing heavily on Jerome's biography of the evangelist, *De viris illustribus*, 7) and writings before launching into a long and elegant elaboration of the metaphor of the gospel as a drug or medicine. The dedication proceeds to describe attempts at spiritual healing made by pagan philosophers and Old Testament figures, the true physician Christ and his gospel cure, and a variety of analogies with the practice of human medical art. Turning to the world of history, and beginning with the classical analogy of the state to a single human body, Erasmus explains how the medicine of the gospel, unequalled by the political prescriptions of pagan philosophers and of Moses, contained such healing for political ills that it won over the entire Roman Empire and beyond, eliminating the pagan religions and even a significant element of Judaism, sweeping away all opposition offered it. This historical development owed its success to humble people, the apostles and their successors, and to a plain, even awkwardly composed, written text, yet one possessing more truth than the artistic productions of writers like Thucydides and Livy. Such is the healing power of this drug, and yet it has become diluted in more recent ages, even in a world full of Christian princes and learned bishops, wealthy and powerful. Erasmus wonders what the reason could be, for its discovery could lead to a cure. Yet at this point, nearly the end of his dedicatory letter, he pulls himself up short and returns to the theme of Luke the physician and his medicine, advising Henry on the best way of taking the necessary doses. He concludes with a few words about the provisional, not authoritative, nature of paraphrase as compared with Holy Writ itself, and reminds the 'less intelligent reader' (*lector crassior*) that he himself never speaks in the *Paraphrase* except *sub evangelistae persona*, in the voice of the evangelist (Ep 1381; LB 7: 271–80).

Here lies the present question: in Luke, Erasmus has one evangelist at least to whom the tradition of the Church gives a definite identity. In the dedicatory letter, he connects Luke's traditional identity with two of the major ways of understanding Christian thought: the healing nature of the doctrine and the assertion of its validity on grounds of its emergence in the course of world history. Will he then exploit this identity as he assumes the voice of the evangelist? Will the reader find Erasmus' Luke speaking distinctively like a physician, distinctively like a historian?

Erasmus, the good rhetorician, knows that among the classical devices to increase the effectiveness of persuasive speech is *prosopopoeia*, personification, or *prosopographia*, description of persons. He discusses the use of this device in the second book of the *De copia*, as part of his fifth method of amplification. There he emphasizes that a writer who recreates the speaking voice of a character already defined by historical or literary tradition must endow his version with the traits that make the character recognizably himself.[2]

Erasmus as an author of biblical paraphrase confronted this very problem: how to compose a text that would, as he hoped, convey the full meaning of Scripture in clearer and more elegant Latin yet preserve the particular manner of the speaker of the text – not just characters whose words are found in the narrative parts of Scripture, such as Jesus or the Baptist, Pontius Pilate or Peter, various classes of suppliants or opponents, and so on – but also the individuality of the writer whose authorship the text claims – David, Paul, James, Peter, John, or the writers of the Gospels. In some of the prefatory letters to the separate *Paraphrases*, he touches on one or another aspect of his personification of their original human authors.

In the preface to the *Paraphrase on Romans* he says he has worked so that the reader who is free from superstitious objection to the whole project of paraphrasing 'may hear the voice of Paul himself' (Ep 710, CWE 42: 3). He commends his *Paraphrase on 1 and 2 Corinthians* as a means by which its dedicatee can have Paul always ready to chat clearly and familiarly with him (CWE Ep 916: 46–51). Clarity, along with good Latinity, is again the stated achievement of the paraphrases on James and 1–3 John (Ep 1179, CWE 44: 172). He calls his *Paraphrase on Hebrews* a Paul who has learned to speak more clearly and at greater length, and in Latin at that (Ep 1181, CWE 44: 212). In all of these places, while the question of the scriptural writer's persona is scarcely touched upon directly, there is an implied claim that the character of Paul or John or James has been maintained and will be recognized by the reader – in part because of the content but surely also in part because of the writer's style.[3] Still, apart from some remarks that John and James write so plainly as hardly to need paraphrasing, while Paul soars above our ability to follow him without the paraphrast's help, these prefaces reveal little about what Erasmus finds distinctive about each writer.

When he comments on his task as a paraphrast of the Gospels, Erasmus takes up some additional considerations. In the dedication to his first Gospel paraphrase, the one on Matthew (published in March 1522), he observes that paraphrasing a Gospel is more challenging than paraphrasing the apostolic letters, because he must paraphrase the very words of Christ, not just those of the apostolic but still human authors. Then too, the variety of persons whose manner of speech, *oratio*, must be represented without the authorial distance for purposes of explanation that other kinds of commentators enjoy imposes very narrow constraints on the paraphrast.[4] Moreover, the fact that a good part of the Gospels consists of simple historical narrative that needs no elaboration may suggest that the paraphrast is doing no more than lighting a lamp at noonday – merely wasting his time. A particular constraint is that the allegories in the Gospels have been variously explained, sometimes almost playfully so, by the ancient commentators, while the paraphrast can only put the allegories in the mouth of either Christ or the evangelist in a way appropriate to the alleged speaker of them. And the parts that, thanks to the prophetic spirit of the evangelists, seem to apply to modern times as much as to apostolic times can scarcely be paraphrased as if they were being said by the evangelists in their own time (Allen Ep 1255: 29–63; CWE Ep 1255: 30–64).

The general outlines of Erasmus' understanding of his task as a Gospel paraphrast can be seen here, but there is little or nothing that indicates special attention to the distinctive character of Matthew as an evangelist. In the dedicatory letter to the *Paraphrase on John* (Ep 1333), however, which followed the publication of Matthew by ten months (January 1523), Erasmus does mark off this evangelist from the other three by John's interest in explicating the dual nature of Christ rather than telling yet another version of his life and teachings; in this case it is John's style and theme that present the paraphrast with particular challenges. Eight months later, in August 1523, Erasmus was finishing the dedication of the *Paraphrase on Luke*. Here, for the first and only time, he makes the received character of the evangelist the main motif of his remarks. The dedicatory letter of the *Paraphrase on Mark* (Ep 1400, December 1523) concerns only conflicts among nations in modern times and the gospel as the medicine to cure them; the dedication of the *Paraphrase on Acts* (end of January 1524) again discusses only contemporary issues.

From these scraps of evidence we can see that Erasmus does undertake to represent the personality or personhood, or persona, or voice of the author he paraphrases. In later years, when he answered the criticisms of Béda and the Paris theologians, one of his constant refrains was that he was only reporting and amplifying what the evangelists had said about conditions of their own time, without reference to modern times – a disingenuous defence, it is true, almost contradicted by the final part of the passage in the dedication to the *Paraphrase on Matthew* summarized above; but still a defence that situates the speaking voice of the paraphrased evangelist in a time and place, and therefore in an identity, different from that of the paraphrast.[5]

Since Erasmus himself, in the dedicatory letter, has so clearly marked Luke's identity as physician and historian, we may reasonably ask whether he has personified the evangelist's voice in matters having to do with medicine and history. But before we attempt an answer, some potential limitations must be noted. First, it would be worse than naive to think that every reference in the *Paraphrase* to healing or to history is an example of the personification of Luke. Both forms of conceptualization are pervasive in Christian thinking, and certainly in Scripture and Church tradition. The task is rather to discern where in the *Paraphrase* the Luke-voice goes beyond language or ideas imbedded in the biblical text. Here, comparison with the paraphrased voice of Matthew (or occasionally the paraphrased voice of John) can help.[6] Further, in considering the voice of the paraphrased Luke, we will look only at that voice speaking to the reader in narrative or direct address, not at the words it reports others as saying. Though these too come to us only through Luke's voice, the question of how much they are personified directly and how much through the point of view of Erasmus' Luke is a separate issue.[7] Nor shall we expect to find a fully realized narrator-character in the manner of a modern or postmodern novelist; rather, we are looking for a paraphrased voice that merely demonstrates, according to Erasmus' own observations in the *De copia*, the traditional attributes of the evangelist Luke.[8]

Luke's Gospel is unique among the four in beginning with a short preface.[9] Erasmus expands this to an essay twenty-six times the length of the original.[10] His Luke-voice begins with a comparison of the pleasure and utility available to readers of human histories, *humanae historiae*, and gospel history, *evangelica narratio*. While knowledge of classical history and classical thinkers – Hannibal, Alexander, Solon, Plato, and Aristotle are among those mentioned – has some value, ignorance of them does no real harm; but hope of salvation rests on knowledge of gospel history and thus has a more stringent requirement of historical reliability, *fides*. The original oral gospel transmitted by the apostles was completely reliable, but Matthew and Mark were inspired to write down an authentic version to protect the gospel from the inevitable introduction of errors, silly stories, and Judaizing tendencies. Now Luke also undertakes to give a continuous account that includes authentic material omitted by the first two evangelists and excludes stories circulating among the people and the outright lies that have been or will be introduced. Still, even this will not include everything that could be told.

Reliability, *fides*, derives first from personal observation of and participation in the events being reported, and then from the accounts of eye-witnesses. Though he was not one of Jesus' disciples, Luke at least saw the fulfilment of Christ's promises in the actions of the apostles. With the aid of the eye-witnesses he has arranged everything in order, and then selected what is most pertinent to gospel faith, *fides*, and godliness, from the preliminaries to Jesus' birth, through his infancy and boyhood, and then his career of miracles and teaching, to his death and resurrection. He foresees a second volume on the sending of the Holy Spirit and the beginning and growth of the church, so that his addressee Theophilus and all other 'lovers of God' will be able to grasp the sense of the course of events in this part of the story more confidently and refute the errors of others (LB 7: 279A–83A).

This brief summary, which I cast in the third person rather than the first and second persons used by the Luke-voice for himself and Theophilus, scarcely does justice to Erasmus' composition. Still, we can see that the paraphrased Luke presents himself as a historian, with a historian's concern for the value of history in general, the importance of his particular undertaking, its (superior) relation to its predecessors and rivals, the reasons why his account can claim to represent the truth, and its utility to future ages.[11] Readers of the *Paraphrase* are thus presented with a framework that shapes their expectations of the text that follows in terms of genre, content, arrangement, reliability, and commitment to Christian faith as revealed by the intersection of divine action and human history in the phenomenon the Luke-voice calls gospel history.

The first confirmation of these expectations follows immediately, along with a demonstration of the usefulness of gospel history. The Gospel opens its narrative with a one-verse time and content reference.[12] In the paraphrase, the Luke-voice expands the reference by a factor of eighteen to an essay that looks forward to the long-anticipated assumption of human form by the Son of God and his fulfilment of the divine plan for human salvation. This event, in particular the virgin birth, is rhetorically contrasted with gentile stories of prodigies and Old Testament narratives of miracles. Part of the divine plan was for the new dispensation to be anticipated by the witness of the old dispensation, typified by John the Baptist and his father Zechariah. The Luke-voice explains the prophecy of Jacob about the tribe of Judah (Gen. 49: 10) and the prophesied role of Herod the son of Antipater, who is the tool of Caesar, along with the fact of Zechariah's priesthood, his genealogy, his place in the intricate priestly organization of Judaism, and the typology of the numbers seven and eight in it (LB 7: 283A–4D). In other words, after the Luke-voice restates his general topic, he sets the historical stage for the account of the birth of the Baptist in terms of Old Testament history, prophecy, and religious law, as well as political circumstances contemporary to Herod. The interpretation of historical events and institutions as types foreshadowing the imminent spiritual realities amounts to a demonstration of the historian's intention to provide a useful work for future readers.[13]

The paraphrase on 2: 1–3, the familiar verses citing Augustus' edict for a general census, also is reworked by a historian's hand.[14] After a sentence of transition between the birth narrative of the Baptist, just concluded, and that of Jesus, the new subject, the Luke-voice describes Caesar Augustus as ruling over many parts of the world and governing the Roman empire after he had brought about widespread pacification.[15] The words 'that all the world should be enrolled' are replaced by more suitably Roman administrative language: *ut ... censerentur omnes provinciae, quae Romanaum imperium agnoscebant* ('that all the provinces that acknowledged Roman rule should be listed for taxation').[16] The Luke-voice then compares the reign of Caesar, actually limited in extent and essentially a form of servitude, with the truly world-wide reign of Christ, divine prince, *princeps*, and commander, *imperator*, who grants true liberty and a donative, a commander's bonus, of eternal life to his enlistees.[17] Quirinius is said to be sent to Syria, on the authority of Augustus and by decree of the Senate, to be provincial governor for this purpose; and this was the first of several censuses he would conduct there (LB 7: 297F–8B). Here the Luke-voice sharpens some of the historical detail, substitutes recognizably Roman terminology for the simple expressions of the Vulgate, and then exploits Roman political language to present Christ as a more authentic kind of Roman emperor than Augustus was.

At the beginning of the third chapter, where the Gospel had completed its account of the infancy and childhood of Jesus, the original evangelist gave another time and context reference, paralleling his opening in chapter 2.[18] Once again, after summarizing the first two chapters and announcing the preaching careers of the Baptist and Jesus as his new topic, the paraphrased Luke enriches the historical specificity of the information. The deaths of Augustus and Herod are noted, as is Augustus' banishment of Herod's son

Archelaus. The tetrarchy Augustus established in place of Herod's kingdom of Judea is described, with explanations that the new Herod is Archelaus' brother and that Philip's kingdom is part of Syria. The etymology of the name Trachonitis is given, and its geographical position, followed by the etymology of the name Abilene and a note that it was later changed to Lysanion by its tetrarch. The term 'tetrarch' is explained: it comes from the division of the kingdom into four territories and is a mark of the end of kingship in Judea. Jerusalem and the Temple are under Pilate's governance, another sign showing that gentiles will supplant Jews in the heavenly kingdom. The fact that the priesthood was held by two individuals instead of one and could be obtained by purchase indicates that the office will soon cease (LB 7: 309B–D).

The paraphrases on chapters 1, 2, and 3, then, are expanded with, among other things, fuller historical contextualization and with typological connections made between events on the historical plane and the spiritual transformations being set in motion. Certainly the historical contextualization takes its cue from the text of the Gospel itself in these places. Yet the degree of elaboration, I suggest, and also the typological interpretation, owe more to Erasmus' positioning of Luke as a historian, and one whose aim is the utility of his history, as the paraphrased preface says. There the Luke-voice had said he was including some events not reported by his predecessors, Matthew and Mark. The birth of the Baptist, and Jesus' conception, birth, and childhood are obviously such additions. So appropriately the paraphrased Luke enlarges on the historical facts (and their meanings) surrounding this part of his narrative.

Throughout the *Paraphrase*, the Luke-voice scatters further details of or allusions to features of civic life, the historical spread of the new faith across the Roman world and beyond its borders, and in particular Roman institutions and events.[19] Most of this is not very different from the kinds of social or historical elaboration that appear in the other *Paraphrases*, though the Roman flavour seems a bit stronger than, for instance, in the *Paraphrase on John*. Yet set in the context of a paraphrased Luke so assertively committed to the role of gospel historian, not biographer or theologian, even these light touches reinforce a reader's impression of a writer who possesses an educated familiarity with the form and content of Roman historiography.

In the vocabulary he uses to describe his work, the paraphrased

Luke also asserts his historiographical purpose in telling the gospel story and explicating the symbolic meaning behind events. In the paraphrase on 5: 1, commenting on the press of the crowd that drove Jesus from the beach at Lake Gennesaret to a small boat that he then used as an off-shore speaker's platform, the Luke-voice bids his reader pay attention 'so that you may discern in the narrative of the event an image of the infant church, growing by leaps and bounds' (*quo perspicias in narratione rei juxta carnem gesta, nascentis et exuberantis Ecclesiae imaginem* [LB 7: 334B]). Similarly, when Jesus brings the son of the widow back to life at 7: 15 and returns him to his mother, the Luke-voice introduces a long allegorical interpretation of the episode by saying: 'And the event happened in this way on the historical plane, but not without signifying spiritual teaching' (*Atque ita quidem res juxta historiam gesta est, non sine signficatione doctrinae spiritualis* [LB 7: 352F]). In the same chapter, the Luke-voice gives another long allegorical interpretation of the dinner at the house of Simon the Pharisee, at which a woman sinner bathes Jesus' feet with her tears. The exegesis is prefaced by the comment, 'In what we have related there was the shadowy outline of an image of the two peoples, Jews and gentiles' (*Atque in his, quae narravimus adumbrata est imago quaedam utriusque populi, Judaeorum ac gentium* [LB 7: 359B]). The Luke-voice begins an extended allegorical analysis of the 'triumphal' entry into Jerusalem by saying: 'And within this narrative of events there is no little mystery/spiritual meaning' (*Subest autem in hac rerum gestarum historia non parum mysterii* [LB 7: 434B, on 19: 40]). At the conclusion of chapter 19, in remarks on the Jewish leadership in the initial stages of their final plot against Jesus' life, he says: 'But what happened at that time on the historical plane often happens on the tropological plane, whenever those who uphold the citadel of religion and who are conspicuous in their assertion of learning conspire with lay princes against Jesus' (*Quod autem id temporis juxta historiam accidit, id frequenter evenit juxta tropologiam, quoties hi, qui religionis arcem tenent, quique sacrae doctrinae professione conspicui sunt, conspirant cum profanis Principibus adversus Jesum* [LB 7: 436E, on 19: 48]). The historian is reminding his reader of the function of good history as he sees it: to provide a tool that can shed light on the truths that lie behind the surface of events. Not incidentally, he is also deploying Latin terms that mean what we call narrative or history: *historia, res gestae, narratio,* and *narrare*.

We have seen Erasmus thus far shaping his *Paraphrase* in part to enlarge upon and highlight the persona of Luke as historian. Erasmus also highlights another quality of the biblical Luke, his self-presentation as an individual author addressing an individual reader. Among the evangelists only Luke speaks of himself at the outset of his Gospel in the first person, in the general introduction at 1: 1–4, and he does so again in the introduction to his second volume, Acts 1: 1. (John has a kind of 'signature' reference to himself, in the third person, which seems intended mainly to affirm the truth of his account: John 19: 35 and 21: 24). In both places, Luke also addresses a specific reader, one Theophilus. In the narrative of Acts, Luke even reports his own participation in the events he is relating, at the well-known points when the narration changes from third person to first person.[20]

In the *Paraphrase*, Erasmus builds on this personalization of the narrator's voice. Direct address to the named reader, Theophilus, usually associated with imperative verb forms, occurs not just once but at least nine times.[21] The Luke-voice also uses a small but still surprising number of what might be called 'true' first-person verbs and pronouns, that is, ones clearly referring, singular or plural, to the person of the Gospel's author, not to the 'we' that means 'we Christians' or 'we mortals' or 'we sinners' and is common throughout the *Paraphrases*.[22] In particular, the second-person singular imperative plus the ethical dative *mihi* appears at least eight times, two of them also with the name Theophilus.[23] Finally, the Luke-voice of the Gospel paraphrase specifically alludes to his presence in the events narrated in Acts, speaking of 'Paul, whose follower I was' (*Paulus, cujus ego sectator fui*: [LB 7: 360E, on 8: 3]). Perhaps a second allusion to Paul by name, in the paraphrase on 9: 17 (LB 7: 369E), is intended to evoke the same association, though Luke does not mention himself there. Krüger suggests that when Erasmus apostrophized Theophilus in this *Paraphrase*, he was slipping into the guise of the evangelist.[24] I think we need to recast the suggestion somewhat: Erasmus has been at pains (or perhaps we should say at liberty) to shape a Luke-voice that is founded on and emphasizes the character of the biblical Luke. The paraphrased Luke engages his reader, Theophilus or the individual reader who succeeds to Theophilus' place in Luke's project, steadily and directly, on an I-to-you basis, in a way that makes him stand out among the paraphrased evangelists, as the biblical Luke does among his biblical peers.[25]

The other half of Luke's traditional identity, that he was a physician, is not evident in the Gospel text itself but rests on Paul's identification of him in Colossians 4: 14 (see note 1). Yet, as already remarked, it is the predominant motif of the dedicatory letter to this *Paraphrase*; so we may look for a physician in Erasmus' Luke-voice as well as a historian. Here too some caution is necessary, for besides the lack of any internal evidence that Luke was a physician, there is the pervasive analogy made in Scripture and everywhere in the Christian tradition – exegetical, theological, homiletic, liturgical, sacramental, pastoral – between all aspects of illness and healing and the conditions, processes, and consequences of spiritual salvation. All four of Erasmus' Gospel paraphrases use medical metaphors freely, whether the immediate text being paraphrased happens to contain cues for them or not. Even so, we will see, I think, that the paraphrased Luke sounds distinctively like a physician, more so than either the Matthew-voice or the John-voice in the two earlier Gospel *Paraphrases*, and certainly more than the original Luke does.[26]

The first, minor, example, in fact, is common to all four paraphrased evangelists. When Erasmus elaborates the preaching career of John the Baptist, he always includes, in exegetical comments given in the evangelist's own voice, some form of the statement that a sick person must acknowledge his own disease in order for the physician's efforts at healing to have any effect – metaphorically applied to the sinner's need to acknowledge and repent of his sin in order to receive forgiveness. The Matthew-voice has a single comment of this kind; the John-voice has two, among other metaphors of light and darkness. The Mark-voice also has two such comments, and a third asserting that John was not the physician nor the bridegroom nor the light. But the Luke-voice has four such comments, the second of which adds that the Baptist offered a remedy, *remedium*, for the sins his hearers were confessing.[27]

In Luke's Gospel, the first event of Jesus' preaching career is the sceptical reception he receives from the members of his home synagogue at Nazareth when he is unsuccessful at healing. According to the Gospel, he tells them that he knows they are quoting the proverb 'Physician, heal thyself' against him.[28] Erasmus' paraphrased Jesus expands on the metaphor of his role as physician and the Pharisees' refusal to take their medicine or trust their doctor (LB 7: 327D–E, on 4: 24). The paraphrased Luke returns to the same imagery in his interpretation of the episode, saying of the Nazareth Jews, in part:

> They were demanding a doctor but were not prepared to swallow the healthful dose of bitter truth; they wanted their bodies healed but neglected the diseases of their souls. Yet the medicine for an ailing soul is truthful, and therefore biting, speech. They preferred a pleasant but fatal poison to a bitter but healing medicine ... Nor had he come to heal bodies soon to die anyway, but souls to live forever. (LB 7: 328E, on 4: 29)

In the parallel account in Matthew 13: 54–8 (there is not an exact parallel in John), Jesus himself makes no reference to physicians or healing; the paraphrased Matthew-voice only compares the inefficacy of the medical art for a patient who will not follow doctor's orders to the inefficacy of a miracle-worker for a seeker who does not have the faith that accepts the possibility of miracles (LB 7: 82F).

The biblical Luke proceeds immediately (4: 31–7) to a contrasting story not in Matthew, Jesus' warm reception in the synagogue at Capernaum, where he heals a man possessed by a demon. The paraphrased Luke inserts a circumstantial comment on the difficulty of healing demoniacs:

> Those who try to free the bodies of people from harmful spirits generally apply every kind of remedy to expel the evil thing, imprecations in set forms of words, fumigations, sprays, potent herbs, and other rituals nearly magical, yet with all of it we rarely see the spirit driven out. And if it does leave, it leaves behind traces of its malice – a severed limb or an incurable disease. (LB 7: 331A)

Next comes, in the Gospel, a two-verse account of Jesus curing Peter's mother-in-law of a fever, followed by another two-verse account of the crowds who sought him out at her house to be healed of their physical ills and to have their demons expelled.[29] The sequence is paralleled in Matthew 8: 14–17, which also says that the healings are the fulfilment of prophecy, quoting Isaiah 53: 4. Erasmus might have taken the prophecy as a cue for the Matthew-voice to expand on the theme of healing, but he did not. The Matthew-voice does emphasize that Peter's mother-in-law was cured instantaneously and completely, without anything like the slow mending of normal human convalescence.[30] On the crowds who then came for healing, the Matthew-voice notes briefly that no disease was so repulsive as to make Jesus turn away or so incurable that it did not leave the sufferer at Jesus' bidding; his freely given healing was an emblem of what he would do in taking away sins, the diseases of the soul.

The Luke-voice makes the same observation about the healing of Peter's mother-in-law. Yet his comments about the crowds who then came to her door for Jesus' healing, though similar to the comment of the paraphrased Matthew, are expanded to about ten times that length, partly by the addition of specific medical details, and partly by a much more elaborate development of their allegorical applications. The Luke-voice explains that Jesus' readiness to offer healing in spite of his own need for rest and the lateness of the hour is a demonstration to all who want their spiritual diseases healed that he is the one to whom they should turn, for no disease is so incurable, so persistent, or so lethal that it does not flee at his touch and bidding. Jesus' actions in healing are also a model of gentleness for the bishops and pastors who will succeed him; he was not put off by disgusting diseases from touching and healing their victims. His successors should do the same, both because he has cleansed them of their spiritual ills and because they are only servants of a divine gift, bringing their people to the mighty physician and praying that he will lay his hands on their minds (LB 7: 331C–2A, on 4: 38–40).

The Luke-voice then goes on to elevate the expulsion of demons, mentioned in verse 41, above healing of physical ills as a sign of power, and to explain mental and demonic illness as a specific allegory for spiritual illness. There are many kinds of physical illnesses, but there are just as many diseases of the spirit, and they are more destructive – unless there are fewer kinds of intemperance than of fever, he adds sarcastically, or unless being hot with fever is more dangerous than being mad with lust! Of physical diseases some are so foul, like pediculosis, that even close friends cannot stand to be near those who suffer them; some are so contagious, such as leprosy or plague, that it is not safe to be near them – though most diseases are at least somewhat contagious. Some are so aggressive, or so well established, that they defeat the resources of medical art. Yet this physician's power is superior to every one of them, his purity is greater than any human ill, his mercy is such that he is repelled by no foulness. He welcomes, touches, heals all. But human physicians, the Luke-voice continues, have the least effect in the diseases that weaken the seat of the spirit, such as *phrenesis,* frenzy, and *lethargus,* depressive illness. And demoniacs, whose spirits and bodies are affected, are the most incurable of all – they are usually not even brought to doctors but are left to heaven's assistance, a pitiable sight. Yet much more truly wretched are those who are driven to morally outrageous acts by their lust for power, though they do not seem so pitiable. How little evil a demoniac suffers or does compared to the storms that drive a prince insane with a spirit of tyranny, and compared to the damage he causes in human affairs. The exegesis continues, not in the language of medicine, with a description of the moral and spiritual benefits available to rulers who have fled to Christ (LB 7: 332A–F, on 4: 41); the Luke-voice appears to have returned to his identity as moralizing historian rather than physician. In the transitional sentence to the next episode, however, medical language reappears: Jesus had come not to heal bodies but souls, though the admiring crowds followed him more in search of bodily health than of spiritual salvation (LB 7: 333B, on 4: 42).

In paraphrasing this sequence of four incidents from the very beginning of Jesus' preaching and healing career, Erasmus has deliberately shaped his Luke-voice to conform to the traditional description of Luke as a physician. His Luke puts into Jesus' mouth an explanation of why patients' expectations of their doctors sometimes inhibit healing and how that fact sheds light on the reception of prophets. The paraphrased Luke himself knows names and characteristics of diseases, treatments for diseases, and the capabilities and limitations of the art of medicine. He has a hierarchy of diseases whose guiding principle is how amenable they are to medical treatment: physical illness, mental illness, demon-possession. He knows the importance of the patient's disposition towards the doctor – and the doctor's towards the patient – in the outcome of medical care. More important, though, to the paraphrased Luke are the analogies that his physician's knowledge provides to the process of conversion to Christ through the forgiveness of sins, which are defined as diseases of the soul. He employs these in explanations of Jesus' reported actions as models for all humans or for the clergy in particular, or as images of spiritual truths not easily comprehended by words alone. From now on, when the reader comes upon the paraphrast's or the Gospel's own applications of medical metaphors or narratives of healing miracles, they will attach themselves in his or her mind to a narrator who has established his identity as a physician and a moralizing one at that.

There are further examples of the Luke-voice using elements of the characterization established early in his narrative of Jesus' career. At 5: 12–14, the Gospel has the first of its two accounts of lepers being healed.[31] The Luke-voice announces that the purpose of the episode is to show that no sin is too foul to forgive if the sinner acknowledges his disease and asks the divine physician for a medicine. The leper's condition is described as so loathsome that the leper falls prone before Jesus so his disfigured face need not be seen. But Jesus, who is absolutely free from the possibility of contagion, touches his face, thus modelling the doctor of souls for the apostles and their heirs. The Jews, by contrast, are the complete reverse of the leper – sanctimoniously clean from all contagious contact in a physical sense, they have true leprosy of the heart and ooze with subcutaneous sins. Jesus removes all diseases (unlike the Jewish priests, who merely attest to the presence or absence of leprosy), does not charge for his services, and does not seek human glory from them (LB 7: 336F–8D). In a comment on the immediately following report that crowds of people desiring to be healed sought out Jesus, the Luke-voice remarks:

> They thought it a great thing, more than human, for a leper's skin to become clean at the touch of a hand, when it is a far greater and more divine act of kindness to dispel from the heart, by means of the medicine of the Gospel word, the fever of a foul lust, the dropsy of greed, the demon of ambition, and other lethal plagues of souls. (LB 7: 338E)

And when Jesus is reported to have retreated into the desert, the Luke-voice adds that such retreats are models for the Gospel teacher, who will come forth when his people need to be fed on the food of the Gospel and their worsening ills require help from the healer (LB 7: 339B, on 5: 16).

The healing of the bedridden paralytic (5: 17–25), which is told fairly simply in the paraphrase on Matthew 9: 1–9, receives a good deal more elaboration from the Luke-voice. When Jesus taught, he breathed a divine power of healing, says the paraphrased evangelist, a cure offered first to the more important part of a human being, for his words healed diseases of souls. Yet healing of bodies concerned him too, since such acts increased faith in the less visible effects he had on souls. The paralytic is described as no better than a corpse (as he is in the Matthew paraphrase too) because all his tendons were affected. In the description of how the paralytic was lowered through the roof, Jesus is called 'gentle physician' and 'merciful physician.' The crowd expects a bodily cure, but Jesus' words of forgiveness indicate the greater importance of healing the soul. The paraphrased narrative continues with an admixture of medical language motivated by the events in the Gospel text (LB 7: 339B–41A).

The Luke-voice introduces the story of the feeding of the five thousand by again noting the priority of teaching over miracle-working, cast in terms of feeding and healing minds before healing and feeding bodies: 'Jesus ... first fed their souls, saying much to them about the kingdom of God; then he healed those who were in the grip of disease and other physical ills' (LB 7: 368D, on 9: 11). After the account of the miracle of loaves and fishes, the Luke-voice concludes:

> Now regard with me this part of the mystery: Our Lord Jesus taught and healed first, and then provided food. The divine word is indeed the food of the soul, but some portion of it is not denied even to the ungodly and to catechumens. For it is medicine for minds and a restorative for the weak. The healthful teaching does the same thing in the souls of sinners that Jesus did by his word and touch in bodily diseases. (LB 7: 369D, on 9: 17)

The association of feeding and healing here and in the paraphrase of 5: 16–17 just described reflects what Erasmus had said in his dedicatory letter to the *Paraphrase*, that dietetics is the other half of a physician's professional concern, along with therapeutics (LB 7: 275–6).

Later in the Gospel there is another miracle, not recorded by the other evangelists, that receives enhancement from the realm of medical knowledge: during a Sabbath-day dinner to which he had been invited by a Pharisee, Jesus healed a man who suffered from dropsy, thus exacerbating the Pharisees' repeated complaint that he did not keep the Sabbath holy.[32] For the Luke-voice this is another opportunity to make the comparison between the sick and their physical illnesses on the one hand and on the other the spiritually diseased and their sins. Erasmus' Luke adds medical details to the Gospel's original bare statement of the illness: dropsy is usually incurable and is marked by a sallow colour and a swollen body. These two symptoms disappear instantly at Jesus' healing touch. But the true dropsy of the soul, says the paraphrased Luke, is apparent in the Pharisees' envy of anyone's glory, even God's, beside their own. As the comparison is elaborated, more of the medical lore about dropsy, and more language particularly appropriate to that disease, is employed. Spiritual dropsy arises from corrupted moral judgment as if from a damaged liver; the Pharisees were externally swollen with empty pride and their internal organs were all corrupt and decayed. Yet the Lord longed to heal their disease with the drug of his health-bringing word. The Pharisees' vainglory was a thirst and swollenness. The man with dropsy was healed easily with a touch because he acknowledged his illness and wished to be cured; spiritual disease cannot be healed unless it is first acknowledged. Everything the Pharisees do is dropsy, that is, a hunt for vainglory (LB 7: 400B–1B, on 14: 2–7).

These are the most developed examples of the Luke-voice explaining the events of the narrative in a way that suggests he is more familiar with medical matters, and more inclined to use them as interpretive schemata, than the other evangelists. Not all the paraphrases of healing miracles receive so much particularly medical detail in their narratives or in the exegetical or homiletic comments on them. Among the other kinds of narrative amplification and the other sets of metaphorical language found everywhere in all the Gospel *Paraphrases*, however, these are prominent enough to keep Luke the physician distinctively before the reader's eye. And because they are there, the many brief occurrences of medical details and metaphors elsewhere in this *Paraphrase* become reminders of this evangelist's medical persona. Appropriately enough, it is only the Luke-voice, for instance, who says that Peter's hasty act in slicing off Malchus' ear during the confusion of Jesus' arrest caused a wound that was more embarrassing than life-threatening but still incurable, because when cartilage is cut it does not mend. Yet Jesus healed it so well that there was no scar (LB 7: 455E–F, on 22: 50–1).[33]

Let us summarize. Recreating the character and voice of the evangelist Luke was not, of course, Erasmus' main purpose in paraphrasing this Gospel; amplifying and clarifying the content of the Gospel was. Still, as one means to that end he was able to exploit the received character of Luke as historian and physician. In the preface, he elaborated and reinforced the evangelist's posture as a historian; he elaborated the historical settings of the narrative in the first three chapters; and throughout he added little touches of allusion and comparison to keep readers reminded that his Luke-voice was contemporary with and familiar with the history and historiography of first-century Rome. Likewise, early in the narrative of Jesus' preaching career he made his Luke-voice speak at length as an experienced physician, knowledgeable of diseases and of their social and psychological ramifications, and he reinforced the reader's awareness of the narrator's professional role with a good dose of reminders throughout the rest of the Gospel. Erasmus also used the evangelist's address in the preface to a named reader, Theophilus, and his reference there to himself in the first person as the basis for later occasional occurrences of direct address from the Luke-voice to Theophilus or any reader after Theophilus; the Luke-voice engages the reader with himself in an I-you relationship.

Two factors are common to each side of this characterization of Luke as physician and as historian. First, Erasmus is at pains to establish each characterization early in the *Paraphrase*: Luke the historian from the very beginning, and Luke the physician from the first stages of Jesus' preaching mission. The characterizing marks occur when a reader is least informed and most curious about the content of the book he or she has opened. Once that character is established, the reader need only be reminded of it by smaller notes in the course of the narrative. The narrator's personal *fides* has been established at the outset and he can proceed by directing the reader's attention more to the story than to himself. Second, the Luke-voice uses both his specialties, history and medicine, as means by which to understand and express the spiritual meaning of the story he tells. Historical events are foreshadowings of the spiritual reality that was unfolding in the life story of Jesus of Nazareth, or types of coming patterns in human history when the Christian message comes into conflict with other forces. Illness, healing, and the art of medicine form the basis of a web of metaphors for individual sin and salvation, and can even be extended to the historical plane and applied to the health of nations.

The reader of the dedicatory letter to Henry VIII has had his expectations of this *Paraphrase* fulfilled. Luke the physician and Luke the historian speak clearly, though not obtrusively, in the (paraphrased) Gospel of Luke the Christian. And Erasmus has indeed spoken *sub evangelistae persona*.

NOTES

1 References to the biblical Gospel of Luke appear simply with chapter and verse numbers, omitting the word 'Luke.' Translations from the Bible are those of the Revised Standard Version (RSV), except in a few instances where the New Revised Standard Version (NRSV) gives a version closer to the Latin and Greek texts Erasmus knew. Luke is called a physician in Col. 4: 14. Both the qualities of his Greek style and the affinity of the remarks in 1: 1–14 of his Gospel to the prefatory themes of classical Greek and Roman historians led to his being regarded as a historian himself. For a review of the early development of this double identification, see Joseph A. Fitzmyer, *The Gospel According to Luke (I–IX)*, 35–41. The Gospel of Luke itself is usually thought to contain no particular evidence in content or language that its author was a physician; Fitzmyer, *Gospel*, 51–3. So additions of a medical kind can be attributed to the deliberate choice of Erasmus. Luke himself claims (1: 3) that he has revised (by additions) the order of events, something a historian would be expected to do, and the paraphrased Luke does not depart from that biblical order. In 'Erasmus' Prescription for Henry VIII: Logotherapy,' Marjorie O'Rourke Boyle discusses Ep 1381, the dedicatory letter to this *Paraphrase*, situating it in the personal relation between the king and Erasmus and in Henry's political circumstances. Her essay provides a complementary perspective to the point of view taken below.

2 *De duplici copia verborum ac rerum*, 2 (ASD I-6: 206–13; CWE 24: 582–7). For the classical background, see the notes to either edition.

3 Style, of course, reflects the man, as Erasmus believes, and speech mirrors the heart even of the divine; see the *Paraphrase on John* (LB 7: 499A; CWE 46: 15–16) and *Adagia*, I.vi.51: *qualis vir, talis oratio.*

4 In a letter of 1522, replying to a reader of the *Paraphrase on Matthew*,

Erasmus notes that paraphrase is not a translation but a kind of commentary with no change of persons; yet it allows something of the paraphrast's own to be added in explanation of the author's meaning (Allen Ep 1274: 34–9; CWE Ep 1274: 37–43).

5 See, e.g., passages in *Divinationes* (LB 9: 491E–F, 493A–B, 493B–C, 493E, 496C), *Elenchus* (LB 9: 497E, 498E, 499D, 499E), and *Supputatio* (LB 9: 520F–1A, 601D–E, 611C–E). In general, cf. Erika Rummel, *Erasmus and His Catholic Critics*, 2: 38–9.

6 I omit the *Paraphrase on Mark* from such comparison because it was composed after the one on Luke; therefore the Mark-voice is likely to have been influenced by what Erasmus had already done in paraphrasing Luke.

7 Erasmus himself alluded to this issue in his comment that the variety of voices was a deterrent to his undertaking the paraphrase of the Gospels: see 129 above.

8 Robert Sider, 'Preface' to *Paraphrase on Mark* (CWE 44: ix–x), says of the *Paraphrase on Mark* that sometimes 'the identity of the historical author of the Gospel fades, and the voice of Erasmus can be heard distinctly.' There may be special reasons why this is more true in Mark than in the other *Paraphrases*, such as the traditional belief, which Erasmus also held, that the Gospel of Mark was no more than a summary of Matthew's; see the Mark-voice's opening to the *Paraphrase on Mark* (LB 7: 158B; CWE 49: 14) and Erasmus' annotations on Mark 1: 1 and on Luke 1: 1, in Anne Reeve, *Erasmus' Annotations on the New Testament: The Gospels*, 112, 152. See also Jacques Chomarat, *Grammaire et rhétorique chez Érasme*, 1: 617; and Friedhelm Krüger, *Humanistische Evangelienauslegung: Desiderius Erasmus von Rotterdam als Ausleger der Evangelien in seine Paraphrasen*, 103–9, 131–50, esp. 148–50.

9 Luke 1: 1–4: 'Since many have undertaken to set down an orderly account of the events that have been fulfilled among us, just as they were handed on to us by those who from the beginning were eyewitnesses and servants of the word, I too decided, after investigating everything carefully from the very first, to write an orderly account for you, most excellent Theophilus, so that you may know the truth concerning the things about which you have been instructed' (NRSV).

10 The fifty Latin words of Luke 1: 1–4 are roughly equivalent to seven lines of Latin in a column of the LB text of the *Paraphrase on Luke*. In LB 7: 279A–83A there are seven lines to the inch and twenty-six column-inches' worth of paraphrase on 1: 1–4. The same calculation, fifty Latin words of the Latin Gospel being equivalent to seven lines, or one inch, of an LB column of the *Paraphrases*, will be used in the rest of this essay.

11 For the relation of Luke 1: 1–4 to the prefaces of classical literature, see Loveday Alexander, *The Preface to Luke's Gospel: Literary Convention and Social Context in Luke 1: 1–4 and Acts 1: 1*. For discussion of the Greek and Roman historical writers' approaches to historiography and the historian's self-presentation, see John Marincola, *Authority and Tradition in Ancient Historiography*.

12 Luke 1: 5: 'In the days of Herod, king of Judea, there was a priest named Zechariah, of the division of Abijah, and he had a wife of the daughters of Aaron, and her name was Elizabeth' (RSV).

13 Such typological interpretation is common, of course, throughout the *Paraphrases*; the point here is that since a declared historian is speaking, historical typology is thereby identified as part of his conception of the utility of history.

14 Luke 2: 1–3: 'In those days a decree went out from Caesar Augustus that all the world should be enrolled. This was the first enrollment, when Quirinius was governor of Syria. And all went to be enrolled, each to his own city' (RSV).

15 The flat declarative language is reminiscent of a Eutropius or an elementary textbook of Roman history: 'Augusto Caesare, qui plerasque mundi regiones obtinebat, ac latissime rebus undique pacatis Romanorum imperium administrabat' (LB 7: 297F).

16 Cf. the Vulgate Latin, *ut describeretur universus orbis*: Erasmus uses the more appropriately Roman vocabulary of *provinciae* and *censeri*, as well as referring to the *imperium Romanum* instead of 'all the world.'

17 *Princeps*, 'first citizen,' is a term from senatorial procedures that Augustus preferred for his unparalleled constitutional position in the state after 31 BC; it rapidly evolved into the first-century AD equivalent of 'emperor,' and is the source of 'prince' and its cognates in the European languages. *Imperator*, 'commander,' was the title awarded to successful Roman generals during the Republic; during the first century AD it evolved into one that could be held only by the emperor. 'Emperor' is its derivative. See the *Oxford Classical Dictionary*, svv. *princeps*, *imperator*. 'Donative' and 'enlistees,' *donativum* and *qui ... dant nomen*, are also regular terms from Roman military life.

18 Luke 3: 1–2: 'In the fifteenth year of the reign of Tiberius Caesar, Pontius Pilate being governor of Judea, and Herod being tetrarch of Galilee, and his brother Philip tetrarch of the region of Ituraea and Trachonitis, and Lysanias tetrarch of Abilene, in the high-priesthood of Annas and Caiaphas ...' (RSV).

19 Civic life: LB 7: 312D–13A (on 3: 14; the behaviour of soldiers in society), 314D–F (on 3: 19; the characteristic behaviour of tyrants), 320C–E (on 4: 5; ambition's offering of human glory and riches).

Spread of the new faith through the known world: LB 7: 452B–C (on 19: 26; the church and its king like the slaves and the master who entrusted money to them), 435B (on 19: 39). Roman institutions and events (in addition to the material in the introductions of chapters 2 and 3, described above): LB 7: 412E (on 16: 11; trustworthiness is proved in smaller things first and then in greater, as the consulship is only reached after good service as aedile or praetor or in the other lesser magistracies); 433E, 434A, 434B (on 19: 38–9; vocabulary of a Roman general's triumph procession applied to Jesus' entry into Jerusalem); 438D (on 20: 3); *novus homo*, 'a new man on the scene,' Roman political slang applied to John the Baptist. On historical amplification, including echoes of individual historians, cf. Chomarat, *Grammaire et rhétorique*, 1: 629–32.

20 The 'we-sections' of Acts: 16: 10–17, 20: 5–15, 21: 1–18, and 27: 1–28: 16.

21 Theophilus is addressed at LB 7: 282F, 309A, 334A, 359F, 440B, 450B, 462C, and 464C. He is not named at 297E, but in light of the use of his name at 282F can be presumed to be the addressee: 'Habes admirabilem ortum praecursoris, nunc accipe mirabiliorem Jesu Christi.' There is a pun on his name immediately following its first occurrence, at 283A.

22 'I/we' pronouns and/or first-person verbs of the 'true' kind occur at least at LB 7: 281C–2F (many times throughout the passage, which is the paraphrase on 1: 1–4), 315B, 359B, 418B, and 429B.

23 Singular imperative plus *mihi* (typically of the kind *hic mihi considera*, 'here, I urge, consider') is found at least at LB 7: 300C, 328F, 334A, 339F, 359F, 397A, 408E, and 410B.

24 Krüger, *Humanistische Evangelienauslegung*, 28.

25 By contrast, the paraphrased John directly engages his reader only occasionally, notably in the paraphrase on John 7: 50: 'jam mihi considera, prudens lector' (LB 7: 562C). There are a few first-person references that might be called 'true,' e.g., in the *Paraphrase on John* in the interior preface, where the John-voice explains his reasons for writing a gospel (on 1: 14–15, LB 7: 498E; CWE 46: 15; also LB 7: 504E–F). The Matthew-voice and Mark-voice, in their respective paraphrases, also speak in the true first person to explain their reasons for writing (on Matt 1: 4 and 17, LB 7: 2C–5D, passim; on Mark 1: 2, LB 7: 158B). The *Paraphrase on Matthew* appears to have only a few other instances of direct engagement with the reader; the *Paraphrase on Mark* is relentlessly exhortatory, relying heavily on imperatives and rhetorical questions.

26 As in the case of the presentation of the Luke-voice as a historian, since the *Paraphrase on Mark* was composed after the one on Luke, it is usually omitted from my comparison.

27 Matthew: LB 7: 13E (on Matt. 3: 5). John: LB 7: 523A–B (on John 3: 19–20). Mark: LB 7: 158C–E (all three on Mark 1: 4). Luke: LB 7: 310D–E (on Luke 3: 7).

28 The whole episode is Luke 4: 16–29; verse 23 reads: 'And he said to them, "Doubtless you will quote to me this proverb, 'Physician, heal yourself; what we have heard you did at Capernaum, do here also in your own country"' (RSV).

29 Luke 4: 38–41: 'And he arose and left the synagogue, and entered Simon's house. Now Simon's mother-in-law was ill with a high fever, and they besought him for her. And he stood over her and rebuked the fever, and it left her; and immediately she rose and served them. Now when the sun was setting all those who had any that were sick with various diseases brought them to him, and he laid his hands on every one of them and healed them. And demons also came out of many, crying, "You are the Son of God!" But he rebuked them, and would not allow them to speak, because they knew that he was the Christ' (RSV).

30 Other examples of a paraphrased evangelist stressing the same point: the paraphrases on Matt. 9: 25 (LB 7: 56F), on John 5: 9 (LB 7: 534E), and on Luke 4: 35 (LB 7: 330F, the healing of the demoniac just noted).

31 Luke 5: 12–14: 'While he was in one of the cities, there came a man full of leprosy; and when he saw Jesus, he fell on his face and besought him, "Lord, if you will, you can make me clean." And he stretched out his hand, and touched him, saying, "I will; be clean." And immediately the leprosy left him. And he charged him to tell no one; but "go and show yourself to the priest, and make an offering for your cleansing, as Moses commanded, for a proof to the people"' (RSV). The parallel account is Matt. 8: 1–4. The language of healing plays a part in the Matthew-voice's expansion of the Gospel text, but the dominant theme is the Mosaic law on leprosy and how and why Jesus' actions and instructions intersect with it. The relative weighting of the themes is shifted by the Luke-voice in favour of medical language.

32 Luke 14: 1–4: 'One sabbath when he went to dine at the house of a ruler who belonged to the Pharisees, they were watching him. And behold, there was a man before him who had dropsy. And Jesus spoke to the lawyers and Pharisees, saying, "Is it lawful to heal on the sabbath, or not?" But they were silent. Then he took him and healed him, and let him go' (RSV).

33 Other instances (not an exhaustive list) of medical language: the need for a sick person to acknowledge his illness: LB 7: 419A–B (on 17: 12–13) and 443F (on 20: 47). The Pharisees' refusal to take their medicine and unwillingness to be healed: LB 7: 342B (on 5: 31), 387D

(on 11: 53), 387E (on 12: 1), 399E (on 13: 34), 426F (on 19: 2), 438C–D (on 20: 9), and 442F–3A (on 20: 45). The medical value of medicine that delivers a strong shock to the body: LB 7: 459B (on 23: 5). Jesus' desire to heal: LB 7: 386D (on 11: 46), 467E (on 24: 17), and 487C (on 24: 41). Sins as diseases and forgiveness as healing: LB 7: 358D (on 7: 44), 401C (on 14: 8), 419A–B (on 17: 12–13), 423D (on 18: 20), and 455C (on 22: 48). What people in general expect (or not) of their doctors: LB 7: 365C (on 8: 41) and 366B (on 8: 49).

SIX

Jesus and His Family in Erasmus' Paraphrases on Luke and John

Irena Backus

Our aim in this study is to examine Erasmus' portrayal of the human Jesus and his family. In order not to exceed the scope of an essay, we shall focus on a selection of passages from the *Paraphrases* that either tell us something about the human environment in which Jesus was born or depict him in a situation where he has to relate to a member of his family. All the passages will be considered in the context of biblical commentaries that Erasmus would have known and could have used as a model, especially the commentaries of Origen, Chrysostom, Ambrose, Bede, and Theophylact, standard medieval compilations such as the *Catena aurea*, and the *Vita Christi* of Ludolph of Saxony (c.1300–78), still popular in the sixteenth century and very largely founded on the Gospel accounts.[1] We shall ask the following questions. First, is it true to say, as was claimed by Jacques Chomarat, that the Jesus of the *Paraphrases* is a failure as a literary creation because his human nature is not allowed to express itself and thus at crucial moments when he could express shock, surprise, or grief, he simply reverts to his divine nature which, by definition, excludes the expression of any emotion? According to Chomarat, the role of the human Jesus for Erasmus is reduced to that of the pedagogue.[2] Second, we shall raise a question hitherto unasked: How does Erasmus portrays Jesus' immediate family – Elizabeth, Zechariah, Mary and Joseph? Do their human natures differ substantially from the

Saviour's? In dealing with these questions we shall naturally have to consider what Erasmus imports into the basic gospel narrative and what he omits to paraphrase or paraphrases only minimally. The passages we have chosen to discuss here are Luke 1–2 and 3: 21–3, and John 2: 1–11. We shall proceed chronologically, beginning with the circumstances of Jesus' birth.

JESUS' FAMILY AND THE CIRCUMSTANCES OF HIS BIRTH

> Luke 1: 5–7: In the days of Herod King of Judaea there was a priest named Zechariah, of the division of the priesthood called after Abijah. His wife also was of priestly descent; her name was Elizabeth. Both of them were upright and devout, blamelessly observing all the commandments and ordinances of the Lord. But they had no children, for Elizabeth was barren, and both were well on in years. (Luke, 1: 5–7; RSV)

The commentators who single out some of the features of the sterile couple that Erasmus also mentions are Bede and Theophylact. Bede emphasizes that John the Baptist as precursor had to have particularly noble parents, just in the eyes of God – which, in Bede's view, can mean that they were not at all just in the eyes of men. He also stresses that John's parentage was divinely ordained. Elderly parents would be all the more impressed by God's gift of fertility and other people all the more ready to listen to John because of his parentage.[3] Theophylact also observes that wives of the just were often sterile, a fact intended to show that the Law required spiritual and not biological children. He insists that the physical old age of John's parents was in blatant contradiction with their spiritual vigour.[4] Neither Bede nor Theophylact attempts to set John's family in their social context or is interested in them as people. Indeed, Theophylact very deliberately transfers the significance of the passage to the spiritual realm.

Erasmus' paraphrase of the two verses is extremely long and detailed. There is no doubt that he had read both Theophylact and Bede; hence, the fundamental interpretation he puts forward is by no means original. It is also likely that he had read Ludolph of Saxony.[5] However, both the sheer length of the paraphrase and its content show that Erasmus' interest in Zechariah and Elizabeth far exceeded the bounds of a biblical commentary. For Erasmus, the couple constitutes the model of a perfect marriage, not because of their physical relationship but because their union was guaranteed by likeness of mind and piety.[6] John the Baptist's parents are thus an exemplary marriage of true minds, whose justice, Erasmus hastens to specify, was to be sharply distinguished not from justice before men in general but from the justice of the Pharisees who – and here Erasmus paraphrases and slants Matthew 6: 2–7 – announced their acts of charity with a flourish of trumpets, offered up long prayers on street corners, and covered their faces while seeking honour and glory.[7] It is interesting to note that Erasmus, unlike earlier commentators of the passage, considers that the couple's pious conduct would have made them just not only in the eyes of God but also in the eyes of men. He portrays them as a chaste couple living in the world and not in seclusion, whose lifestyle is to be contrasted with the lifestyle of 'the Pharisees.' The introduction by Erasmus of the Pharisees into his paraphrase of the passage from Matthew 6: 2–7 should not, in our view, be interpreted as a gesture of wanton anti-Semitism, as it is improbable that his readers would have interpreted 'the Pharisees' as the Jews. More likely, they would have identified, as they were meant to, the Pharisees' multiplication of hypocritical actions with the corrupt practices of the Roman clergy of their own time. John the Baptist's parents, on the other hand, provide an example of a pious Catholic marriage, which does not upset any human or divine norms.

For Erasmus, as for Bede, the couple was chosen by God to be John's parents. However, whereas for Bede it was their advanced age that was a sign of their election, for Erasmus it was the excellence of their priestly lineage and morals, added to which were John's own virtues and his martyrdom.[8] Like Bede, Erasmus stresses that the *novitas* of John's birth was likely to win him a public. However, the principal ingredient of the *novitas* were the moral qualities of John's parents and not their age.

Erasmus distinguishes himself from other commentators of the passage by noting that Zechariah and Elizabeth were not devoid of defects. Their chief defect, he notes, was their excessive dependence on the opinion of their Jewish contemporaries, who were carnal enough to consider sterility a curse. John the Baptist's parents thus emerge as a noble, chaste couple suffering from the unenlightened attitude of their contemporaries who had not yet learnt that the truly devout are either chaste or celibate.[9] Erasmus would publish a treatise on marriage in 1526,[10] in which he argued, among other things, that chaste marriage of the clergy is to be preferred to celibacy, which often results in clandestine liaisons and children being born out or wedlock. Why not, he argued, allow priests to have legitimate children that they can love? Zechariah and Elizabeth provided a perfect illustration of his convictions, especially as Zechariah was a priest who was manifestly married and who, after the angel's injunction, had sexual relations with his wife with a view to procreation.

Erasmus' comments on Luke 1: 20–5 profit from being compared and contrasted with those of Bede, whose exegesis he had certainly read and to some extent adopted.[11] According to Bede, officiating priests in Zechariah's time were not allowed any access to wife and home in the normal run of their duty. They were, however, given short periods of time when they could be with their wives for procreation purposes, since the priesthood of Aaron was hereditary. However, Bede insists that no such interludes be allowed for New Testament priests, whose office is not hereditary but spiritual. Unlike Zechariah, they are fully given over to the altar and have no need for wives. Thus, the sexual relations Zechariah had with his wife were determined solely by historical circumstances. For Erasmus, by contrast, Zechariah's intercourse with Elizabeth was an example to all priests of Erasmus' time. Their coupling was not due to lust but to divine promise and was motivated solely by the wish to produce children, not for themselves but for the common good.[12]

Various explanations for Elizabeth's seclusion (Luke 1: 23) were given by commentators on the passage. Erasmus' explanation, influenced to some extent by Origen, concentrated on the human angle, making Elizabeth into a figure of consolation for all women of a certain age who should happen to conceive. According to Origen, Elizabeth hid because she was ashamed of giving the impression of having given in to lust, albeit within marriage, when past childbearing age. However, still according to Origen, Elizabeth's fears were quelled completely when Mary came to see her and the infant in her womb announced the coming of Jesus.[13] Bede and Theophylact, although extremely terse in their comments on the passage, did not fundamentally disagree with Origen. According to both, Elizabeth was ashamed of conceiving at such an advanced age, even though the curse of sterility was lifted from her. The shame, however, disappeared when she realized that she was due to give birth to a prophet. Erasmus' exegesis, while the same in essence, adds several details that fill out Elizabeth's character. She was pleased to be pregnant (*laeta quidem de conceptu*), but did not wish to give the impression of an old woman who had given in to lust, knowing that people are always apt to suspect the worst.[14] Moreover, and this is the original aspect of Erasmus' interpretation, Elizabeth wanted to wait and make sure that the pregnancy was real so as not to double the dishonour of sterility. Once she was sure of it, she gave all the credit for it to God.[15] While remaining within the traditional exegetical framework, Erasmus manages to invest Elizabeth with real suspicions, hopes, and fears that any woman of his era would have understood. He also makes the point that pregnancy at an advanced age, so long as it is a result of a legitimate desire for children, is a gift from God and should be the object of neither gossip nor scorn.

The parents of John the Baptist, as portrayed by Erasmus, are a model chaste couple with the very highest motives, such as befit a married priest and his wife. It is interesting to note that Noël Béda, who criticized several passages in the *Paraphrases* and who certainly did not share Erasmus' views on marriage of the clergy, made no objections to his portrayal of Zechariah and Elizabeth. As we shall see, however, Béda did object to Erasmus' portrayal of Jesus' parents, and of Mary in particular.

> In the sixth month the angel Gabriel was sent from God to a town in Galilee called Nazareth, with a message for a girl betrothed to a man named Joseph, a descendant of David; the girl's name was Mary. The angel went in and said to her, 'Greetings, most favoured one! The Lord is with you.' (Luke 1: 26–8)

Theophylact, in his exposition of this passage and its sequel, was only concerned with Mary as redeemer of the fault of Eve. He was not interested in the nature of her fear, her anxiety about her virginity, or her obvious humility. He considers that Mary was full of grace in the sense that she pleased God.[16] Erasmus' paraphrase of the passage is very obviously based on the exegesis of Bede. Although Bede does not go into the question of whether Mary deserved the grace bestowed upon her or whether God chose her, he does imply that Mary's own virtue played some part, by speaking of her as one 'who has the grace that no other woman had deserved.'[17] Like Origen and Ambrose before him, he explains at great length that it was most important that Christ be born of a married virgin.[18] However, whereas Origen and Ambrose consider that the prime reason for this was to avoid gossip about possible illicit relations with an unknown father, Bede adds other reasons. First, it was important that Mary's origins be known. As the Scripture is not in the habit of giving genealogies of women, Mary's origins could only be known through Joseph's (Matt. 1: 2–16; Luke 2: 5). Indeed, according to Bede, both were from the house of David. Second, Mary's marital status prevented her from being stoned by the Jews and removed all possibility that the Saviour's mother would be a bad example to other virgins. Third, Joseph could protect her during the flight to Egypt. Fourth, his presence stopped all possible rumours of Mary's being impregnated by the devil.[19]

Bede also comments at length on Mary's rather hesitant and frightened reception of the angelic message. According to him, this was a natural reaction for a virgin being addressed by a male and should serve as an example to other women.[20] Similarly, Mary's reaction to the Annunciation is to be explained by the unease of one who had vowed perpetual virginity and did not wish to lose it. She had read the prophecy in Isaiah 7, but wanted to know *how* she could conceive without losing her virginity.[21] Bede then explains that the intercourse with the Holy Spirit was to take place without lust so that Mary, contrary to the affirmation of the Nestorian heresy, would become truly *theotokos*.[22] Bede's model human virgin thus assumes divinity through giving birth to Jesus. This, as we shall see, is far from being the case for Erasmus, who takes over much of Bede's exegesis but knows exactly when to stop short.

Like his source, Erasmus thinks it important that Mary was a married virgin. The reason given, however, only partly corresponds to the reasons given by Bede. God chose a married virgin because he particularly values humble chaste marriages; Erasmus here takes up the point of the priestly marriage made earlier with respect to Zechariah and Elizabeth. Moreover, Joseph was there to act as a witness to the marvellous event and to ensure that the news of the virgin birth did not spread prematurely.[23] Further on, Erasmus adds another reason, which Bede had also evoked: Joseph was not there to make his wife a mother or to be a father, but to protect his wife's reputation.[24]

Mary's fearful reaction to the angel's message is due, according to Erasmus, to several factors. First, Mary is uneasy at being hailed so magnificently, *quum ipsa nihil magnifice de se sentiret* ('for she had no high ideas of herself'). Without doubting that God could bring about anything he wanted, she did not think for one moment that she would reign with her son.[25] Second and most important, Mary was worried about losing her virginity and did not see how she could bear a son while remaining intact. In this respect, Erasmus remarks, Mary resembles all of us, for 'everyone likes his or her chastity and would wish that this happy state of affairs were permanent, if possible.'[26] Erasmus follows the pattern of Bede's commentary in emphasizing that the angel's reply is intended to reassure Mary. However, his interpretation of the content of the reply is very different from Bede's. Instead of holding that the coupling between Mary and the Holy Spirit is unaccompanied by lust and that she becomes *theotokos* as a result of it, Erasmus asserts that no human seed will be necessary for the conception: the Holy Spirit will simply adapt himself to human powers. Mary who, as in Bede's commentary, is familiar with the prophecy of Isaiah, does not seek to supplement her knowledge by asking the angel exactly how she will conceive. All she is really interested in is keeping her virginity. Once the angel has assured her that this will be the case, she places herself totally in the hands of God.

Erasmus' Mary is a human, married virgin chosen by God through no merit of her own to give birth to the Messiah. She is modest, hesitant but quite clear in her mind that her chief concern is to preserve her virginity whatever happens. It is no wonder that Erasmus' refusal to single Mary out in any way or to suggest that she in some sense deserved the grace bestowed upon her caused Noël Béda to dismiss what he says as 'misguided and schismatical.'[27]

> About this time Mary set out and went straight to a town in the uplands of Judah. She went into Zechariah's house and greeted Elizabeth. (Luke 1: 39–40)

Erasmus was not the first biblical commentator whose attention was caught by the nature of Mary's journey from Nazareth to Judah and her stay with Elizabeth. True to his intention of portraying Mary as a model, fully human, married virgin, he adapted several interpretations of the passage, including that of Ambrose. In commenting on Luke 1: 39 the bishop of Milan enjoins all holy women to show due care and attention to their pregnant relatives, and not to be afraid, even if they are virgins, to leave the house and face dangers. Concerning Mary's journey, Ambrose notes that it is an example to all virgins not to stay in strange houses, not to tarry on street corners, and not to gossip in public. Mary was slow in the home but hurried through public places. Ambrose observes that she spent three months with Elizabeth and does not at any stage imply that it would have been indecent for her to be present at the birth of John the Baptist.[28]

Bede draws no particular moral lessons for virgins from Mary's journey. He does, however, draw the reader's attention to her sense of duty, which he takes to explain her haste in going to see Elizabeth, and to her humility. He states explicitly that Mary stayed to see the birth of John the Baptist.[29] Theophylact notes that Mary was pleased at Elizabeth's good fortune but also, for reasons of caution, wanted to make sure that Elizabeth was really pregnant. He considers that it would have been indecent for Mary, as a virgin, to be present at the birth, not because of the birth itself but because she was not supposed to mingle with the crowd that would gather on that occasion.[30]

Erasmus selects passages from all three commentators so as to accentuate Mary's perfect but human virginity. He notes that one sign of Mary's piety (to be imitated, he implies) is the pleasure she takes in the joy of others, such as Elizabeth, rather than boasting about her own. As an incarnation of virginity, she does not like to be seen in public unless compelled by duty. Erasmus makes much of the fact that Mary greeted no one on her journey to Elizabeth's house. Once there, she stayed with the older woman, ministering to her and restoring her morale.[31] However, she left before the delivery, because virgins may not be present at birth or act as midwives. Although married, Mary is thus portrayed as totally uncontaminated by anything human and physical, be it only greeting or seeing the birth of a baby. The sole contact she is allowed is part of her duty. Whereas other commentators allow Mary some human characteristics, whether caution (Theophylact) or a wish to be present at the birth of John the Baptist (Bede and Ambrose), Erasmus' portrayal of her, although very largely drawn from Ambrose, is by far the least physical. His Mary, although totally human, interacts as little as possible with the physical world.

Noël Béda was particularly struck by Erasmus' statement about Mary greeting no one on her way. He took it to be an allusion to Luke 10: 4 (the Lord's injunction to the seventy-two apostles) and found the interpretation too literal. Luke 10: 4 should be interpreted morally: it is not that God did not want us to greet our neighbour; he simply did not want us to waste time when more important duty called. Mary would certainly have met people she knew on her way and her refusal to greet any of them would have amounted to arrogance, notes Béda not unjustly.[32]

Taken together, Mary, Zechariah, and Elizabeth are portrayed by Erasmus as belonging to a moral elite, whose virtues should be imitated, although they cannot be matched. It is as a moral elite, he implies, that they can permit themselves to do away with legal ceremonies, as is shown by Elizabeth's insistence that the child be called John, although her neighbours and relatives object 'that there is nobody in your family who has that name' (Luke 1: 61). Whereas Theophylact and Bede suggest that Elizabeth named the child John because she had been granted the gift of prophecy,[33] Erasmus opposes Zechariah and Elizabeth, the harbingers of the new faith, to the relatives who wanted to adhere to the letter of the Law. He notes, implicitly following Origen's ninth homily on Luke and a passage from Chrysostom, both cited in the *Catena aurea*, that Zechariah means 'remembering the Lord,' whereas John means 'the grace of God.'[34] Then he adds somewhat bitterly:

> To this day there are some who prefer the name Zechariah to John, those who still cannot bear the abolition of circumcision, new moons, ablutions, holy days, fasts, selection of food, sacrifices, and who in fact clamour: we do not want the name John, we want Zechariah.[35]

It is obvious that for Erasmus John is the first prophet of the New Testament and not the last prophet of the Old. His entire family thus announces a new era in contrast and opposition to those who want to abide by the ceremonies of the Mosaic Law. Erasmus' excursus on the contemporary equivalent of Elizabeth's and Zechariah's friends and relations who wanted all church ceremonies maintained instead of relying on faith aroused the anger of Noël Béda, who found his criticism of the ecclesiastical establishment 'wicked and impious.'[36]

However, Erasmus' point was made: in his mind the vanguard

of the new religious movement were married, chaste priests and their wives. Like Zechariah and Elizabeth, they would not hesitate to modify traditional customs imposed by ecclesiastical law. Less holy than Jesus' parents, Zechariah and Elizabeth are shown nonetheless as working in perfect unison to bring about more pious practices.

JESUS' CHILDHOOD

Erasmus does not give these characters any historical setting and in fact turns out to be very casual about historical details altogether. Zechariah, Elizabeth, Mary, and Joseph are timeless. The two women are depicted with greater attention than the men, but could come from any period in history. Jesus' childhood receives the same, idealized treatment. Two instances of Erasmus' lack of interest in the historical setting are his descriptions of the census in Luke 2: 1 and of the purification in Luke 2: 22. The reader would expect Erasmus to refer to some extra-biblical evidence for the census. In fact, all he does is to repeat in an abridged form the account of Flavius Josephus, which Bede had cited in considerable detail in his commentary on Luke 2: 1–2.[37] Erasmus' main object here is to establish an opposition between Christ's kingdom and Octavian's empire and to assert that the point of the census was to make clear once and for all that Christ's kingdom was much larger than Caesar's. Those who give their allegiance to Caesar, be it in the New Testament or in Erasmus' own day, declare themselves to be captive and find their possessions diminish; those who declare their allegiance to the new prince are free and gain eternal salvation.[38] Erasmus simplifies and adapts the exegesis of Bede and Origen, according to whom Jesus had to be included in the census of the world so that he in turn could include the faithful in his own census by writing their name in the book of life.[39]

Given his interest in the human aspect of Jesus' family, one would expect Erasmus to pick up on the necessity of his having to be included in a human census, but he seems to prefer to contrast the political and spiritual rules. Bede, who had seen the same opposition in the text, turned it into complementarity: the census was ordained not only to bear witness to the coming of a new king who would inscribe his faithful in the book of life, for the new king would do more than that; he would guide earthly rulers so that they ruled more fairly and with greater moderation.[40] Erasmus' simpler, contrastive exegesis removes the human Christ to an apolitical sphere: Christ's rule is neither comparable to nor compatible with any earthly rule and his arrival on earth is not to be linked with any particular period of history.

How can this observation be reconciled with Jane Phillips' view of Erasmus' wish to situate the gospel events in a precise historical context?[41] The contradiction need not be more than apparent. There is no denying Erasmus' use of the vocabulary of Roman pagan historians, to which Phillips draws our attention. It is also true that Erasmus' recourse to this vocabulary sharpens the historical background. However, the historical background does not impinge on Erasmus' exegesis. It is useful to remember that the composition of the *Paraphrase on Luke* coincides with the period when he came under pressure to write against Luther. He resisted that pressure until 1524, claiming that Christ could not be the property of any intellectual or political faction.[42] The *Paraphrase* provides the theological confirmation of this view. The addition of the historical background cannot be considered as anything more than an aesthetic device.

> Eight days later the time came to circumcise him, and he was given the name Jesus, the name given by the angel before he was conceived. Then, after their purification had been completed in accordance with the Law of Moses, they brought him to Jerusalem to present him to the Lord (as prescribed in the law of the Lord: 'Every first-born male shall be deemed to belong to the Lord'), and also to make the offering as stated in the law: 'A pair of turtle doves or two young pigeons.' (Luke 2: 21–4)

Was it also the wish not to tie down Christ historically and politically that made Erasmus misdescribe Mary's purification? More likely, the error was simply due to impatience. After rapidly adapting the exegesis of Bede so as to emphasize Mary's perpetual virginity (which Bede also upheld),[43] Erasmus sets out to show that Mary, although not subject to the usual purification laws – there being nothing impure about the birth – nonetheless did not forgo any of them. Erasmus' demonstration is somewhat half-hearted and his irritation with the rituals quite plain. Implicit in this section of the paraphrase is the idea that the moral elite should not be subjected to what in his view are empty rituals. His exegesis owes something to Origen and Theophylact, both of whom stress that Christ was circumcised so as not to omit any aspect of the Law (in Origen's commentary the assertion can be read as anti-Gnostic polemic), unlike Bede, who sees Christ's circumcision as a symbol of our renewal.[44] As regards Mary's purification, all commentators make the point that Mary did not need to be purified. Erasmus is alone in insisting on the full incongruity of this, by stating repeatedly that the divinely impregnated womb that gave birth to the one who was to purify the entire human race could not possibly require purification itself.[45]

This irritation at Mary's being subjected to a useless rite probably made Erasmus forget the purification laws in Leviticus 12 and paraphrase Luke 2: 21–4 as follows:

> When the *fortieth* day from birth came, on which the Law commands that the male offspring be shown to the Lord and that a gift be offered for *the purification of the mother and the child*, since the normal female birth does not take place without uncleanness of the flesh ...[46] (emphasis added)

In fact, as Noël Béda was quick to point out, after the birth of a male child, the mother and the child were unclean for seven days. On the eighth day, the child was purified by circumcision, which took place in the home, not in the Temple. The mother then remained unclean for another thirty-two days, thirty-three counting the day of the circumcision. After that period she could leave the house to be purified in the Temple. However, the purification in the Temple did not concern the already circumcised child.[47] Erasmus' rather casual treatment of Luke 2: 21–4 enables him to point up the full absurdity of Mary's purification and of the requirement for Jesus, Lord and Redeemer of all, to be redeemed by an animal sacrifice.[48] Erasmus' sense of the inappropriateness of rites and ceremonies, and of their inapplicability to the child of Mary, helps make his Jesus a very aloof, albeit not at all inhuman figure in the *Paraphrase on Luke*.

Most commentators on Luke 2: 40 ('The child grew big and strong ...') tend to emphasize the distinction between Jesus' divine and his human nature. Naturally, it was only according to his human nature that he could be said to grow, Bede and Theophylact explain. As the Word of God, he was eternal and was not supposed to grow or gain in strength.[49] For Erasmus, by contrast, it was only a certain natural grace acquired as he grew older that suggested Jesus was something more than a man. Erasmus' Jesus is in fact portrayed as possessing all the human virtues – modesty, chastity, gentleness, and piety – to an extraordinary degree.[50]

Commenting on Jesus' religious upbringing (at Luke 2: 41), Erasmus distances himself from all his predecessors. Whereas Origen and Theophylact confine themselves to brief remarks about Jesus' scrupulousness in observing the Law and Bede opts for an allegorical interpretation, while also emphasizing the excellence of Jesus' parents, Erasmus carefully presents young Jesus' religious education as a model to all parents and children. It is no surprise that the education Jesus got from his parents is indistinguishable from Erasmus' own ideal of humanist education. No external teacher is necessary. It is the parents' task to guide their offspring from birth, 'to preserve them from lasciviousness and to accustom them to ardent desire for true piety, while they are still of a tender age and while their mind is still impressionable and apt to follow all instruction in virtue.' [51] Jesus may be divine, but his human nature seems to dominate here; as a human child he has to receive religious training, like any boy from a pious sixteenth-century family. It is not customary, however, for twelve-year-old boys to stay behind in Jerusalem, and the only plausible explanation for that event is the intervention of a divine nature that wishes to begin carrying out the Father's commands.

Erasmus' explanation of Jesus' presence and behaviour in the Temple shows that he wished to expound the simultaneity of Jesus' two natures. But he does not succeed. It is the human Jesus that predominates, albeit a highly schematized human Jesus. According to Erasmus, although young and fragile, the Lord in his conversation with the doctors manifests none of the arrogance of abnormally gifted young people. He asks questions like one desirous of knowledge and replies modestly and prudently when questioned in turn.[52] Jesus as a model of an intellectual adolescent contrasts strangely with the Jesus who chose simple people for his disciples and who distrusted false learning, a characterization developed by Erasmus in other sections of the *Paraphrases*.[53]

The intellectual adolescent does not remain a stable feature of Luke 2. It is obvious that the answer he gives his mother in 2: 48–9 is rude to say the least, and what better way to explain the rudeness than by invoking Jesus' divine nature? In his homilies on

Luke, Origen makes no reference to the Lord's behaviour as a human. Emphasizing Jesus' role as the Son of God he notes at Luke 2: 45–6 that he is never to be found among our relatives and friends but only ever in the Temple, that is the church.[54] Erasmus takes over Origen's exegesis and expands it. It is, he notes, a useful mystery (*utile mysterium*) that he who could not be found physically among friends and relatives, was found in the Temple in Jerusalem, which represents both the church militant and the church triumphant, the latter being our native land upon which we hang all our hopes while we are in exile here below.[55] Jesus, in his divine nature, is not to be found in any ecclesiastical institution, but only in the spiritual church (i.e., among the truly devout) and in the church triumphant. The subject of the dispute in the Temple, adds Erasmus sarcastically, is not the squaring of the circle or primary matter or the prime mover, which have nothing to do with Salvation, but the Holy Scripture, through which we may be saved.[56]

Jesus in his divine nature is not to be fixed in any particular church, less still in any school: he is entirely oriented to Scripture and intends nothing other than our salvation. His rude answer to Mary is not to be judged by human criteria. When he tells his mother that he was bound to be in his Father's house and that her search was quite pointless, he is on another, divine level. That still leaves Erasmus with the problem of two Jesuses: the arrogant theologian seems to have very little to do with the humble adolescent. Indeed, the humble, human adolescent, although rather aloof, seems infinitely preferable to the divine Jesus. Erasmus therefore temporarily restores the human adolescent by asserting that the divine Jesus, on seeing his parents' reverent incomprehension, adjusted himself to their weakness and at the same time gave an example to all children of how to obey their parents: 'Children and adolescents who neglect the admonitions of their parents calling them to do good deeds should blush, since Jesus temporarily abandoned his Father's concerns so as not to give the impression of being an insubordinate son.' The example of Jesus' obedience extends beyond relationships between parents and children to include the clergy: 'Simpletons who rebel against their bishops, that is their spiritual fathers, should blush, since Jesus who was the greater obeyed those who were lesser than he; as God he obeyed men.'[57]

Erasmus' main sources here are undoubtedly Origen and Bede,

who also enjoin their readers to follow Jesus' example and obey their parents. Furthermore, Origen sees in Jesus an example not just of filial obedience, but also of the obedience that lesser clerics must show to their bishops.[58] Although both Origen and Bede consider Jesus' human nature as subordinate to his divine, neither elaborates on the distinction between the two natures, which means that neither commits Erasmus' blunder of creating two Jesuses.

Faced with a human Jesus who is fairly aloof and a divine Jesus who is completely inaccessible to human feelings, the reader may find it difficult to sympathize with the Saviour as portrayed by Erasmus. At no point, however, does the human Jesus leave the stage.

THE ADULT JESUS

> Then he went back with them to Nazareth, and continued to be under their authority; his mother treasured up all these things in her heart. As Jesus grew up he advanced in wisdom and in favour with God and men. (Luke 2: 51–2)

Erasmus' comments on this verse do not have a model in the exegetical tradition. His main concern is to show his readers the correct age to take up the ministry of the gospel (*evangelicum munus*). It is the human Jesus that once again serves as an example. He did nothing remarkable until he was thirty, waiting until he had acquired a correct behaviour and learning and had received celestial vocation from the Father.[59] What did Jesus do until the age of thirty? According to Erasmus, as he grew in stature, he commended himself increasingly to men so that they too could make gradual progress in Christian justice. That is to say, before instructing by words and miracles, Christ taught by example.

> When Jesus began his work, he was about thirty years old, the son, as people thought, of Joseph. (Luke 3: 23)

In considering thirty the perfect age for baptism (3: 21–2) and priesthood, Erasmus situates himself well within the exegetical tradition. Although neither Bede nor Theophylact feels compelled to account for Jesus' actions before the age of thirty, both consider that that age is the most perfect. Bede, like Erasmus, is of the opinion that Christ's age is an example and a warning to those who think that one can become a priest and a teacher at any age, especially at a young age.[60] Erasmus adds that old age is also unsuitable, as people's powers fail and they are more prone to be suspected of madness.[61] In sketching out Jesus' actions before the age of thirty and then carefully outlining his motives for becoming a priest at that age, Erasmus portrays the Saviour's transition from the overly gifted, extremely modest adolescent to the perfect priest. The model, although, as we have said, somewhat cold, would not have been thought unattainable by intelligent, well-educated, and pious candidates for the priesthood.

Does Erasmus identify himself with the human Jesus? It is not unreasonable to suppose that Erasmus would have identified with Jesus' desire to give himself an earthly father so as to avoid all suspicion of illegitimacy. This would explain his idiosyncratic exegesis of Luke 3: 23, where he manages to portray a human Jesus who is less than perfect. Earlier exegetes were not at all interested in the moral implications of the presumed identity of the Lord's father. According to Ambrose, Christ wanted to be thought the son of a carpenter, as 'the son of a maker of things,' since his real Father was 'the maker of all things.'[62] For Bede, Jesus wanted to cite Joseph as his father because it was contrary to usage to mention female lineage, and since Joseph and Mary were from the same tribe he implicitly gave his female lineage by mentioning Joseph.[63]

Erasmus gives a more complex explanation: Jesus could not reveal his divine origin until people began believing in him. As it was difficult to persuade them that he was born of a virgin, he took advantage of the popular misbelief about his origins and did not correct it. He did this, according to Erasmus, quite deliberately, feeling that it was no disadvantage to come from a humble home, so long as all suspicion of scandal was avoided. For, Erasmus adds rather sententiously, 'the common opinion of men has it that bad parents hardly ever produce good children.'[64] In his commentary on Luke 2: 41, Theophylact does briefly remark that Mary called Joseph Jesus' father only so as to avoid any suspicion of illegitimacy.[65] However, at no stage does he or any other commentator suggest that Jesus himself was at all anxious about the opinion of others. Erasmus' justification of what he takes to be a white lie on the part of Jesus may be due to his unease about his own illegitimate birth. At the same time, the human Jesus is portrayed as not perfect in profiting from people's gullibility in order to protect his own reputation. The perfect adolescent pupil and priest has a flaw in his character, but it is of no consequence because he is under the constant protection of his divine nature.

> On the third day there was a wedding at Cana-in-Galilee. The mother of Jesus was there, and Jesus and his disciples were guests also. (John 2: 1–3)

The duality of Erasmus' Jesus means that he almost invariably behaves badly as a human whenever he performs miracles according to his divine nature. Although the theological foundation for this apparent discrepancy is perfectly sound and goes back to Augustine,[66] Erasmus' *Paraphrases* by their very nature do not discuss the theological background to Jesus' actions but tend to present it in the guise of his thoughts, motives, and so forth. In the case of the wedding at Cana, Jesus' cruelty to his mother, as brought out by Erasmus, contrasts strangely with the circumstances of the miracle, which was understood as sanctifying marriage and family life.

Erasmus emphasizes first of all that Mary as Jesus' mother was entitled to draw his attention to the lack of wine, but that she showed her deference by not telling him what should be done about it. Jesus' reply to her is intended to show that the Lord performed miracles not to help his relatives but to build up faith in an incredulous people. His *Quid mihi et tibi est mulier?* (John 2: 4: 'Woman, what do have I to do with you' [RSV]) was thus intended to show that maternal authority was quite irrelevant at that moment and that Jesus' divine nature prevailed. Unlike some commentators, such as Thomas Aquinas, who attribute to Mary the obtaining (*procuratio*) of the miracle,[67] Erasmus removes her from it altogether. Indeed, Jesus' opinion of his relatives must have been very low; according to the humanist, his first miracle was deliberately performed in the family circle in order to convince his mother and his relatives of his divinity, concerning which they would have been particularly sceptical because of their blood ties to him.[68] Motives of this type cannot possibly be attributed to Jesus' divine nature. The idea of his 'showing his relatives what he was capable of' can only apply to the human Jesus who, once again, appears in a not very favourable light. As if to remedy this, Erasmus, following Bede, insists that one of the main reasons for the miracle at Cana was Jesus' wish to sanctify marriage, foreseeing that it would subsequently be condemned by some.[69] Jesus also wanted to show that the insipid letter of the Mosaic Law would shortly give place to the full-bodied wine of the Gospel. In order to move the reader's attention decisively away from the less edifying aspects of the human Jesus' behaviour, Erasmus finally puts forward the traditional allegorical interpretation of Mary as the synagogue whose authority was diminishing. She could only point to lack of wine; she could not redeem it herself.[70]

CONCLUSION

The human Jesus and his family as depicted in the *Paraphrases* do not create a pleasant impression. It seems as if Erasmus deliberately wished to break with the medieval tradition instantiated by the apocryphal infancy gospels, by Ludolph of Saxony's *Vita Christi* and by Thomas a Kempis' *Imitatio Christi*, which all, in their different ways, made Jesus and his family into an attainable object of meditation and imitation. He also deliberately departed from the custom of humanists like Christoph Scheurl of Nürnberg, who published apocryphal pieces to do with Jesus' life, such as the *Letter of Lentulus* or the *Letters of Pilate*, in order to situate the Saviour in history and to bring him closer to the faithful.[71] Erasmus deliberately ignored anything that could have added colour or immediacy. Relying very largely on traditional commentaries, which he ably adapted, he created his own biblical characters by adding considerably to the biblical text. He thus portrays Zechariah and Elizabeth as a paradigm of the new priesthood; chastely married, discreet, they have enough moral authority to abolish existing church ceremonies and customs, which do nothing to promote piety. Joseph is hardly referred to by Erasmus. Mary, however, is depicted in great detail as the perfect virgin who, although married, has all the virtues of a nun: aware of her own unworthiness, she shuns all contact with the external world, even omitting to greet neighbours. At the same time, Erasmus makes it plain that Mary is fully human and a recipient of God's grace like any other human.

The human Jesus is by far the most complex character. From a model Renaissance schoolboy, he turns into a priest who deliberately conceals his origins so as to avoid a suspicion of illegitimacy. He credits his mother and his relatives with scepticism about his ability to perform miracles and invariably behaves badly towards them, once his divine nature has started to manifest itself. Erasmus obviously set out to portray the duality of Jesus' nature, but his juxtaposition of Jesus' poor behaviour with the grandeur of God's design is not really successful, as we saw particularly in the episode of the miracle of Cana. Erasmus' human Jesus is not intended to attract, and would seem to provide an antidote to the Jesus of the *Imitatio Christi*, the infancy gospels, and the *Vita Christi*. As well as disparaging philosophy, Erasmus wants to discourage the idea that the Lord and members of his family are attainable through 'one-on-one' spiritual exercises.

NOTES

1 Editio princeps of the *Vita Christi*: Cologne, 1474. The *Vita* went through several editions in the course of the sixteenth century. There is no critical edition to this day. Cf. M.I. Bodenstedt, *The Vita Christi of Ludolphus the Carthusian*.

2 Cf. Jacques Chomarat, *Grammaire et rhétorique chez Érasme*, 1: 639–40: 'Le Christ d'Érasme est bien particulier. Il n'est pas une grande réussite littéraire, s'il est permis de parler en ces termes, mais il est malgré cela d'un profond intérêt ... Sa faiblesse en tant que personnage, c'est la prescience ... Érasme veut bien établir par là la divinité du Christ et de sa mission, mais cela a des effets fâcheux: toutes les fois que le texte évangélique attribue à Jésus de la surprise, du doute, de l'incertitude, de l'étonnement ... la paraphrase d'Érasme explique que cette surprise est feinte, ce doute fictif.'

3 PL 92 (1862): 310.

4 PG 123: 695–6.

5 The text provides no concrete proof that he had, but the popularity of the *Vita Christi* was such that Erasmus was likely to react to it.

6 LB 7: 284D–E: 'Erat enim vere sanctum coniugium non tam coniunctione corporum quam animorum similitudine ac pietatis societate confoederatum.'

7 LB 7: 284E: '... propterea quod essent ambo vere iusti, non iustitia Phariseorum, qui se falsa quadam specie sanctimoniae venditabant oculis hominum ad quaestum et gloriam obscurantes facies suas, praecinente tuba dantes eleemoysnas suas, prolixis precibus in angulis platearum venantes opinionem pietatis ...'

8 LB 7: 284E–F: '... procurante nimirum et hoc divino consilio ut is qui

Christo venienti perhibiturus esset testimonium, esset ipse numeris omnibus populo Iudaeorum commendatus primum generis paterni simul ac materni sacerdotali nobilitate, parentis utriusque inculpata vita, tum suis ipsius raris et admirandis virtutibus ...'

9 LB 7: 285B: 'Nondun enim didicerant carnales Iudaei spiritualem esse populum quem Deus vellet coelesti generatione semper in maius propagari. Nondum audierant esse beatos qui se castrassent propter regnum Dei. Ea res graviter discruciabat animos amborum sed praecipue Elizabet, quae iam probroso cognomine vulgo sterilis vocabatur et ut deploratae sterilitatis mulier inter infelices matronas numerabatur.'

10 Ep 1727, 15 July 1526.

11 Cf. PL 92: 313–14.

12 LB 7: 288C: 'Casti coniugum complexus sunt quos divina promissio copulat, non libido. Sanctus est coitus qui nihil nisi prolem ambit. Pius amor prolis quae non nobis gignitur sed publicae saluti.'

13 PG 13: 184.

14 LB 7: 288C: 'Nec enim ignorabat quam sit pronum ad male suspicandum, simul et male loquendum vulgus hominum.'

15 LB 7: 288C–D: 'Spectabat et illud prudens mulieris animus, non esse iactandum Dei donum apud populum donec certum esset, ne si quid fefelisset sterilitatis probrum, ob frustra speratam anui prolem, conduplicaretur. Verum ubi iam sese certis argumentis cognovisset gravidam, sic suae felicitati gratulata est ut hoc totum quicquid esset, ad Dei bonitatem referret.'

16 PG 123: 701: 'Invenerit gratiam apud Deum, hoc est placuerit Deo.'

17 PL 92: 316D: '... quae nimirum gratiam quae nulla alia meruerat, assequitur ut ipsum videlicet gratiae concipiat et generet auctorem.'

18 Origen, PG 13: 1814–15; Ambrose, CCSL 14: 30–1.

19 PL 92: 316D.

20 PL 92: 317A: 'Trepidare virginum est et ad omnes viri ingressus pavere, omnes viri affatus vereri. Discant mulieres propositum pudoris imitari.'

21 PL 92: 318C.

22 PL 92: 319B.

23 LB 7: 289A–B: 'Humiles delegerat Deus ne quid in hoc coelesti negotio sibi mundus vindicaret. Moris inculpatissimos ac purissimos delegerat ne quid in hoc criminis posset impingi. Casto coniugio iunctos delegerat ut virginei partus arcanum in suum usque tempus caeleretur, simulque ne testis idoneus deesset rei alioquin incredibili quod citra virilem congressum virgo peperisset.'

24 LB 7: 290A–B: 'Non tibi in hoc additus est sponsus ut is te matrem faciat aut tu illum patrem, sed hoc ratione divina providentia tuae incolumitati, tuae famae ac virginitati debitae tranquillitati consultum esse voluit.'

25 LB 7: 289F: '... non praesumebat animo se quoque cum filio regnante regnaturam, nec ignorabat nihil esse tam arduum quod solo nutu non posset Deus.'

26 LB 7: 290A: 'Placet enim utrique castitas et hanc felicitatem nobis, si liceret, cuperemus esse perpetuam.'

27 Noël Béda, *Annotationum in Jacobum Fabrum ... libri duo et in Des. Erasmum Roterodamum liber vnus qui ordine tertius est* (Cologne: P. Quentel, 1526), 247v–8r.

28 CCSL 14: 39–40.

29 PL 92: 323C.

30 PG 123: 707–8, 713–14.

31 LB 7: 291C: 'Siquidem vera pietas potius gaudet de felicitate aliena quam studet iactare suam. Amat secretum virginitas, non evocatur ab aedium intimis nisi provocet officium. In publico properat, in officio lentior est. In toto itinere neminem salutavit Maria donec ventum esset ad Elizabet.'

32 Béda, *Annotationum libri duo*, 248r.

33 Theophylact, PG 123: 713–14; Bede, PL 92: 324B.

34 Thomas Aquinas, *Catena aurea in quatuor Evangelia*, ed. A. Guarienti, 2: 23A–B. Cf. LB 7: 294D: 'Zacharias enim Hebraeis sonat idem quod memor Domini. Ioannes a gratia dictus est.' Origen gives the etymology *memor Domini* for Zechariah, but takes John to mean *demonstrans*. Chrysostom in the passage cited in the *Catena aurea* mentions no etymology for Zechariah, but says that John means *gratia Dei*. Erasmus' conflation of Origen and Chrysostom would suggest that he did use the *Catena aurea* for his *Paraphrases*.

35 LB 7: 294E: 'Et adhuc hodie sunt quibus magis arridet nomen Zachariae, quam Ioannis, nimirum hi qui nondum patiuntur aboleri circumcisionem, neomenias, lotiones, dies festos, ieiunia, delectum ciborum, sacrificia, re videlicet clamitantes: nomen Ioannis nolumus, Zachariam volumus.'

36 Béda, *Annotationum libri duo*, 248r–v.

37 LB 7: 298B: 'Ad eam igitur professionem in Syria peragendam missus est ex auctoritate Caesaris Augusti et Senatus consulto Quirinus eius provinciae praeses. Hic autem erat primus census, qui sub hoc praeside fuit actus in Syria. Nam sub eodem post acti sunt et alii.' For Bede's much lengthier paraphrase of Josephus' account in *Antiquitates Iudaicae* 18.1, see PL 92: 328D.

38 LB 7: 297F–8A: '... ut appareret quanto latius pateret ditio Christi quam Caesaris ... Qui Caesari dant nomen, quid aliud quam servitutem profitentur et rem familiarem comperiunt arctiorem? Qui novo principi dant nomen, libertatem accipiunt cum donatione salutis aeternae.'

39 For Origen's view, see PG 13: 1828.

40 PL 92: 328B.

41 See chapter 5.
42 Allen Ep 1195: 23–30, to Marliano, 1521; Ep 1352: 118–27, 158–82, to Hadrian VI, 22 March 1523.
43 Bede, PL 92: 331B: '... iuxta divinitatis excellentiam unigenitus a Patre et iuxta fraternam societatem primogenitus est omni creaturae.' LB 7: 298F: 'Matri erat unicus filius, nobis erat primogenitus quos sibi spiritu iunctos fratres reddidit et haereditatis aeternae consortes ne solus veniret ad patrem ...'
44 Theophylact, PG 123: 727–8; Origen, PG 13: 1836; cf. Bede, PL 92: 337.
45 LB 7: 301B–C: 'An vero quicquam sordidum poterat esse in foetu, qui coelitus natus in hoc venerat ut solus omne genus hominum purgaret a cunctis vitiorum sordibus?'
46 LB 7: 301A–B: 'Rursum quum adesset dies a partu quadragesimus, quo Lex iubet masculinum foetum exhiberi Domino proque purgatione puerperae simul et pueri nati, quod vulgaris mulierum partus non absque sordibus corporis constet, offerri munus ...'
47 Béda, *Annotationum libri duo*, 248v: '... decrevit Deus tres et triginta dies tantum quorum primus, partu octavus erat, quo circumcidebatur, secundum mandatum Abrahae factum, parvulus. Septem vero et triginta tres numerum quadragenarium reddunt. Quod hic Erasmus asserit plane et Scripturae sacrae obviat et ecclesiae ritui, quae purificationis sanctae Dei matris commemorationem die quadragesimo celebriter agit.'
48 LB 7: 301A: 'Redemptus est exiguo pretio, qui sui sanguinis pretio redempturus erat universum mundum.'
49 Bede, PL 92: 348A: 'Christus in eo quod puer erat, id est habitum humanae fragilitatis induerat, crescere et confortari habebat. In eo vero quod etiam Verbum Dei et Deus aeternus erat, nec confortari indigebat nec habebat augeri.' Cf. Theophylact ad loc.
50 LB 7: 305A–B: 'Augescebat et spiritus robor, in dies magis ac magis sese exserentis vultu, incessu, sermone, factis in quibus nihil erat quod non spiraret modestiam, castitatem, suavitatem, pietatem.'
51 LB 7: 305C–D: '... ab ipsis, ut aiunt, incunabulis arcere ab omni lascivia, sed sanctis moribus veraeque pietatis studiis assuefacere, dum adhuc tenera est aetas, dum adhuc molle et ad omnem virtutis institutionem sequax ingenium.'
52 LB 7: 306C: 'Et tamen interim aberat faustus, aberat procacitas, aberat iactantia, quae vitia pueris adesse solent praecocis ingenii. Interrogabat velut discendi cupidus, interrogatus modestissime simul et prudentissime respondebat.'
53 Notably in the *Epistola ad lectorem* in the *Paraphrase on Matthew*: LB7: **3r–v.
54 PG 13: 1847–8.
55 LB 7: 306C–D: 'Nec hoc interim omnino vacat utili mysterio quod

qui non potuit inveniri inter notos et cognatos secundum carnem, Hierosolymis in Templo repertus est. Siquidem illa civitas religionis opinione celebris gerebat imaginem vel ecclesiae militantis in terris vel triumphantis in coelis. Haec est enim patria nostra ad quem suspiramus, intelligentes quod hic versamur in exilio, non habentes permanentem civitatem.'

56 LB 7: 306D–E.

57 LB 7: 308A–C: 'Erubescant pueri et adolescentes qui negligunt monita parentum ad honesta vocantium quum Iesus ad tempus reliquerit patris negotium ne quam praeberet speciem filii immorigeri. Erubescant idiotae rebelles adversus episcopos suos, videlicet patres spiritales, quum Iesus maior obsequundaret minoribus, Deus hominibus.'

58 Bede, PL 92: 350C. Cf. Origen, PG 13: 1852: 'Discamus filii subiecti esse parentibus nostris; maior minori subiicitur ... Quid loquar de parentibus et filiis? Si Iesus Filius Dei subiicitur Ioseph et Mariae, ego non subiiciar episcopo, qui mihi a Deo ordinatus est pater?'

59 LB 7: 308C: '... nos interim admonens exemplo suo ne quis ad evangelicum munus tenere et importune semet ingerat, priusquam aetatis accessu, moribus inculpatis, doctrina sacra, coelestique vocatione docendi sibi colligat auctoritatem.'

60 Theophylact, PG 123: 743–4; Bede, PL 92: 359D: 'Iesus annorum triginta baptizatur et tunc demum incipit signa facere et docere, legitimum videlicet et maturum tempus ostendens aetatis his qui omnem aetatem vel ad sacerdotium vel ad docendum putant opportunam.'

61 LB 7: 316B, paraphrasing Luke 3: 21: 'Proinde aetas matura delecta est et expectata quod adolescentiae desit auctoritas propter publicam opinionem imperitiae; senectus minus habeat ponderis ob vires ingenii defectas ac suspicionem delirationis.'

62 CCSL 13: 76.

63 PL 92: 361A.

64 LB 7: 316C: 'Siquidem haec est communis opinio, vix unquam e malis parentibus nasci bonos liberos.'

65 PG 123: 733–4.

66 Augustine, *In Ioh*, tract. 8, CCSL 36: 89; *De fide et symbolo*, 4.9, PL 40: 186.

67 Thomas Aquinas, *Super Evangelium S. Ioannis lectura*, ad loc.

68 LB 7: 516B: 'Ab hoc facto dominus Iesus auspicatus est in Cana Galileae miraculorum gestionem, paulatim prolaturus mundo divinae suae virtutis argumenta. Nam primum hoc in re non perinde seria et privatim gestum est, ac propemodum matris et cognatorum affectibus indultum est qui hoc contemptius sentiebant de Iesu quod essent illi sanguinis propinquitate coniuncti.'

69 Cf. Aquinas, *Super Evangelium S. Ioannis lectura*, ad loc. (ed. R. Cai):

'Secundo vero ut errorem quorumdam excluderet qui nuptias damnarent, quia, ut dicit Beda: "si thoro immaculato et nuptiis debita castitate celebratis culpa inesset, nequaquam Dominus ad has venire voluisset."'

70 LB 7: 516D: 'Aderat illic et mater Iesu synagogae typum gerens, cuius auctoritas minuitur: admonet tamen de vino sed ipsa non praestat.'

71 Cf. Irena Backus, 'Christoph Scheurl and His Anthology of New Testament Apocrypha.'

SEVEN

Exegesis and Marriage in Erasmus' *Paraphrases on the New Testament*

Hilmar M. Pabel

In an article published in 1966, Roland Bainton observed: 'The Paraphrases of Erasmus have never received their due.'[1] Similarly, Jacques Chomarat and Friedhelm Krüger, who in the 1980s produced the most substantial treatments of the *Paraphrases on the New Testament* to date, have also lamented the scholarly neglect from which the *Paraphrases* have suffered.[2] In the same year that Bainton published his article, John Aldridge unwittingly proved Bainton's observation. He set up a dubious dichotomy between Erasmus' *Annotations on the New Testament* as a work of exegesis and the *Paraphrases* as 'primarily a work of explaining the meaning of the [scriptural] passage in understandable terms, rather than exegeting the text itself.'[3] Consequently, Aldridge paid no attention to the *Paraphrases* in his study of Erasmus' method of interpreting Scripture, and, unfortunately, Peter Walter's more recent monograph on the same topic barely refers to the *Paraphrases*.[4] While Manfred Hoffmann acknowledges that in the *Paraphrases* and especially in his psalm commentaries Erasmus 'repeatedly accounted for his exegetical approach and presented hints at his hermeneutic as well' and insists that an analysis of Erasmus' theology 'must include his actual exegesis of Old and New Testament texts,' his approach to Erasmus' biblical hermeneutic is too systematic to allow for a detailed consideration of the exegesis evident in the *Paraphrases*.[5]

Chomarat has rightly asked how one can separate the *Annotations* and the *Paraphrases* when they both serve as commentaries on the New Testament. In the one, a discontinuous commentary, the voice of the exegete speaks to us; in the other, a continuous exposition, the voice is that of the text being paraphrased.[6] The *Paraphrases* are in large measure the fruit of Erasmus' philological and exegetical labours in the *Annotations* and constitute a continuous form of exegesis.

Chomarat and Krüger suggest two different but potentially complementary approaches to studying the *Paraphrases*. The former pays close attention to the conspicuous rhetorical dynamic within the *Paraphrases*, whereas the latter is most interested in the modalities of Erasmian exegesis, particularly his application of the allegorical and tropological sense. In the analysis at the end of his book of what one might call Erasmus' political theology,[7] Krüger anticipates a more recent approach. Scholars have begun to read the *Paraphrases* thematically as a rich deposit of Erasmus' religious ideas, probing these sources to elucidate, among other things, his standards for appropriate clerical behaviour, his concepts of justification and holiness, his hostility towards Judaism, and his reading of early Christian history.[8]

One theme that still requires serious attention is Erasmus' concept of marriage in light of the significant New Testament passages upon which the church fathers and medieval thinkers constructed elaborate theologies of marriage and upon which medieval canonists built a canon law of marriage. In this study, I will analyse Erasmian scriptural exegesis in the *Paraphrases* according to three categories: the dignity of marriage, the relative merits of marriage and virginity, and the extent to which the marriage bond was indivisible. Erasmus contributed to the controversy surrounding these three subjects. Against a traditional theological culture that elevated virginity above marriage, he pressed the claims of married life. While he acknowledged the theological and canonistic consensus that a valid, consummated marriage may under no circumstances be dissolved, he hoped that the church would revise its position to help married people in unhappy circumstances. Thus, he has acquired the reputation for helping pave the way for the modern concept of divorce.

As the *Ratio verae theologiae* (1518) makes abundantly clear, the enterprise of theology and of preaching, tasks that in Erasmus' mind were inseparable, must be deeply rooted in a study of

Scripture that required a philological, rhetorical, and literary analysis of the sacred text in order to interpret it. One must, furthermore, not interpret Scripture in a vacuum. Whether he finds support for his positions among the church fathers or exposes the shortcomings of medieval commentators, Erasmus demonstrates in the *Annotations* that a close familiarity with the Christian exegetical tradition is vital for the on-going practice of exegesis. To comprehend fully Erasmian exegesis in the *Paraphrases* requires its own Erasmian analysis. Accordingly, wherever appropriate, I take into account the philological and rhetorical dimensions of that exegesis along with the historical context in which Erasmus operates. Such an approach reveals the complex dynamic of Erasmus' thinking about marriage in the *Paraphrases*. He asserts the dignity of marriage while retaining esteem for virginity and indicates the legitimacy of divorce for the specific case of adultery within the more general context of a rhetoric of the indivisibility of the marriage bond.

THE DIGNITY OF MARRIAGE

One of the most important grounds for the dignity of marriage is its status as one of the seven sacraments. Erasmus always accepted it as a sacrament, as is evident in the *Christiani hominis institutum*, a catechetical poem first published in 1514 (CWE 85: 96/97), in the controversial *Encomium matrimonii* (1518), in the 1526 treatise on marriage, the *Christiani matrimonii institutio* (LB 5: 619E–20B), and in the long catechism *Explanatio symboli apostolorum sive catechismus* that appeared in print in 1533 (CWE 70: 340). In the *Encomium*, Erasmus writes that marriage was first of all the sacraments to be established by God. Whereas the other sacraments were instituted on earth as remedies against sin, marriage alone was instituted in paradise and was meant for the companionship of happiness (ASD I-5: 388). In the *Encomium*, Erasmus also invokes the authority of Paul in Ephesians 5: 32: *Magnum, inquit Paulus, matrimonii sacramentum est, in Christo et in ecclesia* (ASD I-5: 390). The Vulgate translation reads: *sacramentum hoc magnum est ego autem dico in Christo et in ecclesia.* This text from the Vulgate was the crucial scriptural proof text in medieval theology for the sacramental nature of marriage. What is surprising is that Erasmus quotes the Vulgate when he himself had disagreed with its translation. Two years previously, in 1516, in the first edition of his New Testament, he had translated the passage as: *Mysterium hoc magnum est, verum ego loquor de Christo et de ecclesia* (LB 6: 856A). Jacques Lefèvre d'Étaples in 1512 had similarly revised the Vulgate: *hoc mysterium magnum est. ego autem dico in CHRISTO & ecclesia.*[9] Curiously, the French humanist provides no explanation for this controversial reading. By translating *musterion* as *mysterium* and not as *sacramentum* Erasmus, however, indicated his belief that Ephesians 5: 32 could not be used to argue that marriage was a sacrament 'according to the distinctive and exact meaning of the word,' as he specified in the 1522 edition of the *Annotations* (LB 6: 855B). After elaborating upon this opinion, he concludes the note, again in the 1522 and subsequent editions, by pointing out that he does not deny that marriage is a sacrament; however, he calls for an examination of whether the passage could serve as the basis for calling marriage a sacrament in the same way as baptism is so nominated (LB 6: 855E).[10]

It is not surprising that medieval theologians took Ephesians 5: 32 to refer to marriage as a sacrament. At 5: 31 Paul quotes Genesis 2: 24, which speaks of a man leaving his parents to become one flesh with his wife, and then immediately proceeds to say that 'this' is a 'great mystery' or, as the Vulgate would have it, a 'great sacrament.' But he then refers this mystery to Christ and the church. Consequently, Erasmus believes that the great mystery refers not to marriage, but to the relationship between Christ and the church, as is clear from his *Paraphrase on Ephesians* (1520).

Erasmus writes that a man will join himself in such a way to his wife that the two become one 'in the supreme union of bodies and souls' (LB 7: 987D–E), ensuring that the marital bond is not simply a physical one. The paraphrase continues:

> Here there is subsumed a certain marvelous thing [*Subest hic ineffabile quoddam*] and a vast mystery [*ingens arcanum*], how what in Adam and Eve is manifested in the form of a type is mystically [*mystice*] accomplished in Christ and in the church. Whoever closely examines this indivisible bond will comprehend the great mystery that underlies it [*intelliget subesse magnum mysterium*]. For inasmuch as Christ [*ipse*] was one with the Father, so also did he wish all of his followers to be one with him. (LB 7: 987E)

Here the most conspicuous feature of Erasmus' exegetical rhetoric is repetition, evident in the recurrence of the verb *subesse* and in the idea of mystery, expressed twice as a noun (*arcanum, mysterium*), once as an adverb (*mystice*), and, arguably, once as an adjective (*ineffabile*). He emphatically directs attention away from the marriage relationship to the mystery that undergirds it and thus supports his translation and the reasoning for it in the *Annotations*. The paraphrase coheres perfectly with his biblical scholarship; it ties the dignity of marriage to the unity between Christ and the church without even hinting at the notion of sacrament.

Of course, the paraphrase is inconsistent with the *Encomium*, but before we dismiss the traditional rendering of Ephesians 5: 32 in the latter as part of a declamatory exercise, we should note that later in life Erasmus invoked the Vulgate on at least two more occasions. He points out in his treatise on marriage that, given the many symbolic mysteries inherent in marriage, Paul rightly said, *Sacramentum hoc magnum est, ego autem dico in Christo et in ecclesia* (LB 5: 623A), although later in the treatise he writes that Paul calls Christ's relationship with the church a *magnum mysterium* (LB 5: 703B). In 1535, the year before his death, Erasmus published his prayer-book, the *Precationes aliquot novae*. It includes a prayer to be said on the eve of one's wedding ('Sub nuptias'). Rehearsing the reasons for marriage's dignity, the prayer affirms that, through Paul, God had taught that the union between man and woman was 'a great sacrament in Christ and in the church' (LB 5: 1205D). It is difficult to say why Erasmus departs from his scholarly judgment. If it is because he wished to uphold marriage as a sacrament when Protestants were rejecting it as such, then why did he not revise his paraphrase? The *Christiani matrimonii institutio*, the prayers, and the *Paraphrases* all shared the same objective of promoting piety. Yet perhaps because the *Paraphrases* were closely connected with his New Testament scholarship Erasmus felt he could not defy the latter in the former. Since he persisted in the belief that marriage was a sacrament, he allowed himself the licence to leave aside accuracy in translation and interpretation for the sake of discussing the theological symbolism of marriage and of cementing the bond of love between those prayerfully preparing to marry.

In 'Sub nuptias,' Erasmus refers to another source for the dignity of marriage. God adorned marriage with a mystic gift at Cana in Galilee when his Son changed 'tasteless water into choice wine' (LB 5: 1205D). After recounting the story of the miracle at the wedding at Cana (John 2: 9–10) in the *Paraphrase on John* (1523), he pauses to explain the significance of this, Jesus' first sign. This results in a considerable amplification of and extrapolation from John 2: 11. The first explanation that Erasmus adduces for the sign's significance involves Jesus' presence at the wedding: 'For in the first place he wanted to honour weddings with his presence, foreseeing that there would some day be those who condemned them as filthy, though an honourable marriage and an unstained marriage-bed is a thing most pleasing to God' (CWE 46: 40). The original passage says nothing about Jesus' desire to safeguard the reputation of marriage. For Erasmus, John 2: 11 becomes a platform from which to defend marriage, and to consolidate his position he links this passage with Hebrews 13: 4, which reads 'Let marriage be held in honour among all, and let the marriage bed be undefiled' (RSV).[11] The use of one scriptural logion to help expound another is a common practice in the *Paraphrases*. Erasmus, like Christian exegetes before and after him, believed in the textual coherence of the New Testament.

Erasmus also assimilates Hebrews 13: 4 into his paraphrase on 1 Timothy 4: 3. The context is a warning that some people will depart from the faith. They will, among other things, forbid marriage. Erasmus goes beyond the original scriptural text to launch a bitter attack against them:

> Inwardly, such men are sodden with envy, hatred, avarice, ambition, and other diseases diametrically opposed to genuine godliness; nevertheless, in order to procure for themselves a reputation for godliness through their 'novel' and 'wonderful' doctrine, they will follow the example of the Essenes and forbid couples from being joined in lawful wedlock, as if a chaste marriage and a stainless marriage bed were not something honourable in God's view. They will demand to be taken for saints because they live in celibacy, though they are infected with the countless other diseases of their vices. In a word they are not free from lust, only from wives. (CWE 44: 24)

By associating the opponents of marriage with the Essenes, who are never mentioned in the New Testament, Erasmus goes out of his way to make them part of the scriptural past. Yet, precisely because he does this, one may wonder whether, in his mind, the

Essenes actually stand for sixteenth-century champions of celibacy and denigrators of marriage, those who neglect the exhortation to hold marriage in honour. The irony that pervades the description of those who depart from the faith is rhetorically appropriate. In the Vulgate text, their prohibition of marriage is grammatically dependent on their hypocrisy: *Spiritus autem manifeste dicit, quia in novissimis temporibus discedent quidam a fide, attendentes spiritibus erroris, et doctrinis daemoniorum, in hypocrisi loquentium mendacium, et cauteriatam habentium suam conscientiam, prohibentium nubere* ... (1 Timothy 4: 1–3, emphasis added). Erasmus develops the theme of hypocrisy to develop the lack of sincerity, the incongruence between the morals and the ideals of the champions of celibacy. He begins the paraphrase on 1 Timothy 4 by referring to those 'who will abandon the sincerity of evangelical faith' and goes on to comment: 'Under the guise of a feigned godliness they will say things at variance with evangelical truth' (CWE 44: 24).

Erasmus' interpretation of John 2: 11 and 1 Timothy 4: 3 is a tropological one. The two paraphrased passages have the effect of issuing the moral imperative of Hebrews 13: 4. One should honour marriage. Of the three classical goals of oratory – to teach, to move, and to delight – it is clear that the first is operative in both paraphrases. In the *Annotations*, Erasmus writes that the text of Hebrews 13: 4 does not preach in praise of marriage; it teaches (LB 6: 1022B). Accordingly, he integrates the didactic value of this text into his exposition of the other two. Erasmus wishes to teach respect for marriage, but it is equally obvious in the paraphrase on 1 Timothy 4: 3 that he intends to move his audience to hold the denigrators of marriage in contempt. He accomplishes his purpose by amplifying his texts. Whereas the Gospel passage affords no basis for Erasmus' amplification, the paraphrase on the passage from the epistle develops ideas present in the text.

A final amplification that deserves mention in the context of the dignity of marriage is Erasmus' paraphrase on 1 Corinthians 12: 13. He first published the *Paraphrase on 1 Corinthians* in 1519. Initially he adhered closely to the original text. The Vulgate reads: *Etenim in uno Spiritu omnes nos in unum corpus baptizati sumus, sive Iudaei, sive gentiles, sive servi, sive liberi.* Erasmus paraphrases: *Quandoquidem ex aequo participes baptismi per eundem & omnibus communem spiritum in idem corpus compacti sumus, siue Iudaei, siue Graeci, siue serui, siue liberi* ('For as equal partakers of baptism we have been grafted into the same body through the same Spirit common to all, whether Jews or Greeks, slaves or free').[12] Of moment is not the more elegant Erasmian redaction or the correction, in keeping with the philological observation in the *Annotations* (LB 6: 720F), of *gentiles* to read *Graeci*, but the addition to the paraphrase in the revised *Tomus secundus* of 1532 (reissued in 1534), which established the text of the paraphrase for Erasmus' *Opera omnia* of 1540 and of 1703.[13] Erasmus enlarges the scope of the Christian equality endowed by baptism beyond 'Jews or Greeks, slaves or free' to include men and women, the married and the celibate, the powerful and the powerless: *sive mares, sive foeminae, sive coniugati, sive coelibes, sive potentes, sive humiles* (LB 7: 899A–B). Revisiting the paraphrase after thirteen years, Erasmus chooses to make 1 Corinthians 12: 13 an instrument for affirming the spiritual equality of marriage with celibacy. In a Catholic religious and theological culture that had long exalted virginity above the married state, the addition of *sive coniugati, sive coelibes* was highly significant.

MARRIAGE OR VIRGINITY?

Erasmus has acquired the reputation of an advocate for marriage among scholars who are both sympathetic towards and critical of him. Emile Telle, whom we can associate with the latter camp, wrote of the humanist's 'philogamie' as the obverse of his supposed campaign to destroy monasticism.[14] In the treatise on marriage, Erasmus reminds his readers that marriage is a sacrament, but not virginity (LB 5: 620A). He urges married couples not to be disheartened by 'the splendour of virgins and priests' but to take pride in the dignity of marriage by ensuring that its dignity corresponds to a life of piety (LB 5: 623B–C). To examine Erasmus' approach to the relative merits of marriage and virginity in his scriptural exegesis we must turn to the *Paraphrase on Matthew* (1522) and the *Paraphrase on 1 Corinthians* (1519).

The crucial text in Matthew is 19: 10–12, but it is necessary to keep in mind verse 9 for context:

> 9. 'And I say to you [Jesus asserts]: whoever divorces his wife, except for unchastity, and marries another, commits adultery; and he who marries a divorced woman commits adultery.'

> 10. The disciples said to him, 'If such is the case of a man with his wife, it is not expedient to marry.'
> 11. But he said to them, 'Not all men can receive this precept, but only those to whom it is given.
> 12. For there are eunuchs who have been so from birth, and there are eunuchs who have been made eunuchs by men, and there are eunuchs who have made themselves eunuchs for the sake of the kingdom of heaven. He who is able to receive this, let him receive it.' (RSV)

Some forty years ago, Jacques Dupont noted that according to the common or traditional interpretation, espoused by ancient and modern exegetes alike, this passage was about celibacy.[15] The key to the interpretation of the passage is Jesus' final comment in verse 12. If what is to be received is the disciples' belief that it was not expedient to marry, then it makes perfect sense for Thomas Aquinas, for example, to state in his commentary on Matthew that the entire passage was 'about the perfection of the chaste' (*de perfectione continentium*).[16] But if verse 12 refers back to verse 9, then Jesus in the first instance was not issuing a general summons to live in chastity but was rather instructing those who had divorced their wives to refrain from a subsequent marriage in order to enter the kingdom of heaven. This, Dupont believed, was 'the more concrete and more immediate significance' of verse 12, although he did not want to rule out the traditional interpretation.[17]

It appears that, in the West, Jerome's influence was decisive in establishing the exegetical tradition of Matthew 19: 9–12. In his commentary on Matthew, he explained the disciples' disenchantment with marriage. Wives were a 'heavy burden' (*grave pondus*) if one could not send them away except on the grounds of 'fornication.' How could one put up with a woman who was drunk, irascible, possessed of wicked morals, dissolute, gluttonous, fickle, quarrelsome, and abusive? Yet, whether we want to or not, we must endure such a woman, 'for since we were free, we freely subjected ourselves to servitude' (*Cum enim essemus liberi voluntarie nos subiecimus servituti*). Wittingly or unwittingly disagreeing with Origen, who argued that all three categories of eunuchs must be interpreted in a spiritual sense,[18] Jerome held that the first two types of eunuchs must be taken in a literal or 'carnal' sense, but the third type in a spiritual sense. Only those who have become eunuchs for the kingdom of heaven are promised a reward because they have done so for Christ's sake. The other two types of eunuchs are obliged to chastity by necessity; they have not chosen it. When Jesus says at the end of verse 12, 'He who is able to receive it, let him receive it' (*Qui potest capere capiat* in the Vulgate), he exhorts his followers or soldiers (*milites*), urging them on to the 'reward of chastity.' Jerome's paraphrase on this passage is an exhortation that continues the military metaphor: *qui potest pugnare pugnet, superet ac triumphet* ('he who can fight, let him fight, let him conquer, and moreover let him triumph').[19]

Bede followed Jerome's misogynistic understanding of verse 10 as well as his interpretation of the eunuchs and quotes Jerome's military exhortation,[20] but, more important, the *Glossa ordinaria*, the standard medieval interpretation of the Bible, canonized the Hieronymian exegesis while adding some clarifications. The interlinear gloss on *non expedit nubere* of verse 10, for example, indicated that this referred to the goodness of chastity: *id est, bonum est continere.*[21] Commenting on verse 11, Jerome insisted that one should not think that the virgins who have their gift from God acquired it through fate or fortune, but what is given comes to those who ask and wish for it and who work to preserve it.[22] The interlinear gloss places the emphasis squarely upon the divine gift. Only those can receive Jesus' saying to whom it has been given 'since we have not the ability except for God's grace.' The marginal gloss makes clear that the 'precept of chastity' is 'not given to all by God.' In the fifteenth century, the traditional interpretation was alive and well in the theologian and mystic Dionysius the Carthusian. He pointed out in his commentary on Matthew that the disciples believed it was inexpedient to marry not only because marriage was less meritorious than virginity but also on account of servitude and of the misfortunes of the present life, as when a woman is disputatious, gluttonous, impudent, or afflicted with a serious and incurable disease. Those who of their own volition live chastely 'lead the angelic life in the flesh.' Like Jerome, Dionysius notes that the Saviour calls forth his fighters (*pugiles*) 'to the rewards of chastity.'[23]

The patristic roots and the medieval continuation of the interpretation of Matthew 19: 10–12 provide the essential context for Erasmus' paraphrase (LB 7: 103E–4B). Erasmus adheres closely to the exegetical tradition, although he does leave his own peculiar mark in his exposition of the text. In his paraphrase, the disciples respond to Jesus' censure of divorce: 'If this is the situation of husbands, that they cannot be released from a wife, if she is a nuisance [*si displiceat*], it is obvious that one should abstain from marriage.' The potential burden that a wife can be on a husband explains why the disciples had their doubts about marriage: 'Indeed, it is hard service [*dura servitus*] to endure a woman who is peevish, quarrelsome, drunk or beset by another similar vice.' Jesus does not disapprove of his disciples' reply because 'he wanted them to be free of the servitude of marriage [*a servitute matrimonii*].' Not only has Erasmus taken the word *servitus* directly from Jerome; by repeating it he also reinforces the unpleasant concept of the thralldom of marriage.

Erasmus proceeds to emphasize that celibacy, though laudable, is only meant for a few. Jesus explains that, except for those who have the strength to refrain completely from sexual intercourse, 'it is not safe to avoid marriage.' Only a very few could remain chaste 'because this physical impulse [*hic affectus corporis*] is so common to all people that no other impulse was more violent or invincible.' True, 'not to be fettered to marriage' (*non alligari matrimonio*) brings greater freedom, 'but it is safer to be chaste within the confines of marriage than to be defiled by promiscuous intercourse [*vago concubitu pollui*].' While Jesus wants to indicate what was best and invite his followers to it 'with the reward of freedom,' he is not so bold as to insist on what practically surpasses human strength. To consolidate his point Erasmus rephrases Jesus' comment at Matthew 19: 11 to read: 'Not all are capable of this saying, but only those to whom it has been given from above' (*Non omnes capaces sunt huius sermonis, sed hi duntaxat, quibus datum est divinitus*). The Vulgate records Jesus as saying: *Non omnes capiunt verbum istud, sed quibus datum est.* Here we notice, of course, Erasmus' characteristic preference for *sermo* over the Vulgate's *verbum*, although in his New Testament he wrote: *Non omnes capaces sunt huius dicti* (LB 6: 100B). We also observe that Erasmus qualifies Jesus' speech in two important ways. The adverb *divinitus* corresponds to the traditional explanation that the gift of chastity comes from God. The restrictive adverb *duntaxat*, however, is consonant with the increasingly obvious Erasmian agenda in expounding a scriptural text that had long been read as recommending chastity above marriage.

While Erasmus gives expression to the traditional praise of chastity, he wishes to circumscribe chastity within a relatively small number of individuals. In this light, rendering the original

Greek of 19: 11 as *non omnes capaces sunt* instead of the Vulgate's *non omnes capiunt* is significant. According to the marginal gloss on *non omnes capiunt*, Jesus says, '"not all receive." He does not say "[all] are not able to receive," but "not all wish to receive."' Thus, the *Glossa ordinaria* makes clear that refraining completely from sexual relations is a matter of personal choice not of personal ability. Presumably, everyone can be celibate. Erasmus disagrees, and this disagreement reflects his divergent reading of 19: 11. As Erasmus explains in the *Annotations*, the Greek verb *chorousin* does not mean *capiunt* in the sense of *intelligunt* or *apprehendunt*. The verb does not mean 'they understand' or 'they take hold of.' Instead, it has the sense of *capaces sunt* ('they are capable') in the same way that a place is called *capax* ('capacious') that is sufficiently spacious to receive what is placed in it (LB 6: 100C–D). Erasmus' philological position in the *Annotations* underlies his exegesis in the *Paraphrase on Matthew*. Celibacy is certainly a divine gift, but it is also a matter of human capacity, of human strength. Since only few have the strength, Erasmus declares that marriage is morally safer than celibacy, even though it is not morally superior to celibacy. Consequently, in his note on 19: 12, he complains sarcastically that in the category of the eunuchs for the kingdom of heaven, we place those who 'either by cunning or by fear are forced into celibacy.' They can frequent prostitutes, but they may not take a wife. If they acknowledge having a concubine, they are Catholic priests; if they prefer to marry, they are cast into the fire. Parents who intend their sons to be celibates would treat them with greater kindness by castrating them as boys than by casting them 'into this conflagration of lust' (LB 6: 100E).

Erasmus continues his paraphrase by commenting that those to whom the gift of celibacy has been given from above are so consumed by gospel holiness that they disregard the sexual impulse 'freely and of their own will' (*sponte volentesque*). A 'chaste celibacy' deserves praise only if it undertaken 'out of zeal for gospel piety.' We can see that Erasmus is returning to the traditional interpretation by insisting that celibacy must be the result of a free choice and must have a religious orientation. He also follows the conventional wisdom on the three types of eunuchs. Those who are born eunuchs have no inclination for sex owing either to 'a defect of a colder nature' (*vitio naturae frigidioris*) or to some other mysterious natural force. Here again Erasmus has borrowed from Jerome, who speaks of the eunuchs who have a more frigid nature (*qui frigidioris naturae sunt*),[24] but Erasmus makes it clear that there is something wrong about this. Neither these eunuchs, Erasmus continues, nor those 'whom men castrate' deserve any praise for their chastity. The gospel has its own eunuchs, and they are certainly blessed. The paraphrase underlines that they are not literally eunuchs. Those who have castrated themselves for the kingdom of heaven have not suffered any physical dismemberment, but 'out of love for the gospel' they have overcome their impulse for sex.

Jerome's concluding military exhortation becomes in Erasmus' paraphrase an athletic challenge: 'You see the palm of victory set out in the open. Let him compete who runs,[25] and who trusts in his own strength. Let him carry off the prize [*brabium*] who can. Those who compete bravely and willingly will not lack the favour of the president of the games [*favor agonothetae*].' In writing this, Erasmus was obviously thinking of 1 Corinthians 9: 24–5 in which Paul writes that of those who run in a race, only one receives the prize, or *bravium* as we read in the Vulgate. Staying with the Vulgate, we read that the athletes who contend in the games (*in agone*) exercise self-restraint in all matters: *ab omnibus se abstinet*. The athletes' 'abstinence' may have made Erasmus think of the theme of chastity in Matthew.

It seems clear that the prize that Erasmus mentions is meant exclusively for the chaste and not also, as Telle suggests, for married people.[26] Nevertheless, the exact identity of the athletes whom Erasmus cheers on in the paraphrase, the eunuchs for the kingdom of heaven, remains ambiguous. In his opinion, Jesus is not issuing a divine counsel in 19: 11 (LB 6: 100D), and it would seem therefore that the passage in Matthew cannot serve as a justification for mandatory priestly celibacy, an ill-advised rule according to Erasmus.[27] Whereas in his paraphrase on 19: 10 he had already associated celibacy with the disciples' mission to preach the gospel, the four references to the gospel in the paraphrase on 19: 11–12 make no specific connection with the preaching ministry. One could argue that the first mention of the gospel informs the remaining four and, therefore, that the eunuchs stand for a celibate clergy. One could equally argue, however, that the eunuchs refer simply to the few, whether clergy or laypeople, who have the gift of celibacy and refrain from marriage because of their devotion to the gospel.

Dupont noted that interpreters usually have read the logion on the eunuchs in the light of what Paul says about virgins in 1 Corinthians 7.[28] Indeed, the entire chapter serves as a key New Testament text for assessing the relative merits of marriage and celibacy. Jean Héring rightly pointed out: 'This chapter is the most important in the entire Bible for the question of marriage and related subjects.'[29] Yet its significance lies not only within the Scriptures but, more importantly, in the long tradition of Christian exegesis. Accordingly, Peter Brown observed that 1 Corinthians 7 was 'the one chapter that was to determine all Christian thought on marriage and celibacy for well over a millennium.'[30] While Elizabeth Clark holds that the text is 'arguably the most ascetically directive chapter of the New Testament,'[31] other modern exegetes have challenged the decidely ascetic tradition of patristic and medieval interpretation. Acknowledging Paul's preference for celibacy, they nevertheless deny that this was a principled preference based on an ascetical belief in the absolute moral and spiritual superiority of celibacy over marriage and in the immorality of sexual intercourse.[32] Will Deming argues that a 'significant gulf' exists between Paul and the church fathers and that 1 Corinthians 7 should not be placed 'at the beginning of a supposed trajectory of Christian asceticism.'[33]

Jerome, 'the inflexible champion of chastity,'[34] used 1 Corinthians 7 in *Adversus Iovinianum* to refute the claim that marriage and virginity were spiritually equal. His treatise was well known to medieval posterity. Thomas Aquinas cites its authority in his own argument for the superiority of virginity.[35] It seems, however, that Jerome's exegesis of the Pauline text did not enjoy the same type of direct influence on shaping a tradition of scriptural commentary as did his exposition of Matthew 19: 10–12. The *Glossa ordinaria*, for example, does not reflect Jerome's negative attitude towards marriage. In his *Annotations on 1 Corinthians* (1522) Philip Melanchthon specifically criticized Jerome for 'superstitiously exalting virginity.'[36] Yet ten years earlier, in his own commentary on 1 Corinthians 7, Lefèvre, while he did not appear to borrow directly from Jerome's exegesis, nevertheless pointed out the pre-eminence of virginity several times. Both conjugal life and chastity are good. But chastity undertaken for service to Christ is better; it is holier and more pure. Celibacy and a life that avoids 'all carnal contact': such a life is 'by far to be preferred to marriage, for it is holier, more pure, and more spiritual.'[37]

Erasmus' paraphrase on 1 Corinthians 7 reflects the traditional ascetic perspective, but with a characteristically Erasmian twist. Jerome had interpreted Paul's opening comment in verse 1 that it was good not to touch a woman (*bonum est homini mulierem non tangere*) to mean that it was bad to touch a woman. This verse together with the next one, in which Paul writes that because of fornication every man should have his own wife and every woman her own husband, show that marriage is a concession to prevent a greater evil.[38] Erasmus begins his paraphrase much more positively by pointing out that 'there is a certain chaste and lawful use of marriage.' Everyone may avail or not avail himself or herself of 'lawful marriage to the extent that it promotes or thwarts the business of the gospel.' Given the present times, Erasmus' Paul explains, it would for many reasons be 'advantageous [*commodum*] to refrain completely from dealings with wives in order to be more free for the business of the gospel and to have the leisure for improving thought [*bonaeque menti vacare*].' To be sure, marriage is an honourable estate (*honesta res*), but the worldy cares that accompany it distract a person from holy things. Marriage, moreover, has a certain coarse characteristic that for a short time can completely consume a person and make him less human (LB 7: 878C–E).

This last comment is obviously a pejorative reference to sex. Erasmus' ideal, evident in the *Christiani matrimonii institutio*, is a chaste marriage, one in which couples enjoy intercourse primarily for the sake of procreation and as infrequently as possible (LB 5: 658A, 697F–8A, 699F–700A).[39] The only other negative comments about marriage have to do with the servitude that it entails. Erasmus applies Paul's discussion of slavery and freedom in verses 21–3 to marriage and celibacy in his paraphrase on verse 24: 'For the person who has attached himself to the yoke of marriage is in some respects a slave. But he who leads a celibate life enjoys the power of living more freely' (LB 7: 882C–D). At verse 26, Erasmus equates the 'necessity' mentioned by Paul with the duties and cares of marriage. Those who refrain from marriage escape 'this necessity and, as it were, bondage' (LB 7: 882E). Paul recommends in verse 30 that those who have wives should live as if they did not have them. Erasmus writes that for these people 'the bondage of marriage' will be less overwhelming (LB 7: 883C). When Paul assures his readers in verse 36 that the man who marries his betrothed does not sin, Erasmus paraphrases: 'For although we have said that marriage is associated with the disadvantages of servitude and anxiety, it is not, however, associated with sin.' He continues: 'Marriage is a lawful and honourable estate, for certain people also a necessary one' (LB 7: 884A–B).

The praiseworthiness of marriage is a conspicuously Erasmian theme in the paraphrase on 1 Corinthians 7. As we have observed, he opens his paraphrase by commending marriage, and he reiterates its honourable quality. At verse 7 Paul wishes that the Corinthians could be like him, that is unmarried, but acknowledges that everyone has his own gift from God. Erasmus' Paul desires all to be like him. They should either be 'absolutely free from the fetters of marriage' or treat their wives as sisters. Yet he will not require anything of the Corinthians, just as Christ did not dare make demands on his followers:

> He declares them blessed who had castrated themselves from the kingdom of God; he does not reject those who make chaste and moderate use of the right of marriage. Perpetual chastity taken up for the business of Christ is a certain excellent estate. But marriage is an honourable and lawful estate, and God himself established and hallowed it. (LB 7: 879C–D)

Jerome writes that 'in the church there is a diversity of gifts and I concede that marriage is a gift lest I seem to condemn nature.' He concedes that marriage is a divine gift, but he is quick to point out that 'there is a great diversity [*diversitas*] between gift and gift.'[40] One gets the impression from Jerome that marriage is not a gift on the same level as virginity. Erasmus too speaks of the diversity (*varietas*) of divine gifts and makes it clear that not all of these gifts are equal. 'It may perhaps be,' the paraphrase continues,

> that to refrain completely from sexual intercourse is beyond human strength. They are fortunate who have this strength from God, but he has loved this diversity in his people, so that some may achieve distinction in some gifts and others in other gifts, and that this diversity of things contributes wondrously to the harmony and gracefulness of the whole.

No one should criticize another's estate nor regret his own, but everyone 'should as much as he can respond to the gift that he has received from God.' The Erasmian Paul assures his readers: 'There is a chaste type of marriage, there is also an impure type of virginity' (LB 7: 879D).

The exposition of verse 7 reflects in microcosm the protean quality of the paraphrase on the entire chapter. Erasmus constantly shifts from one perspective on marriage to another. Marriage can be unseemly and onerous; it limits personal freedom. Yet it is also honourable and chaste in its own way. Erasmus integrates his descriptions of marriage into a fine balancing act between marriage and virginity. He does not want to praise the latter to the detriment of the former. Christ's eunuchs are blessed, but God is the 'consecrator' of marriage. Celibacy is a more fortunate state of life, but, as in the *Paraphrase on Matthew*, so too in the *Paraphrase on 1 Corinthians* do we read that marriage is safer (LB 7: 883A). The Erasmian Paul in the paraphrase on verse 2 realizes that his audience is especially prone to an 'untamed and violent' sexual impulse. He says: 'Therefore I think it is safer that each man have his own wife and each woman her own husband so that with mutual service the one may remedy the intemperance of the other' (LB 7: 878E). These ideas reappear in the paraphrase on the famous verse 9. The original Paul writes that he who cannot remain chaste should marry, for it is better to marry than to burn. Erasmus' Paul begins by saying that everyone should look to his or her own strength. Those unequal to the task of withstanding the 'violent spurs of sexual desire' are better off if they marry, 'so that in lawful intercourse they may cure their incontinence,' than if 'in celibacy they should wish to be associated with the perils of a more serious infamy as the result of an impulse painfully itching for sexual desire.' Paul neither recommends nor forbids marriage. He leaves everyone to his own decision. Those who are not married should decide whether or not they will marry 'as long as they look to nothing other than Christ' (LB 7: 879F–80A). Marriage and virginity therefore are both matters of personal choice and capability.

Those who marry take on a way of life that is full of cares but, nevertheless, lawful. No one is worse off in Christ's opinion for having a wife, although he is more burdened with worries (LB 7: 882F). Paul contrasts the unmarried with the married (verses

32–4). The former are anxious only to please the Lord; the latter must think about worldly matters and each other, and thus their interests are divided. It is because Erasmus' Paul wishes his audience to be distracted as little as possible by worldly cares that he says in the paraphrase on verse 32: 'celibacy is preferable [*potior*] to the condition of the married' (LB 7: 883D). At verse 38, Paul writes that he who gives his daughter in marriage does well but he who does not does better. Erasmus in amplified form follows the sense of this idea.[41] He adds, however, that in God's eyes it is 'more admirable' in marriage to do what one can to steal away from necessary cares in order to devote oneself to divine worship than 'to abuse the pretext of virginity for the sake of luxury or lazy leisure and a dissolute lifestyle' (LB 7: 884C). Virginity obviously has its own dangers or temptations.

In some respects, Erasmus transmits the traditional ascetic outlook on marriage and virginity in his New Testament exegesis. Virginity ranks higher than marriage, which ideally should reflect the splendour of virginity by demonstrating its own form of chastity. We cannot therefore agree with Telle's categorical statement that Erasmus' interpretation of Matthew 19: 10–12 and 1 Corinthians 7 betrays his 'aversion towards asceticism.'[42] He does value virginity, yet, we must admit, he imposes several qualifications on virginity. It only deserves praise when it is dedicated to Christ and his gospel. Since it is beyond the ability of most mortals, we would expect that relatively few people not only would but, more important, could live in perpetual chastity. Virginity is not a divine counsel for spiritually superior Christians. Unlike Lefèvre, Erasmus never says that it is more spiritual than marriage. Virginity's benefits are practical; they do not make it more virtuous than marriage. Virginity's superiority to marriage is a pragmatic one, for it is more advantageous to promote the cause of the gospel as a celibate person than as a married person. When Erasmus insists that whether one embraces marriage or chastity is a matter of personal choice and capacity, he does not assert that virginity possesses a principled spiritual superiority over marriage and thus approaches modern interpretations of 1 Corinthians 7. This should come as no surprise, for at the beginning of his publishing career he wrote in the *Enchiridion* what was very controversial for his day: 'Being a monk is not a state of holiness but a way of life, which may be beneficial or not according to each person's physical and mental constitution' (CWE 66: 127).

THE MARRIAGE BOND

At least as controversial as the relative merits of marriage and virginity was the question of the permissibility of divorce and remarriage. Protestantism challenged the long-standing position of medieval canon law and theology that a marriage contracted duly between two Christians was absolutely indissoluble. Canon law did make provision for spouses who could no longer tolerate living together to be separated from bed and board, but a separated spouse was not allowed to marry as long as the other was still alive. Sixteenth-century Protestant church polities permitted divorce, usually on the sole grounds of adultery and desertion. The innocent party was accorded the right to remarry.[43]

Modern scholars see Erasmus as undermining the medieval doctrine of the indissolubility of the marriage bond. Telle has stated that he was the first to propose 'with sufficient eloquence the possibility and legitimacy of total divorce,' that is, the complete dissolution of a marriage, allowing the divorced parties to remarry. The note on 1 Corinthians 7: 39, the longest note in the *Annotations* and a veritable treatise unto itself, represents, according to Telle, the first time that 'the concept of divorce in the modern sense was introduced in the world.'[44] While Erasmus concedes that the indissolubility of marriage had become the universally accepted opinion, he pleads the case of those unhappily married. The church authorities should remedy their situation by dissolving their marriages and permitting them to remarry. Erasmus envisages divorce because of adultery, but he also seems to think other causes could justify divorce, although he does not specify them (LB 6: 692D–703D).

The doctrine of the indissolubility of marriage had its roots in the New Testament. In Matthew 5: 31–2 and 19: 3–9, Mark 10: 2–12, and Luke 16:18, Jesus forbids divorce and remarriage. He who divorces his wife and marries another woman is guilty of adultery, and he who marries a divorced woman is equally guilty of adultery. The two passages from Matthew both provide one exception. Jesus' censure does not apply to the husband of an adulterous wife. The exception, expressed as *porneia* in the original Greek, is rendered as *fornicatio* in the Vulgate. In 1 Corinthians 7: 10–11, Paul repeats Jesus' teaching against divorce in absolute terms. Paul sets out his own teaching in verses 12–16. A Christian married to a non-believer should remain married to him or her, but if the non-believer leaves the marriage, the Christian spouse is no longer bound to that person.

Prominent in Erasmus' exposition in the *Paraphrases* of the four gospel passages and of the text from 1 Corinthians is the relationship between the Mosaic Law and Jesus' teaching. Indeed, the relationship between the *Lex Mosaica* and the *Lex Evangelica* is an important theme throughout the *Paraphrases*. The former is inferior to and adumbrated the latter; the latter rendered the former obsolete, particularly with respect to what Erasmus calls its 'carnal ceremonies,' although the moral imperatives of the Ten Commandments are still binding on Christians. Erasmus is quite capable of slighting the Law of Moses in the *Paraphrases*, but he frequently recalls Jesus' affirmation that he has come to fulfil not abolish the Law (Matthew 5: 17).[45] In the *Paraphrase on Luke*, we read that Christ is 'soul of the Law' (LB 7: 325C), and we encounter perhaps the most pithy Erasmian expression of Christ's policy towards the Law: *non abolitio, sed absolutio* (LB 7: 414C). Relating the story of Jesus' transfiguration in Mark and Luke, Erasmus sees special significance in Jesus' conversing with Moses and Elijah: both the Law and the prophets point to Christ (CWE 49: 109; LB 7: 370E). The same event takes on a slightly different meaning in the *Paraphrase on Matthew*, however. Jesus' familiarity with Moses and Elijah shows the apostles that they should not suspect him of abolishing the Law and the prophets (LB 7: 95A–B). The conclusion of Erasmus' paraphrase on the Sermon on the Mount summarizes Jesus' method of fulfilling, that is, perfecting, the Law of Moses: with authority he forbade what the Law conceded and required what the Law did not require. Erasmus adduces divorce as his first example: 'The Law had conceded divorce for any reason; Jesus prohibited all divorce except when adultery occurs' (LB 7: 47D).

Amplifying Jesus' précis of Deuteronomy 24: 1 in Matthew 5: 31, 'Whoever dismisses [*dimiserit*] his wife, let him give her a bill of divorce [*libellum repudii*],' Erasmus provides more complete details of the Mosaic regulation on divorce. Assuming the voice of Jesus, he writes: 'The Law of Moses allows a husband offended by any defect of his wife to dismiss her according to his own judgment, provided that he give the dismissed woman a bill of divorce, which enables her to marry another man and takes away from the first husband the right to take back the woman whom he rejected.' As long as the man who divorces his wife 'for whatever reason' (*quavis de causa*) gives her a bill of divorce, neither will he be deemed an adulterer, nor will anyone consider the divorced woman an adulteress (LB 7: 32C–D). Erasmus' elaboration of the law on divorce is significant, for he shows that Jesus understood it in terms of Jewish law. Divorce completely severed the marriage bond and opened the way for divorced people to remarry. Erasmus reminds gainsayers, presumably theologians and canon lawyers, of this in his note on 1 Corinthians 7: 39, and asks whether Jesus was thinking of their idea of divorce – separation without permission to remarry – when he spoke to Jews about divorce (LB 6: 698E). The implied answer is that by divorce Jesus did not mean the medieval concept of mere separation from bed and board.

Erasmus begins to reconcile the Mosaic Law and Jesus' teaching when he has Jesus point out that 'the Law wished the friendship and harmony between spouses to be everlasting' (LB 7: 32D). In the paraphrase on Matthew 19: 8, Jesus goes so far as to claim: 'Moses wanted the same thing that I teach' (LB 7: 103C). Then, ask the Pharisees in Matthew 19: 7, why did Moses permit divorce? 'On account of the hardness of your hearts,' replies Jesus in 19: 8. This is also his explanation in Mark 10: 5. Erasmus in his exposition of all five New Testament passages that we are examining adds to this explanation the idea that Moses permitted divorce as a lesser evil. In the paraphrase on Matthew 19: 8, Jesus tells the Pharisees that Moses 'did not permit you this because it was right by nature, but, knowing the hardness of your hearts, he made a concession to a lesser evil so that a more serious one might not be committed by you' (LB 7: 103B). Moses, in the paraphrase on Luke 16: 18, 'unwillingly conceded divorce' to prevent 'more horrible crimes' (LB 7: 414E), and in the paraphrase on 1 Corinthians 7: 10 he conceded divorce to the Jews not because he thought it was right but because human beings, whom he feared were vengeful and stubborn by nature would commit 'more horrible things than divorce' if the right of divorce were taken from them (LB 7: 880B). Erasmus provides examples of the *atrocioria facinora*: 'poisoning and murder' in the paraphrase on Matthew 5: 31 and 19: 8 (LB 7: 32D, 103C), 'murder, poisoning, and parricide' in the paraphrase on Mark 10: 5 (CWE 49: 122). In this regard, we can observe a parallel with Jerome. In his comment on Matthew 19: 8, he writes: 'When Moses saw that, on account of the desire for second wives who were either richer, or younger, or more beautiful, first wives were being killed or leading a wretched life, he preferred to yield to discord than to have hatreds and murders persist.'[46]

Erasmus consistently represents divorce as a concession to the Jews, preferable to evil, violent means of ending a marriage. Divorce is never inherently right, and Moses knew this. His unwillingness to concede divorce in the paraphrase on Luke 16: 18 finds a parallel in the paraphrase on Mark 10: 5, where Erasmus affirms that 'he did not at all approve of divorce.' Erasmus proceeds to mention in the paraphrase on the latter verse that Moses 'preferred an *unfair* divorce' to the three crimes mentioned (CWE 49: 122; emphasis added).

It is clear that Jesus' requirements of his followers exceed those of Moses. In the paraphrase on Matthew 5: 31, Jesus announces his wish that those who profess the new law should treat marriage with greater reverence than, presumably, the old Law of Moses. The new law, the Law of the Gospel, condemned divorce and remarriage as adultery, but the Law of Moses did not punish divorced people for remarrying (LB 7: 32D–E). Nevertheless, if the intent of Mosaic Law is to see marriage as holy and not to grant divorce indiscriminately, 'we do not abolish the Law but help it, we who are against divorce except by reason of unchastity [*causa stupri*], which conflicts with the very nature of marriage' (LB 7: 32F). In the paraphrase on Matthew 19: 9, Jesus states that he does not provoke the Law to wrath but renders it more complete. Divorce for any reason at all (*quavis de causa*) is wrong and is 'both contrary to the mind of God and contrary to the will of Moses' (LB 7: 103C).

Erasmus essays a more elaborate reconciliation of the Law of Moses and the Law of the Gospel in the paraphrase on Luke 16: 18. He introduces Jesus' prohibition of divorce with the statement 'What was carnal and unrefined in the Law, this has given way to more perfect things; but what is spiritual, this not only is not made obsolete, but it is also perfected.' After expounding Jesus' prohibition, Erasmus remarks that to require what is more perfect is the mark of someone who perfects, not abrogates, a rule. A father who demonstrates more indulgence to a young son does not contradict himself when he demands more of the son as an adult. The paraphrase on the verse concludes with a reference to Matthew 5: 18. Jesus tells his audience that heaven and earth will pass away more quickly than one jot of the Law. What has been foretold will be fulfilled; so far is Jesus from abolishing the Law (LB 7: 414E–F).

In Matthew 19: 3, the Pharisees ask Jesus whether a man may divorce his wife for any reason (*quacumque ex causa*). Erasmus clearly opposes indiscriminate divorce. He sneers at Jewish reasons for divorce in the paraphrase on Mark 10: 12. Christians must not imitate the hard-heartedness of the 'Judaic spirit.' 'A Jew divorces his wife because of bad breath, runny eyes, or similar faults, when among the followers of the gospel there is only one reason that could sever a marriage, namely when the marital trust has been betrayed' (CWE 49: 123). Divorce is permissible only for adultery. Erasmus introduces this exception from Matthew into his exposition of Mark and of 1 Corinthians 7: 10, but, curiously, he neglects it when he paraphrases Luke 16: 18. Paul repeats Jesus' rule that a wife may not leave her husband and that a husband may not put away his wife. Erasmus, however, has him tell married people that he does not want to be like the Jews and pagans, who severed the bonds of marriage for whatever reasons they liked. 'For the Lord forbade a man to reject his wife for trivial offences.' Jesus made one exception: 'if a wife should have an affair with another man.' Adultery is obviously not a trivial offence. It counts as an exception either because a woman who has pledged herself to one man but joins herself to another has lost the right of marriage or because it seems unfair to require anyone to share house, bed, hearth, and board with a woman who betrays the trust of marriage and has relations with a disgraceful adulterer (LB 7: 880B).

The idea that adultery justifies divorce and takes away the guilty party's legal claim upon a previously contracted marriage recurs in Erasmus' scriptural interpretation. In the paraphrase on Matthew 19: 9, Jesus wants his audience to know that anyone who rejects his wife for any reason at all commits adultery and so presents his wife with an opportunity for adultery unless by chance the woman he divorces deserves to be divorced by reason of adultery. 'For a woman who avails herself of another man has already ceased being a wife and has deprived herself of the right of marriage, having divided the flesh that God wanted to be one and indivisible' (LB 7: 103D). Erasmus explains in the paraphrase on Mark 10: 12 how adultery ends a marriage:

> [a] wife who gives her body to another man has ceased to be a wife, even if she is not divorced. And a husband who gives his body to another woman has ceased to be a husband,

> even before divorce. Just as fire is not fire unless it is hot, so a marriage is no marriage unless two are made into one. One cannot make one flesh out of three or four partners. (CWE 49: 123)

The *Paraphrases* obviously become a vehicle for presenting Erasmus' views on divorce. Before we fault him for exegetical opportunism, we should consider two things. First, he did not invent the exception of adultery as a legitimate cause for divorce. His position on adultery's effect upon a marriage is, to be sure, an extrapolation of Jesus' statements in Matthew 5: 32 and 19: 9, but it does rest on a reasonable scriptural basis. If Jesus prohibits divorce except for adultery, how does exegesis deal with the exception? One can either pass over it in silence or seek to explain it. Erasmus was not the first exegete to imagine the implications of a scriptural logion. Take, for example, Matthew 19: 6: 'What therefore God has joined together, man should not divide.' The meaning seems simple enough: human beings may not undo the bond of marriage wrought by God. But may God undo it? This question underlies Jerome's comment that 'God, who had joined us together, separates us when, by mutual agreement and for the service of God – and may the time be short! – we have wives as if we do not have them.'[47] Jerome in effect provides divine sanction for Paul's instruction that married people should not deny each other sexual intercourse except temporarily and by agreement to spend time in prayer (1 Corinthians 7: 5) and possibly also for the apostle's exhortation that those who have wives should live as they did not have them (1 Corinthians 7: 29).

The second point to consider is that Erasmus' interpolation of the exception of divorce into his paraphrase on Mark 10: 12 and 1 Corinthians 7: 10 was not unprecedented. Jerome mentions the *causa fornicationis* in his exposition of the Pauline passage.[48] In the *Glossa ordinaria*, we encounter the same *causa* three times in connection with 1 Corinthians 7: 10. After Paul writes that a wife should not leave her husband, he adds that, if she does leave, she should not remarry. An interlinear gloss connects the *causa fornicationis* with the wife's departure presumably to explain why she would leave her husband. The man may not divorce his wife, according to another interlinear gloss, 'except for the sake of fornication.' A marginal gloss explains: 'The case that Christ excepted is here passed over in silence since it is very well known, namely the case of fornication.' The marginal gloss on Jesus' prohibition of divorce in Mark 10: 12 quotes Bede, who wrote that Matthew's account is more complete. There is but one carnal and one spiritual reason 'that a wife may be put away.' The former is fornication, the latter is the fear of God, 'as we read that many have done for the sake of religion.' Significantly, Bede concludes that divine law prescribes no case in which one may take another wife while a current wife is still alive.[49]

Erasmus' emphatic criticism of indiscriminate divorce potentially has a double effect. On the one hand, it prepares the reader to expect that there might be some legitimate grounds for divorce. As he points out in his note on Matthew 19: 3 (LB 6: 97F), that is the sense of the *quacumque ex causa* of the Pharisees' question, which he prefers to render as *quilibet ex causa* (LB 6: 98C) or as *ex quavis causa* (LB 6: 97F). On the other hand, his criticism can function as the obverse of another important theme in the *Paraphrases*: the indissolubility of marriage when adultery does not occur.

We have already observed Erasmus' contention that Moses was opposed to divorce. The Law of Moses conceded divorce even though it wished, according to the paraphrase on Matthew 5: 31, that a married couple enjoy perpetual harmony and concord. This was also Erasmus' wish, as he makes clear in his paraphrase on the next verse. A Christian husband, a man endowed with gospel kindness, should either correct his wife's morals or put up with them. A series of rhetorical questions upbraids a Christian husband for thinking of ending his marriage. Why should he look for conflict with his wife when he is at peace even with his enemies? Why should he plan her destruction if he neither becomes angry when harmed nor, when offended, wishes anyone ill? Or how is it that he will not tolerate his wife at home when he endures even a life-threatening enemy (LB 7: 32E–F)? Marriage was instituted so that a woman would bear children for one husband and obey one husband. Yet she has already turned away from her husband if she has sexual relations with another man. 'Therefore,' concludes Erasmus' Jesus, 'neither should serious offences occur among Christian spouses, nor as a result of trivial ones should either he or she seek a divorce, but the one will be immediately reconciled to the other if anything should come to pass through human weakness' (LB 7: 32F–3A).

In the *Paraphrase on Luke*, Jesus declares that both nature and the gospel 'insist that everlasting friendship and an indivisible bond exist not only in marriage but also in every friendship' (*flagitat amicitiam perpetuam, et indivulsam copulam, non solum in matrimonio, verum etiam in omni amicitia*) (LB 7: 414E). *Perpetuum* and *indivulsum* are also the adjectives that modify marriage (*coniugium*) in the *Paraphrase on Mark* (LB 7: 233C–D). These qualities were divinely ordained for marriage in paradise. God joined one man to one woman and wanted their love to be incapable of division. Let man not break apart what God has joined to be indivisible.

The rhetoric of indivisibility manifests itself most forcefully in the paraphrase on Matthew 19: 4–6 (LB 7: 102F–3A). In the scriptural account, Jesus replies to the Pharisees' question whether a man could divorce his wife for any reason with a question of his own: 'Have you not read that he who made humankind from the beginning made them male and female?' The Erasmian Jesus begins his discourse on divorce by affirming the indissolubility of marriage before referring to the biblical account of the creation of humanity:

> Have you not read, he said, that when God created the human race, he instituted the first marriage in such a way that one man was joined to one woman with an indissoluble bond [*ut unus uni indissolubili copula iungeretur*]? For out of the same lump he fashioned the male and the female, so that the human race should be enlarged [*propagaretur*] from their embrace.

God the Creator, not Moses, forged 'the indivisible bond of husband and wife' and said: 'For the sake of mutual love a man will depart from his father and mother and be joined to his wife.' Erasmus portrays the intimacy of the marital union by writing *adglutinabitur uxori suae*: the husband literally becomes glued to his wife. The next two sentences elaborate this theme. Erasmus describes marriage as an *arcta coniunctio* and, to the point of redundancy, underlines the transformation of the duality of man and woman into the unity of husband and wife:

> And the tightly-knit association will be such [*tamque erit arcta coniunctio*] that out of two people there will be made, in a certain sense, one person, who previously had been two.

> Therefore, once they are joined in marriage, they are no longer two but one body so that for a wife to tear herself away from her husband [*a viro divellere*] is tantamount to cutting away a limb from the body.[50]

Matthew 19: 6 concludes: 'What therefore God has joined together, man should not divide' (*Quod ergo Deus coniunxit, homo non separet*). Availing himself again of the adjective *arctus*, Erasmus amplifies this statement in conformity with the preceding rhetoric of indivisibility: 'Therefore what God has once tied together with so tight a bond, let man not divide' (*Quod igitur Deus tam arcto vinculo semel connexuit, ne separet homo*).

In connection with Erasmus' assertions of the permanence of the marriage bond, we should examine his amplification of Paul's counsel in 1 Corinthians 7: 12–16 that a Christian married to a pagan should remain married unless the latter leaves the marriage. Paul paraphrased declares: 'Divorce is so odious a thing that I would not want a marriage, once entered upon, to be put asunder because of a difference in religion.' He urges a Christian woman, if she will listen to him, not to abandon her non-Christian husband if their religious differences do not prompt him to divorce her. Nor should a Christian husband reject a non-Christian wife if she does not demand a divorce because they do not agree in religion (LB 7: 880D).

What Erasmus calls *diversa religio* should ideally not terminate a marriage.[51] The term is a significant one. It appears five times in the paraphrase on 1 Corinthians 7: 12–16. The above references to religious difference and religious disagreement constitute the first three instances: twice in the paraphrase on verse 12, once in the paraphrase on verse 13. In the paraphrase on verse 14, Paul observes that married couples who have the greatest difficulties in staying together are those whom religious difference divides (LB 7: 881A). Yet their situation is not hopeless. A few sentences earlier, Erasmus has Paul say that when a baptized wife has intercourse with a man who is not yet baptized, she is not joined to a pagan but obeys a husband. It is not the case that she is in love with an ungodly man; rather, she bears with a man who could become godly. The husband offers his wife the hope that, although he has not yet acknowledged Christ, he nevertheless does not take offence at her worship of God. What is more, he is not completely pagan and is in some sense a Christian. He lives at peace with his Christian wife and sees 'with favourable eyes' the cross that hangs above their bed. After acknowledging the strain that religious difference puts upon a marriage, Paul concludes that 'this hope' ought to sustain the Christian woman in living together with her husband (LB 7: 880F–1A). Here Erasmus provides a touching amplification of what in comparison seems rather terse. Paul in the original passage simply asserts that the unbelieving man is sanctified by the believing woman and vice versa.

At verse 15 Erasmus still has a Christian wife in mind. If the unbelieving husband wishes to divorce his wife out of hatred for Christ and when there is no hope of changing his mind, there is no reason why the woman should remain any longer with the impious man. He who despises God as the author of marriage puts himself outside the law of marriage. The Christian wife should take advantage of the freedom of divorce, provided by the husband, and serve Christ in peace (LB 7: 881A–B).

After saying that a Christian need not be subject to an unbelieving partner that abandons marriage, Paul comments that God has called us to peace. Erasmus interprets this peace in two ways. On the one hand, it is the result of being liberated from marital responsibility to a non-Christian who wants to sever the ties of marriage. On the other, it is the norm of marital coexistence. Erasmus has Paul say: 'For not for this reason did God call us to the life of the gospel, that we live in quarrelling, but that we do so in concord and peace.' If it is not possible for a couple to live in peace and if the unbelieving husband demands a divorce, the Christian wife should not stay with an unwilling partner. Yet if marital harmony prevails, 'let the wife remain in the hope of changing her husband, and, similarly, let the husband remain in the hope of changing his wife' (LB 7: 881B). The paraphrase on verse 15 explicitly mentions *divortium* three times, a word not in the original Pauline vocabulary of 1 Corinthians 7, yet it ends with an appeal to preserve the bond of marriage between a Christian and an unbeliever.

This leads appropriately to the paraphrase on Paul's two rhetorical questions of verse 16 addressed to a Christian wife or husband: how does she know if she might save her husband, how does he know that he might save his wife? (*Unde enim scis mulier, si virum salvum facies? Aut unde scis vir, si mulierem salvam facies?*). Erasmus imagines the means of conversion: encouragement at home, moderation and gentleness in conduct, and conjugal affection. He refrains from using the Vulgate expression *salvum facere* and avoids making the wife the grammatical agent of salvation, while allowing the husband to play this role. As a result of her efforts, how does the wife know that her husband might 'come to his senses' (*resipiscere*) or 'be saved' (*servari*) with her? How does the husband know that he could save (*servare*) his wife and gain (*lucrificare*) her for Christ? Erasmus adds a third rhetorical question: 'And if this comes to pass, is this not a tremendous gain?' Even if success does not ensue, God will approve of the Christian spouse's good intention. Yet while a successful outcome remains uncertain, the marriage should continue in good hope and no one should change the state of one's life on account of religious difference (LB 7: 881C). In this, the fifth and final instance of Erasmus' reference to *diversa religio*, he again emphasizes maintaining the marital bond.

CONCLUSION

Telle criticized Erasmus for his comment in the paraphrase on 1 Corinthians 7: 36 that, although marriage entails bondage, it is not sinful (LB 7: 884A–B). He expostulated that here Erasmus denies the teaching of Augustine, of the Catholic church, and of Luther and concluded that Erasmian exegesis deprives the Pauline letters and the Gospels of their Christian sense, at least on the question of virginity, and that Erasmus, putting aside the authority of Jerome and Augustine, ends up by rejecting the authority of Scripture itself.[52] V. Norskov Olsen, however, praised Erasmian exegesis as sincerely Christian:

> In his interpretation of the New Testament logia on divorce Erasmus reveals himself as a Christian theologian who seeks to solve an ethical problem within Church and society by finding a solution based on Scripture and centred in Christ. No ecclesiastical institution should stand between the needy and the Good Samaritan. Erasmus appears not as an academic theorist but as a Christian pragmatist who is devoted to his Master in service for his fellow men.[53]

The personal attitudes of scholars towards marriage within the context of the history of doctrine and scriptural interpretation obviously have influenced their own evaluations of Erasmian exegesis. It may be impossible for scholars to think and write with complete, dispassionate objectivity; nevertheless, they would do well not to compare Erasmus to some external and supposedly respectable standard. The best way to analyse his exegesis is to elucidate its internal dynamic while placing it in the appropriate theological context and tradition of exegesis.

The most cursory reading of the *Paraphrases* reveals that amplification is the most fundamental rhetorical device that informs Erasmus' exegesis. Erasmus constantly enriches or enhances New Testament passages, but not only to tease out a tropological or allegorical significance of a particular scriptural text. To be sure, we have noted the tropological dimension of Erasmus' interpretation of John 2: 11 and 1 Timothy 4: 3; yet when he elaborates upon the New Testament teaching on marriage and divorce he stays close to the literal or historical sense of Scripture.

Krüger observes that Erasmus expounds *ad litteram* Christ's prohibition of divorce with the sole exception of adultery in Matthew 5: 32. The significance of this literal interpretation for Krüger lies in what Erasmus does not say in his paraphrase on this verse. Erasmus avoids mentioning contemporary problems, such as clandestine marriages, and any attempt at casuistry. The exegete becomes a pastor, who does not stray into questions of church law and who presents a positive evaluation of the prohibition of divorce while not weakening it.[54] The *Paraphrases* clearly evince a pastoral dynamic, for they are sermons on Scripture. Yet, Erasmus' literal interpretation of the prohibition of divorce may be no less pastoral for what it does say. In his paraphrase on Matthew 5: 31–2 and the other relevant passages that we have studied, Erasmus insists on at least two things: the exception that Christ makes in the case of adultery and the indivisibility of the marriage bond when it is not impugned by adultery. The former leaves open the possibility of a marriage's dissolution in a specific circumstance, the latter upholds the general notion of the indissolubility of marriage.

Erasmian emphasis in the form of the repetition of concepts and of vocabulary is another conspicuous feature of his exegesis. Emphasis imbues Erasmus' interpretation with clarity. Thus, as we have seen, Ephesians 5: 32 proclaims the mystical union between Christ and the church, not the sacramental union between husband and wife. From the paraphrase on 1 Corinthians 7: 12–16 we learn that *religio diversa* should not of itself provide a reason for divorce. In other parts of the paraphrase on 1 Corinthians 7, the reiteration of marriage as an 'honourable estate' helps convey Erasmus' esteem for marriage. Reading the paraphrase on this important Pauline chapter together with that on Matthew 19: 10–12 reveals another point of Erasmian emphasis: while virginity is preferable to marriage, marriage is safer than virginity.

Erasmus thus partially mediates in his own exegesis an enduring tradition of scriptural interpretation while seeking to qualify and limit it. Without a doubt, research into the various Christian traditions of understanding New Testament texts underlies the project of the *Paraphrases*. We have seen, for example, Jerome's influence on the paraphrase on Matthew 19: 10–12, and the precedent in Jerome and in the *Glossa ordinaria* for the interpolation of the *causa fornicationis* in the paraphrase on 1 Corinthians 7: 10. Erasmus took the history of Christian theology and biblical interpretation very seriously, and the seriousness of his approach is evident in his critical evaluation of this history. If he followed an established interpretation, he did so as a result of his own choice, not out of slavish adherence to tradition.

The way Erasmus interprets the New Testament in the *Paraphrases* reveals, among other things, his thinking on marriage as it is also reflected in his other writings. Some might accuse him of abusing Scripture by diluting the value of virginity. Others might praise him for using Scripture to allow for the possibility of divorce. While we can detect a theological agenda in Erasmian exegesis, this should come as no surprise within the context of the history of biblical interpretation. Which Christian theologian did *not* have an agenda when expounding Scripture? Our study of the *Paraphrases* should aim neither to impugn Erasmian exegesis for departing from a supposed univocal sense of Scripture and from a monolithic tradition of interpretation nor to present it as precursor of enlightened religious opinion. We will approach Erasmus' *Paraphrases* more fruitfully if we undertake a much more difficult and complex task, namely, to discover in them not only the variety of rhetorical strategies and hermeneutical approaches but also the interaction of exegesis and theology.

NOTES

This research for this paper was made possible by a grant from the Social Sciences and Humanities Research Council of Canada. I gratefully acknowledge the assistance of Professors Mechtilde O'Mara and Jane Phillips.

With the exception of references to the Revised Standard Version (RSV) all quotations from the Bible are from the Vulgate, either in the original Latin or in English translation.

1 Roland H. Bainton, 'The Paraphrases of Erasmus,' 67.
2 Jacques Chomarat, *Grammaire et rhétorique chez Érasme*, 1: 587; Friedhelm Krüger, *Humanistische Evangelienauslegung: Desiderius Erasmus von Rotterdam als Ausleger der Evangelien in seinen Paraphrasen*, 1.
3 John William Aldridge, *The Hermeneutic of Erasmus*, 60.
4 Peter Walter, *Theologie aus dem Geist der Rhetorik: Zur Schriftauslegung des Erasmus von Rotterdam*.
5 Manfred Hoffmann, *Rhetoric and Theology: The Hermeneutic of Erasmus*, 30, 31.
6 Chomarat, *Grammaire et rhétorique*, 1: 587.
7 Krüger, *Humanistische Evangelienauslegung*, 205–38.
8 Jane E. Phillips, 'The Gospel, the Clergy, and the Laity in Erasmus' *Paraphrase on the Gosepl of John*'; Robert D. Sider, 'The Just and the Holy in Erasmus' New Testament Scholarship'; Hilmar M. Pabel, 'Erasmus of Rotterdam and Judaism: A Reexamination in Light of New Evidence'; Pabel, 'Retelling the History of the Early Church: Erasmus's *Paraphrase on Acts*.' For other thematic approaches to the *Paraphrases*, see Etsuro Kinowaki, 'Erasmus' *Paraphrasis in Epistolam Jacobi* and His Anthropology'; and Phillips, 'Food and Drink in Erasmus' Gospel Paraphrases.'
9 Jacques Lefèvre d'Étaples, *S. Pauli epistolae XIV ex vulgata: Adiecta intelligentia ex Graeco, cum commentariis* (Paris, 1512; repr. Stuttgart, Bad Cannstaat: Frommann/Holzboog, 1978), 39.
10 For the date of Erasmus' additions to the note, see *Erasmus' Annotations on the New Testament: Galatians to the Apocalypse*, ed. Anne Reeve (Leiden: E.J. Brill, 1993), 615.
11 The Vulgate text is: *Honorabile connubium in omnibus et thorus immaculatus*. Erasmus' translation reads: *Honorabile est inter omnes coniugium et cubile impollutum* (LB 6: 1022B). From the *Annotations* it is clear that he preferred *cubile* to *thorus* (LB 6: 1022F), but in his paraphrase he followed the Vulgate, not his own translation: *Primum enim sua praesentia voluit honestare nuptias, praescius olim exorituros, qui eas ut spurcas damnarent, cum res sit Deo gratissima honorabile connubium, et thorus immaculatus* (LB 7: 516C).
12 *Paraphrasis in duas epistolas Pauli ad Corinthos per Erasmus Roterodamum recens ab illo conscripta, & nunc primum typis excusa, ad Christi, Paulique gloriam* (Louvain: Dirk Martens, 1519), p2. The same reading is found in *Paraphrases Erasmi Roterodami in omnes Epistolas*

germanas, et in omnes Canonicas, diligenter ab autore recognitae, ac marginalibus indicibus illustratae (Basel: Johannes Froben, 1521), r5v–r6; *Tomus secundus continens Paraphrasim D. Erasmi Rot. In omneis epistolas apostolicas, summa cura recognitam & ex archetypis & eruditorum animaduersione, ita ut accuratius fieri uix potuerit* (Basel: Johannes Froben, 1523), r7.

13 *Tomus secundus continens Paraphrasim D. Erasmi Roterodami in omneis epistolas apostolicas, summa cura denuo ab ipso autore recognitam, emendatamque, tum ex archetypis, tum eruditorum animaduersione, ita ut accuratius fieri uix poterit* (Basel: Froben, 1532), 128; *Tomus secundus* (Basel: Froben, 1534), 264; *Omnia Opera Des. Erasmi Roterodami*, 9 vols. (Basel: Froben, 1540), 7: 649.

14 Emile V. Telle, *Érasme de Rotterdam et le septième sacrement.*

15 Jacques Dupont, *Mariage et divorce dans l'Évangile: Matthieu 19, 3–12 et parallèles*, 166.

16 *Doctoris Angelici divi Thomae Aquinatis Sacri Ordinis F. F. Praedicatorum Opera Omnia*, ed. Stanislaus Eduard Fretté and Paul Maré, 34 vols. (Paris: Louis Vivès, 1871–80), 19: 507.

17 Dupont, *Mariage et divorce*, 161–220, here 220. Quentin Quesnell, 'Made Themselves Eunuchs for the Kingdom of Heaven (Mt 19, 12),' insists on Dupont's reading, exclusive of the traditional interpretation. For a more recent and different treatment, see Alexander Sand, *Reich Gottes und Eheverzicht im Evangelium nach Matthäus.*

18 Walter Bauer, 'Matth. 19, 12 und die alten Christen,' 238. For Origen's commentary on Matthew 19: 12, see PG 13: 1253–65.

19 CCSL 77: 167–9.

20 PL 92: 86A–B.

21 I have consulted the marginal and interlinear glosses on Matthew 19: 9–12 in vol. 4 of *Biblia latina cum glossa ordinaria: Facsimile Reprint of the Editio Princeps, Adolph Rusch of Strassburg 1480/81*, 4 vols. (Turnhout: Brepols, 1992).

22 CCSL 77: 168.

23 *Doctoris Ecstatici Dionysii Cartusiani Opera Omnia*, 42 vols. (Montreuil: Typis Cartusiae S. M. de Pratis, 1896–1913), 11: 214–15.

24 CCSL 77: 168.

25 LB 7: 104E reads *certet qui volet*, as do two separate editions of the *Paraphrase on Matthew* published by Froben in 1522. For *volet*, third-person singular present subjunctive of *volare*, to fly, I have substituted *velit*, third-person singular present subjunctive of *velle*, to wish. Although *certet qui volet*, translated as 'let him/her compete who runs quickly,' could make sense, in my opinion *certet qui velit* ('let him/her compete who wishes') makes more sense. The sixteenth-century English translator must have had the same opinion: 'Ye see victory set out before you, let hym try that will and knoweth his

owne strenghte.' See *The First Tome or Volume of the Paraphrase of Erasmus upon the Newe Testamente (1548)*, with an introduction by John N. Wall, Jr (Delmar, NY: Scholars' Facsimiles & Reprints, 1975), 78.

26 Telle, *Érasme de Rotterdam et le septième sacrement*, 238.

27 On Erasmus' views on priestly celibacy, see Léon-E Halkin, 'Érasme et le célibat sacerdotal.'

28 Dupont, *Mariage et divorce*, 218.

29 Jean Héring, *The First Epistle of Saint Paul to the Corinthians*, 48.

30 Peter Brown, *The Body and Society: Men, Women and Sexual Renunciation in Early Christianity*, 54.

31 Elizabeth A. Clark, *Reading Renunciation: Asceticism and Scripture in Early Christianity*, 327.

32 Frédéric Godet, *Commentaire sur la première épître aux Corinthiens*, 1: 291, 293, 300, 365–6; Héring, *The First Epistle of Saint Paul to the Corinthians*, 60–1, 65; Jeremy Moiser, 'A Reassessment of Paul's View of Marriage with Reference to 1 Cor. 7'; Brian S. Rosner, *Paul, Scripture and Ethics: A Study of 1 Corinthians 5–7*, 150–1; Ben Witherington, ed., *Women and the Genesis of Christianity*, 124–38; Witherington, *Conflict and Community in Corinth: A Socio-Rhetorical Commentary on 1 and 2 Corinthians*, 174–6; and Will Deming, *Paul on Marriage and Celibacy: The Hellenistic Background of 1 Corinthians 7*.

33 Deming, *Paul on Marriage and Celibacy*, 224.

34 J.N.D. Kelly, *Jerome: His Life, Writings, and Controversies*, 198.

35 *Summa Theologiae* 2a2ae, 152, 4.

36 Philipp Melanchthon, *Annotations on the First Epistle to the Corinthians*, trans. and ed. John Patrick Donnelly (Milwaukee: Marquette University Press, 1995), 93.

37 Lefèvre, *S. Pauli epistolae XIV ex vulgata*, 115v; see also 116v–17.

38 PL 23: 229A–B.

39 On the Erasmian ideal of a chaste marriage, see John B. Payne, *Erasmus: His Theology of the Sacraments*, 111–12; and Alan W. Reese, 'Learning Virginity: Erasmus' Ideal of Christian Marriage.'

40 PL 23: 232B.

41 1 Corinthians 7: 38 has been interpreted in two ways. The traditional view, going back to the church fathers (Clark, *Reading Renunciation*, 321) and evident in Erasmus' New Testament (LB 6: 692B) as well as the paraphrase on the passage, held that the man in question is the woman's father; thus, it is for him to give her in marriage or not. Several modern exegetes, however, argue that the passage refers to a betrothed man who must decide whether or not he will marry his fiancée. On this problem of interpretation, see Héring, *The First Epistle of Saint Paul to the Corinthians*, 62–3 and *The Jerome Biblical Commentary*, ed. Raymond E. Brown et al., 2 vols. (Englewood Cliffs, NJ: Prentice-Hall, 1968), 2: 265–6.

42 Telle, *Érasme de Rotterdam et le septième sacrement*, 243.
43 Jean Gaudemet, *Le mariage en Occident*, 240–67, 284–5; Roderick Phillips, *Putting Asunder: A History of Divorce in Western Society*, 13–94. For an excellent case study of Protestant grounds of divorce, see Robert Kingdon, *Adultery and Divorce in Calvin's Geneva*.
44 Telle, *Érasme de Rotterdam et le septième sacrement*, 206, 209. See also Payne, *Erasmus: His Theology of the Sacraments*, 121–5; and Phillips, *Putting Asunder*, 36–7.
45 On Erasmus and the Law of Moses, see Pabel, 'Erasmus of Rotterdam and Judaism,' 21–6, and for references in the *Paraphrases* to Jesus' intention to fulfil and not abolish the Law, see ibid. 24, n. 79.
46 CCSL 77: 166.
47 Ibid.
48 *Adversus Iovinianum*, PL 23: 233D.
49 CCSL 120: 559.
50 Interestingly enough, the woman is at fault for severing the bond of marriage. At issue in Matthew is whether a husband can divorce his wife, not vice versa. The husband remains the putative agent of divorce in Jesus' reply to the Pharisees, and Jesus condemns divorce except, in effect, in the case of a wife's infidelity. Erasmus remains faithful to the legal and gender dynamics of Matthew. He does not amplify the scriptural text to introduce the idea of equality between men and women. Husbands do not tear themselves away from wives, nor do they, except for the paraphrase on Mark 10: 12, betray conjugal trust. Mark 10: 11 puts men and women on an equal footing inasmuch as Jesus speaks of husbands and wives as initiators of divorce. Erasmus refuses to follow the text, however. In the paraphrase, Jesus speaks only of the husband as initiating a divorce. The wife's agency is limited to instigating adultery (CWE 49: 123).
51 In the *Christiani matrimonii institutio*, *diversa religio* is another way of expressing *dispar cultus* (LB 5: 640F). In canon law, disparity of cult was an impediment to marriage; thus, when a Christian married a non-Christian, their union, in the eyes of the church, was null. Erasmus agrees with the impediment. The situation Paul had in mind was different, however. The couple was already married before one of the spouses converted to Christianity.
52 Telle, *Érasme de Rotterdam et le septième sacrement*, 249–50.
53 V. Norskov Olsen, *The New Testament Logia on Divorce: A Study of Their Interpretation from Erasmus to Milton*, 16–17.
54 Krüger, *Humanistische Evangelienauslegung*, 196.

PART TWO

'A FULL LIBRARY OF DIVINITY BOOKS': THE RECEPTION OF THE *PARAPHRASES*

EIGHT

The Textual Travail of the *Tomus secundus* of the *Paraphrases*

John J. Bateman

Erasmus' *Paraphrase on the New Testament* has come to us in two parts, the *Tomus primus* containing the paraphrases on the four Gospels and the Acts of the Apostles, and the *Tomus secundus* containing the paraphrases on all the Apostolic Epistles. It is typical of the paradoxical history of the work that the *Tomus secundus* should have come into existence two years before the *Tomus primus*. The present study concerns only the history of the text of the paraphrases collected in the *Tomus secundus*. That of the *Tomus primus*, while similar in some respects, is for the most part different from and independent of the *Tomus secundus*.

There were twenty-eight editions of the *Paraphrases on the Epistles*, directly or indirectly authorized by Erasmus, between the first publication in November 1517 and the posthumous *Opera Omnia* of 1540.[1] The purpose of this study is to demonstrate, using primarily the evidence of the editions of the paraphrases on the shorter Pauline epistles, the Epistle to the Hebrews, and the Catholic or General Epistles, the affiliations of the authorized editions and, second, to illustrate the difficulties Erasmus had in licking this particular offspring of his pen into an acceptable shape. The difficulties were caused in part by his own inveterate habit of tinkering with texts, in part by the animadversion of both friendly and hostile critics, but mostly by the men employed to put these works into print:[2] editors, correctors, and, above all, the compositors.

The story can be told in four chapters:

1 The first editions and their immediate reprints
2 The six editions of 1521, 1522, and 1523
3 The revised editions of 1532 and 1534
4 The posthumous editions of 1538 and 1540

The complete story of the history of publication would have to be continued in additional chapters covering the editions from 1540 to 1997 and beyond, but they and the numerous reprints published by other printers during and after Erasmus' lifetime lie outside the present task.

PRAELUDIUM

In chapter 3 of the Epistle to the Philippians, Paul provides some information about his Jewish origins and background. Verse 5 reads in Erasmus' Latin version: *Circumcisus octauo die, Israel ex genere, tribus Beniamin, Hebraeus ex Hebraeis*, etc. The paraphrase on this verse reads in the editions published down through 1523: *non proselytus sed Iudaeus ex Iudaeis oriundus nec e quauis tribu verum e praecipua, nempe Beniamin, vnde et sacerdotes constituuntur.* Noël Béda took exception to this claim about the tribe of Benjamin. In his response to Béda's criticism Erasmus expressed surprise that he could have written such an obviously erroneous statement. 'Since everybody,' he says, 'knows that only the tribe of Levi was responsible for the priesthood and for sacred rituals, this statement can have arisen only from carelessness, not from ignorance. Therefore, I wondered how it had happened. [It must have been that] in transferring the formes,[3] as they call them, one line was left out at the bottom of the page – a common accident. The original sentence said: *Nempe a Beniamin quae semper iuncta fuit tribui Iudae, vnde reges, et tribui Leui, vnde sacerdotes ...*'[4] Is there any evidence that an accident of this kind occurred in the printing of one of the extant editions? None whatsoever. If it did occur, it would have had to have been in the now lost first edition printed most probably by Dirck Martens in Louvain in 1520. But if we, in our imagination, try to set these words into the type employed by Martens for his editions of the paraphrases, we shall quickly discover that they would require not one, but at least one and a quarter lines of type. The truth, of course, is that these words never existed in print until Erasmus invented them for his reply to Béda's criticism.

Erasmus may have thought he had offered a satisfactory explanation of how the erroneous assertion that priests were appointed from the tribe of Benjamin came about. But he had not counted on Béda's pertinacity. The same criticism was advanced once more and was defended once again as a mistake of the typesetters. The second version of the lost line differs a little from the first: *Nempe Beniamin quae semper iuncta fuit tribui Iudae, vnde reges, et Leui, vnde sacerdotes ...*[5] The omission of *tribui* before *Leui* would help squeeze the reconstructed line into a single line of printed text. But the omission of the preposition before Benjamin suggests a reconstruction from memory, not from an autograph manuscript. The final version, which remains in the text to this day, was first printed in the 1532 folio edition: *nempe Beniamin, quae semper iuncta fuit tribui Iudae, vnde reges et Leuitae, vnde et sacerdotes constituuntur*. Now we have kings, Levites, and priests all appointed from the tribe of Judah. How did *Leuitae* come to replace *Leui*? Probably through the intervention of the typesetter who, seeing *et Leui* in his copy and not realizing that it was a brachyology for *tribui Leui*, but thinking that the *et* connected the nouns *reges* and *Leui*, corrected *Leui* to *Leuitae* because he thought *Leui* was a slip by the author. Despite his blithe invention of the lost-line hypothesis, Erasmus was essentially correct in his suspicions about the carelessness of the compositors.

1. THE FIRST EDITIONS AND THEIR IMMEDIATE REPRINTS

Writing on 13 January 1522, in the preface to the *Paraphrase on the Gospel of Matthew*, Erasmus informs his readers that after the idea for the New Testament paraphrases first came to him, he experimented with one or two chapters, but would have given the plan up had not the marvellous agreement of learned friends compelled him to continue (Allen Ep 1255: 6–17). The lack of circumstantial detail is equally marvellous: no year, month, day, place, not even a remark about the weather. Nor do these learned friends have names.

One of them might have been Thomas More. At least there seems to be a connection between More and the *Paraphrase on the Epistle to the Romans*, the first to be written and published. In May 1517 Erasmus sat for a portrait by Quentin Metsys that was to be part of a present for More. The portrait depicts Erasmus starting to write the *Paraphrase on Romans* on the right-hand page of what appears to be a bound volume of blank pages. There is a title in capital letters followed by the opening sentence of the paraphrase.[6] Erasmus himself mentions this fact in a sentence he added to a letter of More's published by Froben in August 1518. On the opposite page there is the word *Gratia*,[7] which at first sight might seem to be a one-word statement of Pauline theology, but *gratia* also means 'thanks' and in the context of the painting suggests Erasmus' gratitude to More. For what? For simply being his friend or, perhaps, for urging him to complete the *Paraphrase on Romans*? If there is any plausibility in this second suggestion, that could take us back to August 1516 when More and Erasmus were guests of John Fisher in Rochester just prior to Erasmus' return to the continent. This is also the occasion of the earliest mention of a paraphrase on the New Testament, though admittedly in a rather different context.

In a letter to Henry Bullock, dated <22> August 1516, after a lengthy complaint about the criticism directed at his edition of the New Testament, Erasmus exclaims, 'What if I had made all the divine books clear by means of a paraphrase so that they could, with no harm to the thought, be read without stumbling and be understood more easily?' (Allen Ep 456: 83–4), a statement that admirably elucidates the primary purpose of the *Paraphrases*. That Erasmus had Paul on his mind in the summer of 1516 is evident not only in letters from friends, most notably John Colet, encouraging him to complete his commentary on the Epistle to the Romans,[8] but Erasmus himself in a letter to Guillaume Budé, apparently written in June 1516, informs the French scholar that having completed a preliminary study of Psalm 1, he is now ready for some serious work on Paul.[9] He probably meant a resumption of the commentary he had begun fifteen years earlier in 1501, but somehow that intention was transformed into the idea to elucidate Paul through a paraphrase.[10] Erasmus himself, writing to Pieter Gillis, probably in October 1517,[11] remarks that 'the paraphrase which I began in the pictures is now complete and has begun to be printed' (Allen Ep 687: 15–16). Does this mean that Erasmus did not begin writing the *Paraphrase on Romans* until May 1517? On 10 May 1517 Beatus Rhenanus wrote to Erasmus from Basel to inform him about various matters concerning the Froben Press and that 'your paraphrase of the Apostolic

Epistles is very eagerly awaited' (Allen Ep 581: 21–4). Erasmus must have written about the future paraphrase to Basel in March from Antwerp or in April from England, a month or more before sitting for the Metsys portrait. In any case his letter did not reach Basel until after 24 April, when Beatus wrote to inform him about affairs at the Froben Press (Ep 575). Precise dates are not possible, but we should probably be safe in assuming that the initial experiment with the paraphrase was made, at the latest, in the winter of 1516–17, with the final version being completed in August or September after Erasmus had settled in Louvain.[12]

A letter to Paolo Barbirio, dated 2 November 1517, states that 'the paraphrase on the Epistle to the Romans is being elegantly printed' (Allen Ep 695: 29–32).[13] The manuscript was thus in the press by the end of October and Erasmus has seen at least one printed sheet. How else could he know that the printing was elegant? The paraphrase itself begins on the third sheet in the book. The preliminary matter, consisting of a letter dedicating the work to Cardinal Grimani, dated Louvain, 13 November 1517, and a detailed argument or summary of the content of the work, was evidently not yet ready when Erasmus gave the work to Martens, though the printer, naturally, had to be informed that there was something still to come.

On 15 November Erasmus informed Pieter Gillis that the printing of the paraphrase was nearly finished (Allen Ep 712: 24) and in a letter to Conrad Geldenhauer, written on the following day, told him that the 'paraphrase is hurrying toward the finish line. A small book, but no one could believe without making the trial himself how much effort it has cost me. It will be sent as soon as Martens has finished printing it' (Allen Ep 714: 7–9). Five days later, on 21 November, it is still not quite finished. The first secure date for the completion of the work is 30 November, when Erasmus sends Thomas More the *libellus Paraphraseos* (Allen Ep 726: 2). The 'little book' is a pot-quarto, approximately 12 × 19.5 centimetres in size, containing nineteen and a half printed sheets. The normal rate of production for a single press, manned by three to four workers, is four sheets a week, so that a book of twenty sheets would take five weeks to complete, which is what the external evidence of the letters suggests. The quires are all quartos except the first which is a quarto in sixes, that is, it consists of one and a half sheets of paper. The first two quires contain the dedicatory letter (a standard feature) and the argument of the epistle (likewise a standard feature of editions of biblical and classical texts), the remaining quires the paraphrase itself. This sets the pattern that will prevail, with a few exceptions, in all subsequent authorized editions of the paraphrases on the Epistles: preface in the form of a letter, argument, paraphrase.

In a letter to Pieter Gillis, unfortunately without a month-date but probably written in early December, Erasmus says, 'I am sending a corrected copy of the paraphrase' (Allen Ep 736: 19–20), on which Allen remarks (note 20) that '[t]he printers note ten corrections on the first two sheets. Erasmus had doubtless found many elsewhere, and corrected them by hand.' Actually there are very few typographical errors in the book. It would appear that the preliminary matter was worked more quickly and carelessly than the text of the paraphrase. Also, the list of errors, which is printed on the back of the title page, shows that sheet 'a' was put through the press twice, the second time to print the errata, and, since there are two separate sets of errata, the sheet may have gone through the press three times. A printer would not normally go to this extra expense, and we would probably be correct to infer that he did so at Erasmus' insistence. Our author is obviously concerned right from the start to have this particular text correctly printed.

Meanwhile the Froben firm in Basel evidently expected to be given the new work, and when news reached them that it was being printed by Martens, Froben and his partner Wolf Lachner were apparently quite disturbed. They communicated their feelings through Beatus Rhenanus sometime in November.[14] Erasmus replied to Beatus on 6 December and to Lachner a day or two later (Epp 732 and 733). In his reply to Beatus, Erasmus explains, 'I was going to send the paraphrase to Basel, as I imagined it would have a good sale. But when I saw that nothing at all [of the works I had sent earlier] was being brought to me, I suspected that they had more than enough work; therefore, I entrusted it to Martens here. I am sending even now a copy which I have somewhat revised. But it would be unkind to compete immediately with what this impoverished printer has just published.'[15] Well, all is fair in love and publishing. Froben and Lachner rushed the work into print as soon as they received it. Thus began, almost by accident it seems, a practice that would continue until the last paraphrase was completed, that on the Epistle to the Hebrews in January 1521. The first edition was printed by Martens in Louvain under Erasmus' direct supervision or, when Martens' press was not available, by Michael Hillen in Antwerp. A corrected copy was dispatched to Basel so that Froben could advertise a new and revised edition.

The revisions in the copy sent to Basel justify the adverb 'somewhat' (*vtcunque*) used above. There are only seven revisions in the text that appear to have been made by Erasmus. Balancing them are six errors made by the typesetters, apart from trivial misspellings, turned sorts, and the like. One may wonder how much the text was really improved in its passage from Louvain to Basel. Yet there are two additions that do convey new information. Following the noun *Paraphrasis* on the title page there is a new clause, *quae commentarii vice possit esse* ('which could be used in place of a commentary'). This is the first indication in print that the paraphrase is a form of commentary. Following the title of the argument, there is a new sentence, *Iam quo res sit dilucidior, argumentum epistolae paucis explicandum* ('And now, for the sake of clarity, we shall set forth the argument of the epistle'), as if we did not know what the function of an argument was. If this statement was written by Erasmus, as seems likely, his purpose is to emphasize the reason for the writing of this new argument, namely to elucidate the subject-matter, a function that is essentially the same as that of the paraphrase itself. There is also an implicit criticism: the arguments found in Greek and Latin manuscripts fail to perform this function. That point evidently struck Erasmus' friend Cuthbert Tunstall, who had been helping Erasmus prepare the second edition of the *Novum Testamentum*. He suggested to Erasmus that he should write new arguments for all the epistles, which Erasmus did in October 1518.[16] He sent to Johann Froben on 22 October the material for the *Novum Testamentum* that had been completed to that date, together with a manuscript copy of the new *argumenta* with instructions to have them printed in front of the respective epistles, which Froben later carried out. At the same time, he gave Dirck Martens a second manuscript so that the arguments could be published as a separate book (Ep 894). Martens' text was later used in the editions of the paraphrases, the Froben text only in the editions of the New Testament. As a result, the arguments come to us in slightly different versions depending on later revisions made in either the *Paraphrase* or the *Novum Testamentum*.

That same October, having completed most of the work for the new edition of the New Testament, Erasmus informed John Fisher and John Colet, two more of the friends who may have encouraged him initially to write the paraphrases, that he was about to return to that task.[17] The product of this work was the *Paraphrases on the Two Epistles to the Corinthians* published by Martens in February or, alternatively, March 1519. There is no date on the title page and no colophon; however, three different dates are found in different parts of the book. At the end of the *Paraphrase on 2 Corinthians* (D4v) there is the statement, surely written by Erasmus, 'The End, for the glory of Jesus Christ and of Paul the Apostle. 1519, the third day before the Calends of February' (30 January). This statement is unique, I believe, in the *Paraphrases* in giving us the day on which one of them was actually completed. The letter dedicating the work to Bishop Erard de la Marck is dated Louvain, 5 February 1519. This letter and the *argumentum*, the text of which Martens would already have had from the book he had printed the previous October, occupy the first three sheets (signed *4, [flower]4, a4) with the *Paraphrase on 1 Corinthians* beginning on the fourth sheet (b). It is likely that, as with the *Paraphrase on Romans*, Erasmus gave Martens the manuscript of the two paraphrases before the dedicatory letter was ready.[18] In fact, in the letter to Erard de la Marck, dated Louvain, 19 February 1519, which accompanied a gift copy of the book, Erasmus claims that there was a contest between the printer and him to see whether Martens could print faster than Erasmus could write (Allen Ep 918: 4–6). If true, this suggests that Erasmus gave Martens the manuscript piecemeal, beginning sometime in January. Printing of the dedicatory letter, the argument, and the two paraphrases was finished or almost finished by 18 February. The text of the paraphrase goes to the last page of sheet D, leaving no room for the device that Martens customarily placed at the end of his books. It looks as though Martens may have asked Erasmus for some additional material to fill a concluding sheet. What was actually provided was the *Apologia pro declamatione de laude matrimonii* in the form of a letter addressed to scholars of the University of Louvain and dated 1 March 1519. Since Froben's reprint was published in March 1519 and does not include the *Apologia*, he too seems to have been sent a copy in February before the final sheet (E) was printed.

The book is the same size (13 × 19.5 cm) and format as the *Paraphrase on Romans*. Though twenty-six pages longer (excluding the *Apologia*), it could, like Romans, still be considered a 'thin book.' Erasmus states that the purpose of his literary gift to the bishop was to enable him to carry about Paul, the unique prelate of our religion, wherever he likes, and Paul will henceforth converse with him clearly and like a friend, with no need for prolix commentaries.[19] The portability of the paraphrases is a new idea, introduced here for the first time. Whether it was Erasmus' suggestion or, more likely, Froben's own idea,[20] a new step was shortly to be taken in the publication of the *Paraphrases*. Froben published in March a quarto edition of the *Paraphrases on Corinthians*, modelled on Martens' edition, and similar to the two quarto editions of the *Paraphrase on Romans* that he had printed in January and November 1518. In April 1519, he published an edition of all three paraphrases in octavo format and in the italic type commonly found in such books-for-the-hand (*enchiridia*). He thus set the program that the Froben firm would follow to their final publication of the Latin text in 1557. But what market did he have in mind? Most likely the same one for which he published Latin Bibles in the same octavo format: primarily for the clergy but also for the educated laity, female and male, who wanted books for private study and meditation or something to read at Mass. A few printers reprinted the Martens edition in quartos when they first appeared, but when the Froben octavos appeared these were the editions that were pirated everywhere, obviously because that was where the major market was. This is evident, for example, from the initial editions of the *Paraphrase on the Gospel according to Matthew*. Froben published this work in March 1522 in folio and in octavo editions. No other printer anywhere published a folio edition of Matthew or of any of the other paraphrases in the sixteenth century,[21] but at least ten other printers reprinted the octavo edition within the next eighteen months.

To return to Louvain and the first editions. At the end of the *Apology for the Declamation in Praise of Marriage* Erasmus promised to give faculty and students at Louvain the *Paraphrase on the Epistle to the Galatians* within a month. He may have finished in April, but Martens did not get it into print until May. The Froben reprint in quarto followed three months later in August. Since the spring book fair was already past, there was evidently no pressure for rapid publication. The work is comparatively short, nine sheets or seventy-two pages in the Martens edition; eight sheets, sixty-four pages, in the Froben reprint. Froben apparently did not think it merited a separate issue in octavo. Thus, it was included in a new octavo edition of the *Paraphrases on Romans and Corinthians*, published in January 1520 by Hieronymus Froben, Johann's son, with funds provided by Johann's second wife, Gertrude Lachner-Froben. (There is undoubtedly a family story here, but we can only imagine it.)

Erasmus in the meantime, after a summer hiatus spent mostly, it seems, in travels back and forth from Louvain to other cities in Belgium – Antwerp, Bruges, Brussels, Mechelen – and editing Cyprian,[22] began in October to work on the paraphrases on the remaining Pauline epistles.[23] He does not seem to have worked on them in the canonical sequence, as we might have expected, since the *Paraphrases on the Epistles to Timothy, Titus, and Philemon* were ready or, perhaps, could be made ready for publication before the paraphrases on the other five short Paulines, Ephesians through Second Thessalonians.

This is not the place to review the history of Erasmus' relations with Edward Lee, even though they frequently impinge in various ways upon the *Paraphrases*.[24] Lee had prepared some 243 annotations upon the *Annotations* that Erasmus had published in the first and second editions of the New Testament.[25] According to Lee, Erasmus had tried to prevent the publication of his work, although Erasmus insisted that he had in fact attempted to promote its publication.[26] After unsuccessful attempts to have his book printed by Jean Thibault or Michael Hillen in Antwerp in May and June 1519, Lee resumed negotiations with Hillen in October and November of that year, only to be told by Hillen that he could do nothing for the next forty days, or until 14 December, because he would have his hands full with Erasmus' paraphrases on the Epistles to Timothy and Titus. Lee took this to mean that Erasmus, by sending the paraphrases to Hillen to print, was in effect bribing Hillen to postpone the printing of Lee's book (Allen Ep 1061: 608–47). Erasmus, naturally, denied that he was doing any such thing; he had turned to Hillen only because Martens at that time was short of workmen.[27] It is not easy to determine the validity of the various assertions, contentions, disclaimers, and, occasionally, actual arguments in these two accounts. Wallace Ferguson notes that Lee's story is full of contradictions, as indeed it is, while Erasmus' story is much more consistent and, apparently for that reason, Ferguson believed it to be more convincing.[28] A more sceptical or suspicious critic is not likely to be so easily persuaded.

For our purposes we need only note that the *Paraphrases on the*

Epistles to Timothy, Titus, and Philemon were in press in November 1519 and were, therefore, published in that month or early in December. The only extant copy has no date on the title page. Unfortunately it is also defective – approximately the final third is missing – so that if there was a date of publication in a colophon, it is now lost.[29] Like the paraphrases on the Epistles to the Romans, Corinthians, and Galatians, it contains a dedicatory letter (called in the table of contents a preface), addressed to Philip of Burgundy, prince-bishop of Utrecht, but dated simply 1519; arguments on each of the four epistles, and the four paraphrases. Allen thought the letter might have been composed while the paraphrase proper was being printed.[30] He is quite likely correct. Unlike Martens' quarto editions, Hillen's is an octavo, though printed in roman, not italic type. The first sheet, signed 'a,' is actually a half-sheet (eight pages) while the remainder of the surviving sheets are full sheets (sixteen pages each). It thus looks as though Hillen had in hand the manuscript of the paraphrase and began printing it before he received the copy for the dedicatory letter and the argument to 1 Timothy. This may be evidence, inconclusive to be sure, that the work, as Lee contended, was hastily thrust upon Hillen. Since Froben printed his edition of the *Paraphrases on the Epistles to Timothy, Titus, and Philemon* at the same time as the *Paraphrases on the Epistles to the Ephesians, Philippians, Colossians, and Thessalonians*, it is probable that Erasmus waited until the latter paraphrases were finished before sending the two volumes containing them all to Basel in February 1520.

No copy of the supposed first edition of the paraphrases on Ephesians through 2 Thessalonians has as yet come to light. We do have some dates that establish the approximate beginning and end of publication. In a letter written to Thomas Wolsey, dated Louvain, 1 February 1519 (for 1520),[31] Erasmus informs the cardinal that he has completed the paraphrases on all the genuine epistles of St Paul.[32] A letter is also extant from Boniface Amerbach to Ulrich Zasius, dated Basel, 1 March 1520, informing him that 'all the paraphrases on the whole of Paul have been completed' and that Boniface will send them when they have been printed (that is, by Froben).[33] For this material to have reached Basel by 1 March it would have had to have been dispatched by February 15 at the latest. The letter dedicating these five paraphrases to Cardinal Lorenzo Campeggi is dated Louvain, 5 February 1519 (again evidently a mistake for 1520). Ten days are probably not enough for the printing of the entire work,[34] so Erasmus must again have given the manuscript of the paraphrases to the printer four or five weeks before completing the front matter.

In the absence of this presumed first edition, we must derive any information about it from Froben's edition, which carries the date March 1520 in the colophon. Still, problems abound with this edition, which Froben published in two separate issues: a quarto in roman type similiar to the quarto editions of the earlier paraphrases on the Epistles to the Romans, Corinthians, and Galatians; and an octavo in italic type. He published at the same time the *Paraphrases on the Epistles to Timothy, Titus, and Philemon,* likewise in quarto and octavo issues. The two issues of the *Paraphrase on the Epistles to Timothy* were set from the Hillen edition independently from each other; I would assume that the same is true of the other paraphrases.[35] Thus, all four issues went through the press about the same time, which would be a sizable undertaking. There are altogether forty-eight and one-half printed sheets; at the normal rate of four sheets a week, this job would take twelve weeks for a single press, two weeks for six presses employing eighteen to twenty-four men. Even though Froben, unlike Martens or Hillen, had a large number of presses and, presumably, the personnel to man them, I suspect that some of this work was subcontracted to other printers in Basel. If so, that could explain some of the anomalies presented by the edition of the paraphrases on Ephesians to 2 Thessalonians.

The first anomaly: Hillen's edition of the paraphrases on 1 Timothy to Philemon contained the arguments on the four Epistles; we know this from the table of contents. Accordingly they appear in Froben's two reprints. However, there are no Arguments in the edition of the paraphrases on Ephesians to 2 Thessalonians. It is easier to assume that they were not in the copy sent to Froben than to believe that for some reason they were omitted from the Basel edition. Did Martens neglect to include them?

Another puzzle is provided by the titles and *finis*-statements of the individual paraphrases. One expects some uniformity in them, and that is essentially what we have in the edition of the *Paraphrases on the Epistles to Timothy, Titus, and Philemon.* Their titles all have the form:

In Epistolam Pauli ad [nomen] Erasmi Roterodami ...

A modified version of this formula with the genitive of the author's name replaced by *per Erasmum Roterodamum*, doubtless due to Erasmus himself,[36] appears in the titles of the *Paraphrase on the Epistle to the Colossians* in both the quarto and the octavo issues and in the octavo issues of the *Paraphrase on the Epistle to the Philippians* and the *Paraphrase on the Second Epistle to the Thessalonians*. A new formula,

> Paraphrasis in Epistolam Pauli ad [nomen] Per Erasmum Roterodamum,

appears in both the quarto and octavo issues of the *Paraphrase on the Epistle to the Ephesians* and in the quarto issues of the *Paraphrase on the Epistle to the Philippians* and the *Paraphrase on the First Epistle to the Thessalonians*. There is some uniformity here, to be sure: the typesetters of Ephesians and Colossians use the same title formula for both issues, but for the other three paraphrases, the typesetter of the quartos goes one way, the setter of the octavos another. There is a similar variation in the *finis*-formulas at the end of each paraphrase. The quartos have

> Paraphrasis in epistolam Pauli ad [nomen] Finis [Eph., Phil., Col.]
>
> Paraphraseos in Epistolam ad [nomen] Finis, per Erasmum Roterodamum [1, 2 Thess.]

The octavo issues all have

> Paraphraseos in epistolam Pauli ad [nomen] per Erasmum Roterodamum, Finis

One can speculate about what is going on here, but there was evidently little supervision and the typesetters were left to decide what was appropriate for the particular work entrusted to them.

There are also numerous places in the text where the typesetter of the quarto issue goes one way, that of the octavo issue another. Many of these variants are typical typographical errors – omission of a word, transposition, dittography, substitution of more familiar for less familiar phrases, foul case or turned sorts that make *nos* into *vos* and vice versa. More intriguing, however, are several variants that look as though the typesetter of the octavo issue has followed a correction in his copy or conceivably made a correction on his own, while the typesetter of the quarto issue has ignored or overlooked it. If we take agreement with the text of the March 1521 edition of the paraphrases on all the epistles (see below) as the test of correctness, then the typesetter of the quarto is right six times, the typesetter of the octavo issue twenty times. If we were to make a similar test with the *Paraphrases on the Epistles to*

Timothy, Titus, and Philemon, we would have the opposite result: the quarto issue is superior to the octavo issue, agreeing with the March 1521 edition twenty-one times against nine times for the octavo.

Fortunately we need not concern ourselves too much with these Froben reprints, since by and large they are a dead end in the history of the text. Still, the present case is a useful example of the difficulty Erasmus had in controlling his text once it went to the print shop. It also illustrates a principle: once a text appears in two settings, variation rules.

One other observation needs to be made at this point. That the paraphrases could be employed as commentaries on their respective epistles was stated on the title page of the Froben reprints of the *Paraphrase on the Epistle to the Romans* and repeated on the title pages of other paraphrases. Commentaries have their own distinctive features, most noticeably their use of a tag or lemma to key the commentary to the text under study. The first editions and reprints of the earlier paraphrases have no marginal or side notes of any kind. Beginning with the present paraphrases we find extracts, chiefly from the Vulgate, printed in the margins. On the title page of the March 1521 edition these lemmata are called 'marginal indices,' but their primary function is to enable the reader to read the paraphrase side-by-side with the biblical text.[37] They can also be useful clues for the history of the text. Thus, in the Froben editions of March 1520 that we have just been examining, there are in the *Paraphrases on the Epistles to Timothy, Titus, and Philemon* twenty-three citations that do not occur in either the first edition or in the March 1521 edition of the complete paraphrase on the Epistles, clear evidence that the 1520 edition was not the copy-text for the 1521 edition. On the other hand, there are no side notes in the 1520 edition of the paraphrases on Ephesians to 2 Thessalonians that do not appear in the 1521 edition, with two exceptions, side notes omitted in the March 1521 edition that reappear in the July 1521 reprint of it. That, of course, is not evidence that the 1521 edition was set from a copy of the 1520 edition, but it could lend support to this possibility, from which we might infer that the March 1520 edition of these five paraphrases was their first printed edition.

Let us return once more to Louvain and the story of the first editions. The letter, mentioned above, written to Cardinal Wolsey on 1 February, informing him that the paraphrases on Paul are now complete, continues with the statement that the work in Erasmus' opinion is one that will live on and the wish that he had been able to place Wolsey's name at the front of one to light the way. Did he know that five days later he was going to dedicate the paraphrases on Ephesians to 2 Thessalonians to Wolsey's rival, Cardinal Campeggi? In any case, he promises Wolsey that he will look for another work to dedicate to him that will have an equally long life (Allen Ep 1060: 53–6). Was he already thinking of continuing with a paraphrase on the Epistles of Peter and Jude, or did he have some grander work in view? The latter, I suspect. In the preface dedicating the *Paraphrases on the Epistles of Peter and Jude* to Wolsey he is quite apologetic about the small size of the book, which does not really measure up to Wolsey's grandeur.[38] The stimulus for the paraphrase was again, it seems, the controversy with Edward Lee. Lee's book had reached Erasmus late in February or early in March.[39] Erasmus replied with a work published in three parts by Michael Hillen in Antwerp.[40] While the work was in press – Erasmus read the proofs himself – he discovered a manuscript of Bede's commentary on the seven Canonical or Catholic Epistles and from it learned that the interlinear and marginal notes in the *Glossa ordinaria* were drawn almost in their entirety from Bede.[41] The *Glossa*, of which he otherwise had a very low opinion,[42] could thus provide a reliable commentary on the Epistles of Peter and Jude that could be used in a paraphrase on them. This, coupled with an effort to prevent any dismay on the part of his English friends and patrons arising from his published responses to Lee, was probably the motive for the composition of the work and its dedication to Cardinal Wolsey. Erasmus had also been encouraged by his English patrons, especially William Warham, the archbishop of Canterbury, to attend the meeting of Henry VIII and Francis I in Calais in June 1520 and may have wished to appear with a *xeniolum* or little gift in hand. As matters turned out he fell ill and could not go to Calais in June, but was able to attend the meeting of Henry VIII and Charles, Duke of Burgundy and now king of Castile and Aragon, in that city in July. But whether he had his gift in hand is more difficult to say.

The dates for the writing of the three paraphrases can be pinned down fairly closely. Erasmus returned to Louvain by 5 May and remained there until the third week of June, when he was again in Antwerp. In a letter to Germain de Brie, dated Antwerp, 25 June 1520, he informs Germain, who had apparently expressed an avid interest in the paraphrases on the epistles of Paul, that he had recently produced a paraphrase on the two Epistles of Peter and the one of Jude (Allen Ep 1117: 123–6); he quotes the title of the work. That gives us a terminal date for the completion of the work, but says nothing about the date of publication.[43]

The book was printed by Dirck Martens but has no date on the title page and lacks a colophon. Likewise the dedicatory letter is undated. Martens had all three parts of the book – dedicatory letter, argument, and paraphrases – in hand before he began printing, but did Erasmus give him the copy for these items before he left for Antwerp in June or after his return to Louvain around 6 July and before his departure for Calais for the meeting of Henry VIII and Duke Charles that took place 11–14 July? In either event, the next we hear of the paraphrases is in a letter to Wolsey dated Antwerp, 7 August 1520, that seems to have accompanied Wolsey's copy (Allen Ep 1132: 10–12). Froben had received a copy of the work by December, since his reprint is dated December 1520 on the title page and January 1521 in the colophon. But did Erasmus send it to him or did he acquire it on his own initiative? There are no changes of any kind other than new typographical errors in the reprint, a fact which suggests that the arrangement made with the paraphrases on the Pauline epistles had broken down. The book was also reprinted by Valentin Schumann in Leipzig sometime before the end of 1520. One wonders whether it was the appearance of the Leipzig edition that prompted Froben to put his own reprint on the market.[44] The Froben program of separate editions of the paraphrases was shortly to come to an end, however.

With the publication of the *Paraphrases on the Epistles of Peter and Jude* Erasmus had reached the end of his endeavours in this kind of study, or so he thought (Allen Ep 1171: 1–5 = ASD VII-6: 117, lines 4–8). He had not reckoned on the persuasive voice of Matthäus Cardinal Schiner. There were several occasions in September and October of 1520 when Erasmus could have met Schiner and listened to his vigorous encouragement to complete his commentaries on the epistles with paraphrases on the epistles of James and John (ASD VII-6: 110). The letter dedicating the *Paraphrase on the Epistle of James* to Schiner is dated Louvain, 16 December 1520. Since typsetting began with the letter, we can assume that printing began a day or two later and, making allowance for the holidays, was probably finished early in January.[45] The preface to the *Paraphrases on the Epistles of John*, likewise dedicated to Schiner, is dated Louvain, 6 January.[46] As with the *Paraphrase on James*, Martens again began the printing with the letter and, if there were no interruptions, would have been finished by the end of January. Both editions are identical in design and format, James containing nine sheets (seventy-two pages), John seven sheets (fifty-six pages). The same design is also followed in the *Paraphrase on the Epistle to the Hebrews*, whose title page is dated January 1521. The letter dedicating the work to Silvestro Gigli is dated 17 January 1521, so again Martens seems to have begun printing soon after receiving the manuscript copy.

2. THE SIX EDITIONS OF 1521, 1522, AND 1523

At some point in the latter half of 1520 it was suggested to Erasmus, or he himself conceived the idea, to publish a revised edition of the paraphrases on all the Pauline epistles. He employed for this task copies of the first editions that he either already had in his possession or could have obtained from Martens and Hillen. If he followed his customary practice, he would make corrections and revisions – for better or worse – in his personal, and quite likely bound, copy of the printed text. A secretary would then transcribe the revisions into a second unbound copy. This second copy would be given or sent to the printer while the copy with the autograph changes would be retained and be available for future comparison.[47] Froben received the revised copies of the paraphrases on the Pauline epistles sometime in January 1521, the revised copies of the three Louvain editions of the paraphrases on the Canonical epistles probably around the middle of February. But evidently he had not yet received the edition of the *Paraphrase on the Epistle to the Hebrews* because the title page of the new edition lists the 'Paraphrase of Erasmus of Rotterdam on all the genuine Epistles of Paul and on all the Canonical <Epistles>, carefully revised by the author and illustrated with indices in the margins.' Froben chose to print the paraphrases in the octavo rather than the quarto format, which makes a more convenient volume to hold in the hand, but a very fat one of fifty-four and a half sheets, or 872 pages. To offset this disadvantage the book was divided into two parts, Romans to 2 Thessalonians and 1 Timothy to 3 John. At some point during the course of printing, however, it was decided to introduce a new division in order to separate the

Pauline epistles from the Catholic epistles, by giving the Catholic epistles their own title page and a new series of signatures (A^8–M^{10}). It really looks as though Froben intended to market the work as two separate editions.[48] It also looks as though printing was complete: the last quire of the paraphrase on the Johannine epistles is a sheet and a half with a colophon (*Basileae apud Io. Frobenium. Anno M.D. XXI*) and the printer's device on the last page, all indications that the book is complete. Then the corrected copy of the edition of the *Paraphrase on the Epistle to the Hebrews* arrived. It receives its own title page, but is signed as a continuation of the paraphrases on the Canonical Epistles (N^8–R^{10}), which adds another five and a half sheets (eighty-eight pages) for a grand total of 960 pages.[49] It is hardly surprising that when Froben reprinted the book four months later in July, he divided it into several sections with separate title pages for Corinthians, Galatians, Ephesians to 2 Thessalonians, and 1 Timothy to Hebrews, and within the last section added a separate title page for the paraphrases on the Canonical Epistles and another for the paraphrase on Hebrews. Thus, as the main title states, 'people are free to cut the book into a handy size as they see fit.' Few buyers, however, would likely go to the expense of having the work bound into seven or eight volumes. Froben's competitors, beginning with Johannes Schoeffer in Mainz, more sensibly reprinted the book in two parts, Romans through Ephesians and Philippians through Hebrews.

Two steps remain before we reach the final form of the *Paraphrases on the Epistles*. Erasmus left Louvain on 28 October, his birthday, to travel to Basel to oversee the publication of the third edition of the *Novum Testamentum*, which eventually appeared in February 1522. The New Testament had been issued in folio format from the beginning. It now seemed desirable, either to Erasmus or to Froben, to publish the *Paraphrases* in the same format. Hence, in February 1522 the first edition in folio appeared with the title, in the form of a letter from Johann Froben to the Reader, 'A Paraphrase on all the epistles of the Apostles received by the Church, that is, Fourteen of Paul, Two of Peter, One of Jude, One of James, Three of John.'[50] It is also likely that at the same time the decision was made to publish the new *Paraphrase on the Gospel of Matthew* in both folio and octavo formats.[51]

One last step remains before the *Paraphrases on the Epistles* attained its final nomenclature. Duke Charles, by then the emperor Charles V, had returned to Brussels on 14 June 1521, and with him Cardinal Schiner, who had no doubt seen the March 1521 edition of the complete *Paraphrases*. Schiner began to urge Erasmus to write a paraphrase on the Gospel according to Matthew.[52] Despite some serious misgivings about the project, Erasmus again succumbed to Schiner's persuasion. Hence, after his arrival in Basel on 15 November to oversee the production of the third edition of the *Novum Testamentum*, he set to work on this paraphrase, which took him one or two months of toil[53] and was apparently competed by 12 February (Allen Ep 1259: 15) and published on 15 March.

The title of the first edition of the *Paraphrase on Matthew*, also in the form of a letter from Johann Froben to the Reader, adds after the announcement of the *Paraphrase on Matthew*: 'Paraphrases on all the Apostolic epistles, that is, of Paul, James, John, Peter, Jude.' The object of this publication in folio format, it would appear, was to present Erasmus' work on the New Testament as an entity: Greek text, Latin translation, *Annotations*, and the *Paraphrases* to provide a more lucid and readable exposition of the meaning of the biblical text. Bibliographers often treat the February edition of the *Paraphrases on the Epistles* as an adjunct to the *Paraphrase on Matthew*, but this is really not correct.[54] Their status as the *Tomus secundus* is first proclaimed in the folio and octavo editions of 1523. Even so, as we shall see, the history of the text of the *Tomus secundus* is independent of that of the eventual *Tomus primus*, which contains the paraphrases on the four Gospels and on the Acts of the Apostles.

In considering the affiliation of the six editions published between 1521 and 1523, it is necessary to keep in mind Erasmus' practice in revising editions (see note 47 above). The title page of the February 1522 folio edition of the complete *Paraphrases on the Epistles* informs us that their text was carefully compared with that of the 'first archetypes' (*archetypis primis*). The phrase is not crystal clear, but surely it is intended to refer to the first editions, which, if true, implies that when he moved from Louvain to Basel in October–November 1521, Erasmus brought with him the copies of the first editions that he himself had corrected,[55] or alternatively had shipped with his library and other possessions.

Second, one needs to keep in mind that the exemplar or copytext for a new edition is a set of unbound sheets that could be, and no doubt often were, distributed to different persons for copying or for typesetting. The individual sheet, not the assembly of sheets that we commonly call a book, is the primary unit of composition and criticism. Within the print shop, not the sheet, but the two formes from which the sheet is printed are the centre of critical attention. But since we shall not be concerned with stop-press corrections and other accidents of the printing process, we shall generally ignore this stage in the production of the text. There were, however, two persons (in any given book, there were probably several at work) in the press whose attention, or rather lack thereof, was crucial to the creation of the printed text: the *castigator*, who performed the functions of copy-editor and proof-reader, and the *typographus* (compositor) on whose eyes and fingers the entire project rested. Depending on their aptitude, experience, and knowledge, both could be minor authors in the making of a text. Indeed, in the matter of orthography and punctuation they were the principal authors.

In the discussion that follows, the individual editions are identified by letters of the alphabet, *A* through *L*, and *BAS* for the Basel 1540 edition of the *Opera omnia*. (See the list of editions, p. 255 below.) The examples cited are identified by the chapter and verse numbers of the respective epistles. The numbers in square brackets refer to the columns and sections in the seventh volume of the Leiden edition (LB) for the thirteen Pauline epistles and to the line numbers of the individual arguments and paraphrases in the Amsterdam edition (ASD) for the epistle to the Hebrews and the seven Catholic epistles. Citations of the text of the New Testament are from the Clementine Vulgate (Vg) and/or from Erasmus' Latin version (Er) as printed in LB 6.

The first thing to be noted is that the Froben reprints of 1518, 1519, and 1520, designated by *B*, play no further rôle in the history of the text.[56] This can be demonstrated in the case of the *Paraphrases on the Epistles to Timothy* and seems probable in the other Pauline epistles. The text of the March 1520 edition of these paraphrases contains twenty readings not found in either the first edition (*A*) or the March 1521 edition (*C*). Consider the following examples:

a) 1 Tim. 1: 2 [1035D2] ... ille nostrae vitae moderator <suos> diuites ac beatos esse voluit

suos *add. B* : *om. A C*

b) 1 Tim. 2: 9 [1042B3] Si quid est in animo muliebrum affectuum

est *C* : haesit *B* : *om. A*

c) 1 Tim. 3: 2 [1043E12] repetitum coniugium non caret ... intemperantis animi suspicione <etiamsi mors alterius coniugum diremerit connubium. Porro diuertio mutata vxor non solum intemperantiae verum etiam morositatis habet suspicionem.>

etiamsi ... suspicionem *add. B* : *om. A C*

d) 1 Tim. 5: 1 [1049B3] Sic enim est tuenda autoritas episcopi vt absit tamen ab omni specie tyrannidis ...

tamen *B* : tum *A C*

Tamen is correct. The typesetter of *A* probably misread an abbreviation in his copy. The error was then missed in correcting the copy for *C*.

e) 1 Tim. 5: 16 [1051D10] Non enim par est vt Christianus ... sibi cognatam viduam destituat et alendam obtrudat Ecclesiae

destituat et ... obtrudat *B* : destituere et ... obtrudere *A C*

f) 1 Tim. 5: 25 [1053D12] ... a palam improborum contubernio est absistendum

absistendum *A C* : abstinendum *B*

g) 1 Tim. 6: 16 [1055E1] ... qui solus inhabitat lucem inaccessam ...

solus *A C* : *om. B*

In reviewing his text Erasmus realized that the adjective *solus* was inappropriate in the relative clause and correctly deleted it in *B*; cf 1 Tim 6: 16 in Vg, Er: *qui solus habet immortalitatem lucem habitans inaccessibilem*. The correction was evidently overlooked in preparing the copy for *C*.

h) 2 Tim. 1:16 [1055E1] Non est meum illis imprecari

Non est meum *C* : non est, meum est *A* : Non meum est *B*

i) 2 Tim. 2: 5 [1060C13] non sat habet vt quomodocunque decertet ...

quocunque *A C* : quocunque modo *B* : quomodocunque *E*

These last two items are an instructive illustration of how Erasmus edited what he himself had written. He obviously did not remember what he had done previously and corrects anew.

j) 2 Tim. 2: 23 [1062E8] dum semper in maius gliscente disputationis calore res tandem in rabiem exit adeoque nullus alii vult concedere

vult *B* : velit *A C–BAS*

In correcting the copy for *C*, Erasmus overlooked the inconsistency between the indicative *exit* and the subjunctive *velit*, an oversight that continued through all subsequent editions.

To this list of variants in the text may be added the twenty-four new side notes in the March 1520 edition (*B*) that do not occur in the March 1521 edition (*C*). It is evident, then, that the exemplar of the March 1521 edition of these paraphrases was a corrected copy of the 1519 Antwerp edition, not the Basel 1520 reprints of this work.

It can be shown in the same way that the July 1521 edition (*D*) was set from a corrected copy of the March 1521 edition. Obvious typographical errors apart, most of the new readings in *D* are simple corrections that could have been made by the castigator at the press or by comparison with the copies of *A* or *B* sent to the press for the March 1521 edition. However, there are several changes that suggest the hand of Erasmus. Note

a) Eph. *finis* [989–90] Paraphraseos ... finis

Paraphraseos *D* : Paraphrasis *C*

The Greek form of the genitive singular is an Erasmian touch that a typesetter is unlikely to have introduced on his own.

b) Col. 2: 23 [1011F8] Praua humilitas est per angelum sperare quod ab ipso Christo petendum erat

sperare *B D–H* : spectare *C*

Spectare fits the context so well that it is difficult to believe that a typesetter would change it. In fact, *spectare* looks very much like Erasmus' own revision about which he may have had second thoughts or, perhaps, one of his secretaries, instructed to compare the text of *C* with *B*, changed *spectare* back to *sperare*.[57]

c) 1 Thess. 4: 16 [1024B11] ... in aduentu Christi vna cum illis rediuiuis subito rapiemur

illis rediuiuis *D–H* : illo rediuiuo *B C*

Obviously when Erasmus first wrote these words he was thinking that at the second coming we would be raptured with Christ, but inspection of the context and, perhaps, a glance at the biblical text made him realize that it was the dead brethren who were to be carried off with the living. A good editor could have made the change, but Erasmus himself seems to be a likelier candidate.

d) 1 Pet. 1: 11 [130–1] ... sciscitati sunt a Spiritu Christi, qui iam tum illis arcano afflatu significabat

sunt ... afflatu *A B D* : *om. C*

This text illustrates the kind of accident that Erasmus imagined had happened in the paraphrase on Philippians 3: 5. The words that should have occupied the first line of page A8v were somehow shifted twenty lines down the page and inserted between the words *qui prius* and *videbatur* (line 144 in ASD). Anyone reading the sequence *sciscitati significabat* would realize that something was amiss; also *sunt*, not *sciscitati* is the catchword at the bottom of page A8r. But correction would require comparison with *A*, the exemplar of *C*, a copy of which would have been available to Erasmus in Louvain or to an editor at the press in Basel. Once the initial correction was made, deletion of the words in the wrong place farther on in the page would present no difficulty.

e) 1 Pet. 3: 9 [476–7] De male merentibus bene mereri ... bene loqui christianae virtutis est

De male merentibus bene mereri *D–H*: De bene merentibus male mereri *A–C*

Erasmus has just said that to do evil to benefactors was the behaviour of a wild animal, to curse those who bless us the behaviour of jesters. He was apparently going to add a third illustration, 'to return evil for good, is the behaviour of' but changed course in midstream to speak about Christian virture. Alternatively, an adjective defining unchristian behaviour was omitted after *male mereri* by the typesetter of the first edition. In either event an anomaly is produced in the text – to return evil for good is the mark of Christian virtue! The required correction is more likely to have come from Erasmus than from a typesetter. Yet revisions of this kind are few and, if Erasmus corrected a copy of the March 1521 edition for the July edition, he seems to have done so while skimming through the text.

A corrected copy of the July 1521 edition subsequently served as the exemplar of the May 1522 octavo edition (*F*) and a corrected copy of that in turn for the 1523 octavo edition (G^1). This sequence of affiliation may be seen from the following variants:

a) Allen Ep 1062, the dedicatory letter to Lorenzo Campeggi

119 ... vt ... Leo ... circulum ... gloriae, quem feliciter orsus est, absoluat

quem *F* G^2: quam *C–E* G^1 *H*

126 ... serenissimus Angliae rex Henricus ...

Henricus *C–E* G^1 *H* : Heinricus *F* G^2

b) Phil. 3: 10 [1000A5] vt vlla *mortali* sapientia possit intelligi

mortali *B C E* G^1 *H* : mortalis *D F* G^2

c) Heb. 7: 7 [470] ... quod minus est ab eo quod maius est benedictionem accipere

est *A C–E* G^1 *H* : *om. F* G^2

d) Heb. 9: 10 [658] ... in variis absolutionibus aliisque purgationibus carnis quae nec in hoc erant instituta

instituta *A–E* G^1 *H* : institutae *F* G^2

The neuter is correct since the relative pronoun *quae* refers to the entire list of 'ceremonies' given in the sentence – discrimination in food and drink as well as 'absolutions' and 'purifications.' The castigator or compositor of *F* took the pronoun to be feminine and corrected the perfect participle accordingly.

e) Heb. 11: 32 [1114] ... factis sui memoriam ...

sui *A–E G*[1] *H* : suis *F G*[2]

f) James 1: 6 [70] ... nihil haesitans

haesitans *A–E G*[1] *H* : haesitatis *F* : haesitatus *G*[2]

g) James 5: 7 [944] ne ... moliamini ..., sed toleretis ...

toleretis *H* : toleratis *E G*[1]: tolerate *A–D F G*[2]

h) 1 Pet. 2: 9 [264] Et qui fisus illi fuerit

fisus *A–E G*[1] *H* : visus *F G*[2]

i) 1 Pet. 4: 12 [676] Ille ... maliciam vobis vertet in bonum, cruciatus mutabit ...

vertet *A–E G*[1] *H* : vertit *F G*[2]

Some of these conjunctive errors linking the May 1522 and the 1523 octavo editions are simply mistakes on the part of the typesetter(s) of *F* that were not caught by the corrector. Others, however, are suggestive and illustrate typical procedures in the revision of a text. Items (f) and (g) are especially illuminating. In (f) the typesetter has made an evident mistake, but working without recourse to other editions the corrector – whether Erasmus himself, one of his secretaries, or a castigator at the press is irrelevant – has made the obvious emendation, which gives good sense but is wrong. In (g) we can probably see Erasmus himself editing his work. The reading in *E* is a mistake by the typesetter; the syntax calls for an imperative, not an indicative. The mistake is overlooked in the correction of the exemplar for the 1523 folio edition, but not in the more careful revision for the 1532 folio edition. But again our corrector, probably Erasmus himself, works by divination and his new reading is an emendation, not a restoration of the original text.

Despite some indications to the contrary, as will be noted below, the February 1522 folio edition (*E*) was also set from a corrected copy of the July 1521 edition as the following agreements indicate:

a) Col. 2: 13 [1010E5] ... per Filii mortem gratis condonatis peccatis omnibus *posthac* cum illo viuatis ...

posthac *B F–H* : post hoc *C D E*

b) 1 Thess. 1: 5 [1017F5] Neque enim sic praedicauimus vobis Euangelium vt praeter verba nihil adferremus vobis ...

adferremus *B C G H* : adferemus *D E F*

This is a good example of how an obvious error (the syntax requires a verb in the subjunctive, not the future indicative) can pass unnoticed through several editions. Compare items (e) and (f) below.

c) 1 Tim. 6: 17 [1056A5] Declaraui quam sit periculosum ...

Declaraui *A–C E H* : Declarauit [*sc* Euangelium] *D F G*

In the context of the paraphrase, which mentions the 'glory of the Gospel' in the immediately preceding sentence, the third-person *declarauit* actually fits the context better than the first person. It is possible, then, that the change from first to third person in *D* was editorial rather than a mistake on the part of the typesetter.

d) Heb. 4: 5 [242] quae refocillaret Hebraeos hospitio terrae Palestinae longo itinere defatigatos

defatigatos *D–H* : fatigatos *A C*

e) Heb. 10: 16 [792] Hoc ... est testamentum quod condam erga illos ...

condam *A* : quondam *C–I*

f) James 3: 6 [599] et inquinet sua lue corpus vniuersum
lue *A C H* : luce *D E F*

The title page of the February 1522 folio edition (*E*) of the Paraphrases, which is in the form of a letter from Johann Froben to the Reader, reads

> In vniuersas epistolas ab Ecclesia receptas, hoc est Pauli quatuordecim, Petri duas, Iudae vnam, Iacobi vnam, Ioannis treis, paraphrasis, hoc est liberior ac dilucidior interpretatio, per Erasmum Roterodamum ex archetypis primis diligenter ab ipso recognitis. Cuius diligentiae nostra quoque cura non defuit. Tuum erit, optime lector, dare operam ne ille Christi gloriae vel nos tuae commoditati frustra sudasse videamur.

At first sight it might seem that the February 1522 edition, like the March 1521 edition, had been set from newly revised copies of the first editions, and several agreements of the text of the 1522 edition with that in the first editions seem to support this assumption:

a) Phil. 4: 21 [1004B3] Salutate cunctos qui iuxta Iesu Christi ...

   Iesu Christi *D F G H* : Christi Iesu *B C E*

   The sequence 'Christ Jesus' is that of the New Testament; 'Jesus Christ' is the more familar order.

b) 1 Tim. 2: 14–15 [1042F6] Qui conuenit vt quae semel marito fuerit magistra praeuaricandi nunc sibi in pietatis doctrina priores vindicet?

   in pietatis *A E F* G^1 *H* : impietatis *B C D* G^2

c) 1 Tim. 2: 14–15 [1043A1] ... ac sat habeat quod quae olim fuit dux ad impietatem nunc comes sit ad pietatem

   impietatem *A B E–H* : pietatem *C D*

All of the passages in which the February 1522 folio agrees with the first editions occur in the Pauline epistles where they slightly outnumber the agreements with the July 1521 edition (eight to five). In the paraphrases on the epistle to the Hebrews and on the seven Catholic Epistles, there are no agreements at all with the first editions (*A*) against the later revised editions (*C* or *D*). Thus, even if a careful comparison of the text in the July 1521 edition was made with that in the first editions, this comparison seems to have been limited to the thirteen Pauline epistles. The only other explanation for this difference in the two parts of the work would be that revised sheets of the first editions were used as the copy-text of the new folio edition, but corrected sheets of the July 1521 edition were used for the remaining epistles.

However, is this inference from the wording of the title page in the 1522 editions correct? Assuming that Erasmus himself is responsible for the text of the title page in these editions, did he write *ex archetypis ... recognitis*. Or did he perhaps write *ex archetypis ... recognita*? Did the typesetter (or possibly Erasmus himself), awash in ablative endings, unconsciously continue with *recognitis* instead of *recognita*? Compare the change made in the participle *recognita* in the title of the 1523 editions:

> Tomus secundus continens paraphrasim Desiderii Erasmi Roterodami in omneis epistolas apostolicas summa cura recognitam et ex archetypis et eruditorum animaduersione ita vt accuratius fieri vix potuerit.

The evidence of the agreements with the text of the July 1521 edition listed above shows that in fact it was the text of the *Paraphrases* in the July 1521 edition that was revised, not that in the first editions.

Mistakes by the typesetters of the February 1522 folio average two per page. This is the only edition of the *Paraphrases* to have an extended list of errata printed on the last sheet. A corrected copy served as the exemplar for the 1523 folio, which, corrections apart, is in many parts of the text virtually a letter-by-letter reprint of the 1522 folio edition. This connection is illustrated by the following passages:

a) Phil. 2: 13 [997B5] ne nesciatis cui tribuendum sit si quid illa vobis suggesserit

   suggesserit *E G H* : successerit *B C D*

b) Phil. 2: 16 [997D2] nec inaniter in hoc Euangelii stadio cucurrisse

   cucurrisse *E G H* : concurrisse *B C D*

c) Col. 1: 18 [1007B11] At ne maiestas illius vos deterreat

   At *E G H* : ac *C D* : aut *B*

d) 1 Thess. 2: 14 [1020D6] sed exerere coepit vim suam in vobis

   vobis *B E G*^{1} *H* : nobis *C D F G*^{2}

e) 1 Thess. 2: 18 [1021B4] sed obstitit haec conanti Satanas

   obstitit *B D F G*^{2} : obstetit *E G*^{1} *H*

f) 2 Tim. 1: 17 [1059E13] nec conquieverit donec inuenisset

   conquieuerit *B E G H* : conquiuerit *A C D F*

g) 1 Pet. 4: 3 [603] ... addictae deditaeque ... commessationibus, compotationibus

compotationibus *A–F* G^2 : om. *E* G^1 *H*

Unlike *E* and *F*, neither the 1523 folio nor the 1523 octavo edition has a month date, so that it is impossible to know which was sent to the press first or whether they went through the press simultaneously. Yet at some point their exemplars must have been compared with each other because while belonging to two separate strands, as it were, of the history of the text, they also have several new readings in common. For example,

a) 1 Thess. 3: 13 [1022E1] ... cum ... palam erit non solum quid quisque gesserit verum etiam quo quisque animo gesserit.

quisque *G H* : quicque *B–F*

b) 2 Tim. 1: 8 [1058B8] praedicas crucem et mortem

et *G H* : ac *A–F*

c) Titus 2: 4 [1071A1] et puellas ... sic instituant vt prudentes sint, ... vt sobriae sint

prudentes *G H* : sobriae *B–F*

vt sobriae sint *om. B*

Correction is complex here. The paraphrase initially followed the text of Erasmus' Latin version of Titus 2: 4–5: *Quo possint modestas reddere adulescentulas, ... vt sobriae sint*. The *vt* clause was then omitted in *B* as redundant, but retained in C. The redundancy was next observed in correcting the text of *E* for the 1523 folio. Comparison with the Vulgate suggested *prudentes* in place of the first *sobriae*; cf. Vg ... *vt prudentiam doceant adulescentulas, ... prudentes* [+ *sobrias* MSS], *castas, sobrias*.

d) Heb. 11: 20 [1025] quod Isaac moriturus, cum ipse nondum accepisset promissam a Deo felicitatem, tamen ausus est *eam* polliceri filiis suis

moriturus *G H* : mortuus *A–F*

eam *G H* : iam *A–F*

e) 1 John 3: 2 [417] Ne quid perturbet animos vestros, charissimi, quod vos habet [*sc.* mundus] despicabiles et abiectos.

quod *A G H* : quos *C–F*

Thus, by the end of 1523 readers had the *Paraphrases on the Epistles* available in two different formats, a folio edition matching the folio edition of the *Novum Testamentum*, intended, presumably, for theologians and other students of the Bible, and an octavo edition for private reading, though the numerous side notes allowed it too to be read alongside the biblical text. The text of the two editions varied at over two hundred places, most of which were the result of mistakes made by the typesetters of the octavo edition, though the typesetters of the folio edition contributed a dozen or so mistakes of their own. Two or three passages apart, none of these variants affected the meaning and most were readily detectable as typographical errors and easily corrected. A few examples of errors in the octavo edition may illustrate the potential challenge to the critical reader:

a) Eph. 5: 32 [987E6] Huius ... copulam [i.e., of marriage] quisquis scrutabitur intelliget

seruabitur G^2

Seruabitur makes some kind of sense, but would even an ingenious critic be able to emend it to *scrutabitur*?

b) 1 Thess. 1: 5 [1017F5] sic praedicauimus vobis Euangelium ...

nobis G^2

This is one of the endless examples of *n* for *u* and vice versa, in this context easily corrected.

c) 1 Tim. 5: 14 [1051C8] neue detur ansa Satanae

causa G^2

One might think at first sight that *causa* was a mental error, but it was more likely mechanical. Intending to set *ansa* the compositor set a *u* in place of *n*, either because of foul case or from turning the piece of type. Glancing over his stick he would have noticed that *ausa* was not right, suspected that he had left out a *c* and inserted it to produce *causa*, which works fine as far as the meaning is concerned.

d) Heb. 13: 17 [1376] Nam id quemadmodum illis est molestum, ita vobis est inutile.

vtile G^2

Erasmus is talking about obedience to church leaders, the absence of which is annoying to them and without advantage to the congregation. Careful readers will realize that something is wrong with this sentence, but are as likely to correct it by inserting a *non* somewhere as by changing *vtile* to *inutile.*

3. THE REVISED EDITIONS OF 1532 AND 1534

At the conclusion of the letter to Lorenzo Campeggi that serves as the preface to the paraphrases on Ephesians to 2 Thessalonians, Erasmus avers that his paraphrases on the Pauline epistles will live because even his habitual critics approved them. In the 1532 edition a side note was inserted opposite this sentence: *Tum dormiebat Bedda* ('Béda was at that time still asleep'). Although Béda's antipathy for Erasmus' views and writings began as early as 1523, his first published criticism of the *Paraphrases* did not appear until 1526.[58] Quite apart from the long series of letters and publications that constitute Erasmus' controversy with Béda and the Faculty of Theology at Paris,[59] we learn from a letter to Thomas More, dated Basel, 30 March 1527, that Erasmus was engaged in 'revising the *Paraphrases*' (Allen Ep 1804: 71). As usual, there is no circumstantial detail, but Allen was probably correct in believing that Erasmus 'had perhaps already been revising the epistles for the edition which did not appear till 1532' (Allen Ep 1804, n. 72). This critical activity, however, seems also to have included the *Paraphrases on the Gospels*, since the next published evidence includes several corrections of statements in these paraphrases as well as those on the epistles.

Evidently feeling some intimations of mortality, Erasmus published in 1529 a list of 'criticized passages' (*loca notata*) that include selections from the *Paraphrases on the Gospels* and from some of the *Paraphrases on the Epistles.*[60] There are only seven selections from the *Paraphrases on the Epistles,*[61] one of which was examined above in the Praeludium. An example from the paraphrase on 1 Corinthians 15: 7 is typical: 'Read, "he was seen by all the disciples." This because of the slanderers. For the common term "apostle" is sometimes said of all those who proclaimed the Lord seen in the flesh.' The slanderer is Noël Béda. In any event, the low number of corrections published in the *Loca Notata* suggests that revision up to this point in time, 1529, was rather desultory. However, between 1529 and the publication of the new folio edition in 1532 the text of the 1523 folio edition was extensively improved, though it was also to suffer corruption in a dozen places by the typesetters. There are close to four hundred changes in the text, of which some 4 per cent appear to be typographical errors, which is perhaps not bad in a volume of 442 pages, set by at least two different compositors. Of the other new readings, 16 per cent are corrections or other changes in grammar, and 80 per cent are improvements in the text, partly through stylistic changes of one kind or another, but mostly through additions ranging from a single *et* to entire sentences.

The exemplar or copy-text for the 1532 edition was the 1523 folio edition (G^1), as the following agreements show:

a) Eph. 3: 3 [979A3] ... ex quorum lectione poteritis agnoscere ...

agnoscere G^1 *H* : cognoscere *B–F* G^2

b) Eph. 3: 8 [979C15] ... praedicem inuestigabiles diuitias Christi ...

inuestigabiles G^1 *H* : imperuestigabiles *B–F* G^2

c) 1 Tim.1: 2 [1035B11] Si parentes impensius diligunt ac peculiarius velutique vere suos agnoscunt liberos

velutique G^1 *H* : veluti *A–F* G^2

d) Heb. 7: 28 [560] idoneus atque perfectus

atque G^1 *H* : ac *A–F* G^2

e) Heb. 12: 11 [1221] imminet atque premit

atque G^1 *H* : ac *A–F* G^2

f) Heb. 12: 23 [1276–7] ad iudicem ... ac spiritus iustorum hominum ...

ac G^1 *H* : ad *A–F* G^2

g) James 1: 17 [187] vt nos Deo commendet

nos *A–F* G^2 : vos G^1 *H*

h) James 5: 12 [986] Neque solum religiosum sit iurare per Deum

sit *A–F* G^2 : *om.* G^1 *H*

i) 1 Pet. 4: 5 [620] mortuos qui ante Christi aduentum iam excesserint e viuis

iam *H* : tum G^1 : *om. A–F* G^2

j) 3 John 6 [16] quos humaniter accepisti venientes

accepisti G^1 *H* : excepisti *A–F* G^2

The new folio edition was followed two years later by the concomitant octavo edition (*I*), the only edition in Erasmus' lifetime to contain both the *Tomus primus* and the *Tomus secundus*. As with the 1532 folio edition of the *Tomus secundus*, the new edition of the *Tomus primus* enabled Erasmus to publish a considerably improved text of the *Paraphrases on the Gospels and on Acts*. However, so far as the text of the *Paraphrases on the Epistles* is concerned, the octavo edition is essentially a reprint of the text of the 1532 edition. Most of the new readings in the octavo edition seem to be mistakes made by the typesetters. A few, however, appear in the later folio editions of 1538 and 1540 and may have been editorial revisions, though whether made by Erasmus or correctors at the press is not always easy to determine. A few examples:

a) Ep 1062: 127–30 Quod serenissimus Angliae Rex Henricus ... vna cum Achate suo R.D. Thoma cardinale Eboracensi, nec dubito quin te quoque consultore, praestitit suae Britanniae

consulto *I K BAS* : consultore *B–H*

Erasmus may have thought in 1521 that Campeggi was one of Henry's advisers, but by 1534 Campeggi's relations with Henry had changed drastically, as Erasmus with his connections to the English court no doubt knew. The omission of the *-re*, which Allen seems to have considered one of the 'inadvertencies' in the 1534 edition, could well have been a subtle recognition of the new state of affairs.

b) Eph. 6: 16 [1009A14] quicquid ignitorum iaculorum versutus hostis in nos torserit hoc scuto repelletur nec sinet vllum ad animi vitalia penetrare.

ad animi vitalia *B–H* : ad animi *om. I K BAS*

c) Col. 2: 2 [1009B12] opulentam Dei Patris beneficentiam ... sese largiter effundentem

effundentem *B–H* : diffundentem *I K BAS*

Effundere is Erasmus' preferred verb in this kind of context: God pours his kindness out. But the object here is all creation and he may have thought that *diffundere* was more apt: God pours his kindness far and wide.

d) 1 Tim. 3: 16 [1046E9] Si doctrinam requirimus, hic est verae pietatis regula quam sequamur.

verae *G*[2] *I K BAS* : vere *A–F G*[1] *H*

The *regula pietatis* is the gospel, but do we have here truly the rule of godliness or the rule of true godliness? Probably the latter, since *pietas* is being contrasted with 'the petty regulations of Judaism' (*Iudaicae constitutiunculae*). But this confusion of the homonyms *vere* and *verae* is ubiquitous in the *Paraphrases*. The reading in G[2] is certainly a typesetter's mistake, but the change in *I* looks more like a deliberate correction.

e) Heb. 7: 23 [539] et habet nonnihil incertudinis sponsor subinde mutatus.

et habet *A* : vt habet *C–H* : vt habeat *I K BAS*

Here again we have one of those interesting sequences that throw light on the development of the text. Erasmus is contrasting the constant change in the person of the Jewish High Priest with the perpetuity of Christ, the new High Priest, in the presence of God. The reading of *A* is certainly what Erasmus originally wrote. The *vt* in C is probably a typographical error; the interchange of *et* and *ut* is quite common. Yet once made it gives an acceptable sense: 'as the continual change of the guarantor brings with it an element of uncertainty,' though in fact it leaves the sentence without a main clause. The change to the subjunctive *habeat*, which might appear to be an improvement in grammar and style, still leaves the sentence without a main clause and makes the meaning even more difficult to understand. One would not like to charge Erasmus with this, but he is not above corrupting his own text.

4. THE POSTHUMOUS EDITIONS OF 1538 AND 1540

These few readings that the 1534 octavo edition shares with the folio editions of 1538 and 1540 bring us to the last and in some ways most puzzling chapter of our story. Erasmus died in July 1536. In his Last Will and Testament he left a sum of money to be used for the publication of his Complete Works, a plan realized in the 1539–40 edition of his *Opera omnia*, in which the *Paraphrases* occupy the seventh volume. Although this project must have been in the planning stage in 1538, the Froben firm decided to issue a new folio edition of the *Tomus secundus* that same year, probably intended as the counterpart of the folio edition of the *Tomus primus* that had appeared in 1535.[62] The new edition was set from a copy of the 1532 edition; in fact, it is almost a page-by-page reprint of it. The new edition also contains numerous new readings. Do these readings stem from Erasmus – he certainly had time before his death to correct one or more copies of the 1532 edition – or are they the work of editors after his death? The evidence is ambivalent.

a) Eph 5: 2 [984E5] ... verum etiam seipsum exposuerit supplicio crucis

   seipsum *B–I* : semetipsum *K BAS*

   Both forms of the reflexive are found in this context. For *seipsum*, see Eph. 5: 25 [987A8] *quam ... non repudiauit vt seipsum pro illius salute redimenda in mortem traderit*. For *semetipsum*, see Eph. 4: 15 [982E9] *vt semetipsum nobis seruandis impenderit*.

b) Phil. 2: 23 [998A11] simulatque videro quo se flectant res meae

   flectant *B–I* : deflectant *K BAS*

c) Col. 1: 22 [1007F3] sed per corporalem mortem Vnigeniti sui ...
   Vnigeniti sui *B–I* : vnigeniti Filii *K BAS*

   Vnigenitus Filius is the expected formula and as the easier reading was more likely to replace the harder one.

d) 1 Tim. 5: 17 [1052E13] et suppetente quod ad vitae mundiciem pertinet

   mundiciem *A–I* : munditiam *K BAS*

The form *munditia* is more common than *mundicies* in classical texts and that may be the reason for the replacement; if so, it was more likely to be made by an editor, since Erasmus has a predilection for less common forms.

e) 1 Tim. 5: 25 [1053B12] a palam improborum contubernio est absistendum

absistendum *A C–I* : abstinendum *B K BAS*

The revisions in *B* and *K* are certainly independent. Since Erasmus made the one, he quite likely made the other.

f) Heb. 11: 9 [966] vnde reuersus tandem coactus est paulum emere locelli

paulum *A–I* : paululum *K BAS*

The diminutive *paululum* with the form *locelli* is stylistically more effective and the kind of revision Erasmus would be likely to make.

g) Jude 3 [22] Inaestimabilis est fidei thesaurus eoque impensius aduigilandum ne vobis interuertatur

est *A–I* : est enim *K BAS*; vobis *A–H* : nobis *K BAS*

In the paraphrase on Jude 3 the paraphrast urges his readers to vie against false apostles to protect the purity of the faith, to labour not only to persist in their own faith but to help others from being seduced by the imposters. The paraphrase continues with the sentence quoted above, in which it is the faith of the readers of the letter ('you') that is at stake. The revision transforms this additional caution into a universal maxim that serves as the ground for the appeal that has just been made. Such a revision could have been made by Erasmus himself; however, a similar revision occurs in the 1540 folio edition that casts doubt on this assumption.

h) Eph. 5: 9 [985D7] Lux hunc habet fructum ...

Lux *B–K* : Lux enim *BAS*

The paraphrase on this verse runs, 'People who walk at night often stumble because they do not see what they ought to avoid. Light has this benefit, that it indicates what is to be followed, what is to be avoided.' The *enim* introduced in the

1540 folio edition changes the apodictic statement into an explanation of what it means to stumble in the night. But is that what Erasmus really wants to say? Or is it an editor's opinion about what is being said here?

l) 1 John 4: 20 [702] Si quis dixerit, 'Diligo Deum,' quum odio prosequatur fratrem suum, mendax est.

prosequatur *A–I* : persequatur *K BAS*

Prosequi with the ablative of a noun expressing an emotional state is a frequent idiom in the *Paraphrases* – to attend with love, friendship, or, as here, hatred. The phrase is thus a periphrastic substitute for the simple verb 'to love,' 'to hate.' Does one persecute with hatred or rather with the instruments of hatred: blows, arrests, executions, and the like? This change could have been made by a typesetter, substituting the more common for the less common expression, or by an editor who thinks he knows better than the author what the author wants to say.

Some similar changes could be the work of a learned editor or, more likely perhaps, a careless compositor:

a) Eph. 5: 19 [986D1] Haec est voluptas, haec hilaritas, ... digna Christianis

hilaritas *B–I* : charitas *K BAS*

Charitas could be defended as a translation of *agape* in the meaning 'love-feast.' But since it involves only replacing the letters *hil* by *ch*, this is most likely a mental error, the more common noun replacing the less common one in the mind of the compositor as he repeats out loud the copy before setting it.

b) 2 Tim. 1: 8 [1059F8] Qualem istic se praestitit, talis erga me fuit et Romae.

praestitit *A–I* : praestiterit *K BAS*

There is no reason for the subjunctive in a simple correlation like this sentence.

c) 1 Thess. (title) IN EPISTOLAM PAVLI ... PRIOREM PARAPHRASIS

PRIOREM *B–G* : *om. H I* : PRIMAM *K BAS*

The omission of *PRIOREM* in *H* was certainly accidental. The use of *Prior* and *Posterior* in place of *Prima* and *Secunda* is characteristic of the March 1521 edition,[63] but *prior* used with one epistle evidently does not guarantee that *posterior* will used for the second epistle. To judge from Erasmus' method of citation in the *Ratio verae theologiae,* he consistently employs *prior* in designating the first of two epistles, but may use either *posterior* or *secunda* when designating the second.[64] Hence the *Prima* found in *K BAS* is probably a correction made by someone at the press and not by Erasmus himself.

It would appear, then, that the 1538 folio edition contains corrections or revisions made by Erasmus but also a large number of changes made by someone else. Erasmus presumably left at his death a copy of the 1532 edition into which he had entered the revisions made for the 1534 octavo edition as well as new revisions for a future edition, probably at the same time he was preparing the copy for the 1535 folio edition of the *Paraphrases on the Gospels and Acts*. This copy would have come into the possession of Hieronymus Froben and Nicholaus Episcopius, who were the executors of Erasmus' Last Will and Testament, together with the other materials that were eventually used for the publication of the *Opera omnia*.[65]

Typesetting for the octavo counterpart to the 1538 folio edition began in late 1539 and was apparently finished in early 1540.[66] Design and typography are similar to that of the 1534 octavo edition. The following examples show that the text is also that of the 1534 edition:

a) 1 Pet. 3: 14 [491–3] ... qua in re possunt laedere? Auferent pecuniam mox alioqui relinquendam, affligent corpus, occident breui morituros.

auferent *A–C K BAS* : auferant *D–I L*

affligent *A–H K BAS* : affligant *I L*

The change to the subjunctive in *D*, whether editorial or a mistake by the typesetter, creates a grammatical inconsistency that is removed in one way in *I* and *L*, another way in *K* and *BAS*.

b) 1 Pet. 3: 21 [363–5] Neque tamen vobis satis est quod per baptismi diluuium periere peccata, periere prauae cupiditates pristinae vitae nisi adsit conscientia per omnem deinde vitam respondens beneficio diuino.

periere peccata *A–H K BAS* : *om. I L*

c) James 5: 4 [924–5] Ecce fraudatus sua mercede messor, qui sudans demessuit segetes vestras, clamat ad Deum et vindictam flagitat

fraudatus *A–H K BAS* : fraudatur *I L*

d) Heb. 2: 13 [129–31] Atqui is [*sc.* Deus Pater] quando promisit se omnia subiecturum pedibus Filii, non est quin et illos seruaturus sit cum quibus et in quibus regnet Filius.

et in quibus *om. I L*

The reading in *I* might very well be a deliberate revision, in which case it would be similar to the situation of the Basel 1520 and 1521 editions, where a correction made for the initial reprint of a first edition was not made in the copy used for the March 1521 edition, since the omission does not occur in the 1538 or 1540 folio editions. Still, omissions resulting from eye-skip are a common mistake of typesetters. The following variant is unquestionably a typographical error:

e) Heb. 11: 8 [960–7] Eiusdem fiduciae fuit quod ... nihil omnibus hisce rebus commotus est Abraham vt diffideret Deo ...

quod *A–H K BAS* : qui *I L*

The 1539–40 octavo has a large number of similar mistakes and is in this kind of negligence comparable to the 1522 folio edition (*E*). On the other hand, it also agrees with the 1540 folio (*BAS*) in several readings:

a) Eph. 3:21 [981A1] per Christum Iesum cuius commercio dotes tantas possidet [*sc.* Ecclesia]

tantas dotes *B–K* : dotes tantas *L BAS*

The transposition could be a coincidence.

b) Col. 2: 9 [1010A11] vt ... non sit quod vmbras ... sectemini

sit *L BAS* : est *B–K*

The correction to the subjunctive is necessary.

c) 1 Thess. Argument [1017–18: 6] Et id quidem agit capite primo et secundo. In caeteris tribus instituit eos ...

tribus *L BAS* : duobus *B–K*

There are five chapters in 1 Thessalonians. The correction is easy, but was evidently overlooked through nine successive editions.

d) Titus 3: 9 [1074B9] Quo aetatis suae anno Solomon genuerit Roboam?

quo ... anno *A–K* : quoto ... anno *L BAS*

e) James 2: 18 [482] sed ex viua fide quae nobis persuasit Deo praestari quicquid praestatur ob ipsum proximo nec ab alio quam ab illo sperandum esse praemium.

ab alio *L BAS* : alió *A–K*

f) 1 John 3: 7 [464–5] Huic qui vere ac totus adhaeret, quod potest ab omni vitiorum inquinamento temperat

quod *A–K* : quoad *L BAS*

These agreements suggest that whoever edited the copy for the 1540 folio edition in the *Opera omnia* may also have prepared the copy for the 1539 octavo, but either in a preliminary way or at most in a perfunctory fashion, because in the majority of instances where the 1540 folio differs from the earlier editions, the 1539 octavo agrees with them, not with the text in the *Opera omnia*.

Though the titles of individual paraphrases and the side notes are treated differently, the text itself of the *Tomus secundus* in the 1540 *Opera omnia* appears to have been set from the 1538 edition. The typography of the two editions is quite different, so this assumption can be established only by conjunctive readings. The 1540 edition contains, with a few exceptions,[67] all the new readings found in the 1538 edition. It introduces an almost equal number of new readings, some of which are necessary corrections; most, however, would be better called false corrections. The edition also contains several misprints, including the omission of an entire clause.[68] Typesetting and proof-reading appear to have been hastily and somewhat negligently done compared to the more careful work in the 1532 and 1538 editions. One reading in particular illustrates the dependence of the 1540 on the 1538 edition:

a) Jude 3 [20] Neque solum in hoc laborate, vt persistatis in fide vestra

laborate *A–I* : laborare *K* : laboraui *BAS*

The interchange of *r* and *t*, which are very similar in appearance in the Froben roman fonts, is a frequent mistake. The infinitive cannot be right, so emendation is called for, but the editor, whoever he was (Simon Grynaeus is a likely candidate), missed the mark. By contrast, the following look like good emendations:

a) Col. 2: 9 [1010A11] vt ... non sit quod vmbras ... sectemini

sit *BAS*: est *B–K*

b) 1 Tim. Argument [1033–4: 14] quaestiones sophistarum inani doctrinae specie sese venditantium

venditantium *B BAS* : venditantes *A C–K*

It is the 'sophists,' not the 'questions' that advertise themselves. The same correction in *B* suggests that it was Erasmus who made this change in the copy for *BAS*.

c) Heb. 6: 4 [382] vt qui semel reliquerint tenebras ... iamque ... experti sint Dei gratuitam liberalitatem

sint *BAS* : sunt *A–K*

Possible, but unnecessary revisions occur at

a) Col. 1: 27 [1008D13] salutem, quam primum credebant solis Iudaeis delatam

delatam *B–K* : delegatam *BAS*

b) Titus 3: 9 [1074B9] Quot annos vixerit Matusalem? Quo aetatis suae *anno* Solomon genuerit Roboam?

Matusalem *A–K* : Metusalem *BAS* ; quo ... anno *A–K* : quoto ... anno *BAS*

c) Heb. 11: 19 [1021] quod in ipso fuerat

fuerat *A–K* : erat *BAS*

This could equally well be an error by the typesetter, who omitted the initial *fu*.

d) James 4: 11 [846] Lex euangelica vetat ne nos vicissim iudicemus.

nos *A–K* : quos *BAS*

Quos would otherwise be an acceptable reading except that the adverb *vicissim*, which when combined as here with a reflexive pronoun functions in Erasmus' Latin as a reciprocal pronoun, is against it: 'Gospel law forbids us to judge one another.' The corrector should have deleted the *vicissim*.

e) 1 John 1: 1 [3] Neque de rebus mediocribus *leuibusue* aut incompertis vobis scribimus

leuibusue *A–K* : neque de leuibus *BAS*[69]

f) 1 John 3: 7 [465] *quod* potest, ab ... inquinamento temperat

quod *A–K* : quoad *BAS*

One final example may serve as a caution for editors:

g) Heb. 10: 26 [833] ... edocti quid expectandum, quid fugiendum

expectandum *A–K* : expetendum *BAS*

What to seek, what to avoid is a common topic in classical ethics and a recurring one in the *Paraphrases*,[70] where it is often joined with the Christian topic, what to expect. So in the paraphrase on 1 Timothy 4: 8 (LB 7: 724A5–9) we are told that 'evangelical piety proclaims whatever must either be sought in the present life or hoped for in the future.' In the paraphrase on Titus 2: 13 (LB 7: 1071F3–6) we are told not to hunt for the petty rewards of this life but to await the extraordinary reward of immortality. What is awaited specifically is the arrival of Jesus Christ and the Last Judgment. The statement in the paraphrase on Hebrews 10: 26 falls into this pattern: 'After we have come to know through the Gospel the truth, having been thoroughly taught what is to be expected [or sought], what is to be avoided, and what rewards await the godly, what the ungodly,' etc. What we seek is a godly life, what we await are the rewards of that life. It might seem that the mention of the rewards after the mention of what is to be expected is a tautology which the emendation in *BAS* would remove. Might Erasmus have made such an emendation? The answer is yes, for he did just that in the paraphrase on 1 John 5: 20, where he changed in the 1532 edition an original 'eternal life which alone is to be expected' to 'which alone is to be sought.'[71]

Persons who wished to obtain a copy of the *Paraphrases* from the Froben firm in 1540 or 1541 had two choices. They could buy the octavo edition, which contained a lightly revised but rather corrupt text of the 1532 edition, or the folio edition, which contained the same text but in a much more heavily revised and edited form. Excluding the mistakes made by the typesetters, which were quite numerous in both octavo and folio editions, the text of the two editions differs substantively in about two hundred places, about the same amount of difference that we find in the folio and octavo editions of 1523. In short, we can say that, in the twenty-three-year history of its publication from November 1517 to 1540 in authorized editions, at no time would a reader find a text of the *Paraphrases on the Epistles* in the form that Erasmus truly wanted to place before his reading public.

The affiliations among the twenty-eight authorized editions are summed up in the Stemma Editionum (below, p. 257). Beyond revising the first editions for the Froben reprints (*B*), Erasmus does not seem to have contributed anything further to their texts. Major revision begins with the copy (A^{cc}) for the March 1521 edition (*C*). Further revision continues without cessation until the last authorized edition in volume seven of the *Opera omnia*, but, as indicated in the preceding discussion, it is not always possible to determine whether a particular correction or revision was made by Erasmus or someone else, especially in the three posthumous editions. Hence ^{c} or ^{cc} (first correction, second correction) should not automatically be assumed to be Erasmus himself.

AUTHORIZED EDITIONS AND THEIR SIGLA

A edd. Louan., Th. Martinus, 1517–21, in 4°;
ed. Antuerp., M. Hillenius, 1519, in 8°.

B edd. Basil., Io. Frobenius, 1518–20, in 4° vel 8°.

C ed. Basil., Io. Frobenius, mense Mart. 1521, in 8°.

D ed. Basil., Io. Frobenius, mense Iul. 1521, in 8°.

E	ed. Basil., Io. Frobenius, mense Feb. 1522, in 2°.
F	ed. Basil., Io. Frobenius, mense Maio 1522, in 8°.
G	consensus G^1 *et* G^2.
G^1	ed. Basil., Io. Frobenius, 1523, in 2°.
G^2	ed. Basil., Io. Frobenius, 1523, in 8°.
H	ed. Basil., Hier. Frobenius et Nic. Episcopius, 1532, in 2°.
I	ed. Basil., Hier. Frobenius et Nic. Episcopius, 1534, in 8°.
K	ed. Basil., Hier. Frobenius et Nic. Episcopius, 1538, in 2°.
L	ed. Basil., Hier. Frobenius et Nic. Episcopius, 1539–40, in 8°.
BAS	ed. Basil., Hier. Frobenius et Nic. Episcopius, 1540, in 2°.

A^c, C^c, D^c, etc: corrected copy of A/C/D etc = exemplar or copy-text.

A^{cc} etc: copy-text with additional corrections

STEMMA EDITIONUM

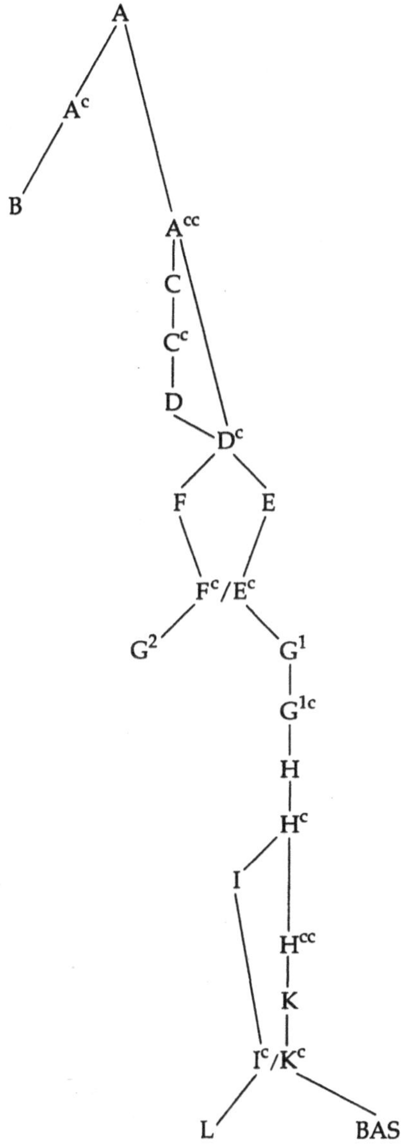

A
A^c
B
A^{cc}
C
C^c
D
D^c
F
E
F^c/E^c
G^2
G^1
G^{1c}
H
H^c
I
H^{cc}
K
I^c/K^c
L
BAS

NOTES

1 There were also twenty or more editions of part or all of these paraphrases by other printers during this same period, but since there is no evidence that Erasmus contributed to any of them, they are omitted from the present study.
2 Only one woman is known to have contributed to this endeavour, Gertrude Lachner-Froben, who financed the publication of one of the editions. Otherwise, so far as I know, the editors, typesetters, and pressmen were all males.
3 The Latin is *in transferendis formis*. I am not sure what operation Erasmus has in mind, but the kind of accident he imagines happened would have to occur during imposition, probably in moving overrun lines to another forme. An accident of this kind did occur in the printing of the March 1521 edition of the collected *Paraphrases*; see p. 235 above.
4 See *Elenchus in N. Bedae censuras*, LB 9: 509A.
5 See *Supputatio calumniarum Natalis Bedae*, LB 9: 692D–E, and *Declarationes ad censuras Lutetiae vulgatas sub nomine Facultatis Theologiae Pariensis*, LB 9: 881F–2A, though the latter work does not cite the reconstructed lost line.
6 See Margaret Mann Phillips, 'The Mystery of the Metsys Portrait.' The evidence of the portrait is suspect since it is one of two copies of the lost original. One copy, now in Hampton Court, England, has the written text; the other, now in Parma, Italy, has no writing of any kind. If the original painting contained a representation of the written text, then Metsys had to have had a handwritten text that Erasmus would have given him at some point, but whether in his own hand or that of one of his secretaries we cannot say. Title and script do not correspond to Erasmus' own practice as known from the autograph manuscripts of the paraphrases on the Gospels of Matthew and John. Erasmus did not bind blank pages before writing on them and the depiction of the paraphrase as a book in the making is Metsys's way of suggesting the completed work. The appearance of the handwritten text, if he did in fact include it in his painting, resembles what one would see in a book and contributes to the impression of the book that the work will become, to be added eventually to the cabinet of Erasmus' publications that forms the background in the painting. A later portrait by Hans Holbein the Younger depicts Erasmus beginning to write the *Paraphrase on the Gospel of Mark*. This portrait was to be a gift to some friend or patron in England, possibly Thomas More because Erasmus is depicted wearing a sapphire ring that More had given him; see Andres Furger-Gunti and Burkhart von Roda, eds, *Erasmus von Rotterdam:*

Vorkämpfer für Frieden und Toleranz, 16. The version with the opening words from the paraphrase (now in the Basel Kunstmuseum) seems to have been a preliminary study for the painting that was actually sent (now in Paris, in the Louvre). The latter, however, depicts Erasmus, pen in hand, staring at the blank page. There is no text and hence no indication of what he is about to write.

7 This word is spelled *Vratia* in the painting, but the *V* must be a misreading of *G* by the painter of the Hampton Court copy.

8 See Allen Epp 423: 39–43; 495: 41–3; 692: 13–33.

9 Allen Ep 421: 112: 'In Psalmum Beatus Vir praelusi. Paulum aggrediar.'

10 See CWE 42: xiv–xv.

11 Allen dates the letter tentatively to October 1517. Cf also Allen Ep 683: 11–15.

12 For Erasmus' movements in 1517 see M.A. Nauwelaerts, 'Érasme à Louvain: Ephémérides d'un séjour de 1517 à 1521.'

13 Cf. also Allen Ep 706: 23, from Thomas More, dated Calais, 5 November <1517>: 'Gaudeo Paraphrasim sub praelo esse.' Erasmus had to have written to More a week or more earlier informing him of this fact.

14 It normally took a fortnight for a messenger to travel from Basel to Louvain. For Erasmus to reply on 6 December meant that Beatus had written around 22 November or earlier and that word about Martens' activity had left Louvain by 7 or 8 November, or soon after the presswork had begun.

15 Allen Ep 732: 15–24. Erasmus goes on to justify his request that Froben postpone publication until Martens has had a chance to sell his own edition.

16 Allen Ep 886: 17–19; cf. Epp 889: 39–40 and 891: 21–4.

17 See Allen Epp 886: 40 and 891: 22–3; also Ep 886: 31–2 to Tunstall.

18 Otherwise Martens would have begun the signatures in the normal fashion with a, b, c, etc.

19 Allen Ep 916: 41–4; compare what Erasmus had to say a year earlier about works of scholastic theology: 'Porro, ut omnia vere, ut omnia recte definierint, praeterquam quod ieiune frigideque tractantur ista, quoto cuique vacat tantum voluminum evolvere? aut quis possit secum Aquinatis Secundae secundam circumferre?' (Allen Ep 858: 57–60, dated Basel, 14 August 1518).

20 Froben's first printed book, published in October 1491, was an octavo edition of the Bible, the first time a Bible was printed in this format.

21 The Erasmus Bibliography in the Rotterdam Public Library records a folio edition of the *Tomus secundus* published in Roshilde, Denmark, in 1534, but this appears to be an error for the folio volume of

Erasmus' arguments and Latin translation of the Pauline epistles, printed that year by Hans Barth; see L.M. Nielsen, *Dansk Bibliografi*, 1: 97 no. 205: *Textus omnium epistolarum beatissimi Pauli apostoli ad castigationem emendatiorum codicum versionis Erasmi*, etc. (Roschildie: n.p., 1534).

22 See Nauwelaerts, 'Érasme à Louvain,' 14–16.

23 Allen Ep 1025: 18–19: 'Hybernis his mensibus reliquas Paraphrases absolvemus adiutore Christo.' The letter is dated Louvain, 16 October 1519, and is addressed to Richard Pace, another of the English friends, who was in Switzerland when Erasmus first began the paraphrases but later took a keen interest in them.

24 For the history of the controversy see Cecilia Asso, *La teologia e la grammatica: La controversia tra Erasmo ed Edward Lee*, 17–58, or Erika Rummel, *Erasmus and His Catholic Critics*, 1: 135–42. For an example of its influence on the interpretation of a biblical text see the *Paraphrase on 1 Peter*, ASD VII–6: 173–4.

25 The *Nouum Instrumentum* (Basel: Johann Froben, 1516) and the *Nouum Testamentum* (Basel: Johann Froben, 1519).

26 The actual facts are probably beyond recovery. See Lee's letter to Erasmus, Ep 1061, and his *Apologia ... ad diluendas quorundam calumnias*, both dated 1 February 1520, and published in his *Annotationes in Annotationes Erasmi* (Paris: Gilles de Gourmont, 1520); the *Apologia*, is reprinted in Asso, *Teologia* 237–49. For Erasmus see Epp 998 (to Lee, dated Louvain, 15 July 1519) and 1053 (to Thomas Lupset, dated Louvain, 13 December 1519), and his *Apologia qua respondet invectivis Lei* (Antwerp: Michael Hillen, 1520), reprinted in Ferguson, *Opuscula*, 223–303.

27 *Apologia qua respondet invectivis Lei*, in Ferguson, 252–6 passim and 286, lines 1210–29 in particular.

28 Ferguson, 230–1.

29 The work, which breaks off in the middle of the paraphrase on 2 Tim. 4: 15 (sig. f7v), is bound with copies of the Basel 1519 editions of Erasmus' *Ratio verae theologiae* and of the *Paraphrase on Romans*, and is located in the Archives (not the Library as reported in CWE 42: xxi) of the Cathedral at Aachen. A photostat exists in the Rotterdam Public Library.

30 Allen Ep 1043, introduction. Allen never saw the extant copy of the book and based this possibility on some similarities in its text to Ep 1053.

31 A similar use of 1519 for 1520 occurs in Ep 1062, the preface to the paraphrases on Ephesians to 2 Thessalonians, dated 5 February 1519. Erasmus does occasionally employ Old Style dating; cf. Epp 537 (an autograph letter), 538, and 539, all written on the same day, 24 February. On the other hand, typographical errors in printing Anno XIX, XX, or XXI are not uncommon.

32 Allen Ep 1060: 52, first published in *Epistolae ad diuersos* (Basel: Froben, August 1521).
33 Alfred Hartmann and B.R. Jenny, eds., *Die Amerbachkorrespondenz*, 2: 231 no. 722, lines 19–21. Cf. also Ep 1064, a résumé of a letter written to Johann Oecolampadius, most likely sent with the budget for Basel.
34 Froben's quarto edition of March 1520 has sixteen and a half sheets, so the Martens edition, if there was one, probably had at least seventeen sheets (Froben's quartos tend to be a little shorter than Martens'), which at the normal rate of four sheets a week would take a single press four weeks to complete. The use of two presses would, of course, double this rate of production.
35 Although they were printed and signed separately, Froben clearly hoped to sell the two editions as packages. An example is provided by the British Library copy (shelf mark 1108.a.23.) in which octavo editions of the *Ratio verae theologiae* (Basel, February 1520), the *Paraclesis* (Basel, February 1520), the March 1520 editions of the paraphrases on 1 Timothy etc., and Ephesians etc., are bound together. A note written on an endpaper states that <the book> was purchased in Augsburg in 1520.
36 This alternation between the genitive of the author's name and the construction with *per* and the accusative occurs throughout the titles of the individual paraphrases. Two autograph versions of the paraphrase on chapter 1 of the Gospel of Matthew survive. In the first and apparently earlier version, Erasmus wrote *In euangelium Matthei paraphrasis Erasmi Roterodami*, in the second version ... *paraphrasis per Erasmum Roterodamum*. He is not consistent in such matters.
37 See *Responsio ad epistolam paraeneticam Alberti Pii*, LB 9: 1116F and *Apologia ad viginti et quattuor libros A. Pii*, LB 9: 1132D. For later developments of the principle, see the remarks of Bernard Roussel, p. 70–1 above.
38 Allen Ep 1112: 1–18 = ASD VII-6: 179, line 1–180, line 20. This is a literary topos and too much stock need not be put in it; cf. Allen Ep 284: 1–6, also to Wolsey regarding a dedication. But in the cover letter with which he seems to have sent the work to Wolsey in England he still refers to it as 'a little book of sorts,' *qualicunque libello*; Allen Ep 1132: 10.
39 Allen Ep 1068 to John Fisher, dated 21 February, shows that Erasmus had not yet seen a copy.
40 The *Apologia qua respondet duabus invectivis Edouardi Lei* in March 1520 and the *Liber quo respondet annotationibus Lei* in April, forthcoming in ASD IX and in English translation in CWE 72.
41 See ASD VII-6: 181 n. 30–1.
42 See H.J. de Jonge, 'Erasmus und die Glossa Ordinaria zum Neuen Testament.'

43 See ASD VII-6: 168–7.
44 Schumann indicates on his title page that the book is a second edition *secundis typis excussae*. Froben omits any statement to this effect, leaving the purchaser to guess whether it is the first edition or a later one.
45 Allen Ep 1177: 45–6, dated Louvain, 31 December 1520, indicates that he has completed the *Paraphrase on James*, but not the paraphrase on the Johannine epistles.
46 No year date is given, but it has to be 1521.
47 See *Responsio ad collationes iuuenis gerontodidascali*, LB 9: 986A.
48 There is a colophon following the *Paraphrase on Philemon* on the penultimate page of the quire, with a blank final page (tt^{8v}).
49 The colophon at the end of the *Paraphrase on Hebrews* is the only place in the book that contains the month date March and thus gives us a terminus for the printing.
50 The octavo edition appeared in May.
51 The folio is dated 15 March 1522, the octavo simply March 1522. The latter was rapidly reprinted and was apparently the more popular of the two formats.
52 See Allen Epp 1248, 1249, 1255: 24–9, and 1342: 66–7. Schiner left Brussels on 30 June; see J.S. Brewer et al., eds., *Letters and Papers, Foreign and Domestic of the Reign of Henry VIII*, 3, nos. 1357 and 1388.
53 One month according to Allen Ep 1255: 82, two months according to Ep 1342: 243–4. Though Allen preferred the former, the latter amount of time seems more likely.
54 Cf., e.g., Irmgard Bezzel, *Erasmusdrucke des sechszehnten Jahrhunderts in bayerischen Bibliotheken*, 402 no. 1469.
55 The alternative would be that Froben had for some reason retained the copies he had received.
56 The sixteen unauthorized reprints by other printers between 1519 and 1523 likewise have no role.
57 For this practice see *Apologia qua respondet invectivis Lei*, Ferguson, 261: 560–5; *Responsio ad annotationes Lei*, ad C (LB 9: 191D–E).
58 See the essay by Erika Rummel, chapter 9 below.
59 See the article on Béda in COE 1: 116–18.
60 See Allen Ep 2095, introduction.
61 One passage each from the paraphrases on Hebrews, 1 Corinthians, Philippians, and Titus, and three passages from the *Paraphrase on Romans*.
62 There was no doubt also a market, even though the 1532 edition may not have been completely sold out. The Froben firm published a separate folio edition in 1541 of the volume of paraphrases in the 1540 *Opera omnia*, probably for sale to those unwilling to purchase the entire *Opera omnia*.

63 Cf. ad Thessalonicenses posteriorem (posteriorem *C–H* : secundam B); ad Timotheum priorem (all editions); ad Timotheum posteriorem Argumentum (posteriorem *C–H* : secundam *A B*); ad Timotheum secundam Paraphrasis (secundam *A B D–H* : posteriorem C). Since there are three Johannine epistles, they are always designated by ordinal numbers in their titles: prima, secunda, tertia.
64 For *prior*, cf. *Ratio verae theologiae*, Holborn, 241: 24, 243: 33; for *posterior*, ibid, 243: 22; for *secunda*, ibid, 241: 27 and 33.
65 Hieronymus Froben, in whose house Erasmus lived during the last year of his life, was, together with his brother-in-law and business partner, Nikolaus Bischoff (Episcopius), one of Erasmus' executors; see the entries for Episcopius and Hieronymus in COE 1: 437–8 and 2: 58–60.
66 The title page has the date 1539, while the colophon has 1540.
67 A striking exception occurs at Eph. 4: 28 (LB 7: 984A1–3): 'Qui ... furto compilabat alios, iam non solum temperet ab alienis, verum etiam vltro de suis impartiat' (suis *A–I BAS* : suo *K*).
68 At Heb. 13: 21 (ASD VII-6: 1383). Many of the side notes are also omitted, but this seems to be the result of the change in the design of the page, which admitted fewer side notes, rather than simple negligence.
69 See the discussion in ASD VII-6: 257 n. 3.
70 Cf. the paraphrase on Rom 2: 17–18 (LB 7: 784A): 'vt ... dignoscas quae fugienda, quae expetenda.'
71 Cf. the paraphrase on 1 John 5: 20 (ASD 7: 844): 'et vita aeterna quae sola est expetenda' (expetenda *H* : expectanda *A–G*).

NINE

Why Noël Béda Did Not Like Erasmus' *Paraphrases*

Erika Rummel

In part, this essay addresses a complaint recently voiced by James Farge: that scholars concerned with Erasmus' controversies, or more generally with controversies between humanists and scholastics, tend to focus on the humanists' arguments.[1] I would like to compensate for this imbalance by focusing on the scholastic side, that is, Noël Béda's critique of Erasmus' *Paraphrases*, considering three aspects: first, Béda's remarks about himself and his party, the scholastic theologians; second, his remarks about Erasmus and his party, the biblical humanists; and third, Béda's method of argumentation as compared with Erasmus.'

First, however, some background information on the polemic between Erasmus and Béda. Béda played a leading role in the faculty of theology at Paris from 1520 on. In 1523, he was approached for an opinion on Erasmus' *Paraphase on Luke*. The Paris printer Konrad Resch wished to reprint the book. For this purpose he needed a privilege from the Parlement, which, in matters touching on religion, routinely consulted the faculty of theology. Béda, who was their consultant on this occasion, found what he considered significant theological errors in the *Paraphrases*. When Erasmus was informed of the objections, he initiated a correspondence with his critic, perhaps to fend off an official investigation or to reach a private understanding with Béda. If this was indeed Erasmus' object, he was unsuccessful. Béda adopted a patronizing tone, and Erasmus replied bluntly. The correspondence therefore exacerbated rather than improved the two men's relationship.[2]

In February 1526, Erasmus raised the ante and officially complained to the faculty of theology about Béda's hostility. He enclosed an apologia, as yet unprinted, entitled *Divinationes* (a legal term referring to a preliminary hearing to determine who will prosecute a case).[3] The faculty was not impressed with Erasmus' arguments and three months later, in May 1526, permitted Béda to publish his critical review of Erasmus' *Paraphrases.* It is this book that forms the basis of my remarks. The tract was entitled *Annotationum ... in Jacobum Fabrum Stapulensem libri duo et in Desiderium Erasmum Roterodamum liber unus*; that is, it combined criticism of Lefèvre's biblical commentaries with criticism of Erasmus' *Paraphrases.*[4]

My first question, then, concerns Béda's remarks about himself and his scholastic colleagues. He tells us that he was motivated, not by personal ambitions, but by concern for the truth and the orthodox faith.[5] This is a commonplace assertion that can be found in the opening paragraphs of many polemics. Polemicists also often stress that they are engaging in polemic unwillingly, that they have not started the quarrel and are merely defending themselves against the accusations of an aggressive opponent. Not so Béda. He candidly admits that he took the initiative, explaining that his book was part of a campaign to mobilize public opinion against men he regarded as dangerous to the orthodox faith.[6] He wanted to complement the work of others who had criticized Erasmus earlier on but had not covered the whole territory. He mentions Edward Lee, Iacobus Stunica, and Petrus Sutor, who had commented on Erasmus' edition of the New Testament;[7] he was now extending their investigation to the *Paraphrases.* In a way, Béda says, this was the more important task, because the *Paraphrases* were being translated into the vernacular and, by their very nature, would have a much larger readership than the New Testament edition.[8]

It is clear, moreover, that Béda saw himself acting, not merely as an individual, but as a representative of scholastic theology and the mouthpiece of the faculty at Paris. He therefore has much to say about scholastic theology. He dwells on two points in particular: (1) scholastic theologians have rendered great service to the church in her battle against heretics; and (2) they have been unfairly characterized as enemies of humanistic studies.

Scholastic theologians contributed to the defence of orthodoxy by systematizing theology and dealing efficiently with problems of biblical interpretation. In these endeavours, they had been so successful that heresy was at one time all but extinct.[9] But, more recently, scholastic theology had met with disdain and neglect; the consequences were obvious: heresies were making a come-back, promoted by people like Erasmus and Lefèvre. In making these claims, Béda is emphatic about the competence of the theologians to explain biblical passages and pronounce on questions of faith. He is equally emphatic in rejecting Erasmus' suggestion that certain biblical passages were obscure in themselves and defied explanation. In Béda's eyes, such remarks merely proved his point. Erasmus' confusion was the result of his neglect of the study of scholastic theology. He was obviously unaware that the questions he was raising had already been satisfactorily explained by the theologians and definitively settled by the church:

> When Erasmus says that attempting to explain discrepancies in the evangelists was like walking in a labyrinth, anyone can see how impious a remark this is. For one cannot cite any apparent discrepancy in the Scriptures that the holy doctors of the church have not long ago reconciled in a Catholic manner or that could not easily be resolved by the theologians ... The meaning of Holy Writ is an inescapable labyrinth only for those who do not follow the thread of the interpretation given by the Catholic doctors and the church.[10]

Second, Erasmus and others of his party wrongly accused scholastic theologians of hostility toward humanists and humanistic studies. The accusation was unjust. The theologians respected humanistic studies:

> For no one is so weak in his head and so lacking in intelligence ... that he does not recognize and praise humane studies and language skills as a gift of God. There is no reason why anyone should disapprove of them. Conversely, no one can approve of ... ungrateful men who abuse God's gifts to the ruination of many people. Let them desist, therefore, let them desist from falsely claiming that professional theologians act out of hatred for *bonae literae,* as they call them, when they object to the humanists' false teaching ... [L]et

> them desist from accusing us of envy if we do not congratulate them on their literary studies, if we do not champion their studies, and finally if we do not praise their books.

Theologians did not object to humanistic studies per se, Béda said, but merely to students pursuing them to the exclusion of more important subjects and indulging in them to the detriment of their souls.[11] Reversing the charge brought against the theologians, Béda accused the humanists in turn of hate-mongering. They openly expressed scorn for the scholastics and reviled them as barbarians, rabbis, and crass fools:

> They say that they spend a lifetime focusing exclusively on philosophical trifles and sophistical arguments, barely greeting Holy Writ from the threshold; that they shrink from reading the theologians of old, the holy doctors of the church; and that they are called scholastic theologians but do not merit the name of theologians at all.[12]

With this quotation I have arrived at my second question: what does Béda have to say about Erasmus and his party? First, and most significantly, Béda calls Erasmus and Lefèvre *humanistae theologizantes*, theologizing humanists,

> men who have ventured to comment on all sacred matters, although they are equipped only with a knowledge of the humanities and of languages ... [T]hey think they ought to be regarded as true and genuine theologians because they have drawn the pure and divine knowledge of theology from its very springs rather than from puddles and they devote themselves to the reading of God's words themselves and to the biblical text rather than to philosophical studies and the writings of scholastic theologians.[13]

Yet it was precisely the neglect of scholastic theology that caused these amateur theologians to fall into grave error. Erasmus called his work a 'paraphrase,' but he was a paraphraser in the negative sense of the word. 'The grammarians tell us that one meaning of the word *paraphrastes* is "wrong interpreter and corruptor"; and *paraphrasis* may denote "a wrong interpretation, one that is alien to the sense."' This was the type of paraphrase offered by Erasmus.[14]

Although Erasmus claimed that he was representing what was said by the evangelist, he often represented his own opinion. Béda gives the following example. Paraphrasing Luke 2, Erasmus had written *Symeon senex puero Iesu bene precatus est* ('Simon wished Jesus well,' or 'prayed on his behalf'). Béda argued that this was not the meaning of the evangelist and that Erasmus' statement amounted to blasphemy. '*Bene precari alicui* means either wishing that some blessing, lacking at present, be conferred on someone by God or by another who can procure this blessing with his prayers, or wishing that someone may keep or increase a blessing he already has.' According to Béda, Simon's blessing was meant for Mary and Joseph. To apply it to Jesus was blasphemy. Erasmus was substituting for the evangelical truth impious words drawn from his own mind. Béda cited Erasmus' disclaimer, 'I want to advise the general reader that it is not I who speaks in the *Paraphrases* anywhere,' and immediately rejected it: 'So saying, this new theologian wants us to believe that everything spoken in the person of Saint Luke must be taken as gospel truth and contains nothing Erasmian ... but Luke never said this; it is Erasmus speaking with his usual audacity.'[15] Such misrepresentations and misinterpretations, said Béda, made it clear that untrained persons must not be permitted to undertake biblical exegesis.[16]

The example just quoted illustrates one element in Béda's portrait of the humanists: their lack of theological training and the errors committed on account of it. A second element that irritated Béda were the priorities of the humanists. In his opinion, they fretted too much about style; they paid more attention to language than to content:

> Lefèvre and Erasmus regard the new style, that is, a more cultured and polished way of treating Holy Writ, a good thing and useful in promoting religion. Wise and experienced men, however, have always judged it imprudent and approaching impiety and sacrilege zealously to superimpose on a humble and pious teaching the pompous and flattering style of heathen literature, as if that by itself could lead to salvation.[17]

Discussing the humanists' emphasis on style, Béda was especially offended by Erasmus' criticism of Paul's idiomatic lapses and solecisms. 'It is the height of blasphemy to complain about the style of Holy Writ, for such complaints suggest that God is an inexperienced writer.' Béda pointed out that Gregory the Great had condemned this attitude, saying explicitly that the Bible was not subject to the rules of the grammarian Donatus.[18] Béda concluded from Erasmus' criticism of Paul's style that he regarded himself superior to the apostle:

> This wretched man plays the instructor, trying to teach God and his apostle to construe correctly, setting himself up as judge over the divine [word]. This pitiful man thinks he is more than a demigod and superior to the apostle in rhetorical polish, putting his confidence in his knowledge of the humanities and his language skills.[19]

So far we have seen that Béda depicts Erasmus and other biblical humanists as incompetent and concerned with style rather than content. A third element in his portrait of the biblical humanists is their connection with Lutheranism. More specifically, Béda held the humanists responsible for creating religious factions: 'They appear to have taught Luther ... rather than having learned from him; indeed they anticipated much of what Luther himself wrote later on.' This statement concerns humanists in general. Interestingly, Béda was less sure about Erasmus' specific relationship with Luther.[20] He did not know, he said, whether Erasmus was a teacher or a follower of Luther; and he left that decision to people who were familiar with the two men's works. Regardless of who had inspired whom, however, Béda detected Lutheran elements in Erasmus' *Paraphrases.* Erasmus, he said, 'promoted the truly servile freedom of the Lutheran faction with his clever art of speaking.'[21] Throughout his book, Béda identified and tagged individual passages in the *Paraphrases* as Lutheran. On one folio page (267r–v), he uses the designation 'Lutheran' six times.

Two examples will illustrate what views Béda regarded as 'Lutheran.' In a comment on Matthew 13, he criticizes Erasmus' views on celibacy, which, he says, put him in league with 'Luther and Lefèvre.' In this passage, he calls Erasmus a 'champion of incontinence' for saying that

> there are few men who can totally abstain [from sexual relations]. This is an error in faith and indeed false. If he had said, there are few who want to abstain, it would have been

> tolerable; but to say there are few who 'can abstain' comes very close to blasphemy. For there is no unmarried man or woman who is not able to abstain from carnal relations, if he or she so wishes.

He concludes that Erasmus, 'together with Luther and Lefèvre was reviving the old heresy [of Jovinian].'[22] The second example comes from Béda's comments on Erasmus' preface to his *Paraphrase on Matthew.* In his prefatory letter, Erasmus had said that the Fathers 'in expounding the allegories ... sometimes behave, in my view, as though they were not wholly serious (*ludere videantur*).' Béda objects: 'The old doctors of the church certainly did not speak in jest or in a playful manner when they discussed the meaning of Scripture; they treated everything seriously.' He then considers the possibility that Erasmus used the word *ludere* in a different sense:

> Now if you chose to use that word *ludere* to indicate *facilitas*, ease or courtesy, I must say that I expect something better from your good mind and intellectual force ...; if you wanted to use the term *ludamus* to indicate the good will and cheerfulness which should prevail among those who dispute in a charitable spirit, explain to me, please: how was I supposed to follow your meaning?

In the end, Béda concludes that Erasmus' use of the term *ludere* is 'arrogant and lacking in respect for the old doctors of the church and promoting the bold attitude of Luther, a chief heretic, who wrote among other things that Dionysius in his *Ecclesiastical Hierarchy* fooled around with allegories, calling this an occupation for men with time on their hands.'[23] The two examples illustrate various modes used by Béda in identifying passages in Erasmus as 'Lutheran.' Sometimes Béda's allegations are vague; at other times he is quite specific, noting literal parallels in the works of Erasmus and Luther.

Although four-fifths of Béda's book concern Lefèvre, and only one-fifth Erasmus' *Paraphrases* – there are 234 folios on Lefèvre, 58 on Erasmus – he clearly considered Erasmus the more dangerous man. He had originally set out to critique only Lefèvre's work, he tells us, but then determined that both men were propagating the same errors. It was not right, therefore, to 'refute the errors of one man, and not reveal those of the other at all.'[24] Of the two men, Lefèvre seemed the more tractable, moreover. He appeared to be receptive to admonitions and was not recalcitrant. In the past, Lefèvre had preferred 'quietly to remove [the offending passages] rather than talking back at length and in an impudent tone, adding new errors to the old ones.' Erasmus, by contrast, was in the habit 'to hold tooth and claw to what he had written,' 'to maintain and defend with remarkable skill and contentiousness what I have condemned in his writings.' Béda concludes: 'I don't think he will ever learn to keep silence.'[25]

I now turn to my third point: Béda's method of argumentation. In some ways, Béda's method resembles Erasmus': he supports his interpretations primarily with references to relevant biblical passages and he appeals to consensus and tradition. This accords with Erasmus' procedure, as explained in his reply to his critics in Spain. He looked for confirmation of his views in 'clear scriptural passages, commonly accepted creeds, and [the pronouncements] of universal synods' (LB 9: 1901C). When quoting authorities, furthermore, Erasmus clearly prefers the testimony of the Fathers to that of medieval authors. Surprisingly, Béda shows the same preference, quoting the Fathers disproportionately more often than scholastic commentators or canon law. Among the patristic authors he cites are Jerome, Gregory the Great, Ambrose, Dionysius, and Origen (usually critically). His favourite authority, however, is Augustine. Perhaps there is an agenda behind this preference: the desire to embarrass Erasmus. When quoting Augustine, Béda liked to point out that Erasmus, a member of the Augustinian order, was apparently unfamiliar with the writings of the founding father:

> It would have been a good thing if Erasmus did not totally devote himself to teaching others and unceasingly write one new book after another, instead of turning inward occasionally. For if he had spent half his life in piously searching for the truth in the writings of the holy fathers, he might have come across this passage in Augustine, his own patron.[26]

In addition to citing the Fathers, Béda, like Erasmus, appeals to the consensus of the church. For example, defending the authenticity of the Pauline letters, he says that they have been 'approved by the usage of the Catholic doctors and the universal church, without controversy.' Similarly, he says of the attribution of the Apostles' Creed: 'None of the doctors of the church has doubted that that holy creed was put together by the apostles.' Conversely, he argues against some of Erasmus' views, declaring that they go against the consensus of the church or cast doubt on universally accepted positions.[27] Needless to say, there is an element of rhetorical exaggeration in such claims. The assertion of the protagonist that he, rather than the opponent, had tradition and consensus on his side, is predicated on the myth that the tradition of the church was monolithic and does not stand up to a rigorous historical examination.

In appealing to Scripture, patristic writings, and the consensus of the church, Béda's argumentation resembles that of Erasmus. There are, however, also significant differences. Erasmus often uses philological arguments, examining the meaning of words according to classical usage or advancing text critical arguments. Béda rarely rests his case on philological arguments. More importantly, Erasmus often argues on both sides of a question. Even if his own preference is evident, he formally suspends judgment and defers to the reader or to the magisterium of the church.[28] Béda never invites discussion and always pronounces firmly and with assurance. Indeed, Béda often dispenses with arguments altogether. He merely pronounces judgment, making no attempt to corroborate his verdict. He lists passages from Erasmus' *Paraphrases* and affixes a one-word label, calling them 'heretical' or 'blasphemous' or 'Lutheran' without explaining how he arrived at this judgment; at other times, he offers interpretations of biblical passages without justification other than saying that his interpretation is self-evident, only wrong-minded people could object to it.[29] This practice, the simple assertion that the opponent's interpretation was wrong, infuriated Erasmus. However, Béda's practice does not stem from arrogance or a similar flaw in his character. He was simply reflecting a general assumption. He regarded it as his right to pass judgment by virtue of his professional standing and his position on the faculty. Most contemporaries would have agreed that this was indeed his privilege. Graduate theologians, and especially members of the prestigious faculty of theology at Paris, had a right to pronounce absolutely on the orthodoxy of a statement. As the *Chartularium* of the university (1414) noted, 'No one would say that the theologians make mistakes or are mistaken ...; even the Holy See is neither reluctant nor embarrassed to consult them.'[30] Erasmus, who did not have an earned degree in theology, did not enjoy the same privilege, Béda pointed out. If Erasmus presumed to differ from Thomas Aquinas, for example, this was inexcusable, even if he prefaced his remarks with polite phrases, saying that he differed from Aquinas 'with due respect.' 'To disagree and oppose statements that have the unanimous approval of later doctors [i.e., the scholastics] is bold and arrogant,' Béda lectured Erasmus. 'To disagree with statements that have been confirmed by the judgment of the church or by steady common usage is not permitted at all and is impious and schismatic.'[31]

Béda, then, took the traditional Catholic position, that religious matters need not (and indeed, must not) be discussed with non-theologians. Not surprisingly, he rejected proposals to open up the study of the Bible to the laity by providing vernacular translations:

> Erasmus zealously attempts to convince us that it is legitimate, good, appropriate, and conducive to the salvation of simple men and women, to make available the sacred writings in the vernacular to people, regardless of sex, age, or status ... I need not elaborate how harmful this is to the Christian cause, for it has already been demonstrated by myself and others, excellent men who have written about this subject recently.[32]

Experience, too, had shown that lay persons were liable to misinterpret the Bible; yet Erasmus had openly said that they understood theological issues better than the scholastic doctors. 'Erasmus should realize the schismatic nature of his remarks, when he glorifies lay persons who presume to argue about Holy Scripture against professors of Scripture.'[33]

To sum up: Béda's statements about scholastic theologians contains an affirmation and a denial: the affirmation that graduate theologians are competent to decide questions of faith; and a denial that the scholastics are hostile toward humanistic studies in principle. His remarks on Erasmus and the biblical humanists contain the corresponding charges. The humanists are incompetent to interpret biblical passages, and it is they who are hostile toward the scholastic theologians and who have their priorities wrong. Furthermore, Béda consistently links the biblical humanists with Luther and regards them as the reformer's inspirational source. Béda's method of argumentation resembles Erasmus' in some ways, but there are important differences, notably Béda's unwillingness to invite discussion. This may stem from a theologian's reluctance to debate with non-theologians, but it is also indicative of epistemological differences. Here I would like to cite Luther's famous characterization of Erasmus as a 'sceptic.' The Christian, says Luther, cannot be a sceptic; he must hold to the tenets of faith with a 'Stoic' assurance.[34] There were not many points on which Béda and Luther agreed, but this was one of them, for in his book against Erasmus, Beda, too, rejects scepticism: *Dubius enim in fide ... infidelis est* ('he who doubts in matters of faith, has no faith').[35] No doubt, epistemological differences account to a large extent for the fact that Erasmus was attacked by both Catholics like Béda and Protestant reformers like Luther.

NOTES

1 See James Farge, 'Texts and Context of a Mentalité: The Parisian University Milieu in the Age of Erasmus,' 3–5.

2 On their correspondence, see CWE Ep 1571, headnote. On Béda's role, see James Farge, *Orthodoxy and Reform in Early Reformation France: The Faculty of Theology of Paris 1500–1543*, esp. 86–96.

3 On the *Divinationes* and the further course of the controversy between Béda and Erasmus see Erika Rummel, *Erasmus and His Catholic Critics*, 2: 29–46.

4 *Annotationum libri duo* (Paris: Bade, 1526). In the colophon of the published book, we read that it was approved by the faculty of theology on 15 February 1525 (section on Lefèvre) and 16 May 1526 (section on Erasmus).

5 Ibid, aa 3v–4r: 'pro veritatis zelo,' 'veritatis zelo motus.' He claimed that Erasmus' works militated against the Catholic faith: ibid, aa 1v: 'tum catholicae fidei adversari, tum christianae pietati.'

6 Ibid, aa 1v: 'ut in eam rem aliorum studia commoverem.'

7 Ibid, 254r; on Lee, Stunica, and Sutor see Rummel, *Erasmus and His Catholic Critics*, 1: 95–120, 145–77, 2: 61–72.

8 *Annotationum libri duo*, Nn iiv.

9 Ibid, Aa 2v: 'eorum studiis zelo ac doctrina eorundem temporum errores extincti omnes fuerint ac suppressi.'

10 Ibid, 235v–6r: 'Quod denique hic dicit Erasmus explicare dissonantes locos in evangelistis nihil aliud esse quam in labyrintho quodam versari, quam impium sit quis non videat? Cum nulla scripturarum dari possit apparens dissonantia quae per sacros

ecclesiae doctores non fuerit iam olim ad catholicam reducta consonantiam aut facile per theologos possit ... Labyrinthus profecto sunt scripturae divinae sensus, unde emergere cuiquam non conceditur, qui catholicorum doctorum et ecclesiae filum non sequitur intelligentiae.'

11 Ibid, Aa 3v–4r: 'Non enim ita hebes ac mentis inops ... fuerit qui humanitatis artem linguarumque peritiam non ut dei dona agnoscat ac laudet. Non certe illa cuique iuste displicere possunt. At rursus placere debet nemini qui de huiuscemodi gratiis ... ingratus ad multorum exitium abusus est. Desinant ergo, desinant theologorum ordini perversis eorum dogmatis sese opponentium falso imputare, id eos odio bonarum (quas dicunt) literarum agere ... bonarum literarum invidiam nobis obiiciant, si non ipsis gratulabimur, si non illorum studiis favebimus ac denique eorum commendabimus libros.'

12 Ibid, aa 1v: '[Theologos] praedicant in solis philosophicis ac argumentorum sophismatumque tricis consenescere vixque divina eloquia a limine salutare, nec minus a veterum theologorum lectione sanctorum videlicet ecclesiae doctorum prorsus abhorrere, et qui denique scholastici licet vocitentur theologi absolutum tamen theologorum nomen haudquaquam merentur.'

13 Ibid, Aa 1v: 'Qui solis humanitatis ac linguarum praesidiis instructi, sacra omnia edissere sunt aggressi ... ac veri germanique theologi censeantur, quippe qui divinam ut aiunt puramque theologiae notitiam propriis e fontibus non e lacunis hauriant, in ipsi divinorum tamen eloquiorum lectioni ac sacrae Bibliae textibus incumbant, non philosophorum disciplinis, non scholasticis theologorum scriptis.'

14 Ibid, 271r: 'Est enim notione una, inquiunt grammatici, ... perversus interpres et depravator, paraphrasis autem dictionum perversa et aliena interpretatio.'

15 Ibid, 249r: 'Per hae vult paraphrastes novus theologus quaecunque in beati Lucae persona locutus est, pro evangelico sensu recipienda omnino esse ... porro non hoc locutus est Lucas, sed pro solita audacia commentatus est Erasmus.'

16 Ibid, Aa 2r: 'sine praevio et monstrante semitam non posse ingredi'; 'absque doctore esse non possunt' (phrases from Jerome, Ep 53.6–7).

17 Ibid, aa 3v: 'Pulchrum sit Fabro et Erasmo visum necnon et promovendae religioni perutile novo dicendi genere, id est, cultius politiusve divinas tractare literas: a prudentibus tamen et expertis viris maxime incautum impietatique ac sacrilegio vicinum semper est iudicatum pietatis et humilitatis doctrinae fastum ac gentilium literarum lenocinia, quasi hae de se saluti conducerent, tamen studiose superinducere.'

18 Ibid, 271r. For Erasmus' position, see Erika Rummel, 'God and Solecism: Erasmus as a Critic of the Bible,' 54–72.

19 *Annotationum libri duo*, 272v: 'Homo miser et miserabilis (quod rhetorica elegantia ac in universum humanitatis et linguarum praesidiis semetipsum apostolo iudicat superiorem, quasi plusquam semideus esset) praeceptorem se exhibit, ut deum et eius apostolum congruentius loqui doceat, iudicem quoque divinorum se constituit.'

20 Ibid, aa 1v: 'Lutherum in multis docuisse potius videntur quam ab eo didicisse'; 'invectamque ecclesiae factionem per istos homines ... in non parvam animarum iacturam.' On Erasmus' relationship with Luther, Béda says: 'seipsum Lutheri aut sequacium praestitit aut praeceptorem aut discipulum' (ibid, 254r).

21 Ibid, 268r.

22 Ibid, 244v, cf. 254r.

23 Erasmus' comment is found at CWE Ep 1255: 46–8. For Béda's reaction, see *Annotationum libri duo*, 235r: 'Certum est veteres ecclesiae doctores divinarum tractando sensus scripturarum nihil ioco aut ludo, sed omnia serio egisse ... si hoc verbum tibi propter facilitatem ponere placuit ego (fateor) maius aliquid expecto a benignitate virium tuarum ... si autem propter hilariatem quae esse inter charissimos disserentes decet putasti dicendum esse "ludamus" ... hoc ipsum edoce, obsecro te, quonam modo assequi valeam ... haec propositio arroganter et in veterum ecclesiae doctorum spretum enunciata est, temeritatique heresiarchae Lutheri favet qua inter alia sic scripsit: In Ecclesiastica Hierarchia Dionysius ludit allegoriis, quod est ociosorum hominum studium.'

24 Ibid, aa 3r–v

25 Ibid, aa 4r–v, 254r.

26 Ibid, 260r–v: 'Bonum quippe fuerat illi non totum sic aliis edocendis incumbere, sine requie novos super novos scribendo libros, sed semet sibi nonnunquam dare. Si enim pia mente veritatem in sanctorum patrum scriptis requirendo, vel aetatis suae dimidium collocasset, illi ex patre suo Augustino forsan occurrisset.'

27 Ibid, Nn iiv, 290r, 291r, 236v.

28 The most famous example of this method is Erasmus' *Diatribe de libero arbitrio* (1524), aimed at Luther, which consists of a comparison of biblical passages for and against the concept of free will. In his reply, Luther condemned Erasmus' 'scepticism.' See below, note 34.

29 Ibid, 257v: 'perverse cogitans.'

30 Henri Denifle and Emile Chatelain, eds., *Chartularium Universitatis Parisiensis*, 4: 295.

31 *Annotationum libri duo*, 291r. On the circumstances in which Erasmus acquired his doctorate of theology, see Paul Grendler, 'How to Get a

Degree in Fifteen Days: Erasmus' Doctorate of Theology from the University of Turin.'

32 Ibid, 236v: 'Quanto studio hic conetur Erasmus convincere licitum pulchrum decens ac simplicium saluti tum virorum tum mulierum expediens esse ut cuilibet sexui, aetati, et statui vulgari lingua sacrae omnes communicentur literae ... at istud quam rei Christianae sit noxium, non est per me aperiendum, quoniam quidem iamiam est id monstratum per nos aliosque recentes et sane egregios scriptores.'

33 Ibid, 265v: 'Videat Erasmus quam schismaticum sit idiotis quasi gloriae dare cum de sacris literis disputando adversus illarum professores congredi praesumant.'

34 *De servo arbitrio*, WA 18: 603.

35 *Annotationum libri duo*, 236v.

TEN

The *Paraphrases* of Erasmus in French

Guy Bedouelle

The first known translation of Erasmus' *Paraphrases* appears to be the one published by Claude La Ville in Lyon in 1543. The book bears the title *Paraphrases ou briesve exposition sur toutes les Epistres canoniques par Didier Erasme de Rotterdam, translaté de Latin en Françoys.*[1] As far as we know, this represents the first publication of this bookseller-printer, who was active in Lyon but also in Valence where, 'in the big street leading to the *place des clercs* next to the sign of the dolphin,' he published the works of Rabelais in sextodecimo: *Gargantua*, the *Second Livre de Pantagruel*, the *Tiers Livre*, and the *Quart Livre.* [2]

In 1548, La Ville published *La Fleur des Sentences certaines, Apophtegmes et Stratagemes*, compiled by Gilles Corozet, and in 1549 *Les Fleurs du Grand Guidon*, by M. Jehan Raoul, surgeon, an edition on which he collaborated with Balthasar Arnoullet, the famous master printer of Lyon. It was also as a joint edition with Arnoullet and three other printers that Claude La Ville published in 1549 *Les Apophtegmes cueilliz par Didier Erasme de Rotterdam, translatez de Latin en Françoys par l'Esleu Macault, secrétaire et vallet de chambre ordinaire du Roy*. The imprint remains that of Claude La Ville.[3]

According to Francis Higman, the motto that adorns the frontispiece of the French translation of the *Paraphrases, Assez tost, si assez bien,* 'is associated with the Genevan bookseller and financier René de Bienassis, known to be active in Geneva from 1545 on.'[4] In 1548, Bienassis, a French exile, published a poem by Calvin to accompany the latter's *Actes du Concile de Trente*.[5] The motto, attributed to Cato and handed down by St Jerome, must be understood by reversing the last two words, *bien assez*.[6] Thus the motto means: 'Soon enough, if indeed enough.'

Some copies of Erasmus' *Paraphrases* in French still exist. Francis Higman found them in Basel (University Library DJV 103), Ghent (U.B. Acc 9080), La Rochelle (Bibliothèque municipale), and London (but this copy was destroyed during the Second World War). The book may also be found in the Bibliothèque Albert Ier in Brussels (II 647 ALP).

The 'translator' addresses the readers without revealing his name. Two hypotheses can be imagined without lingering over them. First, one must bear in mind that the French translation of the commentary on the First Letter to the Corinthians that Jean Girard published in Geneva with the assistance of René de Bienassis, and which also carries the celebrated motto, [7] remains unsigned. Nevertheless, it does not seem that one ought to conclude that he was the translator, for 'the assembled evidence reveals that Bienassis was more bookseller than translator.'[8]

Ought one more plausibly to conclude that the translator of the *Paraphrases* is Antoine Macault, to whom we owe the translation of the *Apophthegms* of Erasmus? This person, who is depicted in a manuscript presenting his edition of Diodorus of Sicily to King Francis I,[9] was an *esleu* (*élu*) – an official responsible for *aides et tailles*, in other words, a collector of royal taxes – named 'secretary and private chamberlain to the King,' as was the case with Clément Marot. The latter, who was a friend of Macault, composed some verses to praise him as a translator. Such is the case with the *Apophthegms* of Erasmus in a text in which Marot successively acknowledges Plutarch, who wrote in Greek, Erasmus, who rendered his words into Latin, and Macault, who produced a French translation. Macault himself, in his preface to Francis I, speaks of both his 'translations of the year' and the 'small labours' that he dedicates to the sovereign 'as an annual rent and a duty to which I placed myself under constraint with both submission and obligation.'[10] There is no doubt that Macault was a prolific and well-known translator, but not of religious works.

The translation of the *Paraphrases* contains neither dedication, postface, nor table of contents. A preface appears on the reverse of the title page: 'The translator to his faithful friends, greetings, through Our Lord Jesus Christ.'[11] The translator judges that he must overcome all his 'detractors and slanderers,' no doubt an allusion to the trials experienced by those who had translated Erasmus into French before him, beginning with the Chevalier de Berquin, executed in April 1529. One thus understands why he should remain anonymous.

Indeed, we know that the *Paraphrases* were condemned by Noël Béda. In 1524, the registers of the Paris Faculty of Theology resounded with discussions of the *Paraphrases on Luke*. Then in 1526, with the publication of Béda's *Annotations* on Lefèvre d'Étaples and on Erasmus we discover that the entire *Paraphrases super quatuor Evangelia et omnes apostolicas epistolas* had come under suspicion. These *Paraphrases* were finally condemned on 16 December 1527, with 112 propositions extracted from this work.[12]

The translator of 1543 therefore knew that he had translated a condemned work but, although aware of his limitations, professed to work only for the glory of Jesus Christ before whom he wanted to present himself with a clean conscience. In accordance with a turn of phrase that traverses centuries of translation, one ought to attribute the blunders to him, the translator. The rest should be referred to God who makes the dumb speak, reveals his wisdom to the little ones and hides it from the wise, and who has made us pass from darkness to light. Behind these words of St Luke, one surely can hear the *Post tenebras lux*, so dear to Geneva.

While the edition of 1543 ought to be understood in the context of the end of the reign of Francis I, the one published in Basel in 1563 is contemporaneous with the regency of Catherine de Medici and the accession of the young Charles IX, who was born in 1550 and became king in 1560. This period brings us to a defining moment for the religious policies of France, the failure of which led to the wars of religion. In September and October 1561, the Colloquy of Poissy failed to produce doctrinal reconciliation. Thus, 'only two ways remained open for a solution to the confessional problem ... either religious unification by force, as had been tried by Henry II, or on the basis of a national unity that would henceforth be distinct from religious unity, in other words, the civil tolerance of the Protestants.'[13] The latter proved to be the course chosen by the Regent in the edict of January 1562, and then, in a more restrictive way, in the edict of Amboise of 19 March 1563. Catherine adopted this policy of tolerance shortly before the massacre of Protestants at Vassy carried out by Catholics under the leadership of François de Guise (March 1562), which was soon followed by the assassination of Guise, thought to be the work of Admiral Coligny. These events unleashed the vengeance that led up to the Saint Bartholomew's Day Massacre (24 August 1572). Thus, the initiative to translate Erasmus' *Paraphrases* into French may be considered one of the last attempts to make Erasmian irenicism prevail.

This folio edition, produced at Basel in the printing house of Ambrosius and Aurelius Froben,[14] successors of Johann Froben (d. 1527) the friend of Erasmus, begins with a preface by the 'translators.' It seems to state that it is the first in the French tongue and to express astonishment at the fact. Yet a comparison with the edition of 1543 shows that it is this very translation that was reproduced without a single change in the paraphrases on the Epistles. Only the marginal glosses had in some places undergone elaboration.

Thus, we can understand the use of the plural 'translators,' as if the translator of the paraphrases on the Gospels associated himself with his predecessor. It happens, however, that on three occasions he reveals himself by using the singular. For example, he writes: '*I* do not know what spirit inhibited us Frenchmen ...'; later in the text he states: 'Nevertheless, *I* will content myself to propose ...'[15] There were thus two stages, the first represented by the 1543 translation of the canonical Epistles in a printing that must have passed sufficiently unnoticed, without attribution, to be reused by a second translator, working on the Gospels for the 1563 edition, whose only sin was one of omission.

The preface is addressed 'to the Most Christian King of France, Charles, the ninth of this name' by the 'translators,' who profess themselves to be 'his humble servants,' thus declaring themselves to be French. We have just seen what to make of this plural form. The translators begin by recalling that Erasmus had dedicated the Gospel *Paraphrases* in Latin to four Christian monarchs of his day, and in particular to Francis I. It was fitting then that the French translation should be dedicated to his grandson. The subjects of the king of France, known for their loyalty to their prince, would be even more so if they were not overwhelmed by the trials of division on account of their sins. They should consequently pray to God to pardon them, each bearing with the other, as St Paul does. In support of this, the translators quote 1 Corinthians 9: 22.

Deployed for particular benefit is the statement 'I have become weak with the weak in order to win the weak.'

Surely the French have become victims of extreme opinions that claim that Catholics and Protestants agree on nothing and that they find themselves as separated as Christians are separated from heretics, Jews, and Mohammedans. Christian charity by contrast would remind us that Catholics and Protestants agree on the 'fundamental points of our religion,' the principal articles of faith, those twelve affirmations found in the Apostles' Creed. Their differences consist of diverging interpretations of certain of these points and of several doctrines and 'ceremonies' added by imposition.

The King and his people should rather trust those pious souls who, the truth being safeguarded, judge that one ought to concede certain points in discussions before the 'weak ones,' as Erasmus said when he tried to reform the prelates in whom he observed abuses. If we had listened to Erasmus and to those kindred spirits who, following in his footsteps, had counselled preferring piety to superstition, we would have avoided the great misfortunes that beset the church.

But the devil led hearts away from the Holy Scriptures, the 'touchstone' capable of judging actions and instruction. That is why Erasmus insisted that not only princes but also all Christians read the Bible and put it into practice. To neglect the Bible would be tantamount to forbidding the public proclamation of a royal edict, or to prefer what somebody had added on to it. God wishes that we know Holy Writ, 'which brings complete peace, union, and concord to true Christians.'

Certain persons claim that now that French translations of the biblical texts have appeared turmoil has occurred. This already happened in the days of the Old Testament with the prophets who had been rejected, and also in New Testament times when Jesus and the apostles were considered as seditious men. Yet how can the Scriptures, which so often urge peace and fraternal communion, become a cause of 'tumults'? Is it not rather that one does not wish to receive the 'pure Word of God'?

If the *Paraphrases* had been translated into French earlier, as they had been into both German and English, things would perhaps have transpired otherwise in the kingdom. Why did not someone take up the task earlier, given that Erasmus was well received by both parties? Erasmus had dedicated his life to glorifying God and to uprooting all superstition, for it is against God. He had been ridiculed by a crowd of ignorant, malicious, inexperienced people. But Erasmus stood firm, 'relying on his well formed conscience.' Have we not seen that certain people, who 'adored him' when he was alive, have outrageously rebuked him after his death?

As for the *Paraphrases*, one must recommend them. They are glosses, but 'taken from a comparative study (*collation*) of the Scriptures themselves'[16] and from the fathers of the church. One finds nothing tawdry there; everything there is neat and 'polished.' Accordingly, as Jacques Chomarat said of the same text of Erasmus: 'A paraphrase does not change the person; as with a translation, one is supposed to hear the author himself.'[17]

Erasmus' own dedicatory letters, especially 'the first,' that is to say, most likely the one that prefaces the Gospel of Matthew and is addressed to Charles V, reveal that he believes that it is necessary to allow everyone to read the Bible, to ensure that they are taught 'purely,' and not to compel 'weak consciences to believe or to act in a way other than what is clearly demonstrated in Holy Scripture.' One cannot force men to do anything against their consciences, any more than did Christ and the disciples who learned from their master 'all sweetness, clemency and gentleness.' For Christ never wished 'the death of a sinner but that he convert and live' (Ezekiel 33: 11).

Does not the king esteem those of his subjects who, for fear of offending him, would refuse to do that which is not expressly contained in his edicts, even if one tries to persuade them? The king ought then to hear the edict of the 'king of kings' (Revelation 19: 16), who counsels sovereigns (Psalm 2: 10, 12) to fear the Lord in order to avoid the terrible judgment of God. Thus, one must not follow the pleasures of the flesh but instead obey the Word of God, which brings 'great repose and peace of conscience.' May the king govern his people in a way that guarantees 'true peace and union.'

The tone of the text is Protestant without any doubt, for, in 1563, references to the 'pure Word of God' and to the attacks against human additions to this Word as the battle against superstition belonged to a Protestant vocabulary. Yet the accent is obviously placed on concord, union, the peace of hearts and, above all, of consciences, a term that recurs time and again and that signals an adherence to the tendency of conciliation and of the search for theological compromise, whatever that might say about the safeguarding of the truth.

The author takes Erasmus for his model. He defends him and castigates those who, having flattered and admired him while he was alive, rejected him after his death. He holds in such high esteem the *Paraphrases on the New Testament* translated into French that he affirms that if it could have been known earlier in France, things would have proceeded 'more peacefully.'

The main Erasmian themes are clearly present. Following the example of Erasmus, the translator privileges 'life,' that is to say, moral behaviour to the detriment of dogma, in particular the reform of prelates. He emphasizes the care one should bestow on the weak and on the sinner, highlights the reading of and commentary on Sacred Scripture drawn from Scripture itself (the 'collation'), and, finally, promotes reconciliation with an eye towards peace both in the church and in civil society. Still, the coherence of his discourse and the argument that he defends certainly constitute a creed capable of being acknowledged by all, a body of beliefs that one would call essential instead of minimalist.

Without saying it explicitly, the translator borrows from Erasmus the idea of a 'summary of the faith' on which Catholics and Protestants could easily agree.[18] Erasmus had developed this idea first of all in a letter to Paul Volz that served as a preface to the 1518 edition of the *Enchiridion*, but the perspective had been above all pedagogic and moral: the 'philosophy of Christ' could be summed up 'in a very few articles.' He again takes up this intuition in a letter of 1 November 1519 to John Slechta, for which the background is the religious situation in Bohemia. In order for the Roman church to persuade, she should present only 'a small number' of truths 'expressed by the Holy Scriptures or without which salvation is not possible.'[19] There follows a small summary of the essentials of the faith: 'all our hope rests in God who freely bestows upon us his gifts through the mediation of his Son. The death of Jesus redeems us, baptism unites us to his body. We ought to live in conformity with his teaching and example.' One can leave to the theologians the complex questions of Christology and the sacraments.

Another text from Erasmus, even closer to the spirit of our French preface, is the letter of 5 January 1523 to John Carondelet, Archbishop of Palermo. This served as the preface to Erasmus' edition of Hilary of Poitiers, the fourth-century church father. The well-known passage reads: 'The sum and substance of our religion is peace and unanimity, something not easy to maintain except on one condition: to define the smallest number of dogmas, and in many things to let each one follow his own judgment.'[20] Erasmus goes on to add that even if one intends to resolve many problems by the next ecumenical council, it would be more fitting, in his view, to postpone them to the Last Day when we will see God 'face to face.' We should bear in mind that this long letter contains the very controversial assertion: 'In the past, faith manifested itself more in life than in the profession of teachings.'[21]

It is not difficult to situate the translator of the Basel edition in the milieu of the theological moderates (*moyenneurs*). Peter G. Bientenholz, in an article published in 1969, then in his book of 1971, suggests the circle of Sébastien Castellion, and even suggests a name: Castellion's friend Léger Grymoult, a proofreader and the translator of other texts into French.[22] The preface to the *Paraphrases* in French seems to hold a middle ground between tendencies represented by two contemporary works, namely, the *Conseil à la France désolée* that Castellion brought out, without an author's name, in October 1562, and the *De officio pii ac publicae tranquillitatis vere amantis viri* by Georges Cassander, which also appeared anonymously at Basel during August of the preceding year. It is the latter work that François Bauduin had put on display a few weeks later at the Colloquy of Poissy.[23]

Mario Turchetti, who has studied the 'moderates' active during this period, considers Cassander more clearly Erasmian than Castellion.[24] Whereas the *Conseil à la France désolée* abounds with appeals to respect the rights of conscience,[25] the work of Cassander clearly develops the theory of the 'fundamental articles' to which Christians would be able to agree, based 'on the foundation of apostolic doctrine.'[26] Cassander affirms: 'One does not separate oneself from the head except by a false doctrine contrary to what the Scriptures teach about Christ our leader. One does not break off from the body, that is the church, except by a loss of charity.'[27] A little further on, Cassander tries to be more precise, without achieving complete clarity: 'Every church that rests on the foundation of the true and apostolic doctrine, contained in the short symbol of faith, and which does not separate itself from communion with the other churches by an impious schism, I consider as the true church, member of the true church and of the Catholic church of Christ. And I say this not only of the churches of the West, but also of the eastern churches.'[28] A memorandum coming from the Cardinal de Châtillon, sent in the autumn of 1561 to Pope Pius IV, is not far from developing similar ideas.[29]

This Erasmian voice that also resonates in the preface to the *Paraphrases* in French seems, then, to be much closer to the theologians of compromise – the *moyenneurs* – than to Castellion, the apostle of the freedom of conscience.[30] For the appeal to conscience contained at the end of the preface of 1563 certainly exhibits traits that appear very frequently in the writings of Castellion, who explained his personal faith through the Apostles' Creed by integrating it into a letter to a friend who had asked him about his convictions.[31] These texts, in any event, witness to the lasting influence of Erasmus in France throughout the 1570s, even if the condemnations made great discretion necessary. Margaret Mann Phillips has shown, above all for the *Adages* and the *Colloquies*, that this influence was not without its distortions.[32] James Hutton has investigated the transmission and reception in France of Erasmus' 'pacifist' works.[33] Our second text shows, obviously from the perspective of Basel, that Erasmus remained important for efforts at reconciliation on account of his intuition about the fundamental articles of faith, but even more because of his conviction that a solid knowledge adapted to the Scriptures was the best remedy for the abuses and quarrels then present in the church.

Translated by Romanus Cessario and Hilmar M. Pabel

APPENDIX

Preface to the French translation of the 1543 edition of the *Paraphrases*

Je ne doute point (mes freres bien aymez) que si de tout temps on eut eu seulement esgard à la detraction des calomniateurs, et de ceux qui ne servent de rien en ce monde, sinon de mesdire et reprendre voyre la verité nous ne jouyrions pas maintenant de tant de savans expositeurs et divins interpretateurs. Maintenant sen aille lenuie et detraction là ou elle voudra. Quant à moy, je ne lairray pour leur sottise de mettre en public e petit talent, que iay receu du Seigneur: combien que je ne soye point ignorant de ma petitesse ne tant stupide ou estourdy, que je ne cognoysse mon ignorance. Je la confesse franchement: et ne me soucye qui en murmure ou qui en detracte, moyennant que la gloyre de nostre Seigneur Iesus Christ soit sauve. Vray est que je ne vous presente pas grand chose (je laisse là ce que nous devons à l'auteur de la Paraphrase) si vous considerez seulement la translation. Mais que me soucye ie d'autre chose, sinon que de pouvoir presenter de nette conscience et pur estomac ce qui m'a esté donné et que mon labeur soyt rapporté à la gloyre de celluy, de qui nous avons tout nostre bien? Je suis bien content de porter sur mes espaules tout le fardeau du langage mal poly, de la traduction non assez fidelement tournée, brief, toute l'ignorance que vous trouverez. Et est bien la raison. Que s'il y a quelque chose qui vous soyt agreable, ne men attribuez rien, je vous prie, mais vous et moy esiouyssons nous en notre bon Dieu, qui sayt tres bien faire parler les muetz quand il luy plaist, et en quelle sorte quil luy plaist, qui revele sa sagesse aux bien petis, et la cache aux sages de ce monde, qui de toutes obscuritéz et renebres nous a remis en pays de grande lumière nous (dy je) qui habitions en la terre et umbre de mort. Bien vous soyt.

NOTES

1 Henri-Louis Baudrier, Julien Baudrier, et al., *Bibliographie lyonnaise: Recherches sur les imprimeurs, libraires, relieurs et fondeurs de lettres de Lyon au XVIe siècle*, 1: 237.

2 Ibid, 1: 237–8. On the editions published in Valence, see L. Desgraves et al., eds., *Répertoire bibliographique des livres imprimés en France au seizième siècle*, 25: 76 (= *Bibliotheca Bibliographica Aureliana*, 65: 76). No information on his activity in Valence appears in Jules Ollivier, 'Notice sur l'origine de l'imprimerie à Valence (Dauphiné),' 13–16.

3 *Bibliographie lyonnaise*, 9: 165; 10: 121, 217. The translator is Antoine Machault or Macault, as with the 1539 and 1547 editions of this version of the *Apophthegms*. See Francis Higman, *Piety and the People: Religious Printing in French, 1511–1551*, 197 E16–18. On the translations of Erasmus' *Apophthegms*, see Jean-Claude Margolin, 'Guillaume Haudent, poète et traducteur des "Apophtegmes" d'Érasme,' reprinted in Margolin, *Érasme dans son miroir et dans son sillage* (VI).

4 On Bienassis, see Rodolphe Peter and Jean-François Gilmont, eds., *Bibliotheca Calviniana: Les oeuvres de Jean Calvin publiées au XVIe siècle*, 1: 244–6.

5 Higman, *Piety and the People*, 129 C9, 133–4.
6 Théophile Dufour, *Le secret des textes: Opuscules inédits de critique et d'histoire*, 84–5.
7 Higman, *Piety and the People*, 135 C31.
8 *Bibliotheca Calviniana*, 1: 245.
9 Chantilly, Musée Condé, MS Fr 1672; cf. James K. Farge, *Biographical Register of Paris Doctors of Theology, 1500–1536*, 370.
10 *Les Apophtegmes cueilliz par Didier Erasme de Rotterdam* (Lyon: Claude La Ville, 1549), 12; preface dated July 1537.
11 *Paraphrases ou briesve exposition sur toutes les Epistres canoniques par Didier Erasme de Rotterdam* (Lyon: Claude La Ville, 1543), verso of the title page; full text in the appendix below.
12 *Registre des procès-verbaux de la Faculté de théologie de l'Université de Paris: De janvier 1524 à novembre 1533*, 137, 177. See also James K. Farge, *Orthodoxy and Reform in Early Reformation France*, 194–5.
13 Joseph Lecler, *Histoire de la tolérance en France au siècle de la Réforme*, 2: 57–8.
14 On Basel and its cultural and religious atmosphere, see the fine book by Alfred Berchthold, *Bâle et l'Europe: Une histoire culturelle.*
15 Peter G. Bientenholz, who published this text in his article, 'Erasmus und der Basler Buchhandel in Frankreich,' in *Scrinium Erasmianum*, 1: 318–23, corrects the passage to read: 'Nous ne sçavons ... nous contenterons-nous ...' (321). While this correction makes logical sense, it is difficult to justify.
16 The term 'collation' in its primary meaning refers to a collection or a textual comparison.
17 Jacques Chomarat, *Grammaire et rhétorique chez Érasme*, 1: 587.
18 On this theme, see Lecler, *Histoire de la tolérance*, 1: 138–49.
19 Allen Ep 1039: 219–43.
20 Allen Ep 1334: 216–20. For the same opinion, see the paraphrase on Matt. 11: 30 (LB 6: 63ff.).
21 Allen Ep 1334: 362: 'olim fides erat magis in vita quam in articulorum professione.'
22 Bientenholz, 'Erasmus und der Basler Buchhandel,' 307; and Bientenholz, *Basle and France in the Sixteenth Century: The Basle Humanists and Printers in Their Contacts with Francophone Culture*, esp. 127, 205.
23 Mario Turchetti, *Concordia o tolleranza: François Bauduin (1520–1573) e i 'moyenneurs,'* 294–9, aptly shows the difference between the two authors.
24 Ibid, 298; Turchetti, 'Une question mal posée: Erasme et la tolérance. L'idée de *sygkatabasis*.'
25 Sébastien Castellion, *Conseil à la France désolée*, ed. Marius F. Valkhoff (Geneva: Droz, 1967).

26 Georges Cassander, *De officio pii ac publicae tranquillitatis vere amantis viri* (n.p., 1562), 15.
27 Ibid.
28 Georges Cassander, *De officio*, 25, trans. Lecler, *Histoire de la tolérance*, 1: 270.
29 Alain Tallon, *La France et le Concile de Trente (1518–1563)*, 709–10.
30 Bientenholz, *Basel and France*, 205, referring to the translators, writes: 'Their approach resembled more clearly that of Bauduin and Cassander, as they urged the young king, and in fact those who ruled France in his name, to remedy the religious strife by encouraging to heed the voice of Erasmus.'
31 Letter of December 1557 to Guillaume Constantin, published in Ferdinand Buisson, *Sébastien Castellion, sa vie et son oeuvre (1515–1563): Étude sur les origines du protestantisme libéral français*, 1: 434.
32 Margaret Mann Phillips, 'Erasmus in France in the later Sixteenth Century.'
33 James Hutton, 'Erasmus and France: The Propaganda for Peace.'

ELEVEN

John Bale's *Image of Both Churches* and the English Paraphrase on Revelation

Gretchen E. Minton

By July 1547, just six months after the death of Henry VIII, the English reformers had already drawn up a set of injunctions that were designed to make official the Protestant agenda that had been cut short by Henry. Among other requirements, these injunctions stipulate that each parish church

> provide within three months ... one book of the whole Bible, of the largest volume, in English. And within one twelve-months ... the Paraphrasis of Erasmus also in English upon the Gospels, and the same set up in some convenient place, within the said church that they have cure of, whereas their parishioners may most commodiously resort unto the same and read the same.

Furthermore, the injunctions require that

> every parson, vicar, curate, chantry priest and stipendiary, being under the degree of Bachelor of Divinity, shall provide and have of his own, within three months ... the New Testament both in Latin and in English, with Paraphrasis upon the same of Erasmus and diligently study the same, conferring the one with the other.[1]

During this same year (1547), John Bale, an English exile who had been on the Continent since 1540 when his patron Thomas Cromwell was executed, was completing a work called the *Image of Both Churches*, which he called an 'exposition or paraphrase' of the 'wonderful and heavenly revelation of St John the Evangelist.'[2] Bale's decision to write a *paraphrase* of the book of Revelation – the one New Testament book that Erasmus did *not* paraphrase – is significant, especially in light of the simultaneous publication of the English translation of Erasmus' *Paraphrases* (to which is added a 'paraphrase' on Revelation). In this essay I shall consider the relationship between Bale's *Image of Both Churches* and Erasmian paraphrase, underlining some of the elements of Erasmus' style and purpose that are evident even in the work of an apocalypticist like Bale, who certainly lacked Erasmus' sense of moderation. I shall seek to situate Bale in the larger context of Erasmian paraphrase in England, by comparing his work with the paraphrase on Revelation that was chosen to conclude the English translation of Erasmus' *Paraphrases*. Finally, I shall argue that these projects reveal an attempt to synthesize two disparate trends in English Protestantism of the time: Erasmian humanism on the one hand, and apocalypticism on the other.

BALE AND ERASMUS

At first glance, no one would seem further removed than Bale from the enterprise of Erasmian humanism. Notorious for his strident anti-Catholicism and rhetorical violence, Bale is not exactly a model for colloquies. Yet the story of his life shows that he, like many of the English reformers, was influenced by the Dutch humanist.[3]

Born in 1495 into a poor family that sent him to a Carmelite friary at the age of twelve, John Bale was from the beginning entrenched in a Roman Catholic world. By 1536, after years of study and work as a Carmelite friar, he openly converted to Protestantism; he left the Order, became a stipendiary priest, and was immediately attacked for his preaching against Roman Catholic ceremonies. He was delivered from prison through the intervention of Thomas Cromwell, who became his patron. During the next few years Bale wrote stage plays and toured the country with a small troupe supported by Cromwell, performing dramas as Protestant propaganda. When Henry ordered Cromwell's execution in 1540, Bale, like many other reformers, fled to the Continent and stayed there until the accession of Edward VI in 1547. Bale spent most of his exile in Antwerp, working on the *Image of Both Churches*, other polemical works, and accounts of Protestant martyrs.[4]

Besides typifying the shift from Roman Catholicism to Protestantism that England as a whole was experiencing in the 1530s and 1540s, Bale's life and writings also point to an important link between English Protestantism and English nationalism. The interest in literary history that Bale already had as a Carmelite was focused upon England. His stage plays and many of his later works were written in the vernacular language so that he could reach a wide (and popular) audience. The Reformation had begun to speak English, in English texts. As well as supporting the campaign of Bible translations into English, Bale composed his own works and commentaries on the Bible in order to help people understand the meaning of Scripture. By identifying the Reformation itself as a sign of the last days, and by reading the events of history as proof of the fulfilment of biblical prophecies, he was instrumental in bringing apocalyptic history to the centre of English Protestant consciousness.

A pervasive feature of Bale's writing is his use of the past and of the writers of the past. His non-dramatic writings are filled with marginal references to previous authors and works. He most commonly quotes or cites the Bible, but he also frequently employs patristic and medieval sources. As his interest in the Apocalypse developed, he turned to the works of the twelfth-century heretic Joachim of Fiore, to Francis Lambert and Albertus Magnus. His view of Lollardy as the predecessor to Protestantism prompted a study of Wycliffe and Huss, and he was quick to pick up the traces of Luther, Tyndale, and other eminent reformers, Continental and English.[5]

When Bale arrived at Cambridge in 1514, Erasmus had just departed, but his influence was felt strongly there for many years afterwards. Despite living near the White Horse Tavern, the young Carmelite seems to have been largely oblivious to the major currents of religious reform associated with the Dutch humanist.[6] He resided at Cambridge for eight years, but, according to his own retrospective testimony, during this time he 'wandered in complete barbarism of scholarship and blindness of mind.'[7] Since he says little about the process of his conversion, apart from mentioning the influence of Thomas, Lord Wentworth of Nettlestead,[8] it is difficult to know whether he was already swayed by the Cambridge reformers, or how much, if anything, he knew of Erasmus before his visit to the Low Countries in the 1520s.

Even before his conversion, Bale held certain views in common with Erasmus, such as a dislike of scholasticism and a feeling that monasteries were too often corrupt. By the time that he converted to Protestantism in the 1530s, the main targets of his attacks on the Roman Catholic church were the corruption of the monasteries and enforced celibacy, both matters that concerned Erasmus as well. Peter Happé observes that

> [s]ome significant doctrinal parallels can be found between Bale's views and those of Erasmus in the *Enchiridion* ... Like Bale, Erasmus repudiated specialist and elitist latin and scholastic philosophy; he produced a critique of monasticism; and he saw chastity and marriage as indistinguishable, and advocated an unsacramental inner religion.[9]

There is evidence in Bale's writings that he was familiar with Erasmus' works. So much might be expected, given their common theological ground and the close association in many quarters between Erasmus' name and the Reformation. The Englishmen with whom Bale kept company were certainly interested in Erasmus' biblical humanism. Cromwell had been instrumental in the publication of several of Erasmus' works in English, including early translations of some of the New Testament paraphrases.[10] As Bale's sympathies with the reformers grew stronger, he could hardly have missed feeling the influence of Erasmus.[11] Many of those whom he lauded in his later writings, such as Cranmer, Tyndale, Bilney, Latimer, and Coverdale, were members of the group that met at the White Horse Tavern. Even had he been ignorant of Erasmianism during his time at Cambridge, it is hard to believe that he would long have remained so.

The evidence for Bale's knowledge of Erasmus goes beyond mere conjecture, however. In the course of his writings he quotes or refers to the *Colloquies, Enchiridion,* the edition of St Jerome, the exposition on the Creed, and other Erasmian works. While it is true that 'on many theological matters Bale went far beyond the position of the Erasmian reformers,'[12] he was perfectly willing to use Erasmus when it suited him, and to disregard the parts of

Erasmian thought that were at odds with his own. Not surprisingly, Bale favours the Erasmus who spoke out against the corruption of the Roman Catholic church. Recalling that '[m]any most able doctors and fathers, since the pope's first rise, have in their famous writings called upon the church's reformation' (520),[13] he includes Erasmus in a list of nearly sixty names; an earlier list joins him with those who have exposed 'that Babylonish harlot Rome' (509). His marginal references to Erasmus in Part 1[14] of the *Image* follow a similar pattern. He cites Erasmus six times, on points such as the corruption of the monasteries (329), the 'superstitious sects' in the Roman Catholic church (347), and problems with scholastic theology (350). Erasmus, says Bale, is one who has 'raised his voice against the unbelieving antichrists' (332) in recent times. The inclusion of Erasmus among the reformers continues throughout the *Image*. Although Bale drops the use of marginal references in the later parts of this work, he nonetheless cites Erasmus several times in the main text. There he appears next to Luther, Calvin, Zwingli, and Oecolampadius among the Continentals, and with Bilney, Tyndale, Cromwell, Ridley, and Coverdale in England.

THE *IMAGE OF BOTH CHURCHES* AS PARAPHRASE

In view of the evidence of Bale's familiarity with Erasmus, we are bound to ask: was his decision to call the *Image* a *paraphrase* informed by the example of Erasmus? To begin answering this question, we must consider how closely the *Image* follows the structure, style, and purpose of Erasmus' *Paraphrases.*

The full title of Bale's work reads: *The Image of bothe churches after the moste wonderfull and heauenly Reuelacion of Sainct John the Euangelist, contayning a very frutefull exposicion or paraphrase upon the same,Wherein it is conferred with the other scripturs and most auctorised historyes. Compiled by John Bale an exile also in this life for the faythfull testimonie of Jesu.* Bale follows a consistent method throughout the *Image,* quoting several verses of the Book of Revelation at a time, then paraphrasing each in turn. The *Image* thus maintains a division between 'the text' and 'the paraphrase,' and these labels are used throughout.[15] Although the quotation of the biblical text does not follow the original practice of Erasmus in the *Paraphrases,* it is not at odds with Erasmian principles. Erasmus meant his paraphrases to be read, not instead of the

Scriptures, but alongside them, as a way of explaining and expanding the often cryptic sense of the Word. Bale formalizes this process so that it is impossible to read his paraphrase *without* the Bible.[16]

The editors of CWE 42 point out that Erasmian paraphrase 'seeks to clarify the text by rephrasing what an author says in the paraphraser's own words. In this respect a paraphrase differs from a translation, in which one attempts to render the author's words themselves.'[17] Like Erasmus, Bale usually speaks in the first person and assumes the voice of the narrator. Thus, the paraphrase accompanying Revelation 1: 9 ('I John your brother and companion in tribulation ...') reads: 'I, the faithful writer of this present revelation, called John the Apostle, your natural loving brother, so entirely coveting your souls' health as mine own, a companion of yours also in adversity, trouble, and persecution, for the truth's sake ...' (268). Sometimes, it is true, Bale uses language such as 'And suddenly I turned back, *saith Saint John*' (269; my emphasis), but he does so generally to indicate the speaking voice (especially helpful in the case of Revelation) and thereafter uses the first person without any identifying noun.

The most significant difference between a paraphrase and a commentary is that the former is 'a continuous narrative rather than an interrupted one.'[18] Despite Bale's inclusion of the biblical text, which does interrupt the narrative to a certain extent, the *Image* does not read like a commentary (nor, more pertinently, like Erasmus' *Annotations*). Instead, it is a continuous retelling of John's vision on Patmos. While it includes much exegesis, the force of the narrative makes it more periphrastic than a commentary would normally be. As Erasmus does in the *Paraphrases*, Bale uses other commentators in order to construct his paraphrase (he lists many of them in the introduction to the *Image*), yet seems intent on providing something different from a commentary.[19] The marginal references show the sources of his material, but in the text itself he rarely interpolates citations of this sort, because they would interrupt the narrative flow. Long digressions – and there are plenty in the *Image* – do not often include citations from other commentators, but instead continue as part of the narrative, with no clear distinction between the various authoritative voices. Bale says this of his use of other authors in his preface: 'Of these commentaries have I taken both example to do this thing, and also counsel to understand the text; to none of them wholly addict, but as I perceived them always agreeing to the scriptures' (258).

Thus Bale's objective is similar to Erasmus': he paraphrases in order to clarify. Both men wanted to use their own text to speak to ordinary people and to elucidate the mysteries inherent in the Scripture, and therefore both wrote in a popular style. Like Erasmus' *Paraphrases*, Bale's paraphrase is a form of exegesis that is intended to clarify the Scripture and to provide an interpretation for the people – in this case, in their own language. Scholars rarely, if ever, call the *Image* a paraphrase, and yet it is closer to being that than it is to being commentary or annotations. These similarities in style and objective between the two men's works suggest that Bale had an understanding of the genre of paraphrase that was informed by Erasmus. Indeed, it seems unlikely that any reformer who was well versed in both English and Continental traditions could have used the term 'paraphrase' without knowingly invoking Erasmian associations.

This said, we should not overlook the differences between the two undertakings, which are many. The most obvious difference in the style of paraphrase between Erasmus and Bale is the latter's historical specificity. Bale was interested in an elucidation of the text that emphasized the relationship between historical events – especially involving the Reformation – and the text of Scripture. For example, Bale says of the earthquake that results from the opening of the sixth seal in Revelation 6: 12:

> Such a terrible earthquake was the general council of Constance against John Huss and Jerome of Prague; and here in England against the king (when he set forth the gospel) the seditious rising of Lincolnshire and the traiterous uproar of Yorkshire in their pilgrimage without grace. (326)

Bale often links the mysteries of the apocalypse to events during his own time, using the Scripture as 'a light to the chronicles' (253). Such an approach would not have made sense to Erasmus, who wrote in his brief *Annotations* on Revelation:

> Jerome testifies to the fact that the Apocalypse was not even, in his own time, accepted by the Greeks. In addition, he states that some learned people had attacked the whole

> narrative, dismissing it as a fiction and heaping many an insult on it, because it contains nothing of apostolic seriousness, but is only a popular history of events, sketched with the appearance of imagery.[20]

Erasmus thought that Revelation should be taken only for illustration, not as an authoritative book of Scripture in its own right, much less as a key to the entire Bible – which is just how Bale used it. He declares at the beginning of the *Image* that

> [t]he very complete sum and whole knitting up is this heavenly book of the universal verities of the bible. All that Moses taught in the law, David in the Psalms, and the prophets in their writings concerning Christ's spiritual kingdom both here and above, meet for this present knowledge, are herein briefly comprehended. (252)

The *Image* is full of examples from history; Bale supplies the events and people that match the prophecies of Scripture.[21] His interpretation does not necessarily preclude references to other events and people, but at every turn it uses the text of the Bible in order to make history clearer – to infuse it with prophetic meaning. Bale wants to clarify the prophecies of the Apocalypse in order to admonish the people in the last days:

> I have considered it no less than my bound duty, under pain of damnation, to admonish Christ's flock by this present revelation of their perils past, and the dangers to come for contempt of the gospel, which now reigneth there above all in the clergy. (255)

This tactic is far removed from Erasmus' spiritual philosophy of Christ. The similar use made of Revelation by apocalypticists such as Beatus of Liebana, Joachim of Fiore, and John Huss was one of the reasons for Erasmus' apprehensions concerning that book.[22]

Bale declares in the *Image* that '[s]ome hateful and ungodly blasphemers there are and ever have been, which will in no wise this book to be of equal authority with the other scriptures of Christ's testament. But damnably wretched are they in the vain imaginations of their sinful hearts' (515). Naturally, Bale makes no connection between Erasmus the supposed champion of the Reformed church and Erasmus the doubter of the Book of Revelation. Bale's insistence upon the authorship of John the Evangelist – even in the title of the *Image* – makes it clear that he was not interested in Erasmus' philological study of Scripture. Rather, it was the idea of making the text available to the people in their own language, and historically relevant, that engaged all his attention. As we shall see, he was not the only Englishman who saw no disjunction between Erasmian paraphrase and apocalypticism.

ERASMUS' *PARAPHRASES* IN ENGLAND AND IN ENGLISH

The 1548 English translation of Erasmus' *Paraphrases* had been many years in the making.[23] Catherine Parr lent extensive support to the project, and much of the work was complete even before the death of Henry. A variety of persons took part. Besides scholars such as Nicholas Udall and Thomas Key, Catherine herself perhaps had a hand in some of the translations, and even Princess Mary assisted in the translation of the Gospel of John. The fact that these English *Paraphrases* went to press so soon after Henry's death suggests that the King had been opposed to their publication, but Catherine's patronage was consistent; several years before Henry's death she had already appointed Nicholas Udall as the general editor.[24] The first volume contained the Gospels and Acts, and was printed by Richard Grafton and Edward Whitchurch, followers of Cromwell who had also printed the Great Bible in 1539.[25] The Protestant agenda behind the English *Paraphrases* was clear; this was the book that the Edwardian Injunctions ordered to be placed in every parish church alongside the Great Bible and the Book of Homilies.

Udall prefaces the first volume with a long dedication to King Edward, making the monarch's role in England's Erasmian reform clear, and then includes a short preface to the reader and another to Catherine Parr which explains that this book is 'for the use and commoditie of suche people as with an earnest zeale, and with deuout studye, dooe houngre and thyrst the simple and plain knowlage of Goddes woorde.'[26] In a revised preface to Catherine Parr the next year, Udall outlines the benefits of Erasmian paraphrase: the fruitful exercise of the learned, the wholesome instruction of English readers, and the edification of ignorant multitudes. Udall defends Erasmus against charges that he is insincere, and asserts that reading this man's work is the route to proper piety. Udall insists that Erasmus 'diligently and moste simply laboureth to bryng to lyght' the grace of the gospel (fol. i v).[27] Furthermore, 'in these his paraphrases ... he laboureth so to enlarge the processe and tenour of the texte, as the sense thereof may bothe euedentlye be gathered, and may well hange together' (ibid). The point is clear: Erasmus' elucidation of the biblical text through paraphrase makes the message of the gospel shine forth more brightly, and the result is the education of all people, who thereby become part of a unified Protestant nation.

Dedicated to the king and endorsed by Catherine Parr, this book had a royal sanction that connected the project of Erasmian paraphrase explicitly to the national Protestant agenda as defined by Cranmer and Lord Protector Somerset. John Wall observes that '[t]he purpose of authorizing use of the Paraphrases was to provide a standard interpretive guide to the New Testament for both clergy and laity. Through commanding use of the Paraphrases, Cranmer sought to bring the whole nation of England to understand the New Testament as Erasmus read it.'[28] However, there was no way to provide the English people with a paraphrase by Erasmus of the Book of Revelation, so a substitute had to be found.

The Edwardian Injunctions required only that Erasmus' paraphrases on the Gospels and Acts be present in every church, but clearly the paraphrases were popular enough to warrant a publication of the rest of them. The second volume, printed the next year (1549) by Whitchurch and under the patronage of Anne Seymour, was edited by Miles Coverdale. The title page reads: 'The second tome or volume of the Paraphrase of Erasmus upon the newe testament: conteynyng the Epistles of S. Paul, and other the Apostles. Whereunto is added a Paraphrase upon the Reuelacion of S. John.' The additional paraphrase was composed by Leo Jud in German, and translated for this volume by an Englishman named Edmund Allen.[29]

Under the direction of Coverdale, the second volume of the *Paraphrases* took on a more radically Protestant character. Coverdale's leanings are clear from his preface to Edward:

> Certes, whan I loke behinde me, and call to remembraunce but euen the shorte daies of my tyme: how sore we haue bene blynded, seduced and hindred from the true waye of

> Christes doctrine: how strongly the wicked delusion of Antichriste (according to S. Paules prophecie) hath preuailed: what sectes of perdicion, what deuelishe doctrines, what straunge inuentions of corrupte menne, what vayne pylgremages ... that moste wicked beast of Rome hathe brought specially in to thys youre realme: howe shamefully and presumptuously (euen after the nature of proude Lucifer) he hathe usurped the Imperiall power thereof: how horrybyle he hathe abused the Maiestie of the Kynges ... in this your realme of Englande. (sig. +.iii)

John King observes that 'Coverdale conferred a stridently polemical tone on the work, particularly through the addition of Tyndale's prologue to Romans and the inclusion of Leo Jud's violently antipapal commentary on Revelation.'[30] The militantly Protestant character of the latter was to be expected: Leo Jud was a Swiss reformer who was a close associate of Zwingli's. He had translated many of Erasmus' works, including the *Paraphrases*, and was a biblical scholar and translator in his own right.[31] Jud's support of Erasmus was not unqualified, however, and his paraphrase on Revelation has little in common with Erasmian paraphrase. Jud cites Erasmus several times in his paraphrase on Revelation but, unlike Bale, he rarely speaks in the first person. The Swiss reformer appears to use fewer sources than either Erasmus or Bale, and his 'paraphrase' on Revelation reads more like a homily or commentary than a continuous narrative.

Coverdale's edition of the *Paraphrases*, like Bale's *Image*, is arranged into small sections of the text of Scripture (taken from the Great Bible) followed by lengthy paraphrases.[32] The way in which the biblical text is broken up is remarkably similar in the two works, in fact.[33] So why did Coverdale include Jud's paraphrase rather than one by the Englishman Bale? Let us suppose, for the sake of argument, that the inclusion of Bale's paraphrase was a real possibility. This is not unlikely. Bale's writings in Latin gained the respect of the Continental reformers, and his fellow English exiles (such as Udall, Grafton, and Whitchurch) would certainly have taken notice of his English works. Coverdale was another of these exiles, and he would have seen Bale's works, and perhaps even the man himself, during this period.[34] The *Image* also had an audience among many who stayed in England. At least part of the work must have been available by 1546, when it attracted enough attention for Bishop Bonner to order any copies found in England to be burned.[35] The popularity of a work like the *Image* would only have increased after Henry died and the exiles, including Bale himself, flocked back to England with their books in hand.

Perhaps someone did suggest that Bale's professed 'paraphrase' on Revelation would be an appropriate substitute for the missing Erasmian text. Even if no such hint was ever given, a comparison of Jud's paraphrase with Bale's will enable us to see more clearly how the Book of Revelation was being written (and read) *in paraphrase* at the end of the 1540s.

PARAPHRASING REVELATION

What could it have been about the *Image* that made it less suitable for Coverdale's and Cranmer's purposes than the work of one of Zwingli's followers? Fidelity to the Erasmian model was apparently not a concern, for while Bale's paraphrase cannot unequivocally be called 'Erasmian' in style, it certainly comes closer than Jud's, which lacks the use of first person and continuous narrative. Both paraphrasts also assert that John the Evangelist is the author of Revelation, ignoring Erasmus' arguments to the contrary. Recalling the tone of the *Image*, we might suppose that Bale's interpretation of Revelation was felt to be too polemical, too full of anti-papal tirades to be included in the English volume of Erasmus' *Paraphrases*. Bale's rhetorical treatment of the Roman Catholic church is indeed intemperate. Yet the same is true of Jud's paraphrase. Jud (in Allen's rendering) complains about the monks, friars, and priests of the Roman Catholic church in the strongest terms, saying that 'thorowe their hypocrysye, [they] haue heaped unto themselues money, goodes and treasures ... And whereas the world should haue learned of them, faith, loue and knowledge, it was nothing but slandered, offended, deceyued and seduced' (fol. ix v–x r). King notes of the Coverdale edition that '[t]he addition of the Tyndale prologue and Jud commentary is hardly compatible with the Erasmian middle way.'[36] Any explanation of why the *Image* may have seemed less fit than Jud's work for inclusion in a translation of Erasmus' *Paraphrases* must be sought elsewhere. Considerations of space can hardly have been decisive: the two works are of comparable length,[37] the Jud/ Allen paraphrase concluding with the same Dürer woodcut of the woman clothed with the sun that is used in the *Image* (which includes several such woodcuts).

A notable difference is that although Jud is more likely to employ specific historical examples than Erasmus, the Swiss reformer's use of history is ultimately less extensive and sophisticated than Bale's. Jud's historical references typically focus only upon the early church, and when he does mention the Reformation, it is not clear how his examples fit into a larger pattern of history as suggested by the Scripture. Bale, by contrast, was primarily interested in history, specifically in the relationship between certain historical events and the prophecies of Revelation.

Following the lead of Francis Lambert, Bale's exegesis in the *Image* suggests that Revelation is a mirror of church history.[38] He interprets each of the seven seals as representing a period of history since the Ascension. First is the time of the Apostles, then the time of heretics and persecution, then the age of Constantine (with its own heresies). Bale associates the fourth seal with the corruption of the papacy (which he dates from the beginning of the seventh century), the fifth seal with the persecution of the saints in all ages, and the sixth seal with the revival of the gospel (starting with Wycliffe). Bale differed from many other apocalypticists of his day by shying away from millenarianism and refusing to identify the antichrist with a specific person. His great strength was his knowledge of historical detail; thus, he interpreted Revelation in a way that allowed him to provide exhaustive lists of names and events in application of specific scriptural passages. This type of interpretation has the effect of making all history, especially that of the Reformation in the sixteenth century, appear as the immediate fulfilment of divine prophecy.

Jud's basic reading of the seven seals is similar to Bale's. (The Swiss reformer was influenced, like his English counterpart, by Joachim of Fiore, Lambert, et al.) However, before providing the historical interpretation, Jud mentions that

> [t]he seven special articles and misteries of the Christian faith maye be opened euen lyke as vii seales throrow the holy goost, in the holy scripture of the olde and newe testament. As the excellent clerke Erasmus doth proue by diuerse testimonies in his paraphrases upon the xxiiii Chapter of luke. (fol. vii v)

This passage exemplifies Jud's reluctance to be historically specific, which causes his exegesis to be much more vague than Bale's. Whereas Jud speaks only briefly about the second seal, saying that it represents the time of martyrs from Stephen to Constantine, Bale lists the types of heresies at this time and the men who were responsible for them, then provides a list of martyrs (*Image*, 313–14). Jud can be historically specific on the subject of the early church – as, for example, when he includes lists of biblical characters, Roman emperors, and church fathers. But he is reluctant to name contemporary names and events, where Bale is most forthcoming. An instructive example is their differing interpretations of Gog and Magog. Jud's paraphrase states that Gog and Magog refer to

> the greate and infinite nomber of the enemyes of God, of the holy doctrine of the gospel, and of all holy congragations of true and faythfull Christians, whiche are called and are in dede the very true Jerusalem, whiche dwell upon earth as citizens of a fortunate, holy, quiet and honorable citie and comunaltie. (fol. xxxiii r)

This very 'Genevan' and general interpretation stands in sharp contrast to Bale's exhaustive listings of people and events to match his exegesis of Gog and Magog as the open and hidden enemies of the church (570–6).

Jud and Bale are substantially in agreement on the abuses of the Roman Catholic church, another subject on which Jud is willing to be somewhat specific. Referring to Revelation 18, he exclaims that 'there was neuer founde more shamefull merchandyse, than that whiche they of the Popes courte, specially the Curtysans, haue exercysed many yeares with other mennes goodes,' and then proceeds to list specific 'atrocities' (fol. xxix v). These lists and examples take both Jud and Bale farther away from the style of Erasmian paraphrase. The departure is partly a consequence of the nature of the Apocalypse itself. Any act of interpretation of this book entails not just a retelling but also a decoding of the symbols that appear in it. Yet if one of these works was going to be used for the 1549 English edition of the *Paraphrases*, the style of its presentation of history may have made Jud's more attractive.

It is reasonable to suggest that Bale's particular brand of historical specificity would have been contrary to the aims of the

Edwardian church. Despite his enthusiasm about Edward himself in his revised conclusion,[39] his recital of names and examples in the *Image* would have made his work seem likely to become quickly outdated, and to entrench divisions between Protestant factions. Neither tendency would have been attractive to individuals who were attempting to create a unified and stable English Protestant church under the rule of the young king. The all-embracing conclusion of Jud's paraphrase would have been more welcome: 'The grace of our Lorde Jesus Christ be with all faithfull electe Christians whiche shall be untyll the ende of the worlde, and specially with them whiche reade this booke with faithe and an holy Christen desyre and mynde. Amen' (fol. xl r).

What is admonition in Bale is exhortation in Jud, and there are historical circumstances to account for the difference. Bale's interpretation of Revelation is influenced throughout by the fact that he was an exile when he wrote it. In his autobiographical sketches, he makes it clear that part of his interest in the Apocalypse was a personal one; he was a stranger almost everywhere he went, often facing harsh opposition for his beliefs. In the *Image* he remarks that he is especially qualified to write on Revelation because he, like John, is an exile:

> I have exiled myself for ever from mine own native country, kindred, friends, acquaintance, (which are the great delights of this life,) and am well contented for Jesus Christ's sake, and for the comfort of my brethren there, to suffer poverty, penury, abjection, reproof, and all that shall come besides. (260)

While this perspective may have been natural for radical English reformers during the first part of the 1540s, by the end of the decade, with Edward's rule established, the exilic vision was no longer so relevant. Instead, any interpretation of the Apocalypse put forth by the Edwardian church needed to de-emphasize the imminent destruction of the established order and to emphasize the unity of Protestantism.

The English were clearly interested in the Apocalypse, and to publish a set of paraphrases on the New Testament without including one of its last book would have been out of the question. Jud's paraphrase may have recommended itself because it was Protestant in tone but relatively general in its historical reference, and because it spoke with the authoritative voice of a Continental reformer. As Irena Backus writes, 'With its insistence on some of the essential points of the Zurich Reformation, its exhortations to devotion, and its simple theology, Jud's *Paraphrase* effectively neutralized all potentially dangerous aspects of the Apocalypse and made it useful reading for the wider mass of the faithful.'[40]

CONCLUSION

In England in the 1540s there was a strong commitment to Erasmian humanism: to putting the Scriptures into the vernacular, to paraphrasing and thereby making plain the sense of the biblical text, and to uniting the people in a common reformed religion. Bale's *Image* and the Coverdale edition of the *Paraphrases* both show how Protestants were combining this Erasmian program with a distinctive emphasis upon the history and prophecy of the book of Revelation. As many scholars have suggested, the aim of the English adoption of Erasmus' *Paraphrases* was to transform the Christian commonwealth by uniting it in a common understanding of the Word. By including a book that Erasmus would have omitted, however, these English reformers departed significantly from their primary model.

Bale was one of the first exponents of an identifiably English apocalypticism, albeit one with strong Continental roots. That apocalypticism was characterized by a historical specificity that left a place open for England as an 'elect nation.'[41] English imaginations would long be stirred by apocalyptic strains, especially in times of trial.[42] Insular interest in the book of Revelation would reach its highest point during the reign of Mary, that one-time translator of Erasmus' *Paraphrase on John*, when many more Protestants, Bale among them, fled to the Continent and many who stayed in England were burned to death. One of the Marian exiles, John Foxe, was a close friend of Bale's. Foxe was greatly influenced by Bale's apocalyptic writings, but he was also a self-styled disciple of Erasmus; he even made a pilgrimage to Rotterdam for the express purpose of seeing Erasmus' city.[43] Foxe appreciated Erasmus' scholarship and his sense of moderation, both attributes he shared. The mingling of Erasmian humanism and apocalypticism that can seem so awkward in Bale and Jud achieves its resolution in the writings of Foxe. Although Foxe, like Bale, first elaborated his apocalyptic ideas in exile, the *Acts and Monuments* would be recognized as a work with the power to speak authoritatively to a united English church. In 1571, it was *Foxe's* book that was ordered into churches, homes, and public places throughout the land.[44]

NOTES

1 The Edwardian Injunctions (1547) in *Documents of the English Reformation*, ed. Gerald Bray, 250, 253.

2 The first two parts of the *Image* had been printed in Antwerp earlier, probably in 1545 (STC 1296.5). The full work was printed by Richard Jugge as soon as Bale returned from exile in 1548.

3 On the life and work of Bale see Peter Happé, *John Bale*; Leslie P. Fairfield, *John Bale: Mythmaker for the English Reformation*; Thora Balslev Blatt, *The Plays of John Bale: A Study of Ideas, Technique and Style*; Honor McCusker, *John Bale: Dramatist and Antiquary*; and Jesse W. Harris, *John Bale: A Study in the Minor Literature of the Reformation*.

4 Hoping for preferment when Edward became king, Bale moved back to England in 1548, but it was not until 1552 that the dubious honour of the bishopric of Ossory in Ireland was urged upon him. Bale's difficulties at Kilkenny were myriad because of the strong Roman Catholic sentiment there, but his time in Ireland was short: when Mary became Queen of England in 1553, he once again fled to the Continent, where he remained until 1559. Returning to England during Elizabeth's reign, Bale spent the last few years of his life as a canon at Canterbury, and died on 15 November 1563.

5 Paul Christianson, *Reformers and Babylon: English Apocalyptic Visions from the Reformation to the Eve of the Civil War*, 15: 'With some exceptions, [Bale] most frequently cited either contemporary reformed scholars or medieval heretics [in the *Image*] – Francois Lambert (48), Sebastian Meyer (26), Martin Luther (14), and Johannes Oecolampadius (11) in the one category, John Wycliffe (20), John Hus (17), and Joachim of Fiora (7) in the other.' On Bale's sources, see also Katharine R. Firth, *The Apocalyptic Tradition in Reformation Britain*, chap. 2; and Richard Bauckham, *Tudor Apocalypse: Sixteenth-Century Apocalypticism, Millenarianism, and the English Reformation*.

6 Fairfield surmises that during Bale's stay in Cambridge, '[h]umanist influences seem to have left [his] traditional piety quite unscathed' (*John Bale*, 13). Nonetheless, the proximity of Erasmus and Bale at this time is tantalizing: 'the young Friar Bale liv[ed] in the Carmelite house just across the narrow lane from Queens' College, where

Erasmus had resided during part of his stay in Cambridge. Bale must have heard a good deal about the famous Dutch scholar, who had only just departed when Bale came to stay in 1514' (ibid, 11).

7 Happé, *John Bale*, 4, quoting Bale's *Scriptorum illustrium maioris Britanniae ... catalogus*, 1:701. The text of the *Catalogus* published in Basel by Oporinus (1557–9) was an expansion of the Wesel edition of 1548, representing the fruit of many years' work both in England and during the author's exiles abroad.

8 *Catalogus*, 1:702; Fairfield, *John Bale*, 34.

9 Happé, *John Bale*, 55.

10 The paraphrases on the Epistles to Titus and Jude were published in the 1530s under Cromwell's patronage: E.J. Devereux, 'The Publication of the English *Paraphrases* of Erasmus,' 350; CWE 42: xxx–xxxi. For other works, see Fairfield, *John Bale*, 121.

11 John N. Wall, Jr, 'Godly and Fruitful Lessons: The English Bible, Erasmus' Paraphrases, and the Book of Homilies,' 49: 'whatever "humanism" was in northern Europe in the early sixteenth century, it was a highly complex and multi-faceted phenomenon, and ... Erasmus was, at least for English humanists, a major and influential spokesman for at least some aspects of it. Instead of thinking of an "Erasmian" party, we might instead want to envision a community of men with shared educational backgrounds, shared goals, and shared methodology, for which Erasmus loomed as the most articulate spokesman.'

12 Fairfield, *John Bale*, 47.

13 Quotations from the *Image of Both Churches* follow the edition in *Select Works of John Bale, D.D.*, ed. Henry Christmas, Parker Society (Cambridge: Cambridge University Press, 1849), 249–640.

14 Only in Part 1 (of three) does Bale add marginal references. In the preface to Part 2, he explains that he included the references in the first part in order 'to ease the readers for search of the places, and to signify unto them that I did nothing therein without authority.' He states that 'undoubtedly the gathering of those places was so laborious unto me, as the making of the commentary; which nevertheless I thought well bestowed for the comfort of my brethren' (380). He claims to have discontinued the practice because 'two cruel enemies have my just labours had in that behalf: of whom the one [the printers] hath them falsified, the other [a critic] blasphemed: which hath caused me to leave them out in all that here followeth' (380–1).

15 The term 'paraphrase' is used only in Parts 1 and 2. In Part 3 it is replaced by 'commentary,' even though the style does not change.

16 Not only does Bale include the biblical text, but he also numbers each phrase of it and inserts the corresponding numbers in the

paraphrase for ease of cross-reference. For the addition of 'marginal indices,' i.e., biblical lemmata, to Erasmus' *Paraphrases* in early editions, see John J. Bateman's essay above p. 226.

17 John B. Payne, Albert Rabil, Jr, and Warren S. Smith, Jr, 'The *Paraphrases* of Erasmus: Origin and Character,' CWE 42: xv–xvi.

18 Ibid, xvi.

19 Albert Rabil, Jr, 'Erasmus's Paraphrases of the New Testament,' 148, notes that in the paraphrases, '[i]n contrast to the annotations, [Erasmus] does not refer to the Fathers upon whom he relies for his interpretations. His exegesis, however, is often dependent upon theirs.' See also the pertinent remarks of John J. Bateman in CWE 44: xv.

20 LB 6: 1123: 'Testatur divus Hieronymus Apocalypsim ne sua quidem aetate fuisse receptam a Graecis. Ad haec quosdm eruditissimos viros, totum hoc argumentum, ceu fictum multis convitiis insectatos fuisse, quasi nihil haberet apostolicae gravitatis, sed vulgatam tantum rerum historiam, figurarum involucris adumbratam.' For Erasmus' view of the Apocalypse, see Irena Backus, *Reformation Readings of the Apocalypse: Geneva, Zurich, and Wittenberg*, 3–6.

21 Bale's historical references are legion. He provides examples from the Old and New Testaments, the early church, the Middle Ages, and from his own period, both in England and on the Continent. For Bale, every name and event of church history somehow fits into the pattern described in Revelation.

22 For Bale's predecessors, see Eugen Weber, *Apocalypses: Prophecies, Cults, and Millennial Beliefs through the Ages*, esp. chapters 4 and 5.

23 Wall, 'Godly and Fruitful Lessons'; Devereux, 'Publication of the English *Paraphrases*'; James K. McConica, *English Humanists and Reformation Politics under Henry VIII and Edward VI*. See also John Craig's essay below (chapter 12).

24 Nicholas Udall, now remembered chiefly for his play *Ralph Roister Doister* and for the controversy surrounding his dismissal as the headmaster of Eton in 1541, was also a first-rate scholar and translator. He published an English edition of the third and fourth books of Erasmus' *Apophthegmata* (1542) and, in 1545, made a translation of the *Paraphrases on Luke*. The latter work attracted the attention of Catherine Parr, who appointed him general editor of the *Paraphrases*. Although he certainly had Protestant leanings, Udall was not as radical as many of his contemporaries; he remained in good favour throughout Henry's reign and also during Mary's. See the entry for him in the *Dictionary of National Biography* (hereafter DNB) and CWE 42: xxxi.

25 The Great Bible, first published in 1539, was planned by Cromwell, with Cranmer's approval. It was edited by Coverdale, and printed

by Grafton and Whitchurch. This was the Bible prescribed by the Edwardian Injunctions in 1547 (also printed by Grafton and Whitchurch). See *Cambridge History of the Bible*, 3: 151–3, and DNB, 'Coverdale, Miles.'

26 *The first tome or volume of the Paraphrase of Erasmus upon the newe testamente*, London, 1548 (31 January), fol. xv v. Quotations from the sixteenth-century English *Paraphrases* respect the orginal orthography, apart from contractions and abbreviations, which are silently expanded.

27 *The seconde tome or volume of the Paraphrase of Erasmus upon the newe testament: conteynyng the Epistles of S. Paul, and other the Apostles. Wherunto is added a paraphrase upon the Reuelacion of S. John*, London, 1549 (16 August). Each paraphrase in this volume is separately foliated.

28 Wall, 'Godly and Fruitful Lessons,' 73.

29 Edmund Allen (1519?–59), took the degree of M.A. at Corpus Christi College, Cambridge in 1537, and then spent much of the next decade on the Continent. He was chaplain to Elizabeth, and eventually was nominated to the see of Rochester. His writings include instructional works such as catechisms, as well as translations of works by Alexander Alex and Philip Melanchthon (DNB). Before translating Jud's paraphrase, Allen had also translated 'On the Apocalypse,' by Conrad Pelican, who had worked closely with Jud and Theodore Bibliander on the translation of the Zurich Bible into dialect: Backus, *Reformation Readings of the Apocalypse*, 88.

30 John N. King, *English Reformation Literature: The Tudor Origins of the Protestant Tradition*, 131.

31 In 1499, Jud matriculated at the University of Basel. There he met Ulrich Zwingli and became his closest associate. Jud had a particular interest in Erasmus, translating the *Enchiridion*, *Querela pacis*, *Institutio principis christiani*, and *Expostulatio Iesu*. His translation of the Paraphrases, *Paraphrasis oder Postille teütsch* (Zurich, 1542), included his own paraphrase on Revelation. See Backus, *Reformation Readings of the Apocalypse*, 87–93; COE 1: 249.

32 On the use of this format in the printing of biblical paraphrases after Erasmus, see also Bernard Roussel's essay above, p. 70–1.

33 An example: at Rev. 1, both Bale and Jud reproduce verses 1–3, then provide a paraphrase; both next quote and paraphrase verses 4–6; Bale quotes and paraphrases verses 7–8 together, whereas Jud takes each verse in turn; they are then in tandem for the rest of the chapter: verses 9–11, 12–16, and 17–20.

34 Like Bale and many others, Coverdale was forced to flee from England after the fall of Cromwell in 1540. Although Bale and Coverdale were contemporaries at Cambridge, there is no direct

evidence that they ever met. Coverdale spent most of his exile in Germany, while Bale was in Belgium; however, the Henrician exiles were a small group (compared to the Marian exiles) and had close relations with each other. Bale's pamphlet, *A Christen Exhortacyon unto Customable Swearers* (Antwerp, c. 1543), has sometimes been attributed to Coverdale, in whole or in part, even though his *Catalogus* (1:704) makes it clear that this is his work; see Fairfield, *John Bale*, 200 note 6.

35 Happé, *John Bale*, 16.

36 King, *English Reformation Literature*, 131.

37 The Allen translation of Jud covers 80 pages. The *Image*, as printed by Jugge in 1548, runs to just over 200, but the pages are half the size.

38 See Fairfield, *John Bale*, 75–85, for a complete discussion of Bale's use of Lambert.

39 '[T]hat most worthy minister of God, King Edward the sixth, afore all other to be remembered ... hath so sore wounded the beast, that he may throw all his superstition into the bottomless lake again (from whence they have come) to the comfort of his people' (*Image*, 640).

40 Backus, *Reformation Readings of the Apocalypse*, 93.

41 Many critics, prompted by William Haller's influential work, *The Elect Nation: The Meaning and Relevance of Foxe's 'Book of Martyrs,'* have held that the English nation is at the centre of Bale's vision of the Christian community. For a recent articulation of this theory, see Andrew Hadfield, *Literature, Politics, and National Identity*. Although the point may have been overstated in some cases (as argued by Firth, *Apocalyptic Tradition*), there can be little doubt that Bale's and Foxe's concentration upon English affairs, albeit in the context of a 'universal' understanding of the church, provided an opportunity for nationalistic interpretations.

42 For apocalypticism in sixteenth-century England, see the studies cited above, note 5, and Avihu Zakai, *Exile and Kingdom: History and Apocalypse in the Puritan Migration to America*, 12–55.

43 See Warren Wooden, *John Foxe*, 6.

44 The story that Foxe's book was ordered by injunction to be placed in every parish church in England has been discredited: Leslie M. Oliver, 'The Seventh Edition of John Foxe's Acts and Monuments,' 245–8. It remains the case, however, that in 1571 all London companies were ordered to purchase and display a copy of the *Acts and Monuments*, that it was set up by the Stationer's Company in Orphan's Court, and that Convocation decreed that every archbishop and bishop should own the book, that it must be in the home of every archdeacon, and, most notably, that a copy of the book should

be placed in all *cathedral* churches: Edward Cardwell, *Synodalia,* 1: 115, 117. See also Thomas S. Freeman, '"Great searching out of bookes and autors": John Foxe as an Ecclesiastical Historian,' 64. These facts do not change the fundamental point behind this often repeated anecdote: the *Acts and Monuments* was an enormously popular and influential book during the last decades of the sixteenth century, and Elizabeth and her advisers saw Foxe's work as an important component of English Protestantism at this time.

TWELVE

Forming a Protestant Consciousness? Erasmus' *Paraphrases* in English Parishes, 1547–1666

John Craig

When John Stavely, a grocer of Southampton, died in 1559, the unnamed appraisers who drew up a detailed inventory of his goods discovered that he possessed in his great shop, along with pounds of pepper, caraway seed, and treacle, three books – two bibles and a 'parafras,' a reference to the English translation of Erasmus' *Paraphrases on the New Testament*. Whether these volumes were for Stavely's use or intended for sale is not known. The 'parafras' was duly valued at 8 shillings.[1] Fourteen years later, in the same town, Richard Goddard the elder, a merchant of substantial wealth, breathed his last. His four friends laboriously tallied up his goods and chattels to a total sum in excess of £2000. Unlike John Stavely, Goddard had a sizeable but (for us) frustratingly anonymous library. His friends recorded thirty-two books in the cupboard in the hall and another fourteen books in the inner counting house, and there was a wainscot cupboard with more books valued at thirteen shillings, four pence. Two books, however, were given places of pre-eminence. There was a Geneva Bible in the chamber over the parlour, while his little parlour with its desk of wainscot, carpet of dornick, forms, and cushions of tapestry and needlework (no fewer than thirty-eight cushions!) was home to a 'bocke of parafraces of Erasmus' that was valued at four shillings.[2] Although the probate inventories of Stavely and Goddard constitute the only explicit reference to ownership of Erasmus' *Paraphrases* among 125 surviving inventories from Southampton from 1447 to 1575, with almost all of these dating from 1550 onwards, it seems clear that both the owners and appraisers recognized something significant in their possession.

Goddard's regard for this work, in particular, comes as something of a surprise. Had he displayed a copy of Foxe's *Acts and Monuments* in his little parlour, there would be less occasion for raised eyebrows. At first glance, the presence of Erasmus strikes one as curiously old-fashioned, out of place in the debates about discipline of the 1570s. Even if we can only guess what the volume was doing in Goddard's parlour – was this a rarely touched ornament of pious show or a well-thumbed text in daily use? – its presence raises larger questions. What significance did the *Paraphrases* possess in Elizabethan England? How was the work regarded and how was it used, if at all? It might be objected that it was only a bible with a running commentary, but the nature of that commentary distinguished it from other bibles. Did those aware of its status as a text required by both Edwardian and Elizabethan injunctions see this work as an icon of the Reformation in England? We shall never have definitive answers to such questions, but the recurring presence of Erasmus' *Paraphrases,* not only in the parlours of wealthy merchants but also in the chapels and libraries of university colleges[3] and, most significantly, chained to desks in hundreds of parish churches, warrants an investigation of the role of this work in English parishes and in the English Reformation.

It is a little sobering to realize that no one has yet produced the 'exhaustive treatise on Erasmus and Erasmianism in Tudor England' whose outline Craig Thompson carefully sketched almost thirty years ago.[4] The lack of historical attention is even more striking when one considers that much of the foundational work was completed in the mid-1960s. J.K. McConica's study of *English Humanists and Reformation Politics under Henry VIII and Edward VI* appeared in 1965 and the two important articles by E.J. Devereux that examined the English translators of Erasmus and the publication of the English *Paraphrases* of Erasmus followed hard upon it.[5] It is almost as if Thompson's challenging call for a comprehensive study of Erasmus' influence on Tudor religion and culture sounded the death knell of Tudor Erasmian studies. That judgment would, of course, be unfair. Part of the reason for the failure to build upon the work of McConica, Devereux, and Thompson is the shift that has occurred in historical scholarship with the explosion of social history and the turn made by many social and religious historians to the study of popular beliefs and practices. If historical research is seen in competitive terms, the story is one of the ascendancy of Thomas over Thompson. In the same year that Thompson published 'Erasmus and Tudor England,' Keith Thomas published his influential study of *Religion and the Decline of Magic*,[6] which helped to direct the attention of historians away from the views of theologians and reformers and towards those of the populace. The result has been a remarkable growth in our understanding of popular beliefs about witchcraft, issues of sex and gender, and the operation of the church courts, to name but a few of the many areas recently explored by historians.[7]

A second and related reason for the neglect of Erasmus in England has to do with the changing nature of the historiography of the English Reformation. This lively field has become and remains hotly contested as Reformation historians continue to debate the relative strength, speed, success, and failure of the reform movement in England.[8] An important consequence of this debate has been a focus upon the local and particular, as historians have moved away from the records of the central archives to the often untapped resources found in county record offices. Hence, much of the most recent work on the English Reformation has been taken up with the problem of explaining the relationships between royal authority and local communities. Robert Whiting's survey of the impact of religious change and Christopher Marsh's of popular religion in sixteenth-century England both engage this issue and both scholars spend a good deal of time trying to explain what moved men and women to accept Protestantism.[9] If the combined efforts of Eamon Duffy, Christopher Haigh, and J.J. Scarisbrick have convinced many scholars that the English church on the eve of the Reformation was alive and well and enjoying a great deal of popular support, their arguments have only heightened the spectacular collapse of this church and the difficulty of explaining its demise.[10]

In a curious way, these historiographical shifts, or what might be called a movement towards an understanding of popular responses in particular parishes, bring one back full circle to many of the questions posed in 1971 by Thompson, who wrote that if 'churches were ordered in 1547 to acquire copies of the *Para-*

phrases in English, that is a noteworthy fact; but what we want to know also is first whether they did so, secondly whether the translations were used and what difference, if any they made to readers.'[11] These are the starting points for this study of the presence of the English translation of Erasmus' *Paraphrases* in English communities.

I

The story of the English translation of Erasmus' *Paraphrases* is well known and needs little elaboration.[12] The project is most closely associated with Catherine Parr, Henry VIII's pious and patient sixth wife, who surrounded herself with reform-minded humanists. This was certainly not the first time that English reformers had sought to popularize Erasmus' writings. The Epistles to Jude and Titus had been translated and published in the early 1530s under Thomas Cromwell's patronage, but Catherine Parr appears to have used her position and patronage to effect a more impressive achievement: an English translation of Erasmus' *Paraphrases* on the four Gospels and Acts of the Apostles. Under her patronage, the lion's share of the work on these books was complete by 1545.[13] This was a collaborative effort involving a number of individuals. Nicholas Udall, poet, playwright, and sometime headmaster of Eton College, who became the general editor of the first volume, translated the *Paraphrase on Luke*. Princess Mary translated part of the *Paraphrase on John* before illness prevented further work; the translation was completed by Francis Malet, her chaplain. The *Paraphrase on Mark* was translated by Thomas Key or Caius, a 'registrary of Oxford.' Although John Strype believed that Catherine herself translated the *Paraphrase on Matthew*, the evidence for this is not known, and the best one can say is that the identity of the translator of the paraphrases of both Matthew and Acts remains a mystery. Despite the hope expressed by Udall in his preface to Catherine of his translation of the *Paraphrase on Luke*, that Henry might not suffer his work 'to lye buiryed in silence, but will one daie, when his godly wisedome shall so thinke expedient, cause the same paraphrase to bee published and set abrode in prient,' his fears were realized and the work remained unpublished until the second year of Edward VI's reign, when it was printed by Edward Whitchurch in January 1548. When it appeared, Udall's editorial efforts were plain to see. He wrote a dedication of the whole work to Edward and prefatory dedications of each of the books to Catherine Parr, with the exception of Mark, where the preface was written by Key. Udall claimed to have checked and occasionally revised the various translations against the Latin original; he also incorporated the text of the Great Bible.

The 1548 volume of the *Paraphrases on the Gospels and Acts* was followed by four other publications. Whitchurch published a second volume, containing Erasmus' *Paraphrases on the Apostolic Epistles* in August 1549, which was followed by another edition, partly reset. Whitchurch reprinted both volumes in 1551–2, the first volume being 'thoroughly corrected' with the addition of 'an exact table according to the notes in the margin of all speciall matters and sentences where mencioned throughout the whole worke with a perfect concordance diligently gathered by Nicholas Udall.'[14]

Even before the first volume had been printed, the work received official standing with Edward VI's royal injunctions of July 1547, which stipulated that the clergy were to provide within three months of the royal visitation, 'one book of the whole Bible of the largest volume, in English,' and within twelve months, 'the Paraphrasis of Erasmus also in English upon the Gospels, and the same set up in some convenient place, within the said church that they have cure of, whereas their parishioners may most commodiously resort unto the same, and read the same.'[15] The cost of these required texts was to be borne jointly by clergy and people, the parson or proprietary paying half the cost of the Bible and *Paraphrases* and the parishioners the other half. The royal injunctions went on to stipulate that 'every parson, vicar, curate, chantry-priest, and stipendiary, being under the degree of a bachelor of divinity, shall provide and have of his own, within three months after this visitation, the New Testament both in Latin and in English, with Paraphrasis upon the same of Erasmus and diligently study the same, conferring the one with the other.'[16] Completing the requirements, the 1547 injunctions for cathedrals stated that cathedral clergy 'shall make a library in some convenient place within their church, within the space of one year next ensuing this visitation, and shall lay in the same St Augustine's, Basil, Gregory Nazianzen, Jerome, Ambrose, Chrysostom, Cyprian, Theophylact, Erasmus and other good writers' works.'[17] Thus, at a stroke, the Crown had made compulsory the purchase of the

English translation of Erasmus' *Paraphrases* by every parish in the realm, by almost every cleric and probably, albeit rather more obliquely, by every cathedral. Furthermore, the function of this text differed with the context. For the laity it was seen as a second Bible full of wholesome teaching, required to be made available within the body of the church for all to come and read, listen to, observe, and wonder at. Here we may see a reflection of the Erasmian dictum that the Word possessed enlightening power. Yet this was also a text for clerical instruction, mediating between the Latin text of the Bible and the English translation. These requirements remained in force throughout Edward VI's reign.

It is worth noting that the royal injunctions only ever specified purchase of the first volume, that is, the translation of the *Paraphrases on the Gospels and Acts*. It is true that this distinction was sometimes blurred, most notably perhaps by Bishop Hooper of Gloucester, who in 1551, during his visitation of the diocese, inquired whether or not the *Paraphrases* 'on the New Testament' had been purchased.[18] And it is not hard to find parishes that purchased both volumes of the *Paraphrases*.[19] Nevertheless, despite the understandable desire on the part of the printer to put about the notion that both volumes fell within the royal directive, the Crown never expanded the injunction to include the second volume or tome of the *Paraphrases*.[20]

This fact may help to explain why the two volumes have often been regarded as quite separate works. McConica has commented that the two volumes of the *Paraphrases* were strikingly different works in both tone and outlook, the first (Gospels and Acts) more truly Erasmian, the second (Epistles) co-opted by the Protestant court party.[21] There is certainly some substance to this claim. The first volume was produced by men such as Nicholas Udall, Francis Malet, and Thomas Key, who were moderate in their reforming stance, conformists under Mary and possessing strong Oxford links.[22] The second volume has the appearance of a maverick Cambridge production, being the work of Miles Coverdale, Thomas Norton, John Olde, Leonard Cox, and Edmund Allen; these were the hotter sort of Protestants, exiles all (with the probable exception of Cox), who included William Tyndale's famous preface to his translation of Romans in their volume as well as a translation of the Zurich reformer Leo Jud's paraphrase of Revelation, a book that Erasmus had not paraphrased.[23]

The making of too sharp a distinction between the two volumes, however, threatens to conceal the way in which Nicholas Udall actively revised the text of the first volume of *Paraphrases*, and in so doing turned the edition of 1548 into the more reformed text of 1551–2. There are three features of this work of revision that are worth considering more closely. The first is the inclusion by Udall of an additional preface 'to the good christian reader,' dated 5 January 1552,[24] in which Udall explained that having perceived that

> the paraphrases of Erasmus upon the new testament, of late set furth in the Englishe tongue, and by the Kynges maiesties injunccions appointed and commaunded to be had in every churche of England, have been an occasion aswel of much more knowlege and understanding of the true sense and veyne of holy scripture to the pastours and curates of this Royalme, as also of muche godly edifying to the vulgare people; I also on my part, for the zeal I have in Christ to ferther the premisses thought with my self that there could not be any piece of labour better bestowed then if the said worke might for the commoditee of all readers be brought to such perfeccion, as in such a worke is to be required. Which thyng I speake not as though it wer not well set foorth alreadie: but because that nothing can at the first be so exactly dooen, but that a second travaile may by diligent filing and poolishing make the same, of verai good a great deale better.[25]

He explained that during the summer months of 1551 he had 'perused the paraphrases upon the fower Evangelistes and the Actes of the Apostles and ... thoroughly conferred them with the latine, to thintent that the English translacion might eche where so aunswer the latine, in as the sense of the autor might in no place be doutfully or derkly expressed.'[26] Udall's concern was not simply with accurate translation. It seems likely that the inclusion of this additional preface was chosen as a way of addressing the critics of Erasmus, fellow translators such as John Olde who had translated Erasmus' paraphrases on a number of Paul's epistles and who, while acclaiming Erasmus as a 'ready strong interpretour in many necessary places' had also stated bluntly that he was a man who might 'bothe be deceaved and deceave.'[27] In response, Udall acknowleged that 'Erasmus wrote in such a dangerous season, as he was of force constreined either to kepe silence, or els to speake within suche limites and compace as the worlde might then beare,' but argued that, 'if the indifferent reader marke and weigh him wel, he shal find, that no writer is more sincere or upright in the true doctrine of our religion then is Erasmus.'[28] This proved the opening gambit in a wholesale embracing of Erasmus by Udall for the English reformed church:

> Neither doth any man better espie his places or more readily take his occasions plainly to expresse any point or article of our religion. No man oftner or more piththily setteth furth the divinitee and godhead of Christ couples with his human nature. No man more substancially teacheth the iustification through feith in Jesus Christ. No man more effectually or clerely declareth the true nature the first institucion, the right use of the Lordes supper. No man more earnestly inveigheth againste all kyndes of idolatrie and supersticion. No man more profoundly discusseth or more fynely deciseth the use of ceremonies. No man more lyvely peincteth or describeth the most detestable discorde and tirannie of the Romishe Babilon. No man more uprightely setteth oute the autoritie of Princes and Magistrates or more strongly perswadeth and confirmeth the obedience of subjects due unto the same. No man more godly exhorteth all sortes of people to the diligent reading and true understanding of the holy scriptures. These and a thousand poinctes more dooeth Erasmus by occasion not onely touche, but also in such sorte moste learnedly handle, that he may iustly be reputed the chief leader and shewer of lyght and the principall opener of a waye unto the Evangelicall trueth nowe in these last tymes by Goddes goodness shyning foorth into the worlde.[29]

The claim for Erasmus as the champion of the 'Evangelicall trueth' and supporter of 'our religion' could hardly be more clearly expressed.

The second notable feature of Udall's revisions is the way in which he both amplified the existing marginal notes and added many more. With the addition of a detailed index, hundreds of marginal notes, and cross references to parallel passages in the gospel narratives, Udall claimed that his work was 'throughout coted in the margin with much more diligence and trueth, then I have yet seen in any newe testament hitherto set forth in any tongue.'[30] The 1548 edition possessed very few marginal notes, the most famous of which perhaps was the note on Mark 11, concerning Christ's entry into Jerusalem, which read: 'The Byshop of Romes pompe is covertly described.'[31] In the 1551–2 edition, Udall revised the note to read: 'A truely comparison of Christe riding into Hierusalem and of the pompous ridyng of the pope and his cardinalles.'[32] This pattern of strengthening and signalling the reformed credentials of the text is clearly apparent from the marginal notes. 'Salvacion cometh of faith and not of works' runs the marginal note on a passage in Mark 10, and alongside Erasmus' statement that 'after that Christ hath once forsaken the worlde, he cannot be shewed nor pointed to with fingers,' Udall notes: 'Howe do the Papists then se him in the Sacrament?'[33]

Finally, Udall, as he indicated in the additional preface, revised the text itself and in particular changed the language to bring it more firmly into the reformed camp. Many of these revisions are minor indeed. Consider, for example, his translation of the passage in Matthew 26 concerning Judas' decision to betray Christ, in which the change wrought is purely stylistic:

> [1548] Therfore Judas gredye and gapyng for the money that was promised him, by and by from that time forward sought for occasion to betraye Jesus.[34]
> [1551–2] Therefore Judas beeyng gredye and gapyng for the money that was promysed hym by and by from that tyme forthwarde, sought occasion and oportunitie to betray Jesus.[35]

Of greater interest is the following comparison in which Udall substituted 'repentance' for 'penance':

> [1548] Jesus saieth unto them, one of you shall betraye me. This he sayde to declare that nothyng at all was hid from hym, and also that the conscience of the traytour beyng touched, might be turned unto penaunce.[36]
> [1551–2] Jesus saieth unto them, one of you shall betraye me. This he sayde to declare that nothyng at all was hid from hym, and also that the conscience of the traytour beyng touched, might be turned unto repentaunce.[37]

Such changes reveal not only the active and continuing involvement of Udall with the second edition, but also how, whether by his initiative or in response to pressure from Archbishop Cranmer and members of the Privy Council, the first volume of the *Paraphrases* was brought solidly into the camp of the reformed English church.[38] With regard to the revised edition of 1551–2, treatment of the English translation of the *Paraphrases* as 'the basis for an Erasmian Church' would appear to be misplaced.[39] A more systematic analysis of this edition might demonstrate what the present glimpse has suggested: that the publication and revision of the *Paraphrases* under Edward VI was a deliberate attempt to co-opt Erasmus as chief spokesman of the evangelical reformed movement in England.

II

It is time now to address Thompson's first question, whether or not English parishes purchased the *Paraphrases*. Was the royal injunction of 1547 obeyed with alacrity or more honoured in the breach? Could it be that thousands of churchwardens across the realm simply omitted to follow the Crown's instructions? Given the rates of illiteracy, and the pressure on parish finance, why would one bother to purchase a hefty book that would probably only collect dust?

In his influential essay on the 'Local Impact of Tudor Reformations,' Ronald Hutton took a sample of 198 sets of sixteenth-century churchwardens' accounts, of which only those for eighteen parishes had complete and detailed records of income and expenditure for the whole period between 1535 and 1570, to argue that most of the parochial evidence displayed a reluctance to accept the Edwardian Reformation, a welcoming of the return to Catholicism under Mary, and more foot dragging when Elizabeth reversed the policies of her half-sister. Hutton concluded that most parishes finally conformed because they lacked any means of resisting the Tudor state. On the specific question of purchase of the *Paraphrases*, Hutton discovered that forty-one parishes of his sample had bought the English translation of the *Paraphrases* before the end of 1548 and that fifty-three had done so by 1553. Another twenty-six parishes purchased the *Paraphrases* under Elizabeth. Unfortunately, it is difficult to retrace Hutton's footsteps, since he does not indicate which parishes he included in his sample, apparently prevented by his publisher for reasons of space. Nor does he say exactly at what date he stops looking for evidence under Elizabeth (1570?). Crucially, he does not say how many of the eighteen parishes with detailed records of expenditure between 1535 and 1570 purchased the *Paraphrases*.[40] Is it possible to be obtain a clearer view?

Although a complete survey of surviving parish accounts could be attempted, the game would probably not be worth the candle. From perhaps almost ten thousand parishes in England, just under one thousand sets of churchwardens' accounts have survived from earliest times to 1690. The representativeness of this evidence is problematic, given the much better survival rate for some southern counties when compared with northern shires. Hutton's recent inventory of accounts has disclosed only four sets of parish accounts from Derbyshire, three from Cumberland, a mere six for Herefordshire, and thirteen for Durham.[41] Even if the northern counties possessed fuller runs of parish accounts, there are good reasons not to rely too heavily on churchwardens' accounts for information about the reception of Erasmus' *Paraphrases*.

First of all, unless churchwardens' accounts include evidence of the actual purchase of the *Paraphrases*, we have no way of knowing whether or not the volume was acquired. The crucial years are those of Edward's reign and the early years of Elizabeth's, and the incompleteness of parish accounting particularly during Edward's reign will often result in a blank. A case in point can be found in the church book of St Ewen's, Bristol, where a full account exists of expenditure in 1548. The parish spent 14s 4d on the English Bible, 4d for the delivery charge, 1s 4d for covering the Bible with leather and another shilling for attaching a chain and lock. There is no mention of the *Paraphrases*, but there is a gap in the accounts from 1548 to 1551; thus, in the absence of any inventory of church goods, we cannot say that the parishioners of St Ewen's in Bristol purchased the *Paraphrases*, but neither can we say that they did not – we simply do not know.[42] Many surviving sets of churchwardens' accounts only commence during Elizabeth's reign and unless the parish drew up an inventory of church goods, parish accounts by themselves simply will not disclose whether or not the parish purchased the *Paraphrases*. Inventories of church goods, sometimes written into a churchwardens' account, can, however, provide evidence of whether or not the parish owned a copy of the *Paraphrases*. Indeed most of the information about parish ownership of this work has come, not from the record of purchase, but from the inventory as evidence of ownership. The difficulty here lies in deciding at what point to stop looking for an inventory, since the evidence of ownership often comes long after the order to purchase. Thus, we only learn that the parish of St Michael's, Lichfield possessed a copy of Erasmus from an inventory drawn up in 1654,[43] and the same is true for the parishes of Tenterden in Kent, Betley in Staffordshire, and Newport in Essex with their inventories of 1642, 1654, and 1661 respectively.[44] Examples might be multiplied. The situation is further complicated by a small clutch of parishes for which no manuscript sources survive but whose copies of Erasmus' *Paraphrases* were still to be seen in their churches in 1923.[45] In short, the evidence available to us is both scrappy and resistant to large generalizations of the kind expressed by percentages.

The establishing of a more solid case for the ownership of the *Paraphrases* depends upon our ability to use a variety of evidence, from records of purchase in churchwardens' accounts to stray memoranda in parish registers,[46] churchwardens' presentments, and parish inventories. The analysis that follows and the accompanying appendices are based upon a range of printed primary sources, together with a selective sampling of parish accounts and ecclesiastical court material from fifteen county record offices, namely Cambridgeshire, Cheshire, Cornwall, Cumbria, Derbyshire, Devon, Essex, Kent, Lincolnshire, Shropshire, Staffordshire, Warwickshire, West Sussex, Wiltshire, and the Guildhall Library in London.

III

There is positive evidence that 162 parishes owned a copy of the *Paraphrases* by 1553. Significantly, these data are derived overwhelmingly from lists of church goods drawn up in response to the work of the Edwardian commissioners appointed to view and eventually to confiscate church goods. It is a neglected feature of these returns, often printed, well known, and of great value to the ecclesiologist interested in the retention or sale of pre-Reformation albs and chalices, that they occasionally list books purchased.[47] The decision to mention books – bibles, prayer books, the *Paraphrases* – appears to have been an idiosyncratic one, taken by whoever drew up the inventory.[48] The absence of books from the list of church goods certainly cannot be interpreted to mean that the parish had not purchased any.[49] In general, these inventories do not seem to have been regarded either by leading parishioners or by the commissioners as a complete list of everything the parish owned, but rather as a list of plate, vestments, ornaments, and so forth that had become superflous to the services as now defined by the Crown. Some of the best evidence comes from London, where fifty-five of ninety-six inventories of city parishes indicate that they owned a copy of the *Paraphrases*. Moreover, this figure is clearly too small, since the parishes of St Mary at Hill and St Michael Cornhill both purchased copies of the *Paraphrases*, as is clear from the surviving churchwardens' accounts, yet listed no books when they drew up their inventories for the commissioners in 1552.[50]

What is striking about the evidence of purchase and ownership, partial and fragmentary though it is, is how it speaks of ready compliance with the Edwardian injunctions. This is true not only in London and Canterbury, Cambridge and Oxford, the more substantial towns of Chester and Ludlow, or medium-sized towns such as Strood in Kent or Louth in Lincolnshire, but also in tiny rural parishes: Wigtoft in Lincolnshire, Ufton in Berkshire, Bramley in Hampshire, Leverington in Cambridgeshire, Badsey in Worcestershire, and the churches of Bix Gibwen and Bix Brand in Oxfordshire.[51] The range of this evidence would seem to indicate a level of compliance with the Edwardian injunction that was extremely high. And this would seem to indicate further that the Crown somehow sought to ensure that parishes purchased the books required by the king's policies and placed pressure upon the visiting commissioners, ecclesiastical officials, parish authorities, and booksellers to accomplish their aims.

Failure to provide copies of the *Paraphrases* might become a political issue. When Robert Ferrar, the Edwardine Bishop of St David's was denounced before the Privy Council in 1551 for a host of offences, it was alleged that the 'churches appropriate to the Bishop have no Paraphrases in English' and that 'the churches of the diocese for the most part and the clergy almost every one, lacke Paraphrases, notwithstanding there hath beene these two yeeres, and yet bee a great number of them to be sold in the Diocesse.' Ferrar's response was equally revealing of the mixed motivations surrounding the provision of the text. He claimed that the churches in his gift were equipped with 'both Bible and

Paraphrases so far as he knoweth' and that one of his accusers, George Constantine, 'covetously ingrossed into his hands a great number of Paraphrases; and this Defendant hath admonished the Clergie to buy, every one, for his discharge: and if the sayd George being Officiall of two Archdeaconries, and other Officials in their Office would declare unto him what Churches do lacke Bibles or Paraphrases, hee would cause it to be amended as much as in him lyeth.' Disputed evidence and unrealized economic advantage aside, the striking feature of the exchange is the determination to see the churches within this remote diocese duly equipped.[52]

If it is not unsafe to extrapolate from 162 parishes to the entire realm, the range of parishes known to have possessed the work would suggest that the *Paraphrases* were probably to be found in most parishes and that this was the result of a deliberate and double policy both of making the text available and of applying pressure to ensure that not only the *Paraphrases* but also the Bible, Book of Common Prayer, and Homilies were acquired. Furthermore, the evidence from churchwardens' accounts indicates that parishioners not only paid for the text but also erected lecterns or desks upon which to set the *Paraphrases* and attached the requisite chains and locks to secure the book in the body of the church.[53]

IV

The argument that purchase of the *Paraphrases* was widespread during Edward's reign makes the question of the fate of this work in Mary's reign considerably more interesting. The evidence on this matter is mixed, reflecting a deep ambiguity on the part of the Marian church about the availability of an English Bible. At an official level, there are two important documents. First, the Marian parliament of November 1554 enacted a statute to revive earlier legislation against Lollardy, which provided the Crown with the authority for suppressing both heresy and heretical literature; another statute created a category of seditious books, defining them as containing any false matter, clause or sentence of slander, reproach and dishonour to the king or queen.[54] More important, however, was the royal proclamation of June 1555 that effectively created an index of prohibited books. The king and queen, 'minding to root out and extinguish all false doctrine and heresies and other occasions of schisms, divisions and sects,' made illegal the possession of any books or writings of twenty-three named reformers, starting with Martin Luther and ending with William Roy and Hall's *Chronicles*. Both Edwardian prayer books were singled out as particularly offensive.[55] Curiously, neither Erasmus nor the English translation of the *Paraphrases* is mentioned. The proclamation of 1555 does mention an Erasmus, but this was Erasmus Sarcerius, not the author of the *Paraphrases*.[56] Since Miles Coverdale was one of the prohibited authors, there was a case for the proscription of the second volume of *Paraphrases*, but not for the first. Despite the well-known opposition to the *Paraphrases* of Stephen Gardiner,[57] now Mary's Lord Chancellor, the Marian authorities apparently made no more attempt to prohibit or do away with the *Paraphrases* than they did to rid English parishes of their copies of the Great Bible.[58] Although churchwardens' accounts from London parishes indicate that Gardiner instructed these parishes to obliterate the scriptural texts that had been painted on their church walls, this measure perhaps speaks more of the fear of the misappropriation of scriptural texts than of opposition to the reading of vernacular Scripture *per se*.[59] Were the *Paraphrases* and Great Bible such slight threats to the restoration of Catholic rites and practice? Or – this is perhaps more likely – were both texts so popular that their official prohibition would have been political folly?

The lack of official proscription of the *Paraphrases* is, however, only part of the story, since it is also clear that there was some, and perhaps much, unofficial action against both the Bible and *Paraphrases*. The parishioners of Morebath, probably in response to the royal proclamation of June 1555, spent 6d in 'caryng of the bybyll and erazamus to Exceter.'[60] The churchwardens of the parish of St Martin in the Fields sold off their Bible, *Paraphrases*, and both service books before the end of 1555.[61] Action against all of the books connected with the Edwardian church explains why the Elizabethan visitors in 1559 asked not only 'what books of God's scripture you have delivered to be burnt or otherwise destroyed and to whom ye have delivered the same,' but also 'whether any man hath burned, or caused the holy Bible to be burned, torn or defaced, or hath conveyed it out of the church that it should not be read of the people, or no.'[62] A small cluster of parishes in the northern province confessed that this had indeed happened. The churchwardens of the parish of Lowdham presented that 'they delivered to Mr Cressye a paraphrases and too communion bookes to be burned,' while the wardens of Estwaite said that 'Sir Richard Barlowe their curate toke awaye their bokes of the communion and the paraphrases.'[63] Book burning can hardly be said to have been widespread, however, for only in eleven parishes in the diocese of York, four in the diocese of Chester, four in the diocese of Durham, and one from the diocese of Carlisle is this said to have happened.[64] Perhaps many more copies were sold off or quietly laid up in a parish chest or private homes. The few cases where book purchases can be traced across the reigns suggests that all these eventualities were represented. Some parishes such as St Michael's Bedwardine near Worcester, Strood and Smarden in Kent, Wandsworth in Surrey, and the London parishes of St Andrew Hubbard or St Michael Cornhill seem to have retained their copies of the *Paraphrases* throughout the Marian period, though whether the volume remained in the parish church or in hiding is impossible to say.[65] Evidence that parishes that purchased the *Paraphrases* during Edward's reign had to replace their copy in Elizabeth's reign exists, but the numbers are relatively small. Outside London, this inquiry has identified eleven parishes to date: St Michael's, Bishop's Stortford; Bramley, Hampshire; Great St Mary's, Cambridge; St Dunstan's, Canterbury; Great Dunmow, Essex; Ludlow, Morebath, Stoke Charity, Hampshire; Thame, West Tarring, Sussex; and Winterslow, Wiltshire.[66] A search of the London city parishes revealed another seven, a number that suggests a more widespread proscription in the capital between 1553 and 1558. That said, parish communities clearly had a range of options available to them, from concealment to combustion – and there was always the possibility of theft. Because the fate of the *Paraphrases* under Mary was in the hands of local officials, it remains largely unknown.

V

Purchase of the *Paraphrases* was ordered again in Elizabeth's reign, the order appearing in the royal injunctions of 1559.[67] This was a throwback to the Edwardian injunction with a minor modification. Once again parishes were commanded to acquire the text and set it up in the body of the church, the costs were to be borne equally between parishioners and incumbent, and all ministers below the degree of M.A. (a slight adjustment from 1547) were to possess their own copy. This much is well known.[68] What has not been noted, however, is the way in which, throughout Elizabeth's long reign, the ecclesiastical authorities maintained pressure on churchwardens to ensure that they possessed a copy of the *Paraphrases*. The question appears with regularity in sets of visitation articles and injunctions from 1559 onwards. And even though a declining interest in the work can be detected in visitation articles from the late 1570s, the question whether or not parishes have Erasmus' *Paraphrases* never entirely disappeared. One of the latest was formulated by William Higgins, archdeacon of Derby, who drew up articles of inquiry in 1641 'to be considered of by the churchwardens and others within the archdeaconry of Derby' as part of his archidiaconal visitation, in which he asked,

> Are the great bible, the service bookes faire and good? Kept clasped or stringed after divine service and well laid up? Have you the bookes of martyrs, Erasmus Paraphrase, and the workes of Bishop Jewell and are they chained in some convenient place? The bookes of homilies? The homily of rebellion? The articles and canons? And are they safely kept for the use of the parish?[69]

The interest of the archdeacon's question goes beyond the fact that the list would tend to reflect the tidy collection of books to be found in many parish churches by this time (although there was never any general order requiring all parish churches to purchase Foxe's *Acts and Monuments*, popularly known as the 'Book of Martyrs').[70] Striking here is the mention of the *Paraphrases* almost a hundred years after the Crown had first instructed parishes to purchase copies of Erasmus' work. How was the question understood? As an aspect of strict conformity? Or was it seen to be utterly old fashioned, the quirk of an eccentric archdeacon? It is not hard to find examples of ecclesiastical articles between 1559 and 1640 that have quietly dropped the reference to Erasmus' *Paraphrases*, as if tacitly to admit that the requirement was out of date.[71] The notion that the *Paraphrases* were no longer at the cutting edge of theological instruction found blunt expression in Bishop Middleton's injunctions of 1583, in which he stated that 'the *Paraphrases* may be provided in every parish church, or rather Bullinger's *Decades* in English, for it is much more profitable,' but no other bishop was prepared to take this line.[72] In spite of these changes, a request for a copy of the *Paraphrases* can be found in the ecclesiastical articles of inquiry drawn up by Bishop Valentine Carey in 1625 for the diocese of Exeter and by Bishop John Williams in 1635 for the diocese of Lincoln.[73]

The detailed records of a visitation conducted by the archdeacon of Chichester in 1579 disclose some of the ways in which parishes responded to this pressure from above. Eighteen parishes within the archdeaconry reported that they had no copy of the *Paraphrases*.[74] The wardens of Lodsworth said that their copy had been stolen, while the wardens of West Dean explained that both volumes of Erasmus had been 'carried awaie by Robert Holland, then our vycar.'[75] Given the requirement for ownership by both parishioners and clergy, confusion on this point might well arise. The wardens of the Nottinghamshire parish of Car Colston were presented in 1576 for failing to possess a copy of the *Paraphrases*. The following year a small delegation from the parish, consisting of the vicar, both wardens, and two sworn men, told the court that 'the Paraphrase of Erasmus which they have is their vicar's and they supposed it to have been their own.' They proceeded to inform the court that they were ready to purchase the volume but did not know if the patron, one Elizabeth Walley, would 'give her part.'[76] Rather more bizarre was the response of the wardens of Houghton in the archdeaconry, who said that they did have a copy of the *Paraphrases* but had lent their volume to the neighbouring parish of Bury, which refused to return it.[77] It appears that parishes would occasionally lend their books for a small fee, most probably to help a nearby parish avoid a citation for failing to purchase the required text. In Salisbury, the parish of St Edmund borrowed a copy of the *Paraphrases* from the neighbouring parish of St Thomas, presumably to avoid action against them by the church courts.[78] Clearly, such practices always ran the danger of backfiring, if we are to believe the wardens of Houghton. More telling perhaps was the situation of the minister of West Stoke, whose response no doubt reflected a common predicament in small rural parishes. When his wardens reported that they lacked the *Paraphrases*, the minister explained, 'Touching the paraphras, I am pore and have charge. There are not xii housholders in the parish and for the most part very poore and not past one or two that can reade.'[79]

Whether or not the court responded with any sympathy to this plea is not known. There is some evidence, however, that where parishioners began to make their own decisions about the books to be retained in the church, the courts reacted severely. The London parish of St Michael, Cornhill purchased a copy of the *Paraphrases* in 1548 and chained it to a desk in the church. The parishioners appear to have hidden their volume during the Marian period as there is no record of a second purchase and in 1560 they simply paid for a chain. Chains notwithstanding, their copy of the *Paraphrases* was probably stolen some time before a vestry meeting held in 1572, when the vestry agreed 'that the boke of Martyrs of Mr Foxe and the Paraphrases of Erasmus shalbe bought for the churche and tyed with a cheyne to the Egle of Brasse' – at which point the memorandum continues in the first-person singular: 'I saye the boke of Martirs and Mr Calvins institutions yf the Paraphrases cannot be had.' In 1573, the parish spent 42s 6d on the *Acts and Monuments* and 8s on a copy of Calvin's *Institutes.* This arrangement continued for fifteen years without complaint until in 1587 the parish hastily paid 3s 8d 'to Mr Sadler for avoiding of an excommunication for not having in our church a paraphrasis of Erasmus' and another 13s 'for a booke called the Paraphrasis of Erasmus.'[80]

Although the events at St Michael, Cornhill demonstrate how quickly a copy of the *Paraphrases* might have been purchased in London in 1587, it is worth reflecting whether or not churchwardens experienced difficulties of supply with a text that was never printed after 1552. In 1567, the churchwardens of the Yorkshire parish of Riesse confessed that 'the paraphraseis they can not get for moneye.'[81] Most of the evidence of Elizabethan purchases comes early in the reign, although a few parishes made purchases in the 1570s and 1580s (and the evidence is mostly for London). The wardens of Ludlow in Shropshire purchased a copy of the *Paraphrases* from London in 1576–7; the London parish of St Benedict Gracechurch also purchased a copy in 1577 and the small parish of Great Packington in Warwickshire bought a copy in 1589–90 from one 'Anthony Jacson of Hawckeswell.'[82] Should we imagine hundreds of unbound copies waiting for purchasers in one of Whitchurch's London warehouses or was the book available in the larger towns of the counties? The parishioners of Morebath were unable to find a copy for sale in 1561 when they sent one of their wardens with money to Exeter. He returned empty-handed, although, given the conservative convictions of this parish, there may have been more to his lack of success than meets the eye.[83] Whatever the difficulties of supply, however, the striking feature of the evidence of purchase and ownership during the Elizabethan period, like that for Edward's reign, is the range of parishes represented. The 110 parishes discovered to date that possessed the *Paraphrases* are scattered throughout the realm, from communities in Cornwall to the mountains of Westmoreland. Their number included remote settlements such as Cartmel in Lancashire, Windermere in Westmoreland, Youlgreave in Derbyshire, and St Breock in Cornwall, as well as the more predictable urban parishes of London, Chester, Ipswich, Salisbury, and Durham.[84]

VI

Beyond the parishes, is it possible to gauge the extent to which the *Paraphrases* made its way into personal libraries? Here one turns to the evidence of probate inventories, and in particular to the work of Elisabeth Leedham-Green, whose study of books in Cambridge inventories analysed the inventories of 187 Cambridge scholars and thirteen privileged persons – surgeons, booksellers, the butler of Christ's, a vintner, the cook at Emmanuel. Not surprisingly, Erasmus was to be found in many of these inventories. Forty-two of these mentioned a complete set of the *Paraphrases* and another fifty-eight listed paraphrases on individual books. None of these entries, however, represented the English translation, which was nowhere to be found: this was all Erasmus in Latin.[85] The same holds true for the work done on the Oxford inventories. The sample is much smaller (perhaps a hundred inventories) and copies of Erasmus abound, but again not in English, with the exception of Thomas Day, fellow of All Souls, who possessed a copy of both volumes of the English translation of Erasmus' *Paraphrases* appraised at 10s in 1570.[86] Outside the universities, an examination of ninety-four inventories from the diocese of Norwich yields intriguing data. Jeffrey Cobb, a gentleman of Norwich, had a copy of the *Paraphrases* of Erasmus in folio, valued at 3s 4d in 1591;[87] Elizabeth Walden, a widow, also of Norwich, had a *Paraphrase* of Erasmus that was valued together at 8s in 1601, the 'together' probably indicating that this was both volumes,[88] and John Sheringham, a yeoman of Norton in Suffolk, when he died in 1590 had 'one large bible, one olde booke of the actes and monuments, the first booke of the paraphrase of Erasmus and two statute bookes'; the collection was appraised with other goods at 9s 8d.[89] Other searches for the *Paraphrases* proved fruitless. Michael Reed's edition of the seventy-two surviving probate inventories for inhabitants of Ipswich between 1583 and 1631 disclosed a small number of books, mostly bibles, but no mention of Erasmus.[90] J.A. Johnston's much wider survey of 590 probate inventories of Lincoln citizens between 1661 and 1714 found that 139 inventories listed books: the Bible was identified in thirty-two of these, four had copies of Foxe's *Acts and Monuments*, two had the Book of Common Prayer, and there were single copies of the Psalter, but once again no mention of the *Paraphrases*, even if much may be hidden behind the generic term 'books.'[91]

Is it possible to go beyond this cataloguing of possession and say something about usage? It is well known that books may be collected and never used. Did the volumes in parish churches or in people's homes simply collect dust? Is there any way of ascertaining whether or not Erasmus' *Paraphrases* had any influence on contemporary theological debate or upon a popular Protestant consciousness?

These questions are both important and extremely difficult to answer. The evidence of widespread parochial ownership would argue in favour of some kind of influence within the parish. Still, the *Paraphrases* were never enjoined to be used in English worship services in the way that the Book of Common Prayer or Homilies were. Nevertheless, when Josua Maler from Switzerland visited Oxford in 1551, he described the chapel services he attended as consisting of a chapter or two from the English Bible and the *Paraphrases* of Erasmus in translation, along with vocal and organ music.[92] And when Sebastian Cabot drew up ordinances for the projected expedition to Cathay of 1553, he ordered that a chapter of either the Bible or the *Paraphrases* be read on a daily basis to the mariners.[93] Is it possible that the *Paraphrases* were used unofficially in parish worship under Edward in place of the Homilies? And if they were used in the Edwardian church, might they not also have been used in the Elizabethan? During the Sunday service a week before Michaelmas 1561, George Brysto of the parish of Stocksbury in Kent so distracted the curate by playing with a dog in the middle part of the church that the curate felt compelled to interrupt his public 'reading of the paraphrases of the gospel' to issue a rebuke.[94] The incorporation of the *Paraphrases* within parish worship may well have been widespread, especially during the 1560s. To think only of usage in the context of a public service of worship, however, is to miss the wider scope of the injunction, which in the first instance required the book to be commodiously set up in the church. How can one judge the influence of a text, chained to a lectern in a parish church? Should we imagine a cluster of people after a Sunday service gathered around the lectern listening to a passage being read aloud, or a scene of silent neglect, the book remaining closed and ignored? Given the excitement attending print and reading in the Reformation period, and the lay interest in the Bible, the former scenario is surely the more plausible, but aside from the evidence in churchwardens' accounts for preservation (e.g., rebinding) and replacement of the *Paraphrases*, the evidence of use is elusive.[95] It is clear, however, that a small but perhaps growing number of Elizabethan parishes were making works of theology available to the laity. Whether in response to popular pressure or clerical initiatives, as parishes began to collect books, questions of use must have been raised. Might parishioners borrow a book? Even if a volume were chained to a lectern, the existence of locks ensured that such works remained portable. Borrowing was evidently practised in the parish of St Peter Mancroft in Norwich, since the churchwardens once noted that 'there remayneth in the handes of Mr Castleton, a boke called the Common places of Musculus the 20 daye of December 1579 that he borrowed owt of the churche.'[96] The parish library of St James, established in Bury St Edmunds in Suffolk in 1595, occasionally lent out volumes, and not only to visiting clergy for whom the library was primarily established. There is evidence that the townsfolk were able to use the library and that it had a copy of Erasmus' *Paraphrases* in English.[97] The parish of Repton established something akin to a modern lending library with rules by 1622–3.[98] From lecterns to libraries, the shards of evidence suggest the possibility of a much greater influence of Erasmus' *Paraphrases* in the English church and in English society than has generally been acknowledged.

VII

According to E.J. Devereux, 'England was indifferent' to the *Paraphrases*.[99] Stephen Gardiner expressed his hostility towards the endeavour, but no one else 'seems to have worried about anything but the ten or twelve shillings the book cost, and Catherine Parr's dream of an Erasmian England came to nothing.'[100] The volumes were 'never printed after 1552, seldom mentioned in visitation articles after the first few years of Queen Elizabeth's reign, and [the] copyright was given up by the queen's printer in 1583 – all of which suggests that ... the English *Paraphrases* of Erasmus ultimately had only slight influence on Anglican thought.'[101] The parochial evidence, partial and fragmentary though it is, suggests the opposite: that the *Paraphrases* was widely purchased and used, that it was instrumental in making the New Testament in English available and known to clergy and people, and that it was the chief means by which Erasmus was claimed for the English reformed church.

That Erasmus was indeed seen in that light is clear from the instructions issued by Archbishop Bancroft in 1610 to the bench of English bishops. Bancroft had arranged for a reissue of Bishop John Jewel's works in one volume, published in the previous year. He has, he says, been

> content that all Bishop Jewel's works should be printed togeither in one volume to the ende that every parrish in England mighte have one of them. In the late queenes tyme of worthy memory, every parrish was driven to buy Erasmus Paraphrase uppon the New Testament and the said bishops Replye against Hardinge, one of the said books delivering plainly to every man's understanding the true sense and meaning of the whole New Testament and the other conteyninge a very notable and learned confutation of all the principall points almost of popery. And therfore forasmuch as the same true causes which moved her late maiestie to impose the said bookes uppon every parrish doe remayne still in force, there beinge more recusantes now then at that tyme, I have thought it my dutie very hartely to intreate your lordship soe to deale with your chancellor, commissary, archdeacons and officiall, as by theire meanes and your owne, with the reste of the preachers and ministers of your diocesse, they may induce theire parishioners to be willinge, every parrish to buye one of the works of Bishop Jewell. And I am soe farre perswaded of your lordships abilitie to prevaile with your clergie herin as I did likewise in as harty manner desier you to sende for as many of the said books ready bounde unto Mr Norton (John Norton, bookseller and printer of London) as there are parishes in your diocesse,

> that hereby the said parrishes may have those bookes neere at hande, which will the better incurrage them to buy them. What you shalbe contente to do herein I knowe his maiestie will take in very good parte, beinge ever of his most princely goodness ready to like and approve of that which may tende to the instruction and benefit of his loving subjects. And besides, you shall bind me very much hereby unto you, in that I gave encouragement to the printing of the said works in one volume to the end that the whole realm might in that sort be furnished with them. And for the prices of them I will take order that they shalbe reasonable.[102]

This statement provides valuable insights into the means by which the episcopate could encourage the purchase of works of religious instruction, even without the sanction of a royal proclamation. The regard with which Bancroft speaks of the *Paraphrases* as late as 1610 is impressive testimony to the work's lingering importance.

Thus, in conclusion, we are brought back to the last of Thompson's questions, concerning the difference made by the availability and use of the *Paraphrases*. For if the weight of the evidence indicates that the 'Protestant' Erasmus of the English *Paraphrases* was indeed a durable presence in the parishes, there is all the more reason to ask what wider influence the work may have exerted in the English church and in English society as a whole. Did it have any impact on the Elizabethan and Jacobean debates over vestments, ceremonies, discipline, kneeling for the sacrament, or the churching of women? How might it have shaped opinions on these and other matters of controversy? And what could it have contributed to the formation of individual, as well as collective, forms of Protestant consciousness among English men and women? Before attempting to answer these questions, we would do well to begin with a close analysis of the contents and tenor of the English *Paraphrases*.[103]

NOTES

1 E. Roberts and K. Parker, eds., *Southampton Probate Inventories 1447–1575*, 1: 164–75, esp. 174.

2 Ibid, 2: 346–71, esp. 348.

3 E.J. Devereux, 'The Publication of the English Paraphrase of Erasmus,' 363–4.
4 Craig Thompson, 'Erasmus and Tudor England.'
5 E.J. Devereux, 'English Translators of Erasmus 1522–57' and 'The Publication of the English *Paraphrases* of Erasmus.'
6 Keith Thomas, *Religion and the Decline of Magic: Studies in Popular Beliefs in Sixteenth and Seventeenth Century England.*
7 See, e.g., Stuart Clark, *Thinking with Demons: The Idea of Witchcraft in Early Modern Europe*; J.A. Sharpe, *Instruments of Darkness: Witchcraft in England 1550–1750*; Laura Gowing, *Domestic Dangers: Women, Words and Sex in Early Modern London*; Martin Ingram, *Church Courts, Sex and Marriage in England, 1570–1640*; and Ralph Houlbrooke, *Church Courts and the People during the English Reformation.*
8 See Christopher Haigh, *The English Reformation Revised* and *English Reformations*; Diarmaid MacCulloch, 'The Myth of the English Reformation'; and Nicholas Tyacke, 'Introduction: Re-thinking the "English Reformation."'
9 Robert Whiting, *The Local Impact of the English Reformation*; Christopher Marsh, *Popular Religion in Sixteenth Century England.*
10 Eamon Duffy, *The Stripping of the Altars*; Christopher Haigh, *English Reformations*; J.J. Scarisbrick, *The Reformation and the English People.*
11 Thompson, 'Erasmus and Tudor England,' 30–1.
12 McConica, *English Humanists and Reformation Politics*, 231–2, 240–8; Devereux, 'The Publication of the English *Paraphrases* of Erasmus'; Thompson, 'Erasmus and Tudor England,' 51–7; John N. Wall, Jr, 'Godly and Fruitful Lessons: The English Bible, Erasmus' Paraphrases, and the Book of Homilies,' esp. 73–85; M. Dowling, *Humanism in the Age of Henry VIII*, 235–7.
13 Wall, 'Godly and Fruitful Lessons,' 80.
14 *The first tome or volume of the Paraphrases of Erasmus upon the newe testament, conteinyng the fower Evangelistes, with the Actes of the Apostles: eftsones conferred with the latine and throughly corrected as it is by the Kinges highnes injunccions commaunded to be had in everie churche of this royalme* (London: Edward Whitchurch, 1551–2). For the publishing details see E.J. Devereux, *Renaissance English Translations of Erasmus: A Bibliography to 1700*, 146–75.
15 W.H. Frere and W.P.M. Kennedy, eds., *Visitation Articles and Injunctions of the Period of the Reformation*, 2: 114–30, here 117–18.
16 Ibid, 2: 122–3.
17 Ibid, 2: 136.
18 Ibid, 2: 294. Hooper's interrogatories for the dioceses of Gloucester and Worcester in 1551/2 asked 'whether there be in the church a Bible of the largest volume and the Paraphrases upon the New Testament in English and whether they be placed in some conven-

ient place of the church so that everybody may come to the same at time convenient.'

19 The parish of St Benet, Gracechurch Street had 'ii bookes of the paraphres of Erasmus the one of them upon the gospels and the other upon the epistels': H.B. Walters, *London Churches at the Reformation*, 189. In London, similar entries can be found for the parishes of All Hallows, Lombard Street, All Hallows, London Wall, St Andrew Undershaft, St Botolph Aldgate, St Dionis Backchurch, St Martin Outwich, St Mary Axe, St Mary Magdalene Milk Street, St Mildred Bread Street, St Pancras Soper Lane, St Peter West Cheap, St Peter Cornhill, and St Stephen Coleman Street. See Walters, *London Churches*, 111, 115, 152, 205, 237, 387, 430, 475, 520, 560, 564, 573, 600.

20 Frere and Kennedy, *Visitation Articles*, 3: 8–29, esp. 10. The injunction stated that within twelve months of the royal visitation each incumbent should obtain a copy of the 'Paraphrase of Erasmus, also in English, upon the Gospels, and the same set up in some convenient place within the said Church that they have cure of, where as their parishioners may most commodiously resort unto the same and read the same out of the time of common service.'

21 McConica, *English Humanists and Reformation Politics*, 248.

22 For Udall's career, see W.L. Edgerton, *Nicholas Udall*. See also G. Walker, *The Politics of Performance in Early Renaissance Drama*, 163–95; Paul White, *Theatre and Reformation: Protestantism, Patronage and Playing in Tudor England*, 126–9; William Peery, 'Udall as Time Server,' 119–21, 138–41, and the rejoinder by W.L. Edgerton, 'The Apostasy of Nicholas Udall.' For a recent analysis of the context within which Udall's career might best be understood, see Richard Rex, 'The Role of English Humanists in the Reformation up to 1559,' 19–40. For Malet and Key, see DNB.

23 Christina Garrett, *The Marian Exiles*, 70–1, 132–4, 241. For Allen, Coverdale, Cox, Norton, and Olde see DNB.

24 See the discussion of the date by Devereux, *Renaissance English Translations of Erasmus*, 168.

25 *The first tome or volume of the Paraphrases* (1551–2), sig. CCvii.

26 Ibid.

27 McConica, *English Humanists and Reformation Politics*, 248.

28 *The first tome or volume of the Paraphrases* (1551–2), sig. CCvii.

29 Ibid.

30 Ibid.

31 *The first tome or volume of the Paraphrases* (1548), fol. 76. Erasmus took the occasion of Christ's entry into Jerusalem to compare Christ's simplicity with the pomp of an ecclesiastical official. Udall translated the passage thus: 'With his dignitie compare me a bishop of

one temple, which hath bought the priesthode or prelacie lasting but for one yeare of a wicked and Heathen kyng for a filthie summe of money. Compare the bare heade of Jesu with his tyare or myter, all glysteryng and shinyng with golde, and precious stones. Compare that sobre and mylde countenance of Jesu, with his face puffed up with pryde: with his grym forheade, with his frowning browes, with his stately loke, with his contencious or uncharitable mouth.' This helps to explain the marginal note.

32 *The first tome or volume of the Paraphrases* (1551–2), fol. 180.

33 Ibid, fols. 178, 189.

34 *The first tome or volume of the Paraphrases* (1548), fol. 116.

35 *The first tome or volume of the Paraphrases* (1551–2), fol. 97.

36 *The first tome or volume of the Paraphrases* (1548), fol. 116.

37 *The first tome or volume of the Paraphrases* (1551–2), fol. 97. Udall did not entirely eliminate the use of 'penaunce' from the text. Two examples can be found at fols. 9 and 55.

38 It seems most probable that Cranmer was behind Udall's decision to revise, but the record is silent. See Diarmaid MacCulloch, *Thomas Cranmer* and *Tudor Church Militant*; and Paul Ayris and David Selwyn, eds., *Thomas Cranmer, Churchman and Scholar*.

39 See Devereux, 'The Publication of the English *Paraphrases* of Erasmus,' 348.

40 Ronald Hutton, 'The Local Impact of the Tudor Reformations,' 114–38, esp. 124–5, 137.

41 Ronald Hutton, *The Rise and Fall of Merry England*, 263–93.

42 B.R. Masters and E. Ralph, eds., *The Church Book of St Ewen's Bristol, 1454–1584*, 183–6.

43 County Record Office (hereafter CRO) Lichfield, D 27/4/1.

44 Betley: CRO Stafford, D689/PC/1/1, p. 40; Tenterden: CRO Maidstone, P364/5/14, Inventory 1642; Newport: CRO Chelmsford, D/P 15/8/1, Inventory 1661.

45 J.C. Cox, *English Church Fittings, Furniture and Accessories*, 195.

46 CRO Chelmsford, D/P 181/1/1: a memorandum in the parish register of Lambourne, Essex stated 'that the Paraphrase of Erasmus belonging to the parish church of Lamborne is in the custodie of Thomas Wynnyt now Parson of Lamborne and is by him to be restored againe to the use of the church. 12 March 1608.'

47 See F.C. Eeles, ed., *The Edwardian Inventories for Buckinghamshire*; Eeles, ed., *The Edwardian Inventories for Bedfordshire*; and S.C. Lomas, ed., *The Edwardian Inventories for Huntingdonshire*.

48 The occasional nature of the inclusion of books in these inventories would seem to bear out this impression. The inventories from Bedfordshire and Huntingdonshire cited above make no mention of books, but the inventories from Buckinghamshire do.

49 In 1552, the parishioners of Thame complained to the King and Privy Council that their churchwardens had sold off all their goods and 'have left almost noo thyng,' but the churchwardens' accounts prove that the wardens had followed the royal injunctions and that some of the money received from the sale of goods had been used for buying the new Prayer Book, Erasmus' *Paraphrases*, four English psalters, and the Homilies. See R. Graham, ed., *The Chantry Certificates and Edwardian Inventories of Church Goods*, xxv, 115–16; and F.G. Lee, *The History, Description, and Antiquities of the Prebendal Church of the Blessed Virgin Mary of Thame in the County and Diocese of Oxford*, 68–9.

50 H. Littlehales, *The Medieval Records of a London City Church (St Mary at Hill)*, 387; W.H. Overall, ed., *The Accounts of the Churchwardens of the Parish of St Michael, Cornhill in the City of London*, 67. Thompson suggested that fifty-seven or fifty-eight London churches owned the *Paraphrases* by 1552, but this figure is based upon a miscounting of the information in Walters, *London Churches at the Reformation*; Thompson, 'Erasmus and Tudor England,' 54–5.

51 See appendix 1.

52 John Foxe, *Acts and Monuments* (London: John Day, 1563), 1087, 1092. I owe this reference to Dr Tom Freeman.

53 See Walters, *London Churches*, 350, 361, 407, 546; and J.C. Cox, *English Church Fittings, Furniture and Accessories*, 195, 197.

54 F.A. Youngs, *The Proclamations of the Tudor Queens*, 197–201.

55 P.L. Hughes and J.F. Larkin, eds., *Tudor Royal Proclamations*, 2: 57–60.

56 Ibid, 2: 59. Erasmus Sarcerius was the author of *Common places of scripture ordrely set forth*, trans. R. Taverner (STC 21752.5).

57 Thompson, 'Erasmus and Tudor England,' 55–6.

58 F.A. Youngs, 'The Tudor Governments and Dissident Religious Books,' 167–90; David Loades, 'The Press under the Early Tudors, A Study in Censorship and Sedition,' 44; Loades, *Politics, Censorship and the English Reformation*, 138–42. See, however, S. Wabuda, 'The Woman with the Rock: The Controversy on Women and Bible Reading,' who argues that the revived heresy laws made all English Bibles illegal. Even if this is right, the evidence still suggests that there was no official attempt to remove the Bible and *Paraphrases* from parishes.

59 The London parish of St Benet Gracechurch paid 3s 4d 'to a plasterer for washing owte and defacing of such Scriptures as in the tyme of King Edward the VIth were written aboute the chirche and walls, we being commanded so to do by the right hon. the Lord bishop of Winchester, Lord Chancellor of England.' J.P. Malcolm, *Londinium Redivivum or An Antient History and Modern Description of London*, 314.

60 J.E. Binney, *The Accounts of the Wardens of the Parish of Morebath, Devon 1520–73*, 186.

61 J.V. Kitto, ed., *St Martin in the Fields: The Accounts of the Churchwardens 1525–1603*, 151. There is no evidence that the parish repurchased the *Paraphrases* under Elizabeth.

62 Frere and Kennedy, *Visitation Articles*, 3: 6, 92. The same questions can be found in Bishop Parkhurst's interrogatories for the diocese of Norwich in 1561: ibid, 3: 105.

63 C.J. Kitching, ed., *The Royal Visitation of 1559, Act book for the Northern Province*, 62–3.

64 Ibid, xxxv.

65 St Michael's Bedwardine: J. Amphlett, *The Churchwardens' Accounts of St Michael's in Bedwardine, Worcester 1539–1603*, 47; London, St Andrew Hubbard: J.C. Crosthwaite, 'Ancient Churchwardens' Accounts of a City Parish' (1849): 276; London, St Michael Cornhill: Overall, *The Accounts of the Churchwardens of the Parish of St Michael, Cornhill in the City of London*, 67, 153. The London parishes paid for new chains for the book(s) at Elizabeth's accession, which indicates that the *Paraphrases* were not to be found tied to a desk during the Marian period.

66 See appendices 1 and 2.

67 Frere and Kennedy, *Visitation Articles*, 3: 10, 13–14. It is noteworthy that although the injunctions only require the *Paraphrases* on the Gospels to be set up in the parish church, ministers were to 'provide and have of his own' the *Paraphrases on the New Testament*, that is, both volumes published by Whitchurch.

68 Thompson, 'Erasmus and Tudor England,' 56; Devereux, 'The Publication of the English *Paraphrases* of Erasmus,' 365.

69 Kenneth Fincham, ed., *Visitation Articles*, 2: 252.

70 David Loades, ed., *John Foxe and the English Reformation*, 144.

71 W.P.M. Kennedy, *Elizabethan Episcopal Administration*, 3: 341. Bancroft's articles for the diocese of London, 1601, make no mention of the *Paraphrases* and neither do Archbishop Sandys' articles for the province of York in 1578 (ibid, 2: 91).

72 Middleton's injunctions for St Davids, 1583: Kennedy, *Elizabethan Episcopal Administration*, 3: 150. Cooper in 1577 required clergy in the diocese of Lincoln under the degree of M.A. to purchase Bullinger's *Decades*, and this anticipated the regulations for clerical study agreed upon in the convocation of 1586 (ibid, 2: 45–6). It is clear that as a text for clerical instruction, the *Paraphrases* were superseded by Bullinger's *Decades*, but the earlier injunction was never rescinded. See Wickham's articles for the diocese of Lincoln (ibid, 3: 188).

73 Fincham, *Visitation Articles*, 2: 1, 99, 252. See also the articles of Bishop George Montaigne for Lincoln diocese in 1618 (ibid, 1: 80).

74 CRO, Chichester, EP1/23/5.
75 CRO, Chichester, EP1/23/5, fol. 25v, 3r.
76 J.T. Godfrey, *Notes on the Churches of Nottinghamshire Hundred of Bingham*, 507.
77 CRO, Chichester, EP1/23/5, fol. 34r.
78 H.J.F. Swayne, *Churchwardens' Accounts of S. Edmund and S. Thomas, Sarum 1443–1702*, 105, 281, 374–5.
79 CRO, Chichester, EP1/23/5, fol. 14r.
80 Overall, *The Accounts of the Churchwardens of the Parish of St Michael, Cornhill in the City of London*, 67, 153, 167, 176, 238.
81 J.S. Purvis, ed., *Tudor Parish Documents of the Diocese of York*, 33.
82 Ludlow: Thomas Wright, ed., *Churchwardens' Accounts of the Town of Ludlow in Shropshire*, 164; St Benet Gracechurch: Malcolm, *Londinium Redivivum*, 327; Great Packington, Warwickshire: CRO, Warwick, DR 801/12, no. 16.
83 J.E. Binney, ed., *The Accounts of the Wardens of the Parish of Morebath*, 205–6, 213. The parish bought a copy of the *Paraphrases* in 1564.
84 See appendix 2.
85 E.S. Leedham-Green, *Books in Cambridge Inventories: Book Lists from Vice-Chancellor's Court Probate Inventories in the Tudor and Stuart Periods*.
86 R.J. Fehrenbach and E.S. Leedham-Green, *Private Libraries in Renaissance England: A Collection and Catalogue of Tudor and Early Stuart Book Lists*. Thomas Day's inventory is found at 3: 196–221.
87 CRO, Norwich Inv. 9/45.
88 CRO, Norwich Inv. 17/13.
89 CRO, Norwich Inv. 7/242.
90 M. Reed, ed., *The Ipswich Probate Inventories 1583–1631*.
91 J.A. Johnston, ed., *Probate Inventories of Lincoln Citizens 1661–1714*.
92 W.D. Robson-Scott, *German Travellers in England 1400–1800*, 25–6 and 'Josua Maler's Visit to England in 1551.'
93 Richard Hakluyt, *The Principal Navigations Voyages Traffiques and Discoveries of the English Nation*, 1: 235. Cabot's order, dated 9 May 1553, read 'that morning and evening prayer, with other common services appointed by the Kings Majestie, and lawes of this Realme to be read and saide in every ship daily by the minister in the Admirall, and the merchant or some other person learned in other ships, and the Bible or paraphrases to be read devoutly and Christianly to Gods honour and for his grace to be obtained, and had by humble and heartie praier of the Navigants accordingly.'
94 The case is cited in David Cressy, *Travesties and Transgressions in Tudor and Stuart England*, 145.
95 The parish of All Saints, Derby had a copy of the *Paraphrases* chained to a movable desk with other books, paid 3s 6d 'for binding Erasmus

Paraphrase' in the 1630s, and repaired their copy again in 1657: J.C. Cox and W.H. St John Hope, *The Chronicles of the Collegiate Church or Free Chapel of All Saints Derby*, 187. Cf. E.R.C. Brinkworth, ed., *South Newington Churchwardens' Accounts, 1553–1684*, 6: 25, 33. It is difficult to interpret the common evidence of 'rent' or torn copies of the Bible and Paraphrases. The wardens of the Yorkshire parish of Swyne reported that 'the paraphrases is torne and lackethe almost v. chapitors': Purvis, *Tudor Parish Documents of the Diocese of York*, 34. See also the presentments from the wardens of Easington and Sigles-thorne: Purvis, *Tudor Parish Documents of the Diocese of York*, 29, 33. When the parish of Great Dunmow spent 20d in 1559/60 on replacing 'xxi chapiters of Jeremye for the byble,' was this the result of the eagerness of certain persons to obtain a portion of printed scripture or the work of those implacably opposed to the vernacular Bible? See W.T. Scott, *Antiquities of an Essex Parish, or Pages from the History of Great Dunmow*, 62.

96 CRO, Norwich PD 26/71, fol. 12v.

97 John Craig, 'The "Cambridge Boies": Thomas Rogers and the "Brethren" in Bury St Edmunds,' 174.

98 J.C. Cox, 'The Registers and Churchwardens' and Constables' Accounts of the Parish of Repton,' 32–3.

99 Devereux, 'English Translators of Erasmus,' 56.

100 Ibid.

101 Devereux, 'The Publication of the English *Paraphrases* of Erasmus,' 367.

102 Fincham, *Visitation Articles*, 1: 96–7.

103 We should not forget, either, that it was not only (or even principally) 'great books' such as the Bible, Foxe's *Acts and Monuments*, and Jewel's *Apology* that found their way into parishioners' hands. The purchasing of smaller and cheaper works such as catechisms, psalters, and books of occasional prayers is also well attested in churchwardens' accounts. In 1627 the parish church of St Nicholas, Great Yarmouth possessed '2 bookes for order of fasting for the time of plague, more two bookes of prayer to be used in time of warr and pestilence, more two bookes of thanksgiving to God for staying the sicknesse, more one booke for the Fift of November,' as well as the more usual Bible, service books, 'fower books of Mr Perkins,' Jewel's works, and homilies: C.H.E. White, ed., *The East Anglian, or Notes and Queries*, n.s. 3: 336. Such examples might easily be multiplied.

APPENDIX 1

English parishes that purchased Erasmus' *Paraphrases* before 1558[1]

Parish	*Purchase*	*Inventory*
Ash, Kent[2]		1552
Ashburton, Devon[3]	1548/9	
Badsey, Worcestershire[4]	1548	
Battersea, Surrey[5]		1552
Beckenham, Kent[6]		1552
Bedwardine, St Michael's Worcs.[7]	1548/9	
Bermondsey, Surrey[8]		1552
Bethersden, Kent[9]	1549	
Bexley, Kent[10]		1552

1 In both appendices, I have included only those parishes for which there is specific evidence that the *Paraphrases* were purchased or owned. I have not included those parishes that probably purchased the *Paraphrases* but did not directly state this. The parish of Halesowen almost certainly purchased a copy of the *Paraphrases* when the accounts in 1548 state that they 'payd for a booke at Winchester' that cost 12s: F. Somers, ed., *Halesowen Churchwardens' Accounts 1487–1582*, 94. There are also a number of parishes like the Surrey parish of St Mary, Horne, which obscured its purchase of the *Paraphrases* in 1552 with a record of 16s 2d 'laid out for bokes nessessari for the church': R.A. Roberts, 'Further Inventories of the Goods and Ornaments of the Churches in the County of Surrey in the Reign of King Edward the Sixth,' 57. The information presented in these appendices should be seen as the tip of an iceberg. They take no account of purchases of the *Paraphrases* by individuals, colleges at Oxford and Cambridge, or parish libraries.

2 M.E.C. Walcott, R.P. Coates, and W.A.S. Robertson, 'Inventories of Parish Church Goods in Kent, A.D. 1552,' 104.

3 A. Hanham, ed., *Churchwardens' Accounts of Ashburton, 1479–1580*, 122.

4 E. Barnard, ed., *Churchwardens' Accounts of the Parish of Badsey, with Aldington, in Worcestershire 1525–71*, 35.

5 J.R.D. Tyssen, *Inventories of the Goods and Ornaments in the Churches of Surrey in the Reign of King Edward the Sixth*, 50.

6 Walcott, Coates, and Robertson, 'Inventories of Parish Church Goods in Kent,' 105.

7 J. Amphlett, ed., *The Churchwardens' Accounts of St Michael's in Bedwardine, Worcester 1539–1603*, 20.

8 Tyssen, *Inventories*, 98.

9 F.R. Mercer, *Churchwardens' Accounts at Betrysden 1515–73*, 5: 89.

10 Walcott, Coates, and Robertson, 'Inventories of Parish Church Goods in Kent,' 108.

Parish	*Purchase*	*Inventory*
Bishops Stortford, Herts.[11]	1549/50	
Bix Gibwen and Bix Brand, Oxford[12]		1552
Bletchingley, Surrey[13]	1547–52	
Boxford, Suffolk[14]	1548	
Bramley, Hampshire[15]	1549	
Bromley, Kent[16]		1552
Calne, Wiltshire[17]		1552
Cambridge, Great St Marys[18]	1550	
Canterbury, Our Lady of Northgate[19]		1552
Canterbury, St Alphege[20]		1552
Canterbury, St Dunstan[21]	1548/9	
Canterbury, St Margaret's[22]		1552
Canterbury, St Mary Bredne[23]		1552
Canterbury, St Paul's[24]		1552
Carlton in Lindrick, Yorkshire[25]	unknown	
Cheam, Surrey[26]		1552
Chelsfield, Kent[27]		1552

11 S.G. Doree, ed., *The Early Churchwardens' Accounts of Bishops Stortford, 1431–1558*, 294.

12 R. Graham, ed., *The Chantry Certificates and Edwardian Inventories of Church Goods*, 96.

13 T. Craib, 'Blechingley Churchwardens' Accounts, 1546–52,' 29. Tyssen, *Inventories*, 103.

14 P. Northeast, ed., *Boxford Churchwardens' Accounts 1530–61*, 54.

15 J.F. Williams, ed., *The Early Churchwardens' Accounts of Hampshire*, 38.

16 Walcott, Coates, and Robertson, 'Inventories of Parish Church Goods in Kent,' 114

17 A. Marsh, *A History of the Borough and Town of Calne*, 372.

18 J.E. Foster, ed., *Churchwardens' Accounts of St Mary the Great, Cambridge 1504–1635*, 120.

19 Walcott, Coates, and Robertson, 'Inventories of Parish Church Goods in Kent,' 122.

20 Ibid, 118.

21 J.M. Cowper, 'Accounts of the Churchwardens of St Dunstan's, Canterbury A.D. 1484–1580,' 112.

22 Walcott, Coates, and Robertson, 'Inventories of Parish Church Goods in Kent,' 121.

23 Ibid, 21.

24 Ibid, 122.

25 C.J. Kitching, ed., *The Royal Visitation of 1559*, 64.

26 Tyssen, *Inventories*, 67.

27 Walcott, Coates, and Robertson, 'Inventories of Parish Church Goods in Kent,' 130.

Parish	*Purchase*	*Inventory*
Chenies, Bucks.[28]		1552
Chertsey, Surrey[29]		1552
Chesham, Bucks[30]		1552
Cheshunt, Herts.[31]		1552
Chester, St Mary-on-the-Hill[32]	1549/50	
Chislehurst, Kent[33]		1552
Cobham, Surrey[34]	1549/50	
Crayford, Kent[35]		1552
Crondall, Hampshire[36]	1549	
Croscombe, Somerset[37]	1550/1	
Darenth, Kent[38]		1552
Dartford, Kent[39]		1552
Dover, St Mary's[40]	1548	
Downe, Kent[41]		1552
Drayton Beauchamp, Bucks.[42]		1552
Dunton, Bucks.[43]		1552
East Donyland, Essex[44]	1547	

28 F.C. Eeles, ed., *The Edwardian Inventories for Buckinghamshire*, 46.

29 Tyssen, *Inventories*, 31.

30 Eeles, *Edwardian Inventories for Buckinghamshire*, 42.

31 J.E. Cussans, ed., *Inventory of Furniture and Ornaments Remaining in All the Parish Churches of Hertfordshire in the Last Year of the Reign of King Edward the Sixth*, 106.

32 J.P. Earwaker, *The History of the Church and Parish of St Mary-on-the-Hill, Chester*, 233.

33 Walcott, Coates, and Robertson, 'Inventories of Parish Church Goods in Kent,' 132.

34 Roberts, 'Further Inventories,' 48.

35 Walcott, Coates, and Robertson, 'Inventories of Parish Church Goods in Kent,' 35.

36 Williams, *Early Churchwardens' Accounts of Hampshire*, 115.

37 Bishop Hobhouse, ed., *Church-Wardens' Accounts of Croscombe, Pilton, Patton, Tintinhull, Morebath and St Michael's Bath. Ranging from AD 1349 to 1560*, 45.

38 Walcott, Coates, and Robertson, 'Inventories of Parish Church Goods in Kent,' 138.

39 Ibid, 141.

40 British Library (BL), Egerton 1912, fol. 35v.

41 Walcott, Coates, and Robertson, 'Inventories of Parish Church Goods in Kent,' 143.

42 Eeles, *Edwardian Inventories for Buckinghamshire*, 72.

43 Ibid, 80–1.

44 C.H.E. White, ed., *The East Anglian, or Notes and Queries*, n.s. 2: 205.

Parish	*Purchase*	*Inventory*
Eastwood, Yorkshire[45]	unknown	
Eltham, Kent[46]		1552
Eynsford, Kent[47]		1552
Farnborough, Kent[48]		1552
Farningham, Kent[49]		1552
Fawkham, Kent[50]		1552
Fetcham, Surrey[51]	1549/50	
Finchamsted, Berkshire[52]		1552
Great Dunmow, Essex[54]	1548/51	
Greenwich, Kent[53]		1552
Halton, Bucks.[55]		1552
Hardwick, Bucks.[56]		1552
Hartley, Kent[57]		1552
Hayes, Kent[58]		1552
Hoggeston, Bucks.[59]		1552
Horton Kirby, Kent[60]		1552
Hughenden, Bucks.[61]		1552
Kingsdown, Kent[62]		1552

45 Kitching, *The Royal Visitation of 1559*, 62–3.
46 Walcott, Coates, and Robertson, 'Inventories of Parish Church Goods in Kent,' 149.
47 Ibid, 152.
48 Ibid, 100.
49 Ibid, 155.
50 Ibid, 156.
51 Roberts, 'Further Inventories,' 54.
52 W. Money, *Parish Church Goods in Berkshire*, 17.
53 W.T. Scott, *Antiquities of an Essex Parish, or Pages from the History of Great Dunmow*, 54.
54 Walcott, Coates, and Robertson, 'Inventories of Parish Church Goods in Kent,' 161.
55 Eeles, *Edwardian Inventories for Buckinghamshire*, 88–9.
56 Ibid, 73–4.
57 Walcott, Coates, and Robertson, 'Inventories of Parish Church Goods in Kent,' 267.
58 Ibid, 269.
59 Eeles, *Edwardian Inventories for Buckinghamshire*, 82.
60 Walcott, Coates, and Robertson, 'Inventories of Parish Church Goods in Kent,' 271.
61 Eeles, *Edwardian Inventories for Buckinghamshire*, 27.
62 Walcott, Coates, and Robertson, 'Inventories of Parish Church Goods in Kent,' 277.

Parish	*Purchase*	*Inventory*
Lee, Kent[63]		1552
Leicester, St Martin's[64]	1553	
Leverington, Cambs.[65]	1552	
Lewes, St Andrew's and St Michael's[66]	1548	
Lewisham, Kent[67]		1552
Little Harwood, Bucks.[68]		1552
Littleton, Worcestershire[69]	1548	
London, All Hallows, Bread St[70]		1552
London, All Hallows the Great[71]		1552
London, All Hallows, Honey Lane[72]		1552
London, All Hallows, Lombard St[73]		1552
London, All Hallows, London Wall[74]		1552
London, All Hallows, Staining[75]	1548	1552
London, St Alphege, London Wall[76]		1552
London, St Andrew Holborn[77]		1548/52
London, St Andrew Hubbard[78]	1548	1552
London, St Andrew Undershaft[79]		1552
London, St Anne and Agnes[80]		1552

63 Ibid, 278.

64 James Thompson, *The History of Leicester*, 462.

65 W.D. Sweeting, 'Leverington Churchwardens' Accounts,' 332.

66 H.M. Whitley, 'The Churchwardens' Accounts of St Andrew's and St Michael's, Lewes from 1522 to 1601,' 53. The two parishes were united in 1546 and purchased both volumes of the *Paraphrases*.

67 Walcott, Coates, and Robertson, 'Inventories of Parish Church Goods in Kent,' 280.

68 Eeles, *Edwardian Inventories for Buckinghamshire*, 85.

69 Barnard, *Churchwardens' Accounts of the Parish of Badsey*, 35.

70 H.B. Walters, *London Churches at the Reformation*, 87.

71 Ibid, 94.

72 Ibid, 101.

73 Ibid, 111.

74 Ibid, 115.

75 Ibid, 121; Guildhall Library (GL), MS 4956/2, fol. 66r.

76 Walters, *London Churches*, 136.

77 Ibid, 141.

78 'Ancient Churchwardens' Accounts of a City Parish,' *The British Magazine, and Monthly Register of Religious and Ecclesiastical Information, Parochial History and Documents respecting the State of the Poor, Progress of Education etc.*, 34 (1848): 676; Walters, *London Churches*, 147.

79 Walters, *London Churches*, 152.

80 Ibid, 162.

Parish	*Purchase*	*Inventory*
London, St Augustine, Watling St[81]		1552
London, St Benet, Gracechurch St[82]		1552
London, St Benet Paul's Wharf[83]		1552
London, St Botolph Aldgate[84]	1550	1552
London, St Botolph Billingsgate[85]		1552
London, St Bride, Fleet Street[86]		1552
London, St Dionis Backchurch[87]		1552
London, St Dunstan in the West[88]	1548	
London, St Ethelburga[89]		1552
London, St Giles Cripplegate[90]		1552
London, St Gregory-by-St Paul's[91]		1552
London, St John Evangelist[92]		1552
London, St Katherine Cree[93]		1552
London, St Lawrence Jewry[94]		1552
London, St Lawrence Pountney[95]		1552
London, St Magnus[96]		1552
London, St Margaret Lothbury[97]		1552
London, St Margaret New Fish Street[98]	1552	
London, St Margaret Pattens[99]	1548	1552
London, St Martin in the Fields[100]	1548/50	

81 Ibid, 179.
82 Ibid, 189.
83 Ibid, 199.
84 Ibid, 205; GL, MS 9325/1, fol. 17v.
85 Ibid, 213.
86 Ibid, 222.
87 Ibid, 237.
88 GL, MS 2968/1, fol. 129r.
89 Walters, *London Churches*, 268.
90 Ibid, 286.
91 Ibid, 293.
92 Ibid, 298.
93 Ibid, 319.
94 Ibid, 328.
95 Ibid, 333.
96 Ibid, 349.
97 Ibid, 350.
98 Ibid, 361.
99 Ibid, 368; GL, MS 4570/1, fol. 98r.
100 J.V. Kitto, *St Martin in the Fields: The Accounts of the Churchwardens 1525–1603*, 130.

Parish	*Purchase*	*Inventory*
London, St Martin Outwich[101]		1552
London, St Martin Pomery[102]		1552
London, St Mary Aldermary[103]		1552
London, St Mary at Hill[104]	1547/8	
London, St Mary Axe[105]		1552
London, St Mary le Bow[106]		1552
London, St Mary Somerset[107]		1552
London, St Mary Staining[108]		1552
London, St Mary Woolchurch[109]		1552
London, St Mary Woolnoth[110]	1547/8	1552
London, St Mary Magdalene Milk St[111]	1549	1552
London, St Matthew Friday St[112]	1547/8	1552
London, St Michael Bassishaw[113]		1552
London, St Michael Cornhill[114]	1548	
London, St Michael le Quern[115]	1548	1552/55
London, St Michael Wood St[116]		1552
London, St Mildred Bread St[117]		1552
London, St Mildred Poultry[118]		1552
London, St Nicholas Olave[119]		1552
London, St Olave, Hart St[120]		1552

101 Walters, *London Churches*, 387.
102 Ibid, 400.
103 Ibid, 427.
104 H. Littlehales, ed., *The Medieval Records of a London City Church (St Mary at Hill)*, 387.
105 Walters, *London Churches*, 430.
106 Ibid, 436.
107 Ibid, 456.
108 Ibid, 459.
109 Ibid, 463.
110 Ibid, 469; GL, MS 1002/1A, fol. 46r.
111 Walters, *London Churches*, 475; GL, MS 2596/1, fol. 98v.
112 Walters, *London Churches*, 486; GL, MS 1016/1, fol. 3r.
113 Walters, *London Churches*, 488.
114 W.H. Overall, ed., *The Accounts of the Churchwardens of the Parish of St Michael, Cornhill in the City of London*, 67.
115 Walters, *London Churches*, 508; GL, MS 2895/1, fols. 126v, 293r.
116 Walters, *London Churches*, 514.
117 Ibid, 520.
118 Ibid, 525.
119 Ibid, 536.
120 Ibid, 541.

Parish	*Purchase*	*Inventory*
London, St Olave, Old Jewry[121]		1552
London, St Olave, Silver St[122]		1552
London, St Pancras, Soper Lane[123]		1552
London, St Peter, West Cheap[124]		1552
London, St Peter upon Cornhill[125]		1552
London, St Stephen, Coleman St[126]		1552
London, St Stephen Walbrook[127]	1548/9	
London, St Thomas Apostle[128]		1552
London, St Vedast, Foster Lane[129]		1552
Long Ditton, Surrey[130]	1549/50	
Long Sutton, Lincolnshire[131]	1549	
Louth, Lincolnshire[132]	1548	
Lowdham, Yorkshire[133]	unknown	
Ludlow, Shropshire[134]	1549	
Maldon, Surrey[135]	1549/50	
Marks Tey, Essex[136]		1552
Marston, Oxfordshire[137]	1553	
Mitcham, Surrey[138]		1552
Morebath, Devon[139]	1549	

121 Ibid, 546.
122 Ibid, 556.
123 Ibid, 560.
124 Ibid, 564.
125 Ibid, 573.
126 Ibid, 600.
127 GL, MS 593/2, fol. 7r.
128 Walters, *London Churches*, 613.
129 Ibid, 624.
130 Roberts, 'Further Inventories,' 50.
131 County Record Office (CRO), Lincoln, Long Sutton 7/1, fol. 38v.
132 CRO, Lincoln, Louth 7/2, fol. 83r.
133 Kitching, *The Royal Visitation of 1559*, 62–3.
134 Thomas Wright, ed., *Churchwardens' Accounts of the Town of Ludlow in Shropshire*, 38.
135 Roberts, 'Further Inventories,' 60
136 White, ed., *The East Anglian, or Notes and Queries*, n.s. 2: 4.
137 F.W. Weaver and G.N. Clark, eds., *Churchwardens' Accounts of Marston, Spelsbury, Pyrton*, 18.
138 Tyssen, *Inventories*, 73.
139 J.E. Binney, ed., *The Accounts of the Wardens of the Parish of Morebath, Devon 1520–73*, 162.

Parish	*Purchase*	*Inventory*
Norwich, St Andrew[140]	1548/9	
Norwich, St Mary Coslany[141]	1549/50	
Sherborne, St Mary's Dorset[142]	1549/50	
Sheriff Hutton, Yorkshire[143]	1548	
Smarden, Kent[144]	1548	
Southwark, St Saviour's, Surrey[145]		1552
Stanford in the Vale, Berkshire[146]		1552
Stoke Charity, Hampshire[147]	1550/1	
Strood, Kent[148]		1555
Swanbourne, Bucks.[149]		1552
Sutton, Surrey[150]		1552
Tewing, Hertfordshire[151]		1552
Thame, Oxfordshire[152]	1549	
Ufton, Berkshire[153]		1552
Wandsworth, Surrey[154]	1547/8	
Warwick, St Nicholas, Warwicks.[155]	1548/9	
West Tarring, Sussex[156]	1547	
White Colne, Essex[157]		1552
Wigtoft, Lincolnshire[158]	1549	

140 J. L'Estrange, 'The Church Goods of St Andrew and St Mary Coslany in the City of Norwich, temp. Edw. VI,' 60.

141 Ibid, 74.

142 Joseph Fowler, 'Post-Reformation Churchwardens' Accounts of St Mary's Sherborne,' 108.

143 J.S. Purvis, 'The Churchwardens' Book of Sheriff Hutton, AD 1524–68,' 185.

144 CRO, Maidstone, P339/5/1, fol. 8v.

145 Tyssen, *Inventories*, 91.

146 Violet House, ed., *Stanford in the Vale Churchwardens' Accounts 1552–1725*, 5.

147 Williams, *Early Churchwardens' Accounts of Hampshire*, 79.

148 H. Plomer, *The Churchwardens' Accounts of St Nicholas, Strood*, 5.

149 Eeles, *Edwardian Inventories for Buckinghamshire*, 82.

150 Tyssen, *Inventories*, 69.

151 Cussans, *Inventory of Furniture and Ornaments*, 99.

152 F.G. Lee, *The History, Description, and Antiquities of the Prebendal Church of the Blessed Virgin Mary of Thame in the County and Diocese of Oxford*, 68–9.

153 Money, *Parish Church Goods in Berkshire*, 41.

154 C.T. Davis, 'Early Churchwardens' Accounts of Wandsworth, 1545–58,' 95.

155 CRO, Warwick, DR 87/1.

156 W.J. Pressey, 'The Churchwardens' Accounts of West Tarring, Sussex,' 243, 245.

157 White, ed.,*The East Anglian, or Notes and Queries*, n.s. 3: 28

158 W. Blades, *Books in Chains*, 78.

Parish	*Purchase*	*Inventory*
Winslow with Shipton, Bucks.[159]		1552
Winterslow, Wiltshire[160]	1552	
Woodmansterne, Surrey[161]		1552
Yatton, Somerset[162]	1548/9	
Yoxall, Staffordshire[163]	1548/9	

159 Eeles, *Edwardian Inventories for Buckinghamshire*, 87.
160 W. Symonds, 'Winterslow Church Reckonings 1542–1661,' 37.
161 Tyssen, *Inventories*, 66
162 Hobhouse, *Church-Wardens' Accounts*, 161.
163 Stafford, D 1851/1/13/20, p. 18.

APPENDIX 2

English parishes that possessed Erasmus' *Paraphrases* after 1558

Parish	*Purchase*	*Inventory*
Addlethorpe, Lincolnshire[1]		1577
Antony, Cornwall[2]		1582
Ashurst, Sussex[3]		1583
Barchesten, Warwickshire[4]		1923
Battersea, Surrey[5]		1590
Bedwardine, St Michaels, Worcs.[6]	1548/9	1561
Berkhampstead, Herts.[7]		1598
Betley, Staffordshire[8]		1654
Bishop's Stortford, Herts.[9]	1560	
Bramley, Hampshire[10]	1561/2	

1 County Record Office (CRO), Lincoln, Addlethorpe 10.
2 CRO, Truro, DDP 7/5/1, p. 88.
3 CRO, Chichester, PAR 11/9/1, p. 27.
4 J.C. Cox, *English Church Fittings, Furniture and Accessories*, 195.
5 J.G. Taylor, *Our Lady of Batersey*, 339. I owe this reference to Mr James Rosenzweig.
6 J. Amphlett, *The Churchwardens' Accounts of St Michael's in Bedwardine, Worcester 1539–1603*, 47.
7 British Library (BL), Add. MS 18773, fol. 28r.
8 CRO, Stafford, D689/PC/1/1, p. 40.
9 J.L. Glasscock, ed., *The Records of St Michael's Parish Church, Bishop's Stortford*, 54.
10 J.F. Williams, ed., *The Early Churchwardens' Accounts of Hampshire*, 45.

Cambridge, Great St Mary's[11]	1561	
Canterbury, St Dunstan's[12]	1561/6	1566
Cartmel, Lancashire[13]		1642
Chester, St Michael, Cheshire[14]	1560	
Chippenham, Wiltshire[15]		1620
Coventry, Holy Trinity, Warwickshire[16]		1627
Derby, All Saints, Derbyshire[17]		1632
Devizes, St Mary's, Wiltshire[18]		1634
Durham, St Nicholas[19]		1666
Egginton, Derbyshire[20]		1923
Ely, St Mary's, Cambridgeshire[21]		1570
Great Dunmow, Essex[22]	1559/60	
Great Packington, Warwickshire[23]	1589/90	
Hadleigh, Suffolk[24]		1589
Hartshorne, Derbyshire[25]		1612
Holme Pierrepont, Nottinghamshire[26]		1633
Houghton-le-Spring, Durham[27]		1617
Ipswich, St Peter's, Suffolk[28]		1566
Kingsthorpe, Northamptonshire[29]		1923

11 J.E. Foster, ed., *Churchwardens' Accounts of St Mary the Great, Cambridge 1504–1635*, 147, 167, 189.

12 J.M. Cowper, 'Accounts of the Churchwardens of St Dunstan's, Canterbury A.D. 1484–1580,' 116, 120.

13 CRO, Kendal, WPR/89/W1, 277.

14 CRO, Chester, P65/8/1, fol. 1r.

15 W.H.B., 'Chippenham Parish Church,' 168.

16 CRO, Warwick, DR 801/12, no. 16.

17 J.C. Cox and W.H. St John Hope, *The Chronicles of the Collegiate Church or Free Chapel of All Saints Derby*, 178.

18 CRO, Trowbridge, P189/2.

19 J. Barmby, ed., *Churchwardens' Accounts of Pittington and Other Parishes in the Diocese of Durham 1580–1700*, 225, 262.

20 Cox, *English Church Fittings*, 195

21 CRO, Cambridge, P68/5/1.

22 W.T. Scott, *Antiquities of an Essex Parish, or Pages from the History of Great Dunmow*, 62.

23 CRO, Warwick, DR 158/19, p. 48.

24 Hadleigh Guildhall, Hadleigh 21/16, fol. 4. The specific evidence concerns rebinding the volume.

25 CRO, Matlock, D976A/PW1.

26 J.T. Godfrey, *Notes on the Churches of Nottinghamshire Hundred of Bingham*, 240.

27 Barmby, *Churchwardens' Accounts*, 292.

28 British Library (BL), Add. MS 25,344, fol. 9v.

29 Cox, *English Church Fittings*, 195

Parish	*Purchase*	*Inventory*
Lambourne, Essex[30]		1608
Landbeach, Cambridgeshire[31]		1613
Leicester, St Margaret's[32]	1559	
Lewes, St Andrew's and St Michael's[33]		1597–8
Lichfield, St Michaels, Staffordshire[34]		1654
Liskeard, Cornwall[35]		1600
London, All Hallows the Less[36]		1644
London, All Hallows, Lombard St[37]		1923
London, All Hallows, London Wall[38]		1572
London, All Hallows Staining[39]	1560	1582
London, St Alban Wood Street[40]		1584
London, St Alphage, London Wall[41]		1587
London, St Andrew Hubbard[42]	1548/1558–60	
London, St Andrew Undershaft[43]		1923
London, St Andrew by the Wardrobe[44]		1635
London, St Bartholomew Exchange[45]		1598

30 CRO, Chelmsford, D/P 181/1/1, note in parish register.

31 CRO, Cambridge, P104/1/2.

32 James Thompson, *The History of Leicester*, 242.

33 H.M. Whitley, 'The Churchwardens' Accounts of St Andrew's and St Michael's, Lewes from 1522 to 1601,' 61.

34 CRO, Lichfield, D 27/4/1.

35 CRO, Truro, DDP 126/4/1, fol. 72v.

36 Guildhall Library (GL), MS 823/1, inventory for 1644.

37 Cox, *English Church Fittings*, 195.

38 GL, MS 5090/2, fol. 14r.

39 GL, MS 4956/2, fos. 87v, 131v–132v. The parish purchased 'a boke of the paraffrases of erosemas of Rotherdame apone the pestelles' in 1560 for 6s 8d and must have retained the first volume purchased in 1548, since the inventory of 1582 records the possession of both volumes.

40 GL, MS 7673/1, inventory 1584. The volume appears to have been stolen by 1619 when another inventory was recorded.

41 GL, MS 1432/2, fol. 21r.

42 J.C. Crosthwaite, 'Ancient Churchwardens' Accounts of a City Parish' (1849): 276. The parish appears to have retained its copy of the *Paraphrases* throughout Mary's reign. In the accounts from 1558–60, there is an expenditure of 6d 'for the fastening of the bible and paraphrase and for nayles,' but no mention of any new purchase of these volumes.

43 Cox, *English Church Fittings*, 195

44 GL, MS 2088/1, inventory for 1635.

45 GL, MS 4383/1, p. 5.

Parish	*Purchase*	*Inventory*
London, St Benet Fink[46]		1611
London, St Benet Gracechurch[47]	1577	
London, St Botolph Aldersgate[48]	1559–60	
London, St Botolph Aldgate[49]	1559–60	
London, St Christopher le Stocks[50]		1583/4
London, St Ethelburga, Bishopsgate[51]		1581/2
London, St Helen Bishopsgate[52]		1602
London, St James Garlickhithe[53]	1560	1563
London, St Lawrence Jewry[54]		1582
London, St Leonard's Eastcheap[55]	unknown	
London, St Margaret New Fish Street[56]		1577
London, St Margaret Pattens[57]		1567
London, St Mary Magdalen, Milk Street[58]	1560–1	1613
London, St Michael Cornhill[59]	1587	
London, St Michael le Quern[60]	1560	1577
London, St Mildred Bread Street[61]		1648
London, St Olave Jewry[62]		1588

46 GL, MS 1303/1, fol. 4r.

47 J.P. Malcolm, *Londinium Redivivum or An Antient History and Modern Description of London*, 327.

48 GL, MS 1454/65.

49 GL, MS 9325/1, fol. 66r.

50 E. Freshfield, ed., *Accomptes of the Churchwardens of the Paryshe of St Christofer's in London 1575–1662*, 17; GL, MS 4423/1, fol. 19v.

51 GL, MS 4241/1, p. 69.

52 GL, MS 6836/1, fol. 68r.

53 GL, MS 4810/1, fols. 12v, 22r. The purchase in 1560 is of a single volume and is perhaps the second volume of *Paraphrases* as the inventory records possession of both volumes.

54 GL, MS 2593/1, fol. 5v.

55 William Blades, *Books in Chains*, 59.

56 GL, MS 1176/1, inventory 1577.

57 GL, MS 4570/2, p. 452.

58 GL, MS 2596/1, fol. 124r. This entry seems to indicate that the parish bought both volumes, but when an inventory was drawn up in 1613, only one book was mentioned: GL, MS 2596/2, Inventory 1613.

59 W.H. Overall, ed., *The Accounts of the Churchwardens of the Parish of St Michael, Cornhill in the City of London*, 176.

60 GL, MS 2895/1, fols. 171r, 286v.

61 GL, MS 3470/1A, fol. 5v.

62 GL, MS 4409/1, fol. 5v.

Parish	*Purchase*	*Inventory*
London, St Pancras Soper Lane[63]		1617
London, St Peter West Cheap[64]	1559–60	
London, St Stephen Walbrook[65]	1561	
Ludlow, Shropshire[66]	1576–7	
Mancetter, Warwickshire[67]		1923
Marlborough, Wiltshire[68]		1574
Melksham, Wiltshire[69]		1575
Menheniot, Cornwall[70]		1578
Mere, Wiltshire[71]	1559–61	
Morebath, Devon[72]	1564	
Newport, Essex[73]		1661
North Elmham, Norfolk[74]		1586
North Newington, Wiltshire[75]		1576
Northill, Bedfordshire[76]		1612
Norwich, St Mary Coslany[77]		1627
Peterborough, St John the Baptist[78]	1565	
Pittington, Durham[79]		1584
Prescot, Lancashire[80]	1564–6	

63 GL, MS 5018/1, fol. 2v.

64 GL, MS 645/1, fol. 58r.

65 GL, MS 593/2, fol. 46r.

66 Thomas Wright, ed., *Churchwardens' Accounts of the Town of Ludlow in Shropshire*, 164.

67 Blades, *Books in Chains*, 65; Cox, *English Church Fittings*, 195.

68 CRO, Trowbridge, 1197/21.

69 CRO, Trowbridge, 1368/55.

70 CRO, Truro, DDP 144/5/2.

71 T.H. Baker, 'The Churchwardens' Accounts of Mere,' 31.

72 J.E. Binney, ed., *The Accounts of the Wardens of the Parish of Morebath, Devon 1520–73*, 219.

73 CRO, Chelmsford, D/P 15/8/1, inventory 1661.

74 C.H.E. White, ed., *The East Anglian, or Notes and Queries*, n.s., 6: 185.

75 E. Kite, 'Notes on the Churchwardens' Accounts of the Parish of North Newnton, Wilts,' 262. The parish bought a copy of the *Paraphrases on the Epistles*.

76 J.E. Farmiloe and R. Nixseaman, *Elizabethan Churchwardens' Accounts*, 59. The parish bought both volumes.

77 J. L'Estrange, 'The Church Goods of St Andrew and St Mary Coslany in the City of Norwich, temp. Edw. VI,' 77.

78 W.T. Mellows, ed., *Peterborough Local Administration*, 169, 171.

79 Barmby, *Churchwardens' Accounts*, 12.

80 F.A. Bailey, ed., *The Churchwardens' Accounts of Prescot, Lancashire 1523–1607*, 55, 59.

Parish	*Purchase*	*Inventory*
Reading, St Mary's, Berkshire[81]	1561	
Repton, Derbyshire[82]		1614
Rotherfield, Sussex[83]		1567
Rowington, Warwickshire[84]		1586
Salisbury, St Thomas, Wiltshire[85]	1560–1	
Smarden, Kent[86]		1636
South Newington, Oxfordshire[87]		1582
St Breock, Cornwall[88]		1560
St Columb Major, Cornwall[89]		1585
St Doddington, Northants[90]		1923
St Neot, Cornwall[91]		1602
St Oswald, Durham[92]		1605
St Peters, Hertfordshire[93]		1586
Staplegrove, Somerset[94]		1591
Stapleton, Shropshire[95]	unknown	
Steeple Ashton, Wiltshire[96]		1581

81 F.N. and A.G. Garry, eds., *The Churchwardens' Accounts of the Parish of St Mary's, Reading, Berks., 1550–1662*, 38. I owe this reference to Mr James Rosenzweig.

82 J.C. Cox, 'The Registers and Churchwardens' and Constables' Accounts of the Parish of Repton,' 32.

83 Canon Goodwyn, 'An Old Churchwardens' Account Book of Rotherfield,' 42.

84 J.W. Ryland, ed., *Records of Rowington*, 2: 90. In 1586 the parish paid 5s for covering 'the paraphras boke.' I owe this reference to Mr James Rosenzweig.

85 H.J.F. Swayne, ed., *Churchwardens' Accounts of S. Edmund and S. Thomas, Sarum 1443–1702*, 281.

86 F. Haslewood, *Memorials of Smarden, Kent*, 252–3.

87 E.R.C. Brinkworth, ed., *South Newington Churchwardens' Accounts, 1553–1684*, 1.

88 CRO, Truro, DDP 19/5/1, fol. 4v.

89 CRO, Truro, DDP 36/8/1, fol. 2r.

90 Cox, *English Church Fittings*, 195.

91 CRO, Truro, DDP 162/5/1.

92 Barmby, *Churchwardens' Accounts*, 141.

93 A. Palmer, *Tudor Churchwardens' Accounts*, 126.

94 BL, Add MS 30278, fol. 8v.

95 CRO, Shrewsbury, 883/568.

96 CRO, Trowbridge, 730/97/1. This is a curious case. Although the inventory records the presence of the *Paraphrases*, the volume that survives to this day in the parish is a 1542 edition of Erasmus' *Annotations* in Latin. There may be another explanation for what appears to be an error on the part of the churchwardens.

Parish	*Purchase*	*Inventory*
Stoke Charity, Hampshire[97]	1560/1	
Strood, Kent[98]		1565
Sutton on Lound, Nottinghamshire[99]	unknown	
Tavistock, Devon[100]	1561/2	
Tenterden, Kent[101]		1642
Thame, Oxfordshire[102]	1565	
Ubley, Somerset[103]		1923
Westbury, Wiltshire[104]		1911
West Tarring, Sussex[105]	1568	
Wimborne, Dorset[106]	unknown	
Windermere, Westmoreland[107]		1923
Winterslow, Wiltshire[108]	1560	
Writtle, Essex[109]		1607
Youlgreave, Derbyshire[110]		1604

97 Williams, *The Early Churchwardens' Accounts of Hampshire*, 86.

98 BL, Additional MS 36,937, fol. 28r; H. Plomer, *The Churchwardens' Accounts of St Nicholas, Strood*, 17.

99 Cambridge University Library, Sel. 3. 84.

100 R.N. Worth, *Calendar of the Tavistock Parish Records*, 26.

101 CRO, Maidstone, P364/5/14, Inventory 1642.

102 F.G. Lee, *The History, Description, and Antiquities of the Prebendal Church of the Blessed Virgin Mary of Thame in the County and Diocese of Oxford*, 78.

103 Cox, *English Church Fittings*, 195

104 E. Kite, 'Notes on North Newnton Churchwardens' Accounts,' 262.

105 W.J. Pressey, 'The Churchwardens' Accounts of West Tarring, Sussex,' 109, 110.

106 Cox, *English Church Fittings*, 197. Cox gives no date for the evidence that the Wimborne parish spent 3s 4d 'for three chaynes of iron with plates and for the fastenyngs of the Bible, Paraphras of Erasmus, and Mr Juells booke in the Church.' The payment is probably from the second decade of the reign of King James.

107 Blades, *Books in Chains*, 37; Cox, *English Church Fittings*, 195.

108 W. Symonds, 'Winterslow Church Reckonings 1542–1661,' 38.

109 CRO, Chelmsford, D/P 50/5/1, no. 23.

110 CRO, Matlock, D3644/42/1.

Bibliography

Adams, Robert M., ed. and trans. *Desiderius Erasmus: The Praise of Folly and Other Writings*. New York: W.W. Norton and Co., 1989.

Aichele, George, et al. (The Bible and Culture Collective). *The Postmodern Bible*. New Haven: Yale University Press, 1995.

Aldridge, John William. *The Hermeneutic of Erasmus*. Richmond, VA: John Knox Press, 1966.

Alexander, Loveday. *The Preface to Luke's Gospel: Literary Convention and Social Context in Luke 1: 1–4 and Acts 1: 1*. Cambridge: Cambridge University Press, 1993.

Amphlett, J., ed. *The Churchwardens' Accounts of St Michael's in Bedwardine, Worcester 1539–1603*. Oxford: Worcestershire Historical Society, 1896.

Asso, Cecilia. *La teologia e la grammatica: La controversia tra Erasmo ed Edward Lee*. Florence: Leo S. Olschki Editore, 1993.

Ayris, P., and David Selwyn, eds. *Thomas Cranmer, Churchman and Scholar*. Woodbridge: Boydell and Brewer, 1993.

B., W.H. 'Chippenham Parish Church.' *Wiltshire Notes and Queries* 5 (1908): 168–9.

Backus, Irena. 'Ulrich Zwingli, Martin Bucer and the Church Fathers.' In *The Reception of the Church Fathers in the West: From the Carolingians to the Maurists*. Ed. Irena Backus. 2 vols. Leiden: E.J. Brill, 1997. 2: 627–60.

– 'Christoph Scheurl and His Anthology of New Testament Apocrypha.' *Apocrypha* 9 (1998): 133–56.

– *Reformation Readings of the Apocalypse: Geneva, Zurich, and Wittenberg*. Oxford: Oxford University Press, 2000.

Bailey, F.A., ed. *The Churchwardens' Accounts of Prescot, Lancashire 1523–1607*. Preston: Record Society of Lancashire and Cheshire, 1953.

Bainton, Roland H. 'The Paraphrases of Erasmus.' *Archiv für Reformationsgeschichte* 57 (1966): 67–76.

Baker, T.H. 'The Churchwardens' Accounts of Mere.' *Wiltshire Archaeological and Natural History Magazine* 35 (1908): 23–92.

Bale, John. *Select Works of John Bale, D.D.* Ed. Henry Christmas. Cambridge: Cambridge University Press for the Parker Society, 1849.

Barmby, J., ed. *Churchwardens' Accounts of Pittington and Other Parishes in the Diocese of Durham, 1580–1700*. Surtees Society 84. Durham: Andrews and Co., 1888.

Barnard, E., ed. *Churchwardens' Accounts of the Parish of Badsey, with Aldington, in Worcestershire, 1525–1571*. Hampstead: Priory Press, 1913.

Bateman, John J. 'From Soul to Soul: Persuasion in Erasmus' *Paraphrases on the NewTestament*.' *Erasmus in English* 15 (1987–88): 7–16.

Bauckham, Richard. *Tudor Apocalypse: Sixteenth-Century Apocalypticism, Millenarianism, and the English Reformation*. Appleford: Sutton Courtenay, 1976.

Baudrier, Henri-Louis, Julien Baudrier, et al. *Bibliographie lyonnaise: Recherches sur les imprimeurs, libraires, relieurs et fondeurs de lettres de Lyon au XVIe siècle*. 12 vols. (1895–1921). Rep. Paris: F. de Nobele, 1964.

Bauer, Walter. 'Matth. 19, 12 und die alten Christen.' In *Neutestamentliche Studien, Georg Heinrici zu seinem 70. Geburtstag*. Ed. Adolf Deißmann and Hans Windisch. Leipzig: J.C. Hinrichs, 1914. 235–44.

Beare, F.W. *The Epistle to the Philippians*. 3d ed. London: Adam and Charles Black, 1973.

Bedouelle, Guy, and Bernard Roussel, eds. *Le temps des Réformes et la Bible*. Paris: Beauchesne, 1989.

Bentley, Jerry H. *Humanists and Holy Writ: New Testament Scholarship in the Renaissance*. Princeton: Princeton University Press, 1983.

Berchthold, Alfred. *Bâle et l'Europe: Une histoire culturelle*. 2 vols. Lausanne: Payot, 1990.

Best, Ernest. *A Critical and Exegetical Commentary on Ephesians*. Edinburgh: T. & T. Clark, 1998.

Bezzel, Irmgard. *Erasmusdrucke des sechszehnten Jahrhunderts in bayerischen Bibliotheken*. Stuttgart: A. Hiersemann, 1979.

Bietenholz, Peter G. *History and Biography in the Work of Erasmus of Rotterdam*. Geneva: Droz, 1966.

– 'Erasmus und der Basler Buchhandel in Frankreich.' In J. Coppens, ed., *Scrinium Erasmianum*, 1: 293–323.

– *Basle and France in the Sixteenth Century: The Basle Humanists and Printers in Their Contacts with Francophone Culture*. Geneva: Droz, 1971.
Binney, J.E., ed. *The Accounts of the Wardens of the Parish of Morebath, Devon 1520–1573*. Exeter: James G. Commin, 1904.
Blades, W. *Books in Chains and Other Bibliographical Papers*. London: Elliot Stock, 1892.
Blatt, Thora Balslev. *The Plays of John Bale: A Study of Ideas, Technique and Style*. Copenhagen: G.E.C. Gad, 1968.
Bodenstedt, M.I. *The Vita Christi of Ludolphus the Carthusian*. Washington: Catholic University of America Press, 1955.
Bond, Ronald B., ed. *Certain Sermons or Homilies (1547) and a Homily against Disobedience and Wilful Rebellion (1570)*. Toronto: University of Toronto Press, 1987.
Bori, Pier Cesare. *L'interprétation infinie: L'herméneutique chrétienne ancienne et ses transformations*. Paris: Seuil, 1998.
Bourdieu, Pierre. *The Field of Cultural Production: Essays on Art and Literature*. Ed. Randal Johnson. New York: Columbia University Press, 1993.
– *The Rules of Art: Genesis and Structure of the Literary Field*. Trans. Susan Emanuel. Stanford: Stanford University Press, 1996.
Boyle, Marjorie O'Rourke. *Erasmus on Language and Method in Theology*. Toronto: University of Toronto Press, 1977.
– 'Erasmus' Prescription for Henry VIII: Logotherapy.' *Renaissance Quarterly* 31 (1978): 161–72.
Bray, Gerald, ed. *Documents of the English Reformation*. Minneapolis: Fortress Press, 1994.
Brewer, J.S., et al., eds. *Letters and Papers, Foreign and Domestic of the Reign of Henry VIII*. 21 vols. London: Longman, Green et al., 1862–1932.
Brinkworth, E.R.C., ed. *South Newington Churchwardens' Accounts, 1553–1684*. Headington, Oxford: Banbury Historical Society, 1964.
Brown, Peter. *The Body and Society: Men, Women and Sexual Renunciation in Early Christianity*. New York: Columbia University Press, 1988.
Buisson, Ferdinand. *Sébastien Castellion, sa vie et son oeuvre (1515–1563): Étude sur les origines du protestantisme libéral français*. 2 vols. (1892). Repr. Nieuwkoop: B. de Graaf, 1964.
Cardwell, Edward, ed. *Synodalia: A Collection of Articles of Religion, Canons, and Proceedings of Convocations in the Province of Canterbury, from the Year 1547 to the Year 1717*. Vol. 1. Oxford, 1842. Repr. Farnborough: Gregg Press, 1966.
Carlson, David R. *English Humanist Books: Writers and Patrons, Manuscript and Print, 1475–1525*. Toronto: University of Toronto Press, 1993.

Cave, Terence. *The Cornucopian Text: Problems of Writing in the French Renaissance*. Oxford: Clarendon Press, 1979.

de Certeau, Michel. *The Practice of Everyday Life*. Trans. Steven Rendall. Berkeley: University of California Press, 1984.

– *The Writing of History*. Trans. Tom Conley. New York: Columbia University Press, 1988.

Chantraine, Georges. 'Le musterion paulinien selon les *Annotations* d'Erasme.' *Revue des sciences religieuses* 58 (1970): 351–82.

Chomarat, Jacques. *Grammaire et rhétorique chez Érasme*. 2 vols. Paris: Les Belles Lettres, 1981.

– 'Grammar and Rhetoric in the Paraphrases of the Gospels by Erasmus.' ERSY 1 (1981): 30–68.

Christianson, Paul. *Reformers and Babylon: English Apocalyptic Visions from the Reformation to the Eve of the Civil War*. Toronto: University of Toronto Press, 1978.

Clark, Elizabeth A. *Reading Renunciation: Asceticism and Scripture in Early Christianity*. Princeton: Princeton University Press, 1999.

Clark, Elizabeth A., and Diane Hatch, eds. and trans. *The Golden Bough, the Oaken Cross: The Virgilian Cento of Faltonia Betitia Proba*. Chico, CA: Scholars Press, 1981.

Clark, Stuart. *Thinking with Demons: The Idea of Witchcraft in Early Modern Europe*. Oxford: Clarendon Press, 1997.

Clausi, Benedetto. *Ridar voce all'antico Padre: L'edizione erasmiana delle 'Lettere' di Gerolamo*. Soveria Mannelli: Rubbettino, 2000.

Collected Works of Erasmus. Toronto: University of Toronto Press, 1974–.

Contemporaries of Erasmus: A Biographical Register of the Renaissance and Reformation. Ed. P.G. Bietenholz and T.B. Deutscher. 3 vols. Toronto: University of Toronto Press, 1985–87.

Coppens, J., ed. *Scrinium Erasmianum*. 2 vols. Leiden: E.J. Brill, 1969.

Cornilliat, François. 'Exemplarities: A Response to Timothy Hampton and Karlheinz Stierle.' *Journal of the History of Ideas* 68 (1998): 613–24.

Corpus christianorum, series latina. Turnhout: Brepols, 1954–.

Corpus scriptorum ecclesiasticorum latinorum. Vienna: 1866–.

Cowper, J.M. 'Accounts of the Churchwardens of St Dunstan's, Canterbury A.D. 1484–1580.' *Archaeologia Cantiana* 17 (1887): 77–149.

Cox, J.C. 'The Registers and Churchwardens' and Constables' Accounts of the Parish of Repton.' *Journal of the Derbyshire Archaeological and Natural History Society* 1 (1879): 27–41.

– *English Church Fittings, Furniture and Accessories*. London: B.T. Batsford, 1923.

Cox, J.C., and W.H. St John Hope, *The Chronicles of the Collegiate Church or Free Chapel of All Saints Derby*. London: Bemrose and Sons, 1881.

Craib, T. 'Blechingley Churchwardens' Accounts, 1546–1552.' *Surrey Archaeological Collections* 29 (1916): 25–33.

Craig, John. 'The "Cambridge Boies": Thomas Rogers and the "Brethren" in Bury St Edmunds.' In S. Wabuda and C. Litzenberger, eds., *Belief and Practice in Reformation England*. Aldershot: Ashgate, 1998. 154–76.

Cressy, David. *Travesties and Transgressions in Tudor and Stuart England*. Oxford: Oxford University Press, 2000.

Crosthwaite, J.C. 'Ancient Churchwardens' Accounts of a City Parish.' *The British Magazine, and Monthly Register of Religious and Ecclesiastical Information, Parochial History and Documents respecting the State of the Poor, Progress of Education etc.* (London: John Petheram) 34 (1848): 15–33, 171–87, 292–307, 395–409, 524–33, 674–81; 35 (1849): 50–7, 178–86, 273–84, 396–405, 520–9, 635–42.

Curtius, Ernst Robert. *European Literature and the Latin Middle Ages*. Trans. Willard R. Trask. Princeton: Princeton University Press, 1953.

Cussans, J.E., ed. *Inventory of Furniture and Ornaments Remaining in All the Parish Churches of Hertfordshire in the Last Year of the Reign of King Edward the Sixth*. Oxford and London: James Parker and Co., 1873.

Davis, C.T. 'Early Churchwardens' Accounts of Wandsworth, 1545–1558.' *Surrey Archaeological Collections* 15 (1900): 80–127.

Delègue, Yves, ed. with the collaboration of Jean-Paul Gillet. *Érasme: Les Préfaces au Novum Testamentum*. Geneva: Labor et Fides, 1990.

Deming, Will. *Paul on Marriage and Celibacy: The Hellenistic Background of 1 Corinthians 7*. Cambridge: Cambridge University Press, 1995.

Denifle, H., and E. Chatelain, eds. *Chartularium Universitatis Parisiensis*. Paris: Delalain, 1897.

Des. Erasmi Roterodami opera omnia. Ed. J. Leclerc. 10 vols. Leiden: 1703–6.

Desgraves, L., et al., eds. *Répertoire bibliographique des livres imprimés en France au seizième siècle*. 30 vols. Baden-Baden: Heitz; V. Koerner, 1968–80.

Desiderius Erasmus Roterodamus: Ausgewählte Werke. Ed. A. and H. Holborn. Munich: C.H. Beck, 1933.

Devereux, E.J. 'English Translators of Erasmus 1522–1557.' In R.J. Shoeck, ed., *Editing Sixteenth Century Texts*. Toronto: University of Toronto Press, 1966. 43–58.

– 'The Publication of the English *Paraphrases* of Erasmus.' *Bulletin of the John Rylands Library* 51 (1969): 348–67.

– *Renaissance English Translations of Erasmus: A Bibliography to 1700*. Toronto: University of Toronto Press, 1983.

Dictionary of National Biography. Oxford: Oxford University Press, 1885–.

Doree, S.G., ed. *The Early Churchwardens' Accounts of Bishops Stortford, 1431–1558*. Hertfordshire Record Publications 10. N.p.: Hertfordshire Record Society, 1994.

Dowling, Maria. *Humanism in the Age of Henry VIII*. London: Croom Helm, 1986.

Duffy, Eamon. *The Stripping of the Altars*. New Haven: Yale University Press, 1992.

Dufour, Théophile. *Le secret des textes: Opuscules inédits de critique et d'histoire*. Lausanne: Payot, 1925.

Dupont, Jacques. *Mariage et divorce dans l'Évangile: Matthieu 19, 3–12 et parallèles*. Bruges: Desclée de Brouwer, 1959.

Duval, Yves-Marie. 'Les premiers rapports de Paulin de Nole avec Jérôme: Moine et philosophe? Poète ou exégète?' In *Polyanthema: Studi di letteratura cristiana antica offerti a Salvatore Costanza*. 2 vols. Messina: Sicania, 1989. 1: 177–216.

Dyck, Andrew R. *A Commentary on Cicero, De Officiis*. 2 vols. Ann Arbor: University of Michigan Press, 1996.

Earwaker, J.P. *The History of the Church and Parish of St Mary-on-the-Hill, Chester*. London: Love and Wyman, 1898.

Eden, Kathy. *Hermeneutics and the Rhetorical Tradition: Chapters in the Ancient Legacy and Its Humanist Reception*. New Haven: Yale University Press, 1997.

Edgerton, W.L. *Nicholas Udall*. New York: Twayne Publishers, 1965.

– 'The Apostasy of Nicholas Udall.' *Notes and Queries* 195 (1950): 223–6.

Eeles, F.C., ed. *The Edwardian Inventories for Bedfordshire*. London: Longmans, Green and Co., 1905.

– *The Edwardian Inventories for Buckinghamshire*. London: Longmans, Green and Co., 1908.

Eisenstein, Elizabeth L. *The Printing Press as an Agent of Change: Communications and Cultural Transformations in Early-Modern Europe*. 2 vols. Cambridge: Cambridge University Press, 1979.

Erasmi opuscula. Ed. W.K. Ferguson. The Hague: M. Nijhoff, 1933.

Fairfield, Leslie P. *John Bale: Mythmaker for the English Reformation*. West Lafayette, IN: Purdue University Press, 1976.

Farge, James K. *Biographical Register of Paris Doctors of Theology, 1500–1536*. Toronto: Pontifical Institute of Mediaeval Studies, 1980.

– *Orthodoxy and Reform in Early Reformation France: The Faculty of Theology of Paris 1500–1543*. Leiden: E.J. Brill, 1985.

– 'Texts and Context of a Mentalité: The Parisian University Milieu in the Age of Erasmus.' In Erika Rummel, ed., *Editing Texts from the Age of Erasmus*. Toronto: University of Toronto Press, 1996. 3–24.

Farge, James K., ed. *Registre des procès-verbaux de la Faculté de théologie de l'Université de Paris: De janvier 1524 à novembre 1533*. Paris: Aux amateurs de livres, 1990.

Farmiloe, J.E., and R. Nixseaman. *Elizabethan Churchwardens' Accounts*. Streatley, Bedfordshire: Bedfordshire Historical Record Society, 1953.

Febvre, Lucien, and Henri-Jean Martin. *The Coming of the Book: The*

Impact of Printing 1450–1800. Trans. David Gerard. Ed. Geoffrey Nowell-Smith and David Wootton. London: New Left Books, 1976.

Fehrenbach, R.J., and E.S. Leedham-Green. *Private Libraries in Renaissance England: A Collection and Catalogue of Tudor and Early Stuart Book Lists*. 5 vols. Binghamton, NY: MRTS, 1990–6.

Fincham, Kenneth, ed. *Visitation Articles and Injunctions of the Early Stuart Church*. 2 vols. Woodbridge, Suffolk: Boydell Press, 1994–8.

Firth, Katharine R. *The Apocalyptic Tradition in Reformation Britain*. Oxford: Oxford University Press, 1979.

Fitzmyer, Joseph A. *The Gospel According to Luke (I–IX)*. New York: Doubleday, 1981.

Fontaine, Jacques. 'L'apport d'Hilaire à une théorie chrétienne de l'esthétique du style (remarques sur In psalmos 13).' In *Hilaire et son temps: Actes du colloque de Poitiers, septembre–octobre 1968*. Paris: Études Augustiniennes, 1969. 287–305.

Foster, J.E., ed. *Churchwardens' Accounts of St Mary the Great, Cambridge 1504–1635*. Cambridge: Cambridge Antiquarian Society, 1905.

Fowler, Joseph. 'Post-Reformation Churchwardens' Accounts of St Mary's Sherborne.' *Somerset and Dorset Notes and Queries* 25 (1950): 7–11, 23–30, 55–9, 64–8, 83–7, 105–9, 122–6, 169–74, 187–9, 206–10, 226–9, 257–62, 268–9, 287–93.

Freeman, Thomas S. '"Great searching out of bookes and autors": John Foxe as an Ecclesiastical Historian.' Ph.D. diss. Rutgers University, 1995.

Frere, W.H., and W.P.M. Kennedy, eds. *Visitation Articles and Injunctions of the Period of the Reformation*. 3 vols. London: Longmans, Green and Co., 1910.

Freshfield, E., ed. *Accomptes of the Churchwardens of the Paryshe of St Christofer's in London 1575–1662*. London: privately printed, 1885.

Furger-Gunti, Andres, and Burkard von Roda, eds. *Erasmus von Rotterdam, Vorkämpfer für Frieden und Toleranz: Ausstellung zum 450. Todestag des Erasmus von Rotterdam*. Basel: Das Museum, 1986.

Garrett, Christina. *The Marian Exiles*. Cambridge: Cambridge University Press, 1938.

Garry, F.N., and A.G. Garry, eds. *The Churchwardens' Accounts of the Parish of St Mary's, Reading, Berks., 1550–1662*. Reading: Blackwell, 1893.

Gaudemet, Jean. *Le mariage en Occident*. Paris: Cerf, 1987.

Gilmont, Jean-François. 'En guise de conclusion ...' In Jean-François Gilmont, ed., *La Réforme et le livre: L'Europe de l'imprimé (1517–v.1570)*: 479–504.

– *La Réforme et le livre: L'Europe de l'imprimé (1517–v.1570)*. Paris: Cerf, 1990. English ed. and trans. Karin Maag. *The Reformation and the Book*. Aldershot: Ashgate, 1998.

Glasscock, J.L., ed. *The Records of St Michael's Parish Church, Bishop's Stortford*. London: Elliot Stock, 1882.

Godet, Frédéric. *Commentaire sur la première épître aux Corinthiens*. 2 vols. 2nd ed. Neuchatel: L.-A. Monnier, 1965.

Godfrey, J.T. *Notes on the Churches of Nottinghamshire Hundred of Bingham*. London: Phillimore and Co., 1907.

Goodwyn, [Canon]. 'An Old Churchwardens' Account Book of Rotherfield.' *Sussex Archaeological Collections* 41 (1898): 25–48.

Gowing, Laura. *Domestic Dangers: Women, Words and Sex in Early Modern London*.

Oxford: Clarendon Press, 1996.

Graham, R., ed. *The Chantry Certificates and Edwardian Inventories of Church Goods*. Oxford: Oxfordshire Record Society, 1919.

Greenslade, S.L., ed. *The Cambridge History of the Bible*. Vol. 3: *The West from the Reformation to the Present Day*. Cambridge: Cambridge University Press, 1963.

Grendler, P. 'How to Get a Degree in Fifteen Days: Erasmus' Doctorate of Theology from the University of Turin.' ERSY 18 (1998): 40–69.

Hadfield, Andrew. *Literature, Politics, and National Identity*. Cambridge: Cambridge University Press, 1994.

Haigh, Christopher, ed. *The English Reformation Revised*. Cambridge: Cambridge University Press, 1987.

– *English Reformations*. Oxford: Oxford University Press, 1993.

Hakluyt, Richard. *The Principal Navigations, Voyages, Traffiques and Discoveries of the English Nation*. Vol. 1. London: J.M. Dent and Sons, 1927.

Halkin, Léon-E. 'Érasme et le célibat sacerdotal.' *Revue d'histoire et de philoshophie religieuses* 57 (1977): 497–511.

Haller, William. *The Elect Nation: The Meaning and Relevance of Foxe's 'Book of Martyrs.'* New York: Harper and Row, 1963.

Hanham, A., ed. *Churchwardens' Accounts of Ashburton, 1479–1580*. Torquay: Devon and Cornwall Record Society, 1970.

Happé, Peter. *John Bale*. New York: Twayne, 1996.

Harris, Jesse W. *John Bale: A Study in the Minor Literature of the Reformation*. Urbana: University of Illinois Press, 1940.

Hartmann, Alfred, and B.R. Jenny, eds. *Die Amerbachkorrespondenz*. 5 vols. Basel: Verlag der Universitätsbibliothek, 1942–58.

Haslewood, F. *Memorials of Smarden, Kent*. Ipswich: privately printed, 1888.

Héring, Jean. *The First Epistle of Saint Paul to the Corinthians*. Trans. A.W. Heathcote and P.J. Allcock. London: Epworth Press, 1962.

Higman, Francis M. *Piety and the People: Religious Printing in French, 1511–1551*. Aldershot: Scolar Press, 1996.

Hobhouse [Bishop], ed. *Church-Wardens' Accounts of Croscombe, Pilton,*

Patton, Tintinhull, Morebath and St Michael's Bath: Ranging from AD 1349 to 1560. London: Somerset Record Society, 1890.

Hoffmann, Manfred. *Rhetoric and Theology: The Hermeneutic of Erasmus*. Toronto: University of Toronto Press, 1994.

Houlbrooke, Ralph. *Church Courts and the People during the English Reformation*. Oxford: Oxford University Press, 1979.

House, Violet, ed. *Stanford in the Vale Churchwardens' Accounts 1552–1725*. N.p.: privately printed, 1987.

Hughes, P.L., and J.F. Larkin, eds. *Tudor Royal Proclamations*. 2 vols. New Haven and London: Yale University Press, 1969.

Hurst, David, trans. *The Commentary on the Seven Catholic Epistles of Bede the Venerable*. Kalamazoo, MI: Cistercian Publications, 1985.

Hussey, Arthur. 'Visitations of the Archdeacon of Canterbury.' *Archaeologia Cantiana* 25 (1902): 11–56; 26 (1904): 17–50; 27 (1905): 213–29.

– 'Archbishop Parker's Visitation, 1569.' *The Home Counties Magazine* 5 (1903): 7–16, 113–19, 208–12, 285–9; 6 (1904): 27–32, 109–14.

Hutton, James. 'Erasmus and France: The Propaganda for Peace.' *Studies in the Renaissance* 8 (1961): 103–27.

Hutton, Ronald. 'The Local Impact of the Tudor Reformations.' In Christopher Haigh, ed., *The English Reformation Revised*. 114–38.

– *The Rise and Fall of Merry England*. Oxford: Oxford University Press, 1995.

IJsewijn, Jozef. 'Erasmus ex poeta theologus sive de literarum instauratarum apud Hollandos incunabulis.' In J. Coppens, ed., *Scrinium Erasmianum*. 1: 375–84.

Ingram, Martin. *Church Courts, Sex and Marriage in England, 1570–1640*. Cambridge: Cambridge University Press, 1987.

Jardine, Lisa. *Erasmus Man of Letters: The Construction of Charisma in Print*. Princeton: Princeton University Press, 1993.

Jeanneret, Michel. 'The Vagaries of Exemplarity: Distortion or Dismissal?' *Journal of the History of Ideas* 68 (1998): 565–79.

Johnston, J.A., ed. *Probate Inventories of Lincoln Citizens 1661–1714*. Woodbridge, Suffolk: Boydell Press, 1991.

de Jonge, H.J. 'Erasmus und die Glossa Ordinaria zum Neuen Testament.' *Nederlands Archief voor Kerkgeschiedenis* 56 (1975): 51–77.

– 'Novum Testamentum a nobis versum: The Essence of Erasmus' Edition of the New Testament.' *Journal of Theological Studies*, new ser. 35 (1984): 394–413.

Kelly, J.N.D. *A Commentary on the Pastoral Epistles*. London: Adam and Charles Black, 1963.

– *Jerome: His Life, Writings, and Controversies*. London: Duckwoth, 1975.

Kennedy, W.P.M. *Elizabethan Episcopal Administration*. 3 vols. London: A.R. Mowbray and Co., 1924.

King, John N. *English Reformation Literature: The Tudor Origins of the Protestant Tradition*. Princeton: Princeton University Press, 1982.

Kingdon, Robert. *Adultery and Divorce in Calvin's Geneva*. Cambridge, MA: Harvard University Press, 1995.

Kinowaki, Etsuro. 'Erasmus' *Paraphrasis in Epistolam Jacobi* and His Anthropology.' In Jacques Chomarat, André Godin, and Jean-Claude Margolin, eds., *Actes du Colloque International Erasme (Tours, 1986)*. Geneva: Droz, 1990. 153–60.

Kitching, C.J., ed. *The Royal Visitation of 1559: Act Book for the Northern Province*. Gateshead: Surtees Society, 1975.

Kite, E. 'Notes on the Churchwardens' Accounts of the Parish of North Newnton, Wilts.' *Wiltshire Notes and Queries* 6 (1911): 261–6.

Kitto, J.V., ed. *St Martin in the Fields: The Accounts of the Churchwardens 1525–1603*. London: Dryden Press, 1901.

Krüger, Friedhelm. *Humanistische Evangelienauslegung: Desiderius Erasmus von Rotterdam als Ausleger der Evangelien in seine Paraphrasen*. Tübingen: J.C.B. Mohr / Paul Siebeck, 1986.

Lacoque, André, and Paul Ricoeur. *Penser la Bible*. Paris: Seuil, 1998.

Lecler, Joseph. *Histoire de la tolérance en France au siècle de la Réforme*. 2 vols. Paris: Aubier, 1955.

Lee, F.G. *The History, Description, and Antiquities of the Prebendal Church of the Blessed Virgin Mary of Thame in the County and Diocese of Oxford*. London: Mitchell and Hughes, 1883.

Leedham-Green, E.S. *Books in Cambridge Inventories: Book Lists from Vice-chancellor's Court Probate Inventories in the Tudor and Stuart Periods*. 2 vols. Cambridge: Cambridge University Press, 1986.

L'Estrange, J. 'The Church Goods of St Andrew and St Mary Coslany in the City of Norwich, temp. Edw. VI.' *Norfolk Archaeology* 7 (1872): 45–78.

Lintott, Andrew. *The Constitution of the Roman Republic*. Oxford: Clarendon Press, 1999.

Littlehales, H. *The Medieval Records of a London City Church (St Mary at Hill)*. London: Kegan Paul, Trench, Trubner and Co., 1905.

Loades, David. 'The Press under the Early Tudors: A Study in Censorship and Sedition.' *Transactions of the Cambridge Bibliographical Society* 4 (1964): 29–50.

– *Politics, Censorship and the English Reformation*. London and New York: Pinter, 1991.

Loades, David, ed. *John Foxe and the English Reformation*. Aldershot: Scolar Press, 1997.

Lomas, S.C., ed. *The Edwardian Inventories for Huntingdonshire*. London: Longmans, Green and Co., 1906.

MacCulloch, Diarmaid. 'The Myth of the English Reformation.' *Journal of British Studies* 30 (1991): 1–19.

– *Thomas Cranmer: A Life*. New Haven: Yale University Press, 1996.
– *Tudor Church Militant: Edward VI and the Protestant Reformation*. London: Allen Lane, 1999.
MacDonald, Dennis Ronald. *The Legend and the Apostle: The Battle for Paul in Story and Canon*. Philadelphia: Westminster Press, 1983.
Malcolm, J.P. *Londinium Redivivum or An Antient History and Modern Description of London*. London: J. Nichols and Son, 1802.
Margolin, Jean-Claude. 'L'art du récit et du conte chez Érasme.' In *Érasme: Le prix des mots et de l'homme*. London: Variorum Reprints, 1986.
– 'Guillaume Haudent, poète et traducteur des "Apophtegmes" d'Érasme.' In *Érasme dans son mirroir et dans son sillage*. London: Variorum Reprints, 1987.
Marincola, John. *Authority and Tradition in Ancient Historiography*. Cambridge: Cambridge University Press, 1997.
Marsh, A. *A History of the Borough and Town of Calne*. Calne: Robert S. Heath, 1903.
Marsh, Christopher. *Popular Religion in Sixteenth Century England*. Basingstoke: Macmillan, 1998.
Marshall, I. Howard. *1 and 2 Thessalonians*. Grand Rapids, MI: William B. Eerdmans, 1983.
Martin, Henri-Jean, and Roger Chartier, eds. *Histoire de l'édition française*. Vol. 1: *Le livre conquérant: Du Moyen Âge au milieu du XVIIe siècle*. N.p.: Promodis, 1982.
Martyn, J. Louis. *Galatians: A New Translation with Introduction and Commentary*. New York: Doubleday, 1997.
Masters, B.R., and E. Ralph, eds. *The Church Book of St Ewen's Bristol, 1454–1584*. London and Ashford: Bristol and Gloucestershire Archaeological Society, 1967.
McConica, James K. *English Humanists and Reformation Politics under Henry VIII and Edward VI*. Oxford: Clarendon Press, 1965.
McCusker, Honor. *John Bale: Dramatist and Antiquary*. Bryn Mawr, 1942.
Mellows, W.T., ed. *Peterborough Local Administration*. Kettering: Northamptonshire Records Society, 1939.
Mercer, F.R. *Churchwardens' Accounts at Betrysden 1515–1573*. Ashford: Kent Archaeological Society, 1928.
Millar, Fergus. *The Emperor in the Roman World (31 B.C.–A.D. 337)*. London: Duckworth, 1977.
Moiser, Jeremy. 'A Reassessment of Paul's View of Marriage with Reference to 1 Cor. 7.' *Journal for the Study of the New Testament* 18 (1983): 103–22.
Money, W. *Parish Church Goods in Berkshire*. Oxford and London: James Parker and Co., 1879.

Nauwelaerts, M.A. 'Érasme à Louvain: Ephémérides d'un séjour de 1517 à 1521.' In J. Coppens, ed., *Scrinium Erasmianum*. 1: 3–24.

Nielsen, L.M. *Dansk Bibliografi*. 2 vols. Copenhagen: Gyldendal, 1919–33.

Northeast, P., ed. *Boxford Churchwardens' Accounts 1530–1561*. Woodbridge, Suffolk: Boydell Press, 1982.

Ogilvie, R.M. *A Commentary on Livy: Books 1–5*. Oxford: Clarendon Press, 1965.

Oliver, Leslie M. 'The Seventh Edition of John Foxe's *Acts and Monuments*.' *Papers of the Bibliographical Society of America* 37 (1943): 245–8.

Ollivier, Jules. 'Notice sur l'origine de l'imprimerie à Valence (Dauphiné).' *Bulletin du Bibliophile* 16 (1835): 13–16.

Olsen, V. Norskov. *The New Testament Logia on Divorce: A Study of Their Interpretation from Erasmus to Milton*. Tübingen: J.C.B. Mohr / Paul Siebeck, 1971.

O'Malley, John W. 'Erasmus and the History of Sacred Rhetoric: The *Ecclesiastes* of 1535.' *ERSY* 5 (1985): 1–29.

Opera omnia Des. Erasmi Roterodami. Amsterdam: North-Holland Publishing Company, 1969–.

Opus epistolarum Des. Erasmi Roterodami. Ed. P.S. Allen, H.M. Allen, and H.W. Garrod. 12 vols. Oxford: Clarendon Press, 1906–58.

O'Sullivan, Orlaith, ed. *The Bible as Book: The Reformation*. London, New Castle, DE: The British Library / Oak Knoll Press, 2000.

Overall, W.H., ed. *The Accounts of the Churchwardens of the Parish of St Michael, Cornhill in the City of London*. London: A.J. Waterlow, n.d.

Pabel, Hilmar M. 'Promoting the Business of the Gospel: Erasmus' Contribution to Pastoral Ministry.' ERSY 15 (1995): 53–70.

– 'Erasmus of Rotterdam and Judaism: A Reexamination in Light of New Evidence.' *Archiv für Reformationsgeschichte* 87 (1996): 9–37.

– 'Retelling the History of the Early Church: Erasmus's *Paraphrase on Acts*.' *Church History* 69 (2000): 63–85.

Palmer, A. *Tudor Churchwardens' Accounts* [for Hertfordshire]. N.p.: Hertfordshire Record Society, 1985.

Parker, Patricia. 'On the Tongue: Cross Gendering, Effeminacy and the Art of Words.' *Style* 23 (1989): 445–65.

Patrologia graeca. Ed. J.-P. Migne. 162 vols. Paris: 1857–66.

Patrologia latina. Ed. J.-P. Migne. 221 vols. Paris: 1844–64.

Payne, John B. *Erasmus: His Theology of the Sacraments*. Richmond, VA: John Knox Press, 1970.

Pease, Arthur Stanley. *M. Tulli Ciceronis De Natura Deorum*. 2 vols. Cambridge, MA: Harvard University Press, 1958.

Peery, W. 'Udall as Time Server.' *Notes and Queries* 194 (1949): 119–21, 138–41.

Pelikan, Jaroslav, Valerie R. Hotchkiss, and David Price. *The Reformation of the Bible / The Bible of the Reformation*. New Haven: Yale University Press, 1996.

Pergnier, Maurice. *Les fondements socio-linguistiques de la traduction*. Rev. ed. Lille: Presses Universitaires de Lille, 1993.

Peter, Rodolphe, and Jean-François Gilmont, eds. *Bibliotheca Calviniana: Les oeuvres de Jean Calvin publiées au XVIe siècle*. Vol. 1: *1532–1554*. Geneva: Droz, 1991.

Phillips, Jane E. 'The Gospel, the Clergy, and the Laity in Erasmus' *Paraphrase on the Gosepl of John*.' ERSY 10 (1990): 85–100.

– 'Food and Drink in Erasmus' Gospel Paraphrases.' ERSY 14 (1994): 24–45.

Phillips, Margaret Mann. 'Erasmus in France in the later Sixteenth Century.'*Journal of The Warburg and Courtauld Institutes* 34 (1971): 246–61.

– 'The Mystery of the Metsys Portrait.' *Erasmus in English* 7 (1975): 18–21.

Phillips, Roderick. *Putting Asunder: A History of Divorce in Western Society*. Cambridge: Cambridge University Press, 1988.

Plomer, H. *The Churchwardens' Accounts of St Nicholas, Strood*. Ashford: Kent Archaeological Society, 1927.

Poinsotte, Jean-Michel. 'Jérôme et la poésie chrétienne.' In Yves-Marie Duval, ed., *Jérôme entre l'Occident et l'Orient: Actes du colloque de Chantilly (septembre 1986)*. Paris: Études Augustiniennes, 1988. 295–303.

Pressey, W.J. 'The Churchwardens' Accounts of West Tarring, Sussex.' *Sussex Notes and Queries* 3 (1930–1) 18–21, 42–6, 77–80, 145–9, 179–84, 209–14, 240–5.

Purvis, J.S. 'The Churchwardens' Book of Sheriff Hutton, AD 1524–1568.' *Yorkshire Archaeological Journal* 36 (1944–7): 178–89.

Purvis, J.S., ed. *Tudor Parish Documents of the Diocese of York*. Cambridge: Cambridge University Press, 1948.

Quesnell, Quentin. 'Made Themselves Eunuchs for the Kingdom of Heaven (Mt 19, 12).' *Catholic Biblical Quarterly* 30 (1968): 335–58.

Rabil, Albert, Jr. 'Erasmus's Paraphrases of the New Testament.' In Richard L. DeMolen, ed., *Essays on the Works of Erasmus*. New Haven: Yale University Press, 1978.

Reed, M., ed. *The Ipswich Probate Inventories 1583–1631*. Woodbridge, Suffolk: Boydell Press, 1981.

Reese, Alan W. 'Learning Virginity: Erasmus' Ideal of Christian Marriage.' *Bibliothèque d'Humanisme et Renaissance* 57 (1995): 551–67.

Reeve, Anne, ed. *Erasmus' Annotations on the New Testament: Galatians to the Apocalypse*. Leiden: E.J. Brill, 1993.

Rex, R. 'The Role of English Humanists in the Reformation up to 1559.' In N. Scott Amos, Andrew Pettegree, and Henk van Nierop, eds., *The Education of a Christian Society*. Aldershot: Ashgate, 1999. 19–40.

Roberts, E., and K. Parker, eds. *Southampton Probate Inventories 1447–1575*. 2 vols. Southampton: Southampton Records Series, 1991–2.

Roberts, Michael. *Biblical Epic and Rhetorical Paraphrase in Late Antiquity.* Liverpool: Francis Cairns, 1985.

Roberts, R.A. 'Further Inventories of the Goods and Ornaments of the Churches in the County of Surrey in the Reign of King Edward the Sixth.' *Surrey Archaeological Collections* 21 (1903): 33–82.

Robson-Scott, W.D. 'Josua Maler's Visit to England in 1551.' *Modern Language Review* (1950): 346–51.

– *German Travellers in England 1400–1800.* Oxford: Oxford University Press, 1953.

Rosner, Brian S. *Paul, Scripture and Ethics: A Study of 1 Corinthians 5–7.* Leiden: E.J. Brill, 1994.

Rummel, Erika. *Erasmus' Annotations on the New Testament: From Philologist to Theologian.* Toronto: University of Toronto Press, 1986.

– 'God and Solecism: Erasmus as a Critic of the Bible.' ERSY 7 (1987): 54–72.

– *Erasmus and His Catholic Critics.* 2 vols. Nieuwkoop: De Graaf, 1989.

Rummel, Erika, ed. *Editing Texts in the Age of Erasmus.* Toronto: University of Toronto Press, 1996.

Ryland, J.W., ed. *Records of Rowington.* Vol. 2. Oxford: Oxford University Press, 1922.

Saenger, Paul, and Kimberly Van Kampen, eds. *The Bible as Book: The First Printed Editions.* London, New Castle, DE: The British Library, Oak Knoll Press, 1999.

Sand, Alexander. *Reich Gottes und Eheverzicht im Evangelium nach Matthäus.* Stuttgart: Verlag Katholisches Bibelwerk, 1983.

Scarisbrick, J.J. *The Reformation and the English People.* Oxford: Blackwell, 1984.

Scott, W.T. *Antiquities of an Essex Parish, or Pages from the History of Great Dunmow.* London: H.S. King and Co., 1873.

Screech, M.A. *Ecstasy and the Praise of Folly.* London: Duckworth, 1980.

Sharpe, J.A. *Instruments of Darkness: Witchcraft in England 1550–1750.* London: Hamish Hamilton, 1996.

Shoeck, R.J. *Erasmus of Europe: The Prince of Humanists, 1501–1536.* Edinburgh: Edinburgh University Press, 1993.

A Short-Title Catalogue of Books Printed In England, Scotland, & Ireland and of English Books Printed Abroad 1475–1640. Ed. A.W. Pollard, G.R. Redgrave, and K. Panzer. 2d ed. 3 vols. London: Bibliographical Society, 1976–91.

Sider, Robert D. '*Concedo nulli*: Erasmus' Motto and the Figure of Paul in the Paraphrases.' *Erasmus in English* 14 (1985–6): 7–10.

– 'Literary Artifice and the Figure of Paul in the Writings of Tertullian.' In William S. Babcock, ed., *Paul and the Legacies of Paul.* Dallas: Southern Methodist University Press, 1990. 99–120.

– 'The Just and the Holy in Erasmus' New Testament Scholarship.' ERSY 11 (1991): 1–27.

Somers, F., ed. *Halesowen Churchwardens' Accounts 1487–1582*. London: Worcestershire Historical Society, 1957.
Swayne, H.J.F., ed. *Churchwardens' Accounts of S. Edmund and S. Thomas, Sarum 1443–1702*. Salisbury: Wiltshire Record Society, 1896.
Sweeting, W.D. 'Leverington Churchwardens' Accounts.' *Fenland Notes and Queries* 7 (1909): 184–90, 203–7, 247–51, 271–5, 297–302, 329–34.
Symonds, W. 'Winterslow Church Reckonings 1542–1661.' *Wiltshire Archaelogical and Natural History Magazine* 36 (1910): 27–49.
Tallon, Alain. *La France et le Concile de Trente (1518–1563)*. Rome: École Française de Rome, 1997.
Taylor, J.G. *Our Lady of Batersey*. Chelsea: George White, 1925.
Telle, Emile V. *Érasme de Rotterdam et le septième sacrement*. Geneva: Droz, 1954.
Thomas, Keith. *Religion and the Decline of Magic: Studies in Popular Beliefs in Sixteenth- and Seventeenth-Century England*. London: Weidenfeld and Nicolson, 1971.
Thompson, Craig. 'Erasmus and Tudor England.' In C. Reedijk, ed., *Actes du Congres Erasme*. Amsterdam: North Holland Publishing Co., 1971. 29–68.
Thompson, James. *The History of Leicester*. Leicester: J.S. Crossley, 1849.
Trapp, J.B. *Erasmus, Colet and More: The Early Tudor Humanists and Their Books*. London: The British Library, 1991.
Turchetti, Mario. *Concordia o tolleranza: François Bauduin (1520–1573) e i 'moyenneurs.'* Geneva: Droz, 1984.
– 'Une question mal posée: Erasme et la tolérance. L'idée de *sygkatabasis*.' *Bibliothèque d'Humanisme et Renaissance* 53 (1991): 379–95.
Tyacke, Nicholas. 'Introduction: Re-thinking the "English Reformation."' In N. Tyacke, ed., *England's Long Reformation 1500–1800*. London: UCL Press, 1998. 1–32.
Tyssen, J.R.D. *Inventories of the Goods and Ornaments in the Churches of Surrey in the Reign of King Edward the Sixth*. London: Wyman and Sons, 1869.
Valkhoff, Marius F., ed. *Sébastien Castellion: Conseil à la France désolée*. Geneva: Droz, 1967.
Versnel, H.S. *Triumphus: An Inquiry into the Origin, Development and Meaning of the Roman Triumph*. Leiden: E.J. Brill, 1970.
Vessey, Mark. 'Conference and Confession: Literary Pragmatics in Augustine's "Apologia contra Hieronymum."' *Journal of Early Christian Studies* 1 (1993): 175–213.
– 'Erasmus' Jerome: The Publishing of a Christian Author.' ERSY 14 (1994): 62–99.
Wabuda, Susan. 'The Woman with the Rock: The Controversy on Women and Bible Reading.' In S. Wabuda and C.J. Litzenberger, eds., *Belief and Practice in Reformation England*. Aldershot: Ashgate, 1998. 40–59.

Walbank, F.W. *A Historical Commentary on Polybius*. 3 vols. Oxford: Clarendon Press, 1957–79.

Walcott, M.E.C., R.P. Coates, and W.A.S. Robertson. 'Inventories of Parish Church Goods in Kent, A.D. 1552.' *Archaeologia Cantiana* 8 (1872): 74–163; 9 (1874): 266–84.

Walker, G. *The Politics of Performance in Early Renaissance Drama*. Cambridge: Cambridge University Press, 1998.

Wall, J.N. 'Godly and Fruitful Lessons: The English Bible, Erasmus' Paraphrases, and the Book of Homilies.' In J. Booty, ed., *The Godly Kingdom of Tudor England: Great Books of the English Reformation*. Wilton, CT: Morehouse-Barlow, 1981. 47–135.

Walter, Peter. *Theologie aus dem Geist der Rhetorik: Zur Schriftauslegung des Erasmus von Rotterdam*. Mainz: Matthias-Grünewald-Verlag, 1991.

Walters, H.B. *London Churches at the Reformation*. London: SPCK, 1939.

Waswo, Richard. *Language and Meaning in the Renaissance*. Princeton: Princeton University Press, 1987.

Weaver, F.W., and G.N. Clark, eds. *Churchwardens' Accounts of Marston, Spelsbury, Pyrton*. Oxford: Oxfordshire Record Society, 1925.

Weber, Eugen. *Apocalypses: Prophecies, Cults, and Millennial Beliefs through the Ages*. Cambridge, MA: Harvard University Press, 1999.

Weinstock, Stefan. *Divus Julius*. Oxford: Clarendon Press, 1971.

White, C.H.E., ed. *The East Anglian, or Notes and Queries on Subjects connected with the Counties of Suffolk, Cambridge, Essex and Norfolk*. New ser., vols. 2–3, 6. London: Elliot Stock, 1887–90, 1895–6.

White, P. *Theatre and Reformation: Protestantism, Patronage and Playing in Tudor England*. Cambridge: Cambridge University Press, 1993.

Whiting, Robert. *The Local Impact of the English Reformation*. Basingstoke: Macmillan, 1998.

Whitley, H.M. 'The Churchwardens' Accounts of St Andrew's and St Michael's, Lewes from 1522 to 1601.' *Sussex Archaeological Collections* 45 (1902): 40–61.

Williams, J.F., ed. *The Early Churchwardens' Accounts of Hampshire*. Winchester: Warren and Son Ltd., 1913.

Witherington, Ben. *Women and the Genesis of Christianity*. Cambridge: Cambridge University Press, 1990.

– *Conflict and Community in Corinth: A Socio-Rhetorical Commentary on 1 and 2 Corinthians*. Grand Rapids, MI: William B. Eerdmans, 1995.

Wooden, Warren. *John Foxe*. Boston: Twayne, 1983.

Worth, R.N. *Calendar of the Tavistock Parish Records*. Plymouth: n.p., 1887.

Wright, Thomas, ed. *Churchwardens' Accounts of the Town of Ludlow in Shropshire*. London: Camden Society, 1869.

Youngs, F.A. 'The Tudor Governments and Dissident Religious Books.' In C.R. Cole and M.E. Moody, eds., *The Dissenting Tradition*. Athens: Ohio University Press, 1975. 167–90.

– *The Proclamations of the Tudor Queens*. Cambridge: Cambridge University Press, 1976.
Zakai, Avihu. *Exile and Kingdom: History and Apocalypse in the Puritan Migration to America*. Cambridge: Cambridge University Press, 1992.
Zim, Rivkah. 'The Reformation: The Trial of God's Word.' In Stephen Prichett, ed., *Reading the Text: Biblical Criticism and Literary Theory*. Oxford: Basil Blackwell, 1991. 64–135.
Ziolkowski, Jan. 'Old Wives' Tales: Classicism and Anti-Classicism from Apuleius to Chaucer.' Paper delivered at the Twenty-Fifth Annual Medieval Workshop, University of British Columbia, November 1995.
– 'The Obscenities of Old Women: Vetularity and Vernacularity.' In Jan M. Ziolkowski, ed., *Obscenity: Social Control and Artistic Creation in the European Middle Ages*. Leiden: E.J. Brill, 1998. 73–89.

Contributors

Irena Backus is professeur titulaire at the Institut d'histoire de la Réformation, University of Geneva. She is a member of the editorial board of the series *Oxford Studies in Historical Theology* and of the journals *Revue des Études Augustiniennes* and *Apocrypha.* She has edited Martin Bucer's *Commentary on the Gospel of John* (1988) and a collective work on *The Reception of the Church Fathers in the West* (1997). She is the author of several monographs, including *Lectures humanistes de Basile de Césarée* (1990), *La patristique et les guerres de religion en France* (1993), and *Reformation Readings of the Apocalypse* (2000). With Jean-François Cottier she is preparing a critical edition of Erasmus' *Paraphrases of the Gospels* for the Amsterdam edition of the works of Erasmus.

John J. Bateman is Professor Emeritus of Classics and Speech Communication at the University of Illinois, Urbana-Champaign. He has also taught at Cornell University and the Universities of Glasgow, Ottawa, and Toronto. He was sometime Head of the Department of the Classics and Director of the School of Humanities at the University of Illinois. He is a member of the New Testament Scholarship Committee for the Collected Works of Erasmus, for which he has translated the Paraphrases on the *Epistles to Timothy, Titus, Philemon, Peter, Jude, James, John, and Hebrews* (CWE 44) and edited the translation of the *Paraphrase on*

Acts (CWE 50). He is editing the *Paraphrasis D. Erasmi Roterodami in omneis Epistolas Apostolicas* for the Amsterdam edition of the works of Erasmus, part 3 of which appeared in 1997 (ASD VII-6).

Guy Bedouelle, O.P., is Professor of Church History at the University of Fribourg, Switzerland. He is the author of numerous studies of sixteenth-century religious culture, notably on Jacques Lefèvre d'Étaples and Erasmus. He has edited a volume of Erasmus' controversial writings for the Toronto edition of the Collected Works (CWE 83) and co-edited *Le temps des Réformes et la Bible*, volume 5 in the series Bible de tous les temps (1989), with Bernard Roussel.

John Craig is Associate Professor of History at Simon Fraser University in British Columbia. He is the author of *Reformation, Politics and Polemics: The Growth of Protestantism in East Anglian Market Towns, 1500–1610* (2001) and co-editor of *The Reformation in English Towns 1500–1640* (1998). He is currently working on a survey of English parish life, entitled *English Parishioners 1500–1700*.

Gretchen E. Minton is Assistant Professor of English at the University of Minnesota at Morris. She has published articles on John Bale and John Foxe and is co-editor of the Arden Edition of Shakespeare's *Timon of Athens*. She is also working on the reception of Augustine in the English Renaissance.

Mechtilde O'Mara, C.S.J., is Professor of Classics Emeritus at St Michael's College in the University of Toronto. She is a member of the Editorial Board for the Collected Works of Erasmus and is collaborating with Edward Phillips on the *Paraphrases on Corinthians, Ephesians, Philippians, Colossians, and Thessalonians* (CWE 43).

Hilmar M. Pabel is Associate Professor of History at Simon Fraser University in British Columbia. He is author of *Conversing with God: Prayer in Erasmus' Pastoral Writings* (1997), editor of *Erasmus' Vision of the Church* (1995), and co-editor with Kathleen M. Comerford of *Early Modern Catholicism: Essays in Honour of John W. O'Malley, SJ* (2001). With Mark Vessey he organized the symposium on 'Erasmus' *Paraphrases on the New Testament*: Composition – Translation – Reception' held in Toronto, 1–2 October 1999.

Jane E. Phillips is Professor of Classics at the University of Kentucky. A member of the Editorial Board for the Collected Works of Erasmus, she is translator and annotator of the *Paraphrase on John* (CWE 46) and of chapters 11–24 of the *Paraphrase on Luke* (CWE 48, forthcoming). She is editor of the *Erasmus of Rotterdam Society Yearbook*.

Bernard Roussel is Directeur d'Études, Section des Sciences Religieuses, at the École Pratique des Hautes Études, Paris, where he holds a chair in Réformes et protestantismes dans l'Europe moderne. He is a member of the Centre d'Étude des Religions du Livre and of the Editorial Committee of the *Bulletin de la Société de l'Histoire du Protestantisme Français*. With Guy Bedouelle he co-edited *Le temps des Réformes et la Bible*, volume 5 in the series Bible de tous les temps (1989). He has published numerous articles on the history of the interpretation of biblical texts in the sixteenth century.

Erika Rummel is Professor of History at Wilfrid Laurier University in Waterloo, Ontario. She is the author of *The Humanist-Scholastic Debate in the Renaissance and Reformation* (1995) and *The Confessionalization of Humanism in Reformation Germany* (2000). She has written a number of books on Erasmus, among them *Erasmus and His Catholic Critics* (1989). She is a member of the editorial board of the Collected Works of Erasmus, contributor to several volumes of that edition, and editor of two collections of Erasmus' writings, *The Erasmus Reader* (1990) and *Erasmus on Women* (1996). She is currently engaged in setting up a project to edit and translate the works of the Strasbourg reformer Wolfgang Capito, to be published in the Corpus Reformatorum Minorum (Geneva).

Robert D. Sider is Professor Emeritus of Classical Languages at Dickinson College, Carlisle, Pennsylvania, and Adjunct Professor of History at the University of Saskatchewan. He is General Editor of Erasmus' New Testament Scholarship for the Collected Works (CWE 41–60) and has contributed as editor and/or translator and annotator to the volumes containing the *Paraphrases on*

Romans and Galatians (CWE 42), the *Paraphrase on Acts* (CWE 50), and the *Annotations on Romans* (CWE 56). As editor of the future CWE 41, to contain prolegomena to the New Testament scholarship, he is also translating and annotating the *Ratio verae theologiae.*

Mark Vessey is Associate Professor of English at the University of British Columbia and holder of a Canada Research Chair in Literature / Christianity and Culture. He is co-editor with William E. Klingshirn of *The Limits of Ancient Christianity: Essays on Late Antique Thought and Culture in Honor of R.A. Markus* (1999) and, with Karla Pollmann and Allan D. Fitzgerald, of *History, Apocalypse and the Secular Imagination: New Essays on Augustine's 'City of God'* (1999). With Hilmar Pabel he organized the symposium on 'Erasmus' *Paraphrases on the New Testament*: Composition – Translation – Reception' held in Toronto, 1–2 October 1999.

Index of Scriptural Passages

OLD TESTAMENT

NEW TESTAMENT

2 Corinthians

Galatians

General Index

Erasmus Studies

A series of studies concerned with Erasmus and related subjects

1 *Under Pretext of Praise: Satiric Mode in Erasmus' Fiction*
Sister Geraldine Thompson

2 *Erasmus on Language and Method in Theology*
Marjorie O'Rourke Boyle

3 *The Politics of Erasmus: A Pacifist Intellectual and His Political Milieu*
James D. Tracy

4 *Phoenix of His Age: Interpretations of Erasmus, c. 1550–1750*
Bruce Mansfield

5 *Christening Pagan Mysteries: Erasmus in Pursuit of Wisdom*
Marjorie O'Rourke Boyle

6 *Renaissance English Translations of Erasmus: A Bibliography to 1700*
E.J. Devereux

7 *Erasmus as a Translator of the Classics*
Erika Rummel

8 *Erasmus'* Annotations on the New Testament: *From Philologist to Theologian*
Erika Rummel

9 *Humanist Play and Belief: The Seriocomic Art of Desiderius Erasmus*
Walter M. Gordon

10 *Erasmus: His Life, Works, and Influence*
Cornelis Augustijn

11 *Interpretations of Erasmus, c1750–1920: Man on His Own*
Bruce Mansfield

12 *Rhetoric and Theology: The Hermeneutic of Erasmus*
Manfred Hoffmann

13 *Conversing with God: Erasmus' Pastoral Writings*
Hilmar M. Pabel

14 *Holy Scripture Speaks: The Production and Reception of Erasmus'* Paraphrases on the New Testament
Hilmar M. Pabel and Mark Vessey (eds.)

15 *Erasmus in the Twentieth Century: Interpretations c1920–2000*
Bruce Mansfield

www.ingramcontent.com/pod-product-compliance
Lightning Source LLC
LaVergne TN
LVHW090800070826
844660LV00022B/1042

* 9 7 8 1 4 8 7 5 2 4 9 2 0 *